THE KINGFISHER BOOK OF
RELIGIONS

All year dates are given using the
Christian conventions B.C. (Before
Christ) and A.D. (Anno Domini), simply
for universality of understanding.

The publishers would like to thank the following editorial
consultants for their help:
Dr. M.A.Zaki Badawi, Principal, The Muslim College, London
Dr. Sue Hamilton, Department of Theology and
Religious Studies, King's College, London
The Reverend Leslie Houlden, formerly Professor of New
Testament Studies, King's College, London
Dr. Nicholas de Lange, Fellow, Wolfson College, Cambridge
Rabbi Judd Kruger Levingston, Principal, Prozdor, Jewish
Theological Seminary of America, New York
Dr. Stewart McFarlane, visiting professor at Chung Hwa
Institute of Buddhist Studies, Taiwan
Dr. Bruce Metzger, Professor of New Testament, Emeritus,
Princeton Theological Seminary, New Jersey
Dr. Eleanor Nesbitt, Department of Religious
Studies, Warwick University
Ranchor Prime, member of the International Consultancy
on Religion, Education and Culture
Rabbi Sylvia Rothschild, Bromley and
District Reform Synagogue
Abdulaziz Sachedina, Department of Religious Studies,
University of Virginia
Inderjit Singh, editor of the *Sikh Messenger*

Edited and designed by Toucan Books Limited, London

For Kingfisher
Managing editor   Miranda Smith
Senior editor   Aimee Johnson
Art director   Mike Davis

KINGFISHER
a Houghton Mifflin Company imprint
215 Park Avenue South
New York, New York 10003
www.houghtonmifflinbooks.com

First published in 1999
4 6 8 10 9 7 5 3

3TR/0602/MID/MA/157MA

Copyright © Kingfisher Publications Plc 1999

LIBRARY OF CONGRESS CATALOGING-IN-PUBLICATION DATA
Barnes, Trevor.
The Kingfisher book of religions / Trevor Barnes. — 1st ed.
p. cm.
Includes index.
Summary: Explains the origins, development, beliefs, festivals,
and ceremonies of various world faiths and where they are practiced,
including Hinduism, Buddhism, Judaism, Christianity, Islam, and
traditional religions of Australian aborigines and Native Americans.
1. Religions—Juvenile literature. [1. Religions.] I. Title.
BL92.B35 1999
291—dc21 98-53303   CIP AC

ISBN 0-7534-5199-9

Color separations by Modern Age
Printed in Hong Kong

THE KINGFISHER BOOK OF
RELIGIONS

Festivals, ceremonies, and beliefs from around the world

TREVOR BARNES

KING*f*ISHER

NEW YORK

CONTENTS

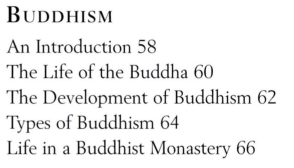

WHAT IS RELIGION?

Some questions are easy to answer. "What time is it?", "What color is grass?", "What is two plus two?" Other questions are much harder. "Where was I before I was born?", "Where will I go when I die?", "Who created the world?" Such questions (and more) have been asked throughout the history of humanity, and at different stages in their development, different tribes, societies, and peoples have supplied different answers that made sense at the time.

> ### "You shall love your neighbor as yourself."
>
> Leviticus 19:18

Religion tries to answer the big questions in life. "Why is there suffering in the world?", "Is there life after death?", "How should I live my life on Earth?", "If God created the world, who created God?" Of course, you do not have to be religious to ask—philosophy and science pose the same questions. But for most of our history, philosophy and science have themselves been part of the religious understanding of the world. Both have shared the deeply human sense of mystery at the wonder of creation.

There are things that cannot be fully explained by our intellect or our reason. The Christian writer C. S. Lewis once gave this example: Imagine you are in a room with a dead body at night. It would probably make you feel nervous or even afraid. But why? A dead body cannot hurt you, make fun of you, or say cruel things to you.

Above This Nepali girl is believed to be a living goddess, a reincarnation of Kumari, goddess of power. At the age of 12 or 13 (at puberty), she resumes a normal life and another girl is chosen by the Hindu priests.

Right These Muslim girls are learning the Koran in Arabic at an evening class in a mosque in the north of England.

Above Santiago de Compostela in northern Spain is traditionally thought to house the bones of St. James. Since the Middle Ages, it has been an important place of pilgrimage for Christians from all over the world.

In fact, the dead body cannot do you any harm, and yet it has a strange power to generate troubling thoughts. "If the body is dead, where has its life gone?", "When I am dead, will I end up there, too?", "Will the body come back to haunt me as a ghost?" The strange, irrational sensation of awe and unease that a "harmless," motionless corpse provokes has been called "numinous." That is to say, it suggests a divine or spiritual presence outside ourselves. We may feel the presence of the numinous at any time—in a mosque, or a temple, or gazing up at the stars in the night sky. We may feel it at the birth of a brother or sister, or at the death of a grandparent. In prehistoric times, people probably felt it when thunder roared or lightning struck. It is that strange "something" that we cannot satisfactorily explain, but that suggests another world beyond the one that we can see. A sense of the numinous is at the heart of all the world's religions.

> **"Not one of you is a believer until he loves for his brother what he loves for himself."**
>
> *Hadith* of the Prophet Muhammad

In the name of religion

Some religions believe in one god who created heaven and Earth. Others believe in the existence of several gods, who take strange forms and control human lives. Some, like Buddhism, do not believe in the idea of a god at all. Great cruelty has been committed in the name of religion, but also great acts of kindness and self-sacrifice. At their best, religions teach that proper respect for the divine should be mirrored in proper respect for the whole of creation.

Right A Jewish family recalls the events of the Exodus—the deliverance of the Jews from slavery in Egypt—at the annual Passover meal.

THE STORY OF THE WORLD'S RELIGIONS

W hat is the link between a golden temple in northwest India and a huge red rock in central Australia? What does a totem pole in North America have in common with a stone circle in the south of England? Why do millions of people every year make a special journey to a wall in Jerusalem, a church in Rome, and a black cube in Mecca? The answer to all these questions involves one word—religion, a phenomenon common to all people in all times. From Salt Lake City, headquarters of the Church of Jesus Christ of Latter-day Saints (Mormons) in Utah, to Kandy in Sri Lanka where it is believed that the Buddha's tooth is housed in a famous temple, people have constructed buildings and monuments to their faith. Or, as with Mount Tai in China, they have looked to elements of the natural world in awe and wonder. The common link is a sense of the sacred in life.

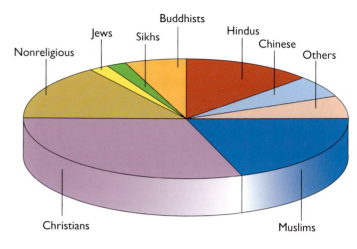

Above Religions such as Christianity and Islam have large groups of followers in many parts of the world. Others, like the Chinese religions, tend to be confined to one particular region.

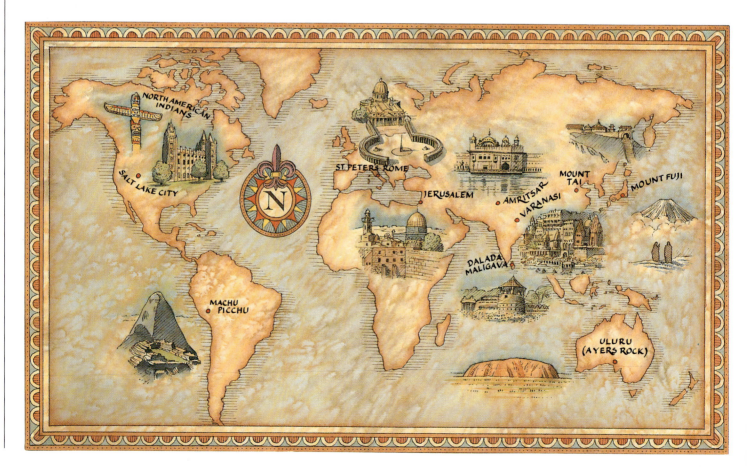

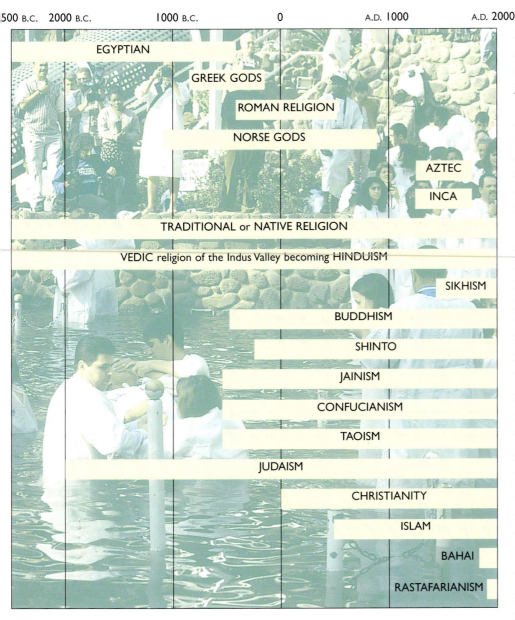

2500 B.C.	2000 B.C.	1000 B.C.	0	A.D. 1000	A.D. 2000

EGYPTIAN

GREEK GODS

ROMAN RELIGION

NORSE GODS

AZTEC

INCA

TRADITIONAL or NATIVE RELIGION

VEDIC religion of the Indus Valley becoming HINDUISM

SIKHISM

BUDDHISM

SHINTO

JAINISM

CONFUCIANISM

TAOISM

JUDAISM

CHRISTIANITY

ISLAM

BAHAI

RASTAFARIANISM

Left Some religions (Christianity and Islam, for example) are easily dated since the historical facts of their founders' lives are well documented. Others, like the religion of the ancient Egyptians, are more difficult to locate in time. Similarly, the religion the West has come to know as Hinduism has not always existed in that form. It has developed over long periods of time, making precise dating impossible.

When did religion begin?

Religion is as old as humankind, which first looked to powers outside itself for protection and reassurance. Early peoples worshiped the sun and the rain as sources of life and fertility, and trembled as the thunder seemed to be roaring its displeasure. They asked unseen gods for help in times of need and thanked them in times of plenty. The gods they worshiped may have been illusions but the comfort they brought was real. For many millions of people, faith is as real today as it was in the time of Moses, the Buddha, Mahavira, Jesus Christ, the Prophet Muhammad, or Guru Nanak.

Religion in people's lives

Religion in one form or another plays a part in the lives of most of the world's population, sometimes dictating what they eat, where they live, what they wear, who they marry, and how they think. Fired by the same religious impulse, believers do different things. Buddhist monks shave their heads, for example, while many Sikhs never cut their hair at all. Some worship with loud music and vibrant dance, while others sit still in complete silence. While some religions hold out the promise of a future life in the hereafter, all religions (whether they believe in one God, many gods, or no god) will encourage a life that requires goodness in the here and now.

Left Most religions have their sacred places, some made by humans like Aztec pyramids, others natural like Uluru (Ayers Rock) or Mount Tai in China.

9

ANCIENT RELIGIONS: AN INTRODUCTION

Remember that what we call ancient religions were once modern religions. In their time, they satisfied many of the same spiritual longings and answered many of the same spiritual questions that living religions do today. More modern religions have since evolved to meet humanity's changing needs.

Mythology or religion

The gods of ancient Greece and Rome, the deities of ancient Egypt, and the superhuman figures of the ancient Scandinavian world live on in myths and legends, but have lost the power to connect with us. The Greek and Roman gods were worshiped and feared, but rarely loved. They changed shape and appeared on Earth, but seldom intervened in human affairs, giving the impression that they were distant, cold, and sometimes even cruel. By contrast, in the Hebrew Bible, God parts the Red Sea to let his chosen people flee from Egypt. He sustains them with food from heaven. In the New Testament, God so loves the world that he sacrifices his only son to save it. In the Koran, God is compassionate and gives humanity a special place in his creation.

Spirits in nature

The natural world played a large part in shaping early religions. The sun and rain were fertility sources that influenced lives. It was only a short step from there to worshiping these powerful elements as divine beings who controlled people's fates.

Left In ancient times, the gods were often associated with the elemental forces of nature. Here, the Norse goddess Freya holds her hand to her breast, which symbolizes fruitfulness and fertility.

Below These cave paintings were made by hunters around 17,000 B.C. in Lascaux, southwest France. By representing the animals in picture form, they believed they could exercise some control over them.

Left Stonehenge, perhaps the most famous of the ancient stone circles, was built between 3000 and 1500 B.C. on Salisbury Plain in Wiltshire, southwest England. It is believed to have been used for the worship of fertility gods and goddesses, as well as for complex astronomical calculations.

A natural impulse

Cave paintings made around 17,000 B.C., such as those in the caves at Lascaux in southwest France, show how early men and women expressed their wonder at the natural world around them. Around this time, female figurines representing a mother goddess began to appear throughout Europe. As stable societies based on farming and agriculture began to emerge, rituals developed to express the relationship between humanity and an unseen spirit world. Eventually, buildings were constructed specifically for prayer and sacrifice, gods and goddesses were given their own temples or shrines, and stories were told to be passed on from generation to generation. Like the living religions of today, the ancient religions tried to give meaning to the joy, tragedy, and mystery of human life.

Above Zeus (known to the Romans as Jupiter) was the supreme god of the ancient Greeks. He was believed to be the ultimate ruler of humankind.

ANCIENT EGYPT

The sun god Ra was a principal deity in ancient Egyptian religion. He was worshiped as the creator of all life, and because he lived in the sky, he was often depicted with a falcon's head. As a powerful force whose daily journey across the sky controlled everyone's life, he was associated with the ruling pharaohs who became known as the Sons of Ra.

Amun Ra

At various points in the history of ancient Egypt, gods were associated with individual cities. When alliances were made between them, the local gods also joined forces. So, when the city of Heliopolis (now El-Matariya), whose protector god was Ra, made a pact with Thebes (now Luxor), whose protector god was Amun, a joint deity known as Amun Ra emerged. For a time, he became the ruling god of the whole nation.

Gods and nature

In addition to Amun Ra, there were many other local gods who were associated with natural forces. Isis was the fertility goddess and queen of all the gods. Osiris was her husband, and later combined with Ra to become the supreme god of Egypt and king of the dead. Horus, the sky god, had a hawk's head. Thoth, the moon god and god of learning, had the head of an ibis, while Anubis, god of the dead, had a jackal's head. Ptah was a creator god and god of craftspeople.

One god

There were many attempts to limit the number of gods, but they were largely resisted by the priests, whose importance depended on the gods.

Above Isis and her husband Osiris were important deities in the Egyptian pantheon (collection) of gods. It was believed that Osiris was killed by his brother Seth, but brought back to life by Isis, queen of the gods. Osiris became king of the dead and ruled the underworld.

Left The solid gold death mask of the young pharaoh Tutankhamen became famous when it was discovered by the British archaeologist Howard Carter in 1922. The contents of Tutankhamen's tomb remained hidden from robbers and were found intact.

Right Many animals, particularly birds and cats, were sacred to the Egyptians, who mummified them and buried them alongside the dead for company in the afterlife. The fertility goddess Bastet was depicted as a cat.

The most successful attempt was by Amenhotep IV (*c*.1379–1362 B.C.), husband of Queen Nefertiti, who tried to impose a form of monotheism (belief in a single god) based on Aten (the fiery disk of the sun). Suppressing all other gods and declaring Aten to be the only source of life, he changed his own name to Akhenaten (spirit of Aten) and closed all the temples that were dedicated to other gods.

The afterlife

Akhenaten was succeeded by Tutankhamen, who was only a boy when he ascended the throne. He abandoned the worship of Aten and reinstated the worship of Amun and the other gods. These gods often included the pharaohs themselves, who were given divine status by the priests and were believed to live on after death. The pyramids are symbols of the immortality that they hoped to achieve. When the pharaohs died, their bodies were preserved, or mummified, and buried with their possessions, which, it was thought, would be useful to them in the afterlife.

Left The Temple at Luxor (ancient Thebes) was one of the principal sites of worship. It was led by a professional class of priests and headed by the pharaoh himself, who was also thought to be divine.

ANCIENT GREECE

The Greeks had many gods, but the focus of their worship was a group of 12 principal deities believed to live on Mount Olympus under Zeus, ruler of the gods. Stories of the gods were recited aloud and passed on by word of mouth. Eventually, they were written down in two major works of poetry called the *Iliad* and the *Odyssey*, both attributed to the poet Homer, who lived in the 700s B.C. These epic poems tell of the lives of two heroic men—Achilles and Odysseus—whose adventures show how personal struggle, fate, and the influence of the gods work together in human lives. Each god or goddess was believed to have human qualities (such as courage, kindness, fertility, or musical or artistic skill), but behaved in a superhuman way. The gods rewarded good and brave actions, but became angry if people became proud or boastful.

Places of worship

Temples were constructed on the highest part of the city, known as the "acropolis." The most famous temple is the Parthenon in Athens, dedicated to the city's patron goddess, Athena, the goddess of wisdom.

Above Zeus was the head of the family of gods on Mount Olympus, who were believed to control the weather and to affect the course of people's lives. Hera, his wife, was the goddess of marriage.

Ares, god of war, and the son of Zeus and Hera.

Hephaestus, god of fire and metalworking.

Aphrodite, goddess of love and beauty.

Artemis, goddess of hunting and wild beasts.

Right Delphi, on the slopes of Mount Parnassus, was home to the Temple of Apollo, patron of music and poetry, and the god who most symbolized the spirit of ancient Greece.

Ordinary people had shrines to their favorite gods at home, or they worshiped in secret, following what were known as "mystery religions." The most famous of these was the cult of Dionysus, the god of wine. People who had been initiated into the mysteries met for a more intense experience of worship and celebration.

Below Apollo and (below right) Demeter, goddess of agriculture and harvests. Demeter is associated with cereal crops and traditionally carries a sheaf of wheat.

New ideas

Gradually, however, poets and philosophers began to think that a literal belief in these distant and indifferent gods was a rather unsatisfactory way of explaining what life was all about. In particular, Socrates, his disciple Plato, and Aristotle developed systems of thought that came to be accepted by much of the Western world as a truer understanding of how the world works. The gods eventually became part of a mythological world that, although it explained an aspect of human experience, was no longer thought to be historically true.

Hestia, goddess of the hearth and family life.

Poseidon, god of the sea, with his distinctive trident.

Athena, goddess of warfare, wisdom, and arts and crafts.

Hermes, god of travelers and messenger of the gods.

ANCIENT ROME

T he word "religion" comes from the Latin word *religio*, which, for the ancient Romans, can be translated as both a bond (between humans and gods) and an obligation (on humans to worship gods).

A public religion
Religion was principally a public matter because it was believed that the gods protected the state. The Romans took the Greek gods and adapted them for their own use. So Zeus, the king of the gods, became Jupiter to the Romans, and Hera, his wife, became Juno. The name of Hermes, the messenger of the gods, was changed to Mercury. Athena, goddess of war and wisdom, became Minerva, while Aphrodite, goddess of love and beauty, became Venus. Ares, the god of war, became Mars. Demeter, goddess of the fruitful Earth, became Ceres, while Artemis, goddess of the moon and hunting, became Diana. Apollo, the god of music, poetry, and the arts, kept the same name.

Temple worship
Roman religion was essentially concerned with the performance of specific actions or rites. It did not try to make citizens into better people. Public religious rituals were carried out by a special class of priest, the *pontifex* or *pontifex maximus* (high priest). The ordinary citizens took no part in the rituals; nor were they expected to attend the temple for worship.

Above *Winged Mercury was the messenger of the gods as well as the god of trade and merchants.*

Above This Roman mosaic pavement shows Neptune, the god of the seas and rivers. He rode the waves in a chariot drawn by seahorses and carried a three-pronged spear, or trident, in his hand. When Neptune was in a bad mood, he caused earthquakes, storms, disastrous floods, plagues, and famines.

Below This relief from the Temple of Neptune in Rome shows a sacrifice to Mars, the god of war.

Private devotion

At important times in their lives, people consulted an oracle for guidance from a particular god. Often the oracle was situated near water. A favorite was the shrine to Aesculapius, god of healing and the patron of doctors, who carried a staff coiled with snakes. People visited the shrine in the hope that they might be cured of sickness. Other shrines were associated with fertility and were visited by women who wanted to have a child. Divination, or foretelling the future, was also popular. Augurs, or people skilled in the art, read signs in the stars or in the natural world and claimed to be interpreting the gods' wishes. As in ancient Greece, there were a number of so-called mystery cults that attracted people who wanted a more intense religious experience. For a time, Christianity, which overlapped with the many pagan gods and goddesses of the age, was itself considered a mystery religion with its own rites and its own select membership.

Below In Roman houses, there were often shrines to the lares and penates, household gods who were associated with farming and food. Here, a lar holds a drinking horn and a bowl for offerings made to the gods.

NORSE AND CELTIC RELIGIONS

Norse and Celtic religions developed in the cold countries of northern and western Europe and present-day Scandinavia. The climate undoubtedly played a part in forming the characters of these gods, who, unlike the light and airy gods of the Mediterranean, were often dark and gloomy.

Elemental gods

In Norse religions, there were gods of thunder, rain, and wind, who were often involved in bloody battles against giants and monsters. Although there is evidence that these gods were worshiped in prehistoric times, they particularly appealed to the Vikings—the traders and warriors who ravaged much of northern Europe between A.D. 700 and 1100. Exciting tales of their mythical adventures were recited aloud at banquets and were eventually written down in poems, such as the *Havamal*, or long tales of heroes and gods, called sagas.

Norse mythology

Odin, the god of war, (also known as Woden or Wotan) was the father of the gods. He is often shown riding across the sky on an eight-legged horse. He is said to have had only one eye and to have been fierce in battle and wise in peace. He was served by the Valkyries—warrior maidens who took those who had died in battle up into the heavenly hall reserved for heroes, and known as Valhalla. The other great god was Thor. He was the strongest of the principal deities and is depicted as a giant carrying a mighty hammer.

Above The Druids were ancient Celtic priests, teachers, and judges. They worshiped in sacred clearings in the forest, or by lakes and springs, and cut mistletoe as a sign of fertility. They were also thought to practice human sacrifice.

Left The traditional Celtic cross was a religious symbol before Christianity arrived in Europe. The Christianity of the early 5th- and 6th-century missionaries, such as Patrick and Columba, was influenced by Celtic culture, in particular by its concern for the natural world.

> "Flocks die, friends die, you yourself die likewise. But if one has won an honored name, then that can never die."

The *Havamal*

Ragnarok

Although the gods were thought to be superhuman, they were not immortal, and Norse religion looked to the day of Ragnarok, when the gods themselves would perish in battle. From this destruction would be born a new world that would worship one almighty god. This belief was influenced by Christianity, which was spreading across Europe at that time.

The Celts

Little is known for certain about the religious practices of the Celts, who occupied large parts of western Europe including pre-Roman Britain, Ireland, and northwestern France in the Iron Age. What is known comes largely from Roman sources, which are inclined to interpret Celtic religion unfavorably. There is some evidence that they worshiped gods from other cultures, including Mercury and Mars, but they added local gods of their own.

Fertility cults

The figure of a naked male god wearing horns or antlers is a recurring symbol in Celtic mythology, as is the Earth Mother—both of whom are associated with fertility. The Celtic tribes treated the natural world as sacred—particularly wells, springs, lakes, and rivers, which were seen as sources of life.

Above In Norse mythology, the universe was divided into nine different worlds linked by the World Tree, Yggdrasil. *The Earth was known as* Midgard. *The gods were called the* Aesir *and they lived in the world known as* Asgard. *This was surrounded by the sea and by a gigantic serpent, the offspring of the trickster god, Loki. Here, Thor is shown fishing for the serpent, the symbol of evil. It escaped, however, thanks to the intervention of the giant Hymir (also shown right).*

ZOROASTRIANISM

Although Zoroastrianism is an ancient faith, it is still a living religion practiced by some 200,000 people living mainly in Iran and in India, where they are known as Parsees.

Zoroaster

Zoroastrianism is a monotheistic religion founded by the prophet Zoroaster, also known as Zarathustra. Although he is traditionally thought to have lived in the 500s B.C., recent scholarship suggests he could have been born as long ago as 1200 B.C. Little is known for certain of his early life in what is now northeast Iran, but it is believed that he was inspired to teach and spread the faith after receiving a series of visions from the Supreme God, Ahura Mazda, at the age of 30. After his death, many legends appeared, in which he was described as a magician, an astrologer, a mathematician, and a philosopher. It is more likely, however, that in his lifetime he was a practicing priest within the Aryan tradition, which used the household fire as the focus of a belief system and drew on the power of the natural elements of rain, wind, and sun.

Good and evil

Zoroaster developed a religion based on the coming of a savior, the resurrection of the dead, and a day of judgment when wrongdoers will go to hell and the just will be rewarded in heaven. Much of his thinking has been absorbed by other faiths—Judaism, Christianity, and Islam, in particular.

Above This relief shows griffins, which are sacred mythological creatures— half-man and half-animal. They are traditionally found on doorposts and gateways to protect against evil.

Left The fire altar is the focus of worship in Zoroastrian "fire temples." Here, the altar is guarded by double images of Shapur I (A.D. 241–272).

Above and below *At the age of seven, children are initiated into the faith and presented with the* kusti, *the sacred cord that is wrapped three times around the waist over a white tunic. During prayers (five times daily), worshipers face a source of light and undo the* kusti.

Zoroaster taught that Ahura Mazda created life and all that was good, but that he was locked in a struggle with Angra Mainyu, the Spirit of Evil, who would one day be destroyed by the forces of goodness.

Zoroastrianism stresses that individuals have free will to choose between good or evil, and that their deeds will be judged as they cross the Chinvat Bridge between life and death. For the righteous, it is wide, but for the wicked, it narrows to the width of a blade.

The magi

The Three Wise Men, who were the first non-Jews present shortly after Christ's birth, and who gave gifts of gold, myrrh, and frankincense, are believed by some to have been Zoroastrian priests, or magi. Today, the magi carry out worship in "fire temples." The sacred fire represents the purity of God, source of light and life.

AZTEC AND INCA BELIEFS

Before the arrival of Christopher Columbus from Spain in 1492, Central America had a history of Amerindian (American Indian) culture stretching back to the 1100s B.C. The Aztecs and the Incas represent the high point of that civilization, which was destroyed by Spanish invaders in the A.D. 1500s.

Left *Quetzalcóatl was the Aztec god of learning and priesthood. He is often depicted as a plumed serpent.*

The Aztecs

The Aztecs believed that the universe was made up of different levels. At the bottom was the underworld: a cold, dark, inhospitable realm reserved for those who did not go to paradise. At the top were two heavenly beings who had created humanity. In between was the Earth. The forces of heaven and the underworld came together at the Great Temple in Tenochtitlan, the Aztec capital.

Sun worship

In order for the Aztec civilization to survive, the sun god Huitzilopochtli needed to remain strong. Human sacrifice (usually of enemy warriors captured in battle) became a central feature of their religious practices because the Aztecs believed they had to feed the sun god with blood every day. The live victim was held down on an altar while a priest used a sharp stone knife to cut out the still-beating heart. The heart and the blood were then fed to the god, who would continue to protect them. Every year, thousands of people lost their lives in this way. When Aztec warriors died, they were thought to join the sun for four years before returning to Earth as hummingbirds.

Below *The Aztec deity Huitzilopochtli was sometimes depicted as a snake. This image is made of wood and covered with turquoise stones.*

The Incas

The Incas first settled in the Cuzco region of the Andes in present-day Peru about A.D. 1200. They believed that certain places or objects possessed a supernatural power. These could be mountains, rivers, buildings, or ancient shrines and were known as *huacas*. The *huacas* were treated with great reverence and became key elements in what Incas believed was a sacred landscape centered on their capital, Cuzco.

The Inca gods

The Incas' main god was Viracocha, the creator of all things, who was believed to have made the sun, the moon, and all humanity. Alongside him were Inti, the sun god, and Illapa, the weather god. As with the Aztecs, worship of the sun was very important because it was the source of life, ripening crops and bringing heat and light.

In times of crisis, human sacrifice was carried out, but usually the sacrifices involved killing a llama or offering corn beer. Ancestor worship was very important in Inca life and, like the Egyptians, they practiced the art of mummification, which meant embalming their dead and treating them as sacred objects. The Incas believed that after death good people joined the sun in heaven and revealed themselves on Earth as *huacas*.

TRADITIONAL BELIEFS: AN INTRODUCTION

Unlike the global missionary religions of Christianity and Islam, which have been exported far beyond their place of origin in the Middle East, and unlike the Jewish faith, which is practiced by adherents all over the world, traditional religions survive in remote areas among comparatively small communities or tribes.

Below This North American totem pole, richly carved with gods and goddesses, reflects the creation stories that are passed down through the generations.

The natural world

It is misleading to refer to tribal peoples as primitive, because although their cultures may not have developed in the same way as ours, they did develop elaborate societies with ritual practices that suggest they are far more religious than many other peoples. Tribal peoples live close to the natural world, which they rely on for food and shelter. They have an instinctive understanding of the fragility of life and realize that they are at the mercy of the elements. Consequently, they look to forces greater than themselves for protection and help in times of uncertainty or danger.

Creation stories

Many of these tribal societies are nonliterate; that is to say, they do not practice the art of writing. Instead, they tell stories or sing songs, which often take them back to the mythological time when the Earth was created. They tell stories of gods and goddesses who grow angry if they are not treated with proper respect, and who reward those who carry out their religious duties properly. These creation stories are part of a tribe's spiritual heritage and are passed down by word of mouth, from generation to generation.

> "Behold this buffalo, O Grandfather, which you have given us. From him the people live and with him they walk the sacred path."
>
> Sioux Indian prayer

Left This mask belongs to the Yoruba people of Nigeria. Elements of a god's spiritual power are thought to be passed on to the wearer of the mask.

Above The creation stories of the Aborigines are reenacted in rituals of song and dance known as corroborees. They recall the Dreamtime, when fantastic creatures roamed the Earth and left their mark on the landscape.

The spirit world

As well as a creator god, there are believed to be many more individual spirits whose help can be sought in everyday life. These may be associated with special places (for example, a clearing in the forest or a particular rock), or with tribal activities (hunting, pottery, and farming). The spirit world is divided into good and evil. Evil spirits, associated with witches and demons, are thought to bring disasters to the tribe (a failed harvest, a drought, or defeat by an enemy) and for individuals (sickness, or the death of a child). At such times, the people turn to shamans, who possess powers to counteract the evil spirits and return people to health.

Respect for the gods also mirrors respect for parents. Boys and girls are expected to show reverence toward their elders and care for them in old age. An Akan proverb from Ghana says, "If your parents take care of you up to the time you cut your teeth, you take care of them when they lose theirs."

ABORIGINAL AND MAORI BELIEFS

To the Aboriginal people of Australia, the land is a sacred place, crisscrossed by energy and unseen spiritual forces. For them, the spirit world is inseparable from the natural world, and elements of the landscape such as mountains, trees, and water holes are treated as holy sites.

The Dreamtime

The landscape is believed to have come into being at a distant time in history known as the Dreamtime. At that time, fantastic beings, half-human and half-animal, peopled the world. They left their mark (literally) on the Earth, so that a footprint became a valley, for example, or a thumbprint a lake. Aborigines believe that these beings are their distant ancestors. Each person is believed to have been born with his or her own Dreaming, so that someone with, say, a Honey Ant Dreaming can point to a honey ant and say, "This is my great-great-great-great grandfather."

Harmony with nature

Stories from the Dreamtime are passed down through the generations, depicted on bark paintings and reenacted in dance, song, and ritual. The spirits of the ancestors are everywhere, in the land (*manta*) and in people (*anangu*). The traditional life of the Aborigine is lived close to nature and they are taught, according to the Laws of the Dreamtime, to treat it with great respect. In return, they will have nothing to fear from it.

Above *Aborigines look back to their ancestral past, which they believe was populated by fantastic creatures, and believe that they are directly related to elements of the natural world. This modern painting is of a Snake Dreaming.*

Left *This bark painting depicts a Wandjina—an ancestral being from the sea and sky that brings rain and controls the fertility of the land and the animals.*

Left Maoris greet each other by pressing their noses together in a hongi. It is a symbol of welcome and friendship.

The Aborigines killed only what they needed to eat, and developed such a close understanding of the natural environment that they could follow the tracks of a kangaroo over huge distances. Breaking Laws of the Dreamtime would, they believed, bring catastrophe, and losing their land would be like losing their souls. This is what many Aborigines believe has happened today. White settlers, who began colonizing the continent 300 years ago, have gradually forced them off their ancestral lands into cities and reservations cut off from their historic past.

The Maoris

In the beginning, according to Maori tradition, Sky Father and Earth Mother held each other in darkness in a deep embrace. Between them lay their children—the gods of wind, forest, sea, and food, and a god known as "the fierce one." To reach the light, the children had to force their parents apart, which the forest god Tane did by putting his head on his mother and his feet on his father and pushing hard. This separation was necessary for humanity, but it was also sad, and that sadness is expressed by the rain, which falls like tears from the sky.

Although their creation stories differ from those of the Aborigines, the Maoris, who came to Aotearoa (New Zealand) from an ancient homeland called Hawaiki in about 750 B.C., share with them a communal life based on respect for the land. When a child is born, the father or priest recites a prayer, or *karakia*, an appeal to the gods for special power. At death, it is believed that the spirit returns to the ancestral homeland.

Below The Maori meetinghouse, richly carved with scenes from the past, is part of communal life. The foreground of the meetinghouse is sacred, and it is here that bodies are brought before burial.

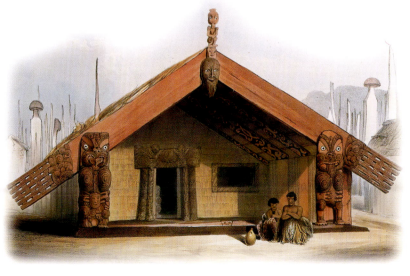

NATIVE AMERICANS

Native American tribes were well established throughout North America by the time Europeans arrived in the 1500s. There were many different tribes, each with its own language, culture, and religion. While some elements of their religions overlapped, there were many differences in their religious rituals.

The Great Spirit
Many Native Americans believe that the world has been created by a Great Spirit, and that there are other spiritual powers all around them, usually in the form of the natural landscape, which they consider sacred. This Great Spirit has many names: for the Sioux it is Wakan Tanka, for the Hopi it is Masau, for the Iroquois it is Orenda, and for the Ojibwa it is Kitche Manitou.

Creation myths
Native Americans have elaborate creation myths that they tell to their children and reenact in ritual dances. The Iroquois, for example, believe that, before the Earth was made, everyone lived in the sky. When the Sky Chief's daughter fell through a hole into the waters below, she was rescued by two swans. At her request, other animals took turns diving into the waves, until eventually a toad dived down and returned to the surface with a mouthful of soil. The toad spat it out onto the shell of a turtle and from this, the Earth grew.

__Right__ A medicine mask dance is performed by the Iroquois of the Northeast (today's Ontario) to invoke the powers of the spirit world for healing purposes.

Guardian spirits

In addition to the creator gods, Native Americans look to guardian spirits who, if treated with respect and given offerings of food and tobacco, will take care of them and bless them with strength, health, and a long life. They also believe in evil spirits who must be fought or avoided. The Navajo and the Apache have a particular dread of ghosts, which they think could cause them harm. The medicine man is an important figure in the tribe. He is a shaman, a priest, and a healer, and is thought to have close contact with the spirit world.

Close to nature

Some early Native Americans settled down and established agricultural communities, while others were nomadic hunters wandering from place to place, but they were all influenced by the cycle of the seasons. At key times in the year—the migration of the buffalo, the return of fish upstream from the sea, or the ripening of the corn and tobacco crops—they would offer up prayers of thanksgiving.

Above The hunters of the plains had a very special relationship with the buffalo on which they relied for food and clothing. The Plains Indians killed only what they needed and, in some tribes, asked the animal's pardon through prayer before killing it.

Right A revelation mask, made by the Kwakiutl Indian tribe from the Northwest, opens up to reveal a second mask. These masks portray trickster gods, who show the tribe that the world is not always as it seems.

Fighting for survival

Native Americans suffered the same fate as the Aborigines of Australia when they were invaded and their traditional homelands were overrun. The American government has tried to ban certain religious rituals (particularly the use of peyote, a hallucinogenic cactus which was believed to bring closer contact with the spirit world). Recently, they have supported the Native American beliefs, which have in turn influenced some New Age beliefs.

AFRICAN RELIGION

I t is thought that about 15 percent of the African population practices some form of local or native religion alongside the continent's most widespread religions: Christianity and Islam.

Creation stories

Creation stories vary from tribe to tribe. The Dinka people of southern Sudan tell of a woman who accidentally pierced a hole in the sky while she was hoeing the ground. The sky god was angry and sent disease and death through the tear she had made. From that moment, suffering entered the world. The Barotse people of Zambia have a different story. They tell of a time when the creator, Nyambi, lived happily on Earth with his wife Nasilele, and the human beings he had created. Their leader, Kamonu, was an ambitious man who annoyed the gods so much with his wicked ways that they decided to leave him and the Earth behind. Nyambi sought the help of a giant spider, which wove a web up to the heavens.

As Nyambi and Nasilele escaped, they were followed by Kamonu, who had built a wooden tower. This crashed to the ground, leaving Kamonu stranded on Earth, able to see the gods only in the form of the sun and the moon.

Other gods

African tribes have a strong sense of an unseen spirit world behind the everyday world they see, touch, hear, and smell. The link between these two worlds is the shaman, or witch doctor. As well as practicing traditional medicine, the people believe that he can travel through the spirit world while in a trance.

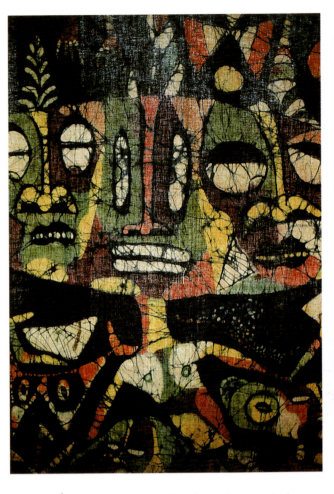

Above Eshu, the trickster god of Nigeria, is depicted on batik. As in Native American beliefs, these spirits of mischief demonstrate that the world is not a predictable place, but has many surprises to offer.

Left In the Juju dance of Cameroon, dancers dressed as forest spirits tell the story of the destruction of the forests and the natural environment.

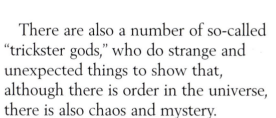

Right In some parts of West Africa, men have their own stool, which is elaborately carved and is said to contain part of the man's spirit. The men often carry their stools to tribal meetings.

Above In Zambia, a ng'anga, or shaman, treats a patient. It is believed that some sicknesses are caused by a breakdown in relationships between humans and the natural world. The ng'anga tries to restore that balance by calling on higher powers.

There are also a number of so-called "trickster gods," who do strange and unexpected things to show that, although there is order in the universe, there is also chaos and mystery.

The gods are usually at the service of a supreme god, who has a variety of names. It is Amma for the Dogon tribe in Mali, Chukwu for the Igbo of Nigeria, and Vidye Mukulu for the Baluba of the Democratic Republic of Congo (formerly Zaire).

Community life

A sense of community and cooperation is vital to tribal African societies. Their world is a network of interdependent relationships, in which the strong help the weak, the young protect the old, and the elders instruct the children. This is summed up in the African proverb, "It takes a village to raise a child." Young men and women are expected to get married soon after initiation into adulthood. It is extremely rare for someone not to marry. They are also expected to have children so that they can fulfill their spiritual obligations to become an ancestor. The spirits of the dead are thought to live on and visit the Earth. Small wooden cages are sometimes found outside homes, where a spirit can stay during these visits.

HINDUISM: AN INTRODUCTION

The origin of the word Hindu is to be found in the word *Sindhu*, which refers to the Indus River, which runs northwest of India in present-day Pakistan. Hinduism is inextricably linked to the land of India itself and has come to mean that cluster of religious beliefs and practices that has grown up over the past 4,500 years on the Indian subcontinent.

The word Hinduism is a modern one that came into being as recently as the 1800s. Hindus themselves refer to their religion in a number of different ways (*see page 44*). One of these is *dharma*, a Sanskrit word with two meanings. The first is the cosmic law by which all creation is governed; and the second is appropriate conduct, or the proper way of behaving to achieve one's spiritual goals.

Right Cows are considered sacred in India and can be seen wandering freely through villages, towns, and cities.

Hinduism was born out of one of the world's oldest civilizations, but unlike other religions, it has no single founder, prophet, or messenger. Instead, it represents a gradual development of thought, philosophy, and devotion. It is not a creed (with rules and set beliefs), but a way of life that seeks to free believers from worldly attachments so that they can appreciate what is true and eternal.

Although eight out of ten people in India (which has a population of around 900 million) describe themselves as Hindu, their approach to the religion, and the way in which they practice it, varies from region to region.

Right A flowing river is a living symbol for Hindus, who see human life as an ongoing cycle from the source of the river to the sea, and back again to the source. Here at Varanasi, pilgrims bathe in the Ganges River as part of their religious devotions.

The belief in reincarnation

The different Hindu traditions are all linked by common threads. One of these is a belief in reincarnation—that when people die they are born again into a new life somewhere in the material world, their new identity (or incarnation) dictated by the good (or bad) deeds they have done while alive. This belief in the ongoing cycle of life, from birth to death to rebirth, is contained in the word *samsara*. The spiritual goal of Hindus is to purify themselves in each successive life so that eventually they will achieve *moksha*—release from the cycle of time, and deliverance into the ultimate reality of eternity itself. This eternity is known as *Brahman*, the godhead (source and origin of all creation).

During the early period of its development, Hindu society was divided into four classes (*varnas*). At the top were the *Brahmins*, who were learned in the scriptures and were permitted to become priests. Beneath them were the *Kshatriyas*, or warrior class, followed by the tradesmen and farmers, known as *Vaishyas*. Last came the *Shudras*, or laborers and servants. Today, the Indian government is trying to improve the lives of the lowest group, the *Dalit* ("the oppressed"). Sometimes known as the "untouchables," they usually do the most menial work. But attitudes toward many of these people are still largely negative. The hardship of their lives is made bearable by the belief that in a future incarnation they may climb higher up the spiritual ladder.

THE HOLY MEN

Sadhus, or Hindu holy men, lead a life of self-denial, practicing self-discipline and avoiding all sensual pleasure in order to develop greater spiritual powers. They have a solitary life, wandering from place to place and begging for just enough to survive. They also wear very few clothes (some wear no clothing at all) and sometimes perform acts of extreme penance such as prolonged fasting or living alone in remote mountain caves during the winter. Ordinary Indian men and women respect the *sadhus'* chosen way of life and will often ask them for advice on how best to lead their own lives. Their dramatic appearance is accepted as a completely normal feature of Indian life. The spiritual is an inseparable part of everyday life for most of the Indian population.

THE ORIGINS OF HINDUISM

Hinduism has its origins in the civilization that developed some 4,500 years ago along the Indus Valley, a corridor of fertile land stretching from the Himalayas through present-day Pakistan to the Arabian Sea. This civilization flourished from c.2500–B.C. 1500, and produced a highly developed culture centered on two cities: Mohenjo-Daro and Harappa.

Early history

Archaeological excavations made in 1921 revealed that these cities, the first on the Indian subcontinent, were enormous in size and elaborate in construction. The streets were laid out in a grid pattern and the buildings were solid with high defenses. What also came to light were numerous clay figurines depicting a mother goddess. She seems to have been worshiped as a source of life and creation and is a forerunner of the mother goddess Mahadevi in classical Hinduism.

The Vedic period

Some scholars claim that around 1500 B.C., tribes of Aryan people from the Caucasus region of Central Asia invaded the Indus Valley and the northwest plains of the Indian subcontinent. They brought with them their traditions and their language (which later became Sanskrit) and mixed elements of their own culture with the existing culture of the Indus Valley. Others say that it was development within the tradition, not invasion by an outside force, that brought about changes to the religion.

Left This terracotta model from Mohenjo-Daro may be of the mother goddess, who represented life, fertility, and the fruits of the Earth. She was worshiped as someone who provided and cared for humankind.

A typical Harrapan house had an open courtyard. Thick, windowless walls kept the inside of the house cool.

The brick houses had a sophisticated drainage system, and many had grain storerooms.

*Below At its peak, Mohenjo-Daro
had a population of around 30,000.
Many of the buildings were made of
baked bricks—and the bricks were
made to a uniform size.*

*Below This model chariot with
bullocks was found in Harappa.
Such artifacts suggest that this
was an increasingly sophisticated
civilization that recognized a
connection between the natural
and the spiritual worlds.*

The public bathing
house may have
been used for
ritual purification.

By *c.*900 B.C., the oral
tradition had given way to
the written tradition and the
religious beliefs were put into writing in the form
of the sacred texts we know as the four *Vedas*
(*see page 38*). The Vedic religion that developed
during this period is based on the ritual
sacrifice of animals to many different gods,
especially Indra, the god of war and storms,
and Agni, the god of fire. Vedic gods have
much in common with ancient Greek and
Roman gods, who also represented the
elements and the forces of nature.

The *Puranas*

About 1,800 years ago, religious ideas and practices crystallized
into the kind of Hinduism broadly recognized today. During this
period, the completion of the epic poems the *Mahabharata* and the
Ramayana marked a cultural and religious step forward. Creation
stories and stories about the lives of the gods appeared in another
collection of sacred texts, known as the *Puranas* (*see pages 38–39*).
Rules were eventually drawn up to govern the way that Hindus
should lead their lives. These included four stages, or *ashramas*,
which Hindus should ideally experience if they are to reach *moksha*—
liberation from the ongoing cycle of birth, death, and rebirth. The four
stages are: being a student to learn about the sacred literature; being a
householder to develop responsibility in society; being a contemplative
to reflect and meditate on important things in life; and being an
ascetic and to renounce the pleasures of the world.

35

HINDU GODS AND GODDESSES

Hindus believe in one god as the ultimate source of reality and existence. They describe their god as Brahman, the unseen, all-powerful force responsible for bringing all creation into being, and to which all creation will ultimately return. Brahman is neutral and impersonal and has to be approached through a series of personal deities, both male and female. The principal deities are Brahma, Vishnu, Shiva, and the goddess Mahadevi, but there are many other gods. These include gods from the Vedic period.

Below Ganesh, the Remover of Obstacles, is portrayed as a man with an elephant's head. Ganesh is often honored at the start of a journey. Traditionally, he is very fond of candy and most statues to him show him holding some candy in his hand.

Right Hanuman is the clever monkey god who came to the aid of Rama when he was fighting the demon, Ravana, King of Lanka. Hanuman is worshiped as a source of protection.

The deities from this period represent the forces of nature and include Agni, Indra, and Varuna. Agni is the god of fire and the life force of nature. Varuna maintains the cosmic order, has the power to punish and reward, and is worshiped as god of the waters and oceans. Indra is the god of the sky and the rain. These gods are addressed in the thousand or so hymns that make up the sacred text known as the *Rig Veda* (*see page* 38).

In addition to the main gods, there are lesser gods such as Vayu, the god of wind, and Surya, the god of the sun. Hindus believe that there are elements of the divine in all living things, so particular animals are worshiped as part of the divine plan. In four of his incarnations, the god Vishnu assumes the form of an animal. He appears as a fish, a tortoise, a boar, and a man-lion.

Two other gods that are particularly important in Hindu worship are Hanuman, the monkey god, and Ganesh, one of the two sons of Shiva. Ganesh is a very popular god in India. It is said that following a misunderstanding, Ganesh's father, Shiva, accidentally beheaded him. When he realized his mistake, he was so upset that he promised to replace his head with the head of the first living thing he saw —which happened to be an elephant. Ganesh, who is known as the Remover of Obstacles, and is worshiped as the god of learning, is portrayed with a human body (with a large pot belly!) and an elephant's head with one tusk. Hindus often have a favorite deity and may have a special shrine in the home.

Right Indra is the sky god and the god of rain. He is often portrayed wearing a turban or a fiery tiara. He sits astride an elephant and speeds across the sky.

THE SACRED WRITINGS

The earliest of the Hindu scriptures are the four texts known collectively as the *Vedas*, which were begun before B.C. 1000. They are the first examples of Hindu written tradition. The oldest of the *Vedas* is the *Rig Veda*, which contains more than 1,000 hymns written in Sanskrit and is addressed to the elemental gods of Earth, fire, air, and water.

Much later, an important collection of philosophical works known as the *Upanishads* appeared. These try to explain the meaning of existence and to provide answers to the big questions in life, such as where we come from, why we are here, and what will happen to us when we die. The *Vedas* and the *Upanishads* are regarded as the revealed words of God and not a single syllable of them can be changed. In addition to a collection known as the *Puranas*, which contains stories of the lives and adventures of the gods, there are two other important works of Hindu literature, called the *Mahabharata* and the *Ramayana*.

Above *A chariot fight takes place between Bhima and Arjuna, two Pandava brothers, and Drona, leader of the opposing forces.*

The *Mahabharata*

The *Mahabharata* was written in its present form between 300 and 100 B.C. and is probably the largest single poem in the world, containing about 200,000 lines. This epic poem tells the story of the war between the five Pandava brothers, helped by their distant relative Krishna, and their 100 cousins, who live in Kurukshetra, near what is now Delhi. The war, caused by a dispute over who is the rightful ruler, is long and bitter. Although the five brothers eventually win, the story gains its power from the different attitudes shown by the brothers to the realities of fighting. For example, the third brother, called Arjuna, is a superb fighter and commander, but objects to warfare. As the story unfolds, the reader is presented with discussions about every aspect of Hindu life, including its laws, politics, geography, astronomy, and science. Consequently, what emerges alongside an exciting story of warfare is a kind of textbook of Hindu thinking.

"These words of glory to the God who is light shall be words supreme among things that are great. I glorify Varuna almighty, the god who is loving toward him who adores. We praise you with our thoughts, O God. We praise you as the sun praises you in the morning; may we find joy in being your servants."

Extract from the *Rig Veda* in honor of Varuna, the upholder of the cosmic order

Above The Ramayana *is more than 50,000 lines long, and was written down around 200* B.C. *It tells the adventures of Prince Rama of Ayodhya, seen here sitting with his brothers and companions, having rescued his wife Sita from the clutches of Ravana, the ten-headed demon king of Lanka.*

Right Om *is the sacred word for god and is repeated in* mantra, *or prayers. Its deep humming sound is supposed to be a living contact with the divine presence.*

The Bhagavad Gita

A central section of the *Mahabharata* is known as the *Bhagavad Gita* (the Song of the Lord). It is a conversation between Arjuna and his charioteer (who is none other than Krishna, the incarnation of Vishnu), but it also explores the essential questions of life. It is a meditation on the nature of God and an exploration of the ways of achieving liberation (*moksha*) through work, devotion, and knowledge. If the *Mahabharata* is sometimes described as an encyclopedia of Hindu life, the 18 chapters that make up the Bhagavad Gita are often regarded as the "bible" of Hinduism.

THE HINDU TRINITY

The Hindu idea of God is contained in the word *Brahman*, which means "the origin and the cause of all existence." Brahman appears to humans in various forms and is worshiped in the shape of different gods and goddesses. Chief among these are three male gods: Brahma, Vishnu, and Shiva—the Hindu Trinity. Brahma is the creator who brings the universe into existence; Vishnu preserves life and all living things; Shiva is the destroyer (also known as the Lord of Time), who destroys the world. This ongoing cycle of creation, preservation, and destruction is at the center of Hindu belief. There is no real end or beginning to life. The beginning is an end and the end is a new beginning.

Brahma the creator
Since Brahma is the lord of all creation, he is considered to be above human worship and very few temples are dedicated to him. When he is shown in paintings and carvings, he is often seen with four faces and four arms, and sometimes on a swan or a lotus flower.

Above Brahma sits upon the lotus from which he was born at the time of creation. His wife is Sarasvati, the goddess of learning.

Below Shiva the destroyer dances in a circle of fire. At his feet lies a demon he has killed.

Vishnu the preserver
Vishnu is responsible for controlling human fate. He appears in ten incarnations, or *avatars*. The two most important are Krishna, the most popular god, and Rama. Vishnu is often portrayed riding majestically across the heavens on an eagle (Garuda). In his hand, he may hold a discus, symbolizing the sun, or a mace, suggesting the power of nature.

Above A group of young Indian women pray in front of a shrine representing the Hindu mother goddess, Mahadevi.

Matsya the fish saved humanity from the flood.

Kurma the turtle carried the world on his back.

Varaha the boar raised the Earth with his tusks.

Narasimha, half-man and half-lion, defeated evil demons.

Vamana the dwarf defeated demons.

Rama fights against evil in the world and upholds virtue and law.

Krishna is renowned as a warrior, a teacher, and a lover.

Parasurama (Rama with an axe) defeated the warrior caste.

Kalki, who will appear riding a white horse, is yet to come.

Buddha is "the enlightened one" and the founder of Buddhism.

Above The protective power of Vishnu (shown in the center of the picture in the form of Krishna with his consort Radha) appears on Earth in ten incarnations, or avatars, which prevent evil in the world.

Shiva the destroyer

Shiva is a god in whom all opposites meet and are resolved into one. So, while Shiva is believed to be responsible for destroying creation, he is also thought to be responsible for re-creating it. Shiva's wife appears in many forms, each representing an aspect of his character. Kali is fierce and is depicted surrounded by skulls or carrying severed heads and limbs. Parvati is known for her kindness and gentleness and is often shown with her son Ganesh, who has an elephant's head and one tusk.

HINDU WORSHIP

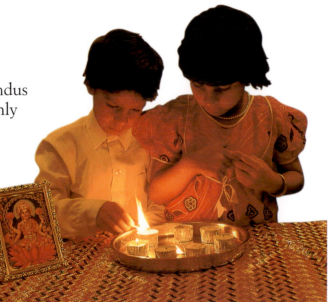

Daily worship is known as *puja* and for most Hindus is usually carried out in the home. A shrine richly decorated with pictures or statues (*murtis*) of favorite gods is set aside for this purpose. Wealthier families sometimes set aside a whole room as a shrine and worship there individually or as a family. *Puja* begins with the simplest but most important prayer (*mantra*)—the saying of the sacred word *Om* to make contact with the divine. This is followed by the recitation of other *mantras* from the scriptures and the offering of gifts (candy, money, fruit, etc.) to a particular god.

Worship is also carried out in the temple (*mandir*) under the supervision of a high-caste priest, or *Brahmin*. Although Hindus believe that their god is everywhere, they also believe that the temple is his special home. Only the priest is allowed to come close to the divine presence which "resides" in the inner sanctuary of the building, in the holy of holies known as the *garbhagriha* (womb-house).

Above *Children light candles to celebrate Diwali, the festival of lights.*

Below *Women pray in a Hindu temple on the Indonesian island of Bali.*

Before worship begins, members of the congregation carry out elaborate rituals of purification, which may involve washing the feet, rinsing the mouth, or preparing special food. The priest leads the worship by reading from the sacred texts and saying *mantras*. Small devotional lamps (*divas*) are lit, and after worship, the people share the food that has been blessed and offered to the gods.

> **"Lights are lit in Hindu households to guide Lakshmi, the goddess of fortune, into the home."**
>
> From the *Mahabharata*

Making a pilgrimage

Pilgrimage is an important part of Hindu worship and involves making the effort to travel to a sacred site. As such, it is considered an act of worship in itself. Particularly holy are sites associated with the birth or life of a god, such as Ayodhya, the legendary birthplace of Lord Rama; Kurukshetra, where the great war described in the *Mahabharata* is said to have taken place; Varanasi, also known as "the city of light," and believed to be the home of Lord Shiva; and Mathura, the birthplace of Lord Krishna. In addition, many Hindus will make a special journey to fords (safe crossing places in rivers). These symbolize the crossing from one life to another and the transition from *samsara* to *moksha* (*see page 33*), which every devout Hindu hopes to make. The most sacred river in India is the Ganges, named after Ganga, the river goddess. Bathing in its waters is an act of devotion, and bathing at the pilgrimage site of Varanasi is thought to be particularly special.

Above The Dusserah festival takes place in September or October. Effigies are burned in a reenactment of the triumph of Rama, Lakshman, and Hanuman over the demon Ravana, recorded in the epic Ramayana.

HINDU FESTIVALS

MARCH **Holi:** the festival (*left*) when people from all backgrounds mingle and throw colored powder (symbolizing fertility) over each other. It is celebrated with bonfires and street parties.
Shivaratri: a national celebration honoring Shiva.

AUGUST **Janmashtami:** the birthday of Krishna.

SEPTEMBER **Dusserah:** celebrating the triumph of good over evil.
Ganesh Chaturthi: the birthday of Ganesh.

OCTOBER **Diwali:** the festival of lights in honor of Rama's safe return from exile.

SOME HINDU BELIEFS

The word Hinduism was coined comparatively recently. It was introduced in the 1800s to describe a cluster of ancient Indian beliefs and religious practices. Hindus themselves are more inclined to refer to Hinduism by other names— *Dharma, Sanatana Dharma* (everlasting *Dharma*), or *Varnashramadharma*. These need some explanation because each word describes, in an Indian way, what people living in the West understand by Hinduism.

The four goals in life

Traditional Hinduism says that there are four goals in life. *Dharma*, the first goal, is the performance of duties appropriate to one's position in life. It also involves living a good life by being kind to others, telling the truth, helping one's neighbor, loving humanity, and being prepared to make sacrifices for other people. Everlasting *Dharma—Sanatana Dharma—*stresses this idea. The second goal of Hindu life is *artha*, the achievement of material prosperity or the pursuit of legitimate worldly success. The third is *kama*, the enjoyment of legitimate pleasure. And the fourth is *moksha*, the ultimate release from attachment to this world.

The four classes and the four stages of life

Hindu society is broadly divided into four *varnas*, or classes (priests, warriors, farmers or tradesmen, and servants or laborers), an earthly scheme that some Hindus believe reflects the divine pattern. They also believe that everyone should pass through four stages in life (*ashramas*)—as a student, as a householder, as a contemplative, and as an ascetic. The word *Varnashramadharma* describes Hindus as the people who "follow the way of the four classes and four stages of life."

Above This is one of 12 great wheels (symbolizing samsara—the wheel of life), intricately carved in stone on the temple of Surya the sun god at Konaraka, on the east coast of India.

Left Young Hindu boys have their heads ritually shaved. This marks, in a formal way, a stage of development in life.

Above Ritual is very important in Hindu worship and practice. Here, a couple exchange vows before committing themselves to marriage.

> "... the end of wisdom is Brahman, beginningless, supreme ... he sees all, he hears all. He is in all, and he is."
>
> Bhagavad Gita 13:12–13

The four stages are the spiritual milestones in a Hindu's time on Earth. The role of student is crucial as it stresses the importance of education and the acquisition of knowledge to achieve enlightenment. The role of the householder underlines the importance of the family. Hindus should then withdraw from the world as contemplatives, before becoming ascetics and cutting themselves off completely in preparation for death. This pattern is not followed rigidly by everyone, but it remains a powerful ideal for Hindus.

Birth and reincarnation

Each individual is believed to have an eternal soul (*atman*), which can be born millions of times into millions of forms or incarnations. The law of *karma* dictates how many times and how many forms. *Karma* is the moral law of the universe, the cosmic principle by which the world and all living things operate. Good deeds done in this life ensure progress in the next. Life is an ongoing cycle of birth, death, and rebirth (*samsara*). When people die, the soul leaves the body but is reborn into another body—human or animal. The precise nature of this new identity, or reincarnation, is determined by how well or badly a person has acted in previous lives. This process of reincarnation ends only when Hindus have achieved release (*moksha*) from *samsara* by freeing themselves from all attachments to worldly pleasure. Then, the soul returns to the eternal stillness of the divine *Brahman*, or godhead.

JAINISM: AN INTRODUCTION

The guiding principle of Jainism is respect for life and all living things. Tradition says that the religion was founded in the 500s B.C. by Mahavira (the Great Hero) in the Ganges Basin in northeast India. Like the Buddha, who was a contemporary, Mahavira was born into a high-caste family, but at the age of 29, he renounced his wealth to live as a wandering beggar. Tired of the ongoing cycle of birth, death, and rebirth, and dissatisfied with the prevailing religious teachings, he set out to find enlightenment for himself through practices that were increasingly ascetic (without material comforts). It is said that his first act was to tear out all his hair before leaving home. After 12 years of wandering, he achieved perfect knowledge (*kevala*) through fasting and meditation. Once he had attained enlightenment, Mahavira gathered a small group of followers around him and taught and preached for the next 30 years before starving himself to death in the village of Pava, near to where he was born. Pava is still an important pilgrimage site for Jain followers.

Above In 1975, on the 2,500th anniversary of the enlightenment of their founder, Mahavira, the Jains decided to adopt the symbol of the open palm.

The *Jinas*

Jains take their name from the word *Jina*—someone who has conquered attachment to the world and won victory of knowledge and enlightenment.

There are said to be 24 *Jinas* (also known as *Tirthankaras*, or "fordmakers"), of whom Mahavira is the last. These are spiritual guides able "to make a ford across the ocean of rebirth" to allow people to achieve release from the cycle of death and achieve liberation from rebirth.

Right Shvetambara monks and nuns wear masks to prevent them from breathing in tiny insects and killing them.

Left Every 12 or 13 years, the head of the immense statue of Lord Bahubali is anointed with offerings (turmeric water in this case) during a festival. The statue, erected in A.D. 981, towers over the Jain holy site of Sravanabegola in Karnataka State, India.

Below This is a Jain celebration near Jabalpur in India.

The Five Great Vows

In Jainism, monks and nuns take Five Great Vows (*Mahavratas*) to help them on their path toward enlightenment. These are *ahimsa*: not to harm any living thing; *satya*: to speak the truth; *asteya*: not to steal; *brahmacharya*: to abstain from sexual activity; and *aparigraha*: to give up all worldly things and human attachments. The vow of nonviolence or noninjury is central to Jainism, and novice monks are given a broom to sweep away living creatures so they do not tread on them accidentally and kill them.

By A.D. 100, the religion had split into two sects. The *Digambaras* (literally, "sky clad") believed that their total renunciation of worldly possessions meant that they should renounce clothing and (men, not women) should go completely naked. The *Shvetambaras* ("white clad") believed that monks and nuns could wear simple white robes.

There are thought to be about four million Jains worldwide, most of whom live on the Indian subcontinent, where they are members of the merchant, banking, and business communities.

JAIN BELIEF AND WORSHIP

Jains do not believe in one god, nor do they pray to gods to help them. Instead, they rely on spiritual teachers to train them in meditation and self-discipline, which will enable them to be released from the prison of day-to-day existence into the joy of ultimate liberation. Ordinary Jains, as well as monks and nuns, practice asceticism because they believe that only through controlling natural desires and appetites can a person be free of the material world.

Central to this belief is the concept of *karma*, which is different from that of the Hindus and Buddhists (*see pages 45 and 59*). For Jains, *karma* is composed of fine particles that stick to the soul, like mud sticks to a shoe, gradually building up and weighing it down. Doing bad deeds creates heavy *karma*, which prevents the soul's liberation, but doing good deeds causes the *karma* to be washed away, eventually allowing the liberated soul (*siddha*) to rise up to the heights of the universe, where it can live forever in spiritual freedom.

Above This typically ornate carving is from the 14th-century Jain temple of Chaumukha.

Right Jain temples are beautiful works of architecture, often richly decorated and carved to show reverence for the sacred images (pujas) of the Tirthankaras placed inside. This one is in the Indian state of Gujarat. Worship may involve quiet meditation or the repetition of a mantra (a word or syllable believed to possess spiritual power). The worshiper may also decorate an image with flowers or anoint it with special liquids.

Sources of *karma*

Jains believe that the principal sources of *karma* are: attachment to possessions and the material things in life; the expression of anger, pride, deceit, or greed; and false belief. The rejection of material things can be used to the advantage of others, and Jains are known for their charitable giving and the way they use their wealth to build temples, hospitals, and schools. Jains are encouraged to strengthen their devotional life by setting aside 48 minutes every day in which to practice meditation and to live one complete day as a monk during the major festival of Pajjusana.

Below Many Jains have a shrine in their home for daily worship. They rise before dawn and invoke the Five Supreme Beings, who represent stages along the path to spiritual liberation.

SIKHISM: AN INTRODUCTION

The Sikh religion was founded in the 1400s by Guru Nanak (*guru* means spiritual guide or teacher) in the area of present-day Pakistan and northwest India known as Punjab. It was a time of tension between Hindus and Muslims. Guru Nanak believed such religious conflicts were harmful and gathered around him a small group of followers who, like him, were searching for an understanding of God uncluttered by ritual. "There is neither Hindu nor Muslim. So whose path shall I follow?" he wondered. And he concluded, "I shall follow the path of God."

Sikhs believe in one god whom they call *Satguru*, or true teacher. They believe God created the world and all things in it, but that God is not visible in Creation. As a result, God's will has to be made known through wise and holy teachers, or gurus. Sikhism has ten human gurus (Guru Nanak and his nine successors) and a final guru not in the form of a person, but of a book—the *Adi Granth* (literally, the first book). This is a collection of the writings of the gurus and is honored in the same way as the ten human gurus— hence its more usual name, the *Guru Granth Sahib*.

Guru Nanak founded a religion based on the simple desire to get close to God and to do God's will. He also believed that true love of God is impossible without love of humanity, so he taught that men and women should be kind to their neighbors and share the fruits of their labors. In the beginning, Guru Nanak and his disciples formed a close-knit community devoted to singing and meditating on the Divine Name (*Nam*). Guru Nanak's hymns live on in Sikh worship practiced today.

Above As a mark of equality, Sikhs often eat communally in a shared dining room, or langar, *attached to the temple, or* gurdwara. *The gurdwara is also a community center and a base for charitable work in the community.*

Above Today, most of the Sikh population live in the agricultural state of Punjab in northwest India and Pakistan.

Right Guru Nanak (A.D. 1469–1539) was the founder of Sikhism and the first of the Ten Gurus, or teachers, of the faith. After a religious experience at the age of 30, he became a wandering preacher before eventually settling in Kartarpur (in present-day Pakistan), where he built the first Sikh temple.

THE TEN GURUS

The development of Sikhism is inseparable from the lives of the Ten Gurus who shaped the religion over the first two centuries of its existence. The religion was founded by Guru Nanak in the A.D. 1400s, when he began to attract a group of followers who wanted a simpler, purer form of devotion, uncluttered by ritual. Originally, the group led an intensely spiritual life, meditating on the name of God and singing the devotional hymns Nanak had written. They lived a communal life and followed three basic rules: *kirt karo* (hard work); *nam japo* (worship of the Divine Name); and *vand cauko* (sharing the fruits of their labors).

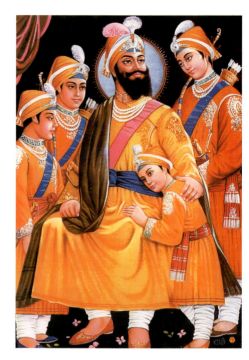

Above *Guru Gobind Singh is surrounded by his sons. He was the last of the living gurus, and is chiefly remembered for founding the Khalsa and for his decision to treat the Sikh holy scripture as if it were itself a living guru.*

A succession of gurus

Nanak's successor was Guru Angad (1504–1552), who is chiefly remembered for composing the Gurmukhi script in which the Punjabi language was written down for worship. The third guru was Amar Das (1479–1574), who founded the town of Goindval in Punjab, where Sikhs gathered twice a year to renew friendships and to deepen their faith. The fourth guru, Guru Ram Das (1534–1581), moved the Sikh's spiritual center from Goindval to what is now Amritsar. The fifth guru, Guru Arjan (1563–1606), was the son of Guru Ram Das, who built the Golden Temple. The Sikhs' next leader, Guru Hargobind (1595–1644), transformed the community (the *Panth*) into a more militant force. Guru Har Rai (1630–1661) was the seventh Guru. He was followed by Har Krishan (1656–64) and then by Guru Tegh Bahadur (1621–1675) and Guru Gobind Singh (1666–1708).

Left *This Sikh is being initiated into the Khalsa (community of the pure) in the distinctive uniform worn by Guru Gobind Singh. He carries a ceremonial sword symbolizing his willingness to defend the faith against outside aggression.*

Above Sikh elders transport the Guru Granth Sahib to the temple, where it is installed with great ceremony.

The *Guru Granth Sahib*

Guru Gobind Singh, the tenth and last living guru, is regarded with almost as much veneration as the founder, Guru Nanak. He was responsible for two key developments that have shaped the Sikh identity to this day. The first was the foundation of the *Khalsa*—the community of "pure" Sikhs, who were prepared to die for their faith. They are baptized with holy water (*amrit*), given the name *Singh*, meaning "lion" (female members were called *Kaur* meaning "princess"), and told to wear a distinctive uniform that marked them out as brave soldier-saints. His second innovation was to place authority over the Sikh community, not in the person of a living guru, but in the Sikh holy scripture. From then on, it was known as the *Guru Granth Sahib*.

Left The Guru Granth Sahib, also known as the Adi Granth (the first book), is the Sikhs' holiest scripture.

AMRITSAR

Amritsar is the Sikh holy city in the state of Punjab in northwest India and Pakistan. It is here that the Golden Temple was completed in 1601, by the fifth guru, Guru Arjan. The Golden Temple, also known in Punjabi as the Harimandir Sahib (house of God), is Sikhism's holiest shrine. By day, it houses the holy scripture, the *Guru Granth Sahib*. At night, the scripture is stored in a nearby building, the Akal Takht. While the Golden Temple is devoted to worship, the Akal Takht, or seat of temporal power, is a kind of parliament and conference hall where political and social matters are discussed.

Daily worship at the Golden Temple starts at four o'clock in the morning—an hour before the *Guru Granth Sahib* is installed each day—and continues until midnight. Hymns (*kirtan*) from the scriptures are sung all day long, and the temple attracts a constant stream of visitors and pilgrims. During the early 1800s, the Temple's two upper stories were covered with gold leaf. The name by which it is known to foreigners, the Golden Temple, dates from this time.

Although it is a focal point of worship, the Golden Temple is part of a much larger complex of guest houses, conference centers, dining halls, watchtowers, cloisters, and a museum. At the entrance to the Temple compound is a gateway called the Darshani Deorhi, above which are stored the golden spades that were used to dig the lake. In front of the gateway is a cardamom tree, where a small shrine marks the spot where Guru Arjan is believed to have sat while he supervised the excavation of the pool.

> "All creatures on their actions are judged in God's court, just and true."
>
> *Guru Granth Sahib*

Left Pictures of the Ten Sikh Gurus and other religious souvenirs are sold to the hundreds of thousands of visitors who make a pilgrimage to the Golden Temple each year.

Left and below The Golden Temple, which by day houses the Sikh scripture, the Guru Granth Sahib, is Sikhism's holiest shrine. Visitors and pilgrims reach it by a 200-foot causeway built across the Lake of Immortality. Moving across the lake to the shrine is in itself a solemn act of worship.

The temple complex has been the scene of many conflicts throughout its history. In the 1700s, it witnessed frequent fighting between the Sikhs and the Moguls—Muslims from Afghanistan. The latest conflict was in 1984, when Indian security forces stormed the Golden Temple and shot dead a Sikh activist, the leader of a movement for Sikh independence. In the fighting that followed, the Akal Takht was virtually destroyed and had to be rebuilt. Later the same year, the Indian Prime Minister, Indira Gandhi, was assassinated in a retaliation that prompted a massacre of Sikhs and several years of fighting between the Indian authorities and Sikh separatists.

Right A Sikh woman reads the holy scripture, Guru Granth Sahib.

LIFE AS A SIKH

The turban is the most distinctive feature of Sikh dress but it is only one element of the traditional customs and practices of the faith. When a man is initiated into the Khalsa (becomes a full member of the Sikh religion), he must wear the Five Ks—so-called because the Punjabi words describing them each begin with a "K." They are: *kesh*, uncut hair covered by the turban; the *kirpan*, a short sword symbolizing resistance against evil; the *kara*, a steel bracelet symbolizing faithfulness to God (originally protection for the sword arm); the *khanga*, a comb symbolizing personal hygiene; and the *kach*, knee-length breeches symbolizing purity. Meat slaughtered in the Muslim way along with tobacco and alcohol are forbidden, as are stealing, gambling, and unfaithfulness to one's marriage partner. Sikhs should get up early, bathe, then meditate on the name of God (*Nam*). Each day, they should read or recite from the scriptures and, if possible, join a congregation (*sangat*) at the temple (*gurdwara*) where they can listen to the words of the gurus and do charitable work.

At the center of temple worship is the Sikh holy scripture, the *Guru Granth Sahib*. Members of the congregation must kneel in its presence and approach it barefoot and with the head covered. On special occasions, a temple supervisor, or *Granthi*, may lead the worship, waving a type of fan or whisk (a *chauri*) over the text as he reads the words aloud. At the end of the recitation of hymns, the congregation joins in the collective prayer (*ardas*).

Left This Sikh wears the traditional costume demonstrating the Five Ks— kesh, kirpan, kara, khanga, *and* kach.

Above At a Sikh wedding, the bride often wears traditional Punjabi red. Gifts of money are made to the couple, and passages from the Guru Granth Sahib are read out to bless the marriage.

Right The Khanda is a sign often used for Sikhism. The central, double-edged sword symbolizes belief in one god. The two outer blades represent spiritual and temporal power.

The *Guru Granth Sahib* also plays a part in family ceremonies. For example, when naming newborn babies the book is opened at random and the first letter of the first hymn on that page is used as the first letter of the baby's name. At a marriage ceremony (*anand karaj*), the bride and groom walk around the holy book four times as a sign of its importance in their future life together. A section of the scripture known as the *Kirtan Sohila* is read at funeral services. The dead person is dressed in the traditional Five Ks and the body is cremated as soon as possible, usually on the day of death. To mark births, deaths, and marriages, Sikhs often hold an "akhand path," a continuous 48-hour reading of the *Guru Granth Sahib* timed to end at dawn on the day of the particular event being celebrated. Sikh festivals (*gurpurbs*) usually commemorate the birth or death of one of the Ten Gurus or an event associated with his life.

Right This young girl wears traditional costume at the festival for Guru Gobind Singh's birthday.

SIKH FESTIVALS

DECEMBER/JANUARY Guru Gobind Singh's birthday.

FEBRUARY **Hola Mohalla:** the fair in Anandpur in honor of Guru Gobind Singh.

APRIL **Baisakhi:** a celebration of the foundation of the Khalsa.

AUGUST A celebration of the completion of the *Guru Granth Sahib*.

OCTOBER Guru Nanak's birthday.
Diwali: a Hindu festival used by Sikhs to mark the release from prison of Guru Hargobind.

BUDDHISM: AN INTRODUCTION

Buddhism began in northeast India around 450 B.C. It is based on the teachings of Siddhartha Gautama, who became known as the Buddha, or "Enlightened One." Buddhism emerged from the other religious ideas of the time, predominantly those of the Brahmins. The Buddha frequently overturned or reinterpreted the teachings of others, and his own approach was in many respects quite new. Life, he said, is constantly changing and people should not look for happiness in wealth or possessions, beauty or fame, because these things will disappear. Instead, he taught that we should see things as they really are and, by freeing ourselves from greed, selfishness, ignorance, anger, fear, passion, and all the things that keep us attached to this "unreal" world, achieve a state of enlightenment known as *nirvana*.

Below This reclining Buddha is from Bangkok in Thailand. The Buddha taught that he was not the only "Enlightened One." There were many more buddhas before him and many more to come. The aim of life should be to strive to be an enlightened one, or buddha, oneself.

After he had achieved enlightenment the Buddha wandered from place to place with a small group of disciples, but during the rainy season, settled in one spot where he established a more stable community. This community (*sangha*) became the basis for the monastic life which continues to be important in Buddhism throughout the world today.

The law of cause and effect

Buddhists do not worship a person or a god, but follow a system of thoughts, meditation, and spiritual exercise based on the Buddha's teachings, or *dharma*. These teachings were written down long after the Buddha's death. In his lifetime, they were passed on by word of mouth by his followers, who carefully memorized them. Buddhism teaches that all our thoughts have consequences both for ourselves and for others. This law of cause and effect, known as *karma*, dictates that the consequence of good deeds, words, and thoughts is rebirth into a better life. Similarly, when those who do not accept personal responsibility for the things they do in life are reborn, they will find that they are further away from the ultimate goal of *nirvana*.

Above The monastic life is important in Buddhism. Monks observe a strict way of life that involves having only a few basic possessions and being completely dependent on ordinary people for their one daily meal, shelter, and clothing. In return, they teach and help people.

There are five basic rules that all practicing Buddhists agree to follow: not to kill; not to steal; not to lie; to abstain from sexual misconduct; and to avoid intoxicants such as drugs and alcohol. The Buddha also taught that compassion and kindness are the most important principles for a person to live by.

Buddhism spread to nearby countries and, eventually, to the West, where it has adapted to the culture of the time and place, and become increasingly popular.

Right Buddhism began in India and spread out into the neighboring countries and beyond. Worldwide, there are over 300 million followers. This Buddha on a turquoise throne is from the Chinese Ming dynasty (1368–1644).

THE LIFE OF THE BUDDHA

There are many myths and legends surrounding the life of the Buddha, but most scholars accept that Buddhism's historical founder lived between 485 and 405 B.C. Siddhartha Gautama came from a prosperous family and led a privileged life. At the age of 29, he is said to have observed three things that prompted him to embark on his spiritual quest: illness; aging; and death and decay. Tradition has it that he met a holy man who, despite his poverty, was happy. At that moment, Siddhartha Gautama realized that life's pleasures are illusions, and that the only road to contentment lies in what is real and true. He decided to leave his home and devote himself to the quest for truth.

Left The Buddha is said to have attained nirvana *beneath the Bodhi tree, or tree of enlightenment.*

"I am is a vain thought. I am not is a vain thought. I shall be is a vain thought. I shall not be is a vain thought. Vain thoughts are a sickness. But after overcoming all vain thoughts one is called a silent thinker."

The words of the Buddha

The Four Noble Truths

At first he became an ascetic; meditating, fasting, and practicing severe exercises of self-denial that made his hair fall out and ruined his health, leaving him weak and emaciated. After six years he decided such extremes of self-discipline were unsatisfactory and the best route to enlightenment was along a path of moderation. One night, his life changed forever when, seated beneath a tree (later called the Bodhi tree, or tree of enlightenment), he began a deep and prolonged meditation. In the course of his meditation he attained a state of perfect knowledge and perfect peace (*nirvana*). This was the moment when he gained insight into The Four Noble Truths—the core of Buddhist teaching.

Above This statue shows the Buddha *before he achieved enlightenment. Extreme self-denial had left him thin and weak. He later abandoned such practices in favor of moderation.*

Right *The Buddha's teaching is often symbolized by a wheel (seen here in his left hand). In his first sermon in Benares, the Buddha declared that he was setting in motion "the wheel of dharma."*

THE FOUR NOBLE TRUTHS

• All existence is unsatisfactoriness.
• Unsatisfactoriness is caused by the craving (*tanha*) for something permanent in the world when no such permanence exists.
• The cessation of unsatisfactoriness, *nirvana*, can be attained.
• *Nirvana* can be reached following The Noble Eightfold Path.

THE NOBLE EIGHTFOLD PATH

Each of these eight steps to *nirvana* contains the word *samma*, or right.
Right knowledge
Right attitude
Right speech
Right action
Right livelihood
Right effort
Right state of mind
Right concentration

Shortly after this he gathered around him five companions, who became his first disciples. Traveling around India for the next 45 years, he lived the life of a beggar and teacher. The Buddha died at the age of 80 in the town of Kushinagara. Among his last words to his followers were, "Do not cry. Have I not told you that it is in the nature of all things, however dear they may be to us, that we must part with them and leave them?"

THE DEVELOPMENT OF BUDDHISM

After the Buddha's death, his followers decided to preserve his teachings. This was not easy because nothing had been written down—indeed, it was not until more than 350 years later that the first Buddhist writings appeared. To bring the master's ideas together, Buddhist monks held a council in Rajagriha and agreed that their conclusions should be reviewed 100 years later in Vesali. But it was the third Buddhist council, held at Pataliputta, that proved the most significant. Monks gathered to try to agree on the Buddha's message, and, though at first there was considerable agreement, there were also the first signs of a deep division.

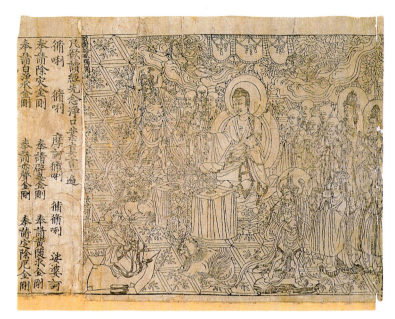

Above A page of the Chinese translation of the so-called Diamond Sutta. *This version appeared in the* A.D. *800s and is the oldest printed book in the world. The* Diamond Sutta *belongs to the collection of* Mahayana *scriptures known as* The Perfection of Wisdom Suttas.

Two schools of thought

Out of this emerged two distinct forms of Buddhism—early and late. The only surviving school of early Buddhism is known as *Theravada*, and all later schools are collectively referred to as *Mahayana*. The main difference between early and late Buddhism is the interpretation of the various teachings. However, they also use different texts. *Theravada* means "the teaching of the elders." Its scriptures contain three sets of teachings that were originally written on palm leaves and stored in wicker baskets (hence the other name by which they are known—the *tripitaka*, or three baskets). The *Sutta Pitaka*, or "basket of doctrinal teachings," is believed to contain the teachings of the Buddha himself. The *Vinaya Pitaka*, or "basket of monastic disciplinary rules," contains more material about the Buddha and lays down the rules of discipline for the monastic community. The *Abhidhamma Pitaka*, or "basket of higher teaching," is for serious scholars. The *Mahayana* tradition, or "Great Vehicle," has its own texts, or *suttas*.

Left The lotus flower, a water lily with its roots in the mud, features frequently in Buddhist imagery. It symbolizes the belief that enlightenment (the flower) can be achieved in the midst of human suffering (the mud and slime beneath the water).

Above Buddhists believe that stupas (ancient burial mounds) contain relics of early Buddhist holy men, or even of the Buddha himself. Many stupas, like this one in Nepal, have become important places of pilgrimage.

One of the distinctive features of *Theravada* Buddhism is the idea of the *arhat*. This is a person who has achieved enlightenment through the teaching of another enlightened being (a buddha). Theravadins believe that only monks can achieve such a state and so try to spend some of their lives in a monastery. Mahayana Buddhists, on the other hand, believe that everyone is capable of achieving enlightenment. They attach great importance to the concept of the *bodhisattva*, a semi-divine being who has achieved enlightenment, but who has voluntarily renounced *nirvana*, to stay in the world to help others. By the A.D. 1000s, Buddhism had declined in influence in India, but was flourishing in many other Asian countries.

"**When I attain this highest perfect wisdom, I will deliver all sentient beings into the eternal peace of *nirvana*.**"

The Buddha's words, taken from the *Diamond Sutta*

63

Types of Buddhism

Buddhism spread beyond India to central and southeastern Asia and adapted to the culture of the countries in which it took root. Different varieties of Buddhist practice emerged—*Mahayana* Buddhism, in particular, includes several distinctive traditions.

Chinese Buddhism

Buddhism arrived in China by A.D. 100 and was practiced alongside Confucianism and Taoism (*see pages 74–81*). By the A.D. 300s, many of the texts had been translated from Sanskrit into Chinese, and many of the *bodhisattvas* had their Chinese equivalents. For example, Avalokiteshvara, the Bodhisattva of Compassion, became Kuan Yin (believed to take the form of a young woman who is ready to help people in trouble).

Tibetan Buddhism

Tibet has its own forms of Buddhism, which combine magic and spirit worship with a type of *Mahayana* Buddhism known as *Vajrayana* ("the vehicle of the thunderbolt"). *Vajrayana* is based on ancient texts called *tantras* and involves ritual practices, such as meditation and chanting *mantras* (words believed to have powerful energies).

Of the many schools of Tibetan Buddhism, the best known is the Gelukpa tradition (also known as the Yellow Hats). This monastic tradition stresses the importance of living teachers (*lamas*) to instruct novices in the ways of Buddhist thought. The leader of this school is the Dalai Lama ("lama as great as the ocean"), who is believed to be a reincarnation of the Bodhisattva Avalokiteshvara. When the Dalai Lama dies, other lamas search for a child they believe to be the reincarnation of the "compassionate one," and he becomes the next Dalai Lama. Following their occupation of Tibet in 1951, the Chinese attempted to control the monasteries, and Tibetan Buddhism is still struggling to keep its traditions intact.

Above The 14th Dalai Lama, here receiving worshipers, fled from Tibet in 1959 because he and his followers feared persecution by the Chinese.

Left The wheel is an important symbol in Buddhism, as it suggests the cycle of birth, death, and reincarnation. The 12 spokes may also represent the Four Noble Truths and the Noble Eightfold Path.

Japanese Buddhism

Buddhism reached Japan in the
A.D. 500s, arriving from China
via Korea. The most popular
school of Japanese Buddhism is
Jodo Shu, or "Pure Land." This is
based on a *Mahayana* text that tells of a Buddha called Amitabha
(or Amida), who lives in a distant world known as the Pure Land.
Faith in the Amida Buddha and meditation on his name will, it is
believed, lead to rebirth in that heavenly land where *nirvana* can
easily be reached. However, the school best known in the West
is Zen, which derives its name from the Chinese *ch'an*, meaning
"meditation." Zen concentrates on meditation and intuition above
worship, and prefers study as a way of
achieving sudden enlightenment (*satori*).
Other means of achieving *nirvana* include
zazen (sitting cross-legged in the lotus
position) and answering a *koan*, or riddle.
The purpose of these riddles (such as "What
is the sound of one hand clapping?") is to
surprise students into looking at things
differently, and in doing so, to challenge
the conventional patterns of thought that
prevent them from achieving enlightenment.

Above Mandalas *are maps of the cosmos.
They are believed to possess spiritual energy
and are used as an aid to meditation in
Tantric Buddhism. They are painted,
carved, or, as here, made out of sand.*

Left A Zen garden is often used in meditation.
Its simple patterns of raked sand suggest the
natural shapes of rivers, mountains, and waves.*

LIFE IN A BUDDHIST MONASTERY

In some Asian countries, such as Thailand, boys as young as eight are sent to monasteries to learn how to be Buddhist monks. Life for these novice monks is demanding. Every morning at five o'clock, they are woken up by a bell and spend the two hours before breakfast meditating in silence.

After a breakfast of rice and vegetables, there are prayers, which continue until nine. For the rest of the morning, there are classes where the young monks have to learn Buddhist holy writings word for word. Lunch is followed by an hour-long discussion, during which groups of novices test each other's knowledge of the scriptures and philosophy. In the afternoon, there are still more classes, and from five until six-thirty, another debate. Dinner is followed by an hour's study of the sacred texts that they have memorized in the morning. After this, the monks may either retire to bed or, if they feel like it, pursue their own meditation in private.

Above A senior monk teaches two young novices (junior monks) in a monastery in Burma (Myanmar).

In Tibetan belief, the golden turrets on the roof will lift the building above the waters on the day when a great flood sweeps the land.

Right The Potala was the center of Tibetan Buddhism. It was built on a rocky outcrop near Lhasa, the capital of Tibet, and was the traditional home of the Dalai Lama, the spiritual leader of Tibetan Buddhists, before he was forced to flee to India in 1959.

The tomb of the fifth Dalai Lama (1617–1682) was filled with jewels and gold vases, and studded with turquoise, rubies, amethysts, sapphires, and diamonds.

The Sangha

The Sangha, as the community of Buddhist monks is called, has formed the backbone of Buddhist society since it was set up by the Buddha himself to preserve and spread his teaching. According to Buddhist doctrine, the life of a monk should be as simple as possible to avoid distraction from spiritual tasks. Life in a Buddhist monastery is not only hard, but also very strict. There are almost 250 rules in the *Vinaya*, the monks' rule book. The monks are not allowed to work for money, to cook their own food, or to live under the same roof as a woman. One of the most serious offenses is quarreling with someone.

There are precise instructions about every aspect of the monks' religious life. They are allowed only a few essential possessions, such as a three-part monk's robe, a water strainer, a razor, a needle, and a bowl to collect alms (gifts of food and clothing).

Life in the monastery revolves around meditation, the study of the scriptures, and taking part in religious ceremonies. Traditionally, monks go out into the community to collect alms, and in return offer spiritual guidance. People may also invite monks to their homes to share a meal. Buddhist society is one in which monks and lay people depend on each other.

With its 1,000 rooms, the Potala was a temple, a palace, a storehouse, a monastery, and a meeting place.

The Great Western Assembly Hall was one of the main places where monks, officials, and pilgrims gathered.

Right These young Burmese novices are allowed few possessions because they must be pure in spirit and free of human concerns.

SHINTO: AN INTRODUCTION

Shinto, which means "way of the gods," originated in prehistoric Japan. According to legend, the gods who controlled the natural elements, such as thunder, wind, and rain came down to Earth to inhabit the mountains, streams, rocks, trees, and other special parts of the landscape. In time, these were given the name *kami* (spirits) and were honored with their own *jinja* (shrine). Shinto has no founder or divine creator, and no particular set of beliefs, but it is practiced by most Japanese people as a folk religion alongside the more formalized rituals of Buddhism. It is quite common for people to turn to Shinto for celebrating births and marriages, and to Buddhism when carrying out funerals.

Shinto legend

Shinto's oldest literary works are the *Kojiki* and the *Nihonshoki*, both written in the A.D. 700s. They contain the Japanese creation myths and legends. It is said that Izanagi and his sister Izanami, who were the last of seven generations of gods, were commanded to form the islands of Japan by dipping a spear into the sea and letting the droplets of salt water form the land. The supreme deity is believed to be Amaterasu, goddess of the sun and daughter of Izanagi and Izanami. Amaterasu is honored at one of Japan's major shrines at Ise, and, even into the 1900s, was said to be a distant ancestor of the ruling imperial family.

Other lesser spirits are honored in order to bring good luck, wealth, and happiness. Unless they are approached with great reverence, these spirits become very angry. Legend has it that the distinguished poet and teacher Sugawara Michizane, who lived in the A.D. 800s, was exiled from court after accusations made by envious courtiers.

Above This Shinto shrine is at Itsukushima-jinja on Miyajima Island in Japan. The torii *was erected in 1875 and is a famous symbol of the Shinto religion.*

Left The most famous mountain in Japan is Mount Fuji. It is also one of the most important natural shrines. Many pilgrims visit the mountain, which has become a symbol of Japan's national identity. This hand-colored woodblock print, Fuji above the lightning, *is by Hokusai.*

Above This colorful print from the 1800s illustrates one of the famous stories from Shinto mythology. The sun goddess, Amaterasu, emerges from her cave to bring light and order to the world.

Below This map shows the location of Japanese Shinto shrines that are marked by a torii.

After Michizane's death, terrible things began to happen to the people of Kyoto. Thunder and lightning struck the palace, storms and droughts affected the city, and people began to die in strange circumstances. Only after they had calmed Michizane's angry spirit did the trouble stop. To this day, his shrine is visited by those wishing for success on tests.

The revival of classical Shinto

In the early centuries of the first millennium B.C., Buddhism, as it spread throughout Japan, absorbed, rather than discarded, local beliefs. As a result, the *kami* were regarded as buddhas or bodhisattvas and were incorporated into Buddhist practice. In the late 1800s and early 1900s, however, scholars had rediscovered the ancient texts and a revival of classical Shinto began. The country looked to its mythical past to build up a strong and proud nation. In 1868, Shinto shrines were cleansed of their Buddhist influences, and a system of "State Shinto" was imposed. Schools taught that the imperial family was related to the gods and insisted on total submission to the will of the emperor, who was believed to be divine. After the defeat of Japan in World War II in 1945, the emperor renounced his divine status, and an American-style constitution decreed that politics and religion should be separate.

SHINTO WORSHIP

Shinto worship (*matsuri*) is both public and private and revolves around the life-cycle events of a family or community. It is common, for example, for pregnant women to visit a shrine to ask for the safe delivery of their child. Thirty-two days after a male child is born (33 days for a girl), the baby is carried to the shrine by the mother or grandmother for a *hatsu miya-mairi*, or first shrine visit, and brought into the presence of the *kami* for a blessing. Later in childhood, the *shichi-go-san* (seven-five-three) festival is held. Parents with three- or seven-year-old sons, or five-year-old daughters, bring them to the shrine for a purification rite, or *harai*. During this service, a wand with paper streamers may be waved over the children's heads to remove bad influences from their lives and to purify them for the future.

Above *Shinto worshipers hang up a prayer board, or* ema, *outside a shrine and write their requests on it.*

Below *The* Tori no Ichi *festival was originally a celebration of the god of battle, but now celebrates good luck. Here, a man holds a lucky charm made of straw.*

Above This shrine has a shimenawa—
*a thick rope threaded with folded white
paper to denote a sacred space.*

Entering the shrine

Elaborate rituals surround entry to the shrine. It is approached through a *torii*, a wooden or stone archway that separates the outside world from the sacred space within. At the entrance is a trough of running water where worshipers wash their hands and rinse their mouths. Then they proceed to the prayer hall, or *haiden*, where the *kami* are alerted to their presence by two claps of the hands. After putting money into the offertory box, ringing a bell, and making a deep ritual bow to the *kami*, worshipers can offer their prayers. In one part of the shrine complex is a wall on which visitors can hang an *ema*. This is a five-sided wooden board on which worshipers write their requests, which may be anything from curing a disease or giving up smoking, to winning the lottery. At the New Year festival these prayer boards are burned to make room for the following year's prayers.

Above A priest burns the previous
*year's prayer boards in a ceremony
at the Shinto Shrine in Ise, Japan.*

The *honden*

Beyond the *haiden* is the *honden*, the main hall where the *kami* live. Only priests may enter this space. During festival times, the image of the *kami* is taken out of the main shrine and placed in a *mikoshi*, or portable shrine. It is then paraded through the town so that the whole community can be blessed by the spirits. *Fudas*, or charms, are sold to help bring good luck and ward off evil spirits. These are then taken home and put on a *kami* shelf, where they remain for a year, protecting the family from misfortune.

Sometimes, if someone cannot go to a shrine, a priest goes out to offer prayers in the name of the *kami*. He might go to a construction site to purify it and to ask for the building (a bank, say, or the headquarters of an industrial corporation) to be blessed by the spirits' presence. Priests will even bless a new car in the hope that it will not be involved in an accident.

Right Children's Day
*takes place once a year in
November at the Meiji Shrine,
the most popular shrine in
Tokyo. Parents bring their
children to receive a
blessing for the future.*

CHINESE RELIGIONS: AN INTRODUCTION

Chinese religion is not one single system of belief, like Judaism, Christianity, or Islam. It contains four main elements that are practiced alongside each other. These are Confucianism, Taoism, Buddhism, and folk religion. Chinese people have been influenced by the ideas contained in all four traditions and often combine the rituals of one with the ceremonies of another.

Early history

Until the late 1800s, China was ruled by powerful clans or families, known as dynasties. The earliest record of religious activity dates from the Shang dynasty around 1700 B.C. The discovery of oracle bones and shells provides evidence that the ancient Chinese practiced a system of divination, or forecasting the future, and believed that unseen spirits affected the lives of ordinary people. Before someone embarked on a new project or set out on a journey, a diviner (someone skilled in the interpretation of supernatural messages) asked the spirits what was in store for them.

Above *Firecrackers are lit to celebrate the New Year festival in honor of the kitchen god, Tsao Chun. He watches what goes on in the household and is believed to control people's lives. At New Year, he is thought to report back to heaven, which grants good fortune for good behavior and bad luck for bad deeds.*

A bone or turtle shell was heated until it cracked, then the diviner looked at the pattern of the cracks and interpreted the spirit's answer. The question and answer were engraved on the bone or shell and were then stored away.

The spirits were apparently consulted on all aspects of human life, including warfare, medicine, farming, and even the weather.

Left *Ancestor worship is important in Chinese religion, and people regularly pay their respects at their ancestors' graves. Families also have shrines in their homes to honor their dead relatives.*

The importance of ancestors

As well as forecasting the future, the Chinese looked to their past. Confucius (551–479 B.C.), from whom the belief system known as Confucianism takes its name, encouraged the practice of ancestor worship that had been in existence since ancient times. Confucius was a sage, or wise man, who taught that kindness (*jen*) toward humanity is one of the most important qualities to develop. He also taught the principle of filial piety, or respect for parents. If children honored their father and mother, he believed, they would become respectful adults who would, in turn, respect their legitimate rulers and form the basis of a stable society. This respect for parents and elders carried on even after death in the form of ancestor worship. To this day, elaborate rituals surround Chinese funerals and many people believe that if a body is buried without proper ceremony, it will not find its way to heaven, but will hang around as a troublesome ghost.

Three different religions

Taoism is said to have been founded by Lao-tzu in the 500s B.C. The Tao means "the way," and reaching it through meditation, chanting, and physical exercise is thought to be a means of achieving immortality. Buddhism came to China before A.D. 100 and influenced the development of both Confucianism and Taoism. The fourth tradition—popular, or folk, religion—involves worshiping a variety of gods drawn from myths and legends.

Above Confucius, Lao-tzu, and the Buddha all lived at around the same time. This symbolic picture shows how different religions have coexisted in China.

Right Oracle bones were used by the ancient Chinese as a way of divining the future.

THE DEVELOPMENT OF CONFUCIANISM

The Western name given to this Chinese tradition of belief emerged in the A.D. 1500s and 1600s, when Christian missionaries began to come across the writings of K'ung Fu-tzu, whose name they translated into Latin. Confucius was not a prophet or a messiah, but a mild-mannered teacher who believed that kindness (*jen*) toward one's fellow human beings and respect for parents (filial piety) were the basis of a harmonious society. He was born into a minor aristocratic family and spent his early life as a civil servant in government offices. It was not until he reached the age of 50 that Confucius became well known and traveled the country spreading his ideas.

Above *This illustration shows Emperor Teaon-Kwang reviewing his guards at the Palace of Peking. The Confucian model of the ideal state centered on a just emperor ruling his people wisely and with compassion. A harmonious rule would be granted by the "Heavenly Mandate," or divine approval. If the Heavenly Mandate were withdrawn, disaster might occur.*

Heaven and Earth

Confucianism is primarily concerned with moral conduct on Earth, but it also contains a spiritual dimension in that Confucius believed that humanity was guided by a higher power that he called "heaven." This early teaching was developed by another teacher called Meng-tzu (*c.*371–289 B.C.), known in the West as Mencius, who believed there was a direct connection between that divine power and human life.

The early Confucians taught that heaven disapproved of chaos and approved of harmony. Harmony came to be seen as a balance of two opposite but complementary forces known as the yin and the yang.

Left *Confucius, portrayed here in a scroll from the 1600s, put great emphasis on harmony in the family and in society.*

Above This painting from the 1600s shows different generations (sage, scholar, and infant) studying the yin and yang symbol. In traditional Chinese thought, yang represents all that is above, hot, light, hard, active, and male. Yin stands for all that is below, cold, dark, soft, passive, and female. Opposites were considered to be complementary aspects of a single whole.

Above The unity of opposite but complementary forces—the yin and the yang—is represented in this symbol. Each half contains the "seed" of its opposite.

Reading the signs

It was believed that divine approval of a government was signaled by the "Heavenly Mandate," which rewarded an emperor with good weather, generous harvests, obedient subjects, and so on. Teams of government officials trained in Confucian thought traveled the country looking for signs, or portents. After monitoring the mood of the people, the state of the crops, and even the weather, they would report back to the emperor, who then had an indication as to how his rule was progressing. In time, this monitoring process was more formally established as a system known as "The Theory of Portents."

Confucian philosophy was consolidated from A.D. 1000 onward, with teachers such as Chu Hsi (1130–1200) and Wang Yangming (1472–1529). These teachers (collectively known as the Neo-, or new, Confucians) combined early Confucian thought with elements of Taoism and Buddhism and produced a system that lasted from the medieval period to the late 1800s.

CONFUCIAN PRACTICE

The essential message of Confucianism is that all things visible (on Earth) and invisible (in heaven) are interdependent. In the sphere of personal behavior, it teaches that the right conduct on Earth —which involves respect and compassion—is its own reward and is in keeping with the ultimate harmony of the universe. In the sphere of public affairs, Confucianism says that a just emperor will be blessed with a stable and strong empire, according to the terms of the Heavenly Mandate.

The texts

The practice of divination was an important way for individuals and governments to read the mind of the heavenly forces. The methods are explained in one of the five Confucian scriptures: the *I Ching*, or *Book of Changes*. The others are the *Shih Ching* (*Book of Odes*), the *Shu Ching* (*Book of History*), the *Li Chi* (*Book of Rites*), and the *Ch'un-ch'iu* (*The Annals of Spring and Autumn*). These classic texts, together with the *Four Books of Confucianism*, are the backbone of Confucian literature. They contain poetry, philosophy, rules for divination and ritual, history, and the sayings of Confucius and his followers, as well as stories about the origins of Chinese society.

Above Education is central to Confucianism. Pupils are encouraged to study hard and to show respect for their teachers and elders.

Left The practice of divination (foretelling the future), which was put into systematic form in the I Ching, *continues in popular form today. Fortune-tellers and geomancers (those advising on where to site objects and houses to bring good fortune) are a regular part of Chinese life.*

Above The man on the right is about to throw down the sticks he is holding. The pattern of sticks will be matched against the predictions in the I Ching (Book of Changes) to determine what the future holds. The I Ching is an elaborate system of divination (foretelling the future) that uses sticks or coins to produce combinations of straight (yang) lines or broken (yin) lines. Consulting the I Ching was an important part of state practice.

Good behavior

Just as the relationship between heaven and Earth was important so, too, were relationships between human beings. Confucius's golden rule is contained in his words, "Do not do to others what you do not wish to be done to you." This basic moral principle runs through all Confucian scripture.

Confucianism is characterized by its great respect for learning and study. Under the emperors, up until the late A.D. 1800s, an elaborate examination system was the basis of employment and promotion. The authorities encouraged the study of Confucian texts and tested potential recruits on aspects of Confucian philosophy. Although criticized by some for its inflexibility, the examination system succeeded in promoting an ethic of hard work and public service, so that, even after the Communist takeover of China, the principles of hard work and study still survived.

THE ORIGINS OF TAOISM

Tao means "the way," in which people live a life of moderation, avoiding extremes of any kind. The secret of happiness is to live naturally without trying to be different or change things. Although very little is known about his life, the founder of Taoism is traditionally taken to be the poet and sage Lao-tzu, to whom the central text of Taoism is attributed—the *Tao-te-Ching* (Classic of the Way and its Power), dating from around the 500s B.C.

Above Mountains and rivers hold a special spiritual significance in Taoism. Sages sought comfort in the magnificence of the natural world and, freed from the tyranny of acquiring material possessions, they could reflect on the harmony of heaven, nature, and humankind.

Philosophy or religion

There are two elements to Tao. The first, *Tao-chia*, or philosophical Taoism, develops the political idea of a sage ruler or emperor ruling through wisdom, not force. The second, *Tao-chiao*, promotes a more mystical or religious understanding of the world. With proper practice, it says, people can free themselves from the dreary acquisition of material possessions and find liberation on a spiritual level, culminating in immortality.

The texts

The *Tao-te-Ching* and the *Chuang Tzu*, the two classic Taoist texts, teach that by harmonizing the forces of yin and yang (*see page 74*) a person can achieve a state of mind that takes good fortune and bad in its stride without complaint. Long life and immortality are believed to be the rewards of following the Tao. Immortality is understood in two ways: eternal life in a transformed body; and, in a more symbolic sense, release from the worries of the everyday world, and spiritual liberation that exists outside time.

Left Ge Changgeng was a calligrapher and wise man who wrote works on Taoism. He associated with Liu Hai, one of the Immortals, whose symbol was the three-legged toad, a mystical creature thought to exist only on the moon. The toad is also the symbol of moneymaking and is shown here with a string of gold coins on its head.

> "To be unsnared by vulgar ways, to make no vain show of material things, to bring no hardship on others . . . There were those who believed that the "art of the Way" lay in those things."
>
> *Chuang Tzu*

Doing and being

Taoists teach that to achieve progress one should practice *wu-wei*, or "active inaction." This seems contradictory, but it involves making a positive attempt not to fight against the flow of universal energy (*ch'i*), but move with it and enter into a balanced state of being. This is illustrated in the writings of Chuang-tzu, who describes the work of a palace cook and master butcher named Ting. Ting is so skilled in the art of carving that his knife seems to encounter no resistance as it slices up an ox for the evening's banquet. The king is amazed and asks the cook where he learned such skills. Ting replies that by concentrating on the right way (the Tao) of doing the job, he can effortlessly find the empty spaces between the muscle and the soft flesh. He does not have to think with his active mind about the business of carving. Instead, he allows his spirit, or consciousness, (*shen*) to take him along, with the result that the beast is effortlessly sliced. In other words, he is *being* a butcher rather than *doing* the butchering. Taoism teaches people to go beyond mere intellect and to appeal to a higher power or consciousness that will take them along with the flow of life.

Right Little is known about Lao-tzu, the founder of Taoism, but one legend portrays him as a scholar in the Chou dynasty. Traveling on an ox, he is said to have come to a border post, where he was asked to write down his teachings. This he did in the form of the Tao-te-Ching. *After that, he vanished and was never seen again.*

79

TAOIST PRACTICE

Taoists believe that an energy (*ch'i*) runs through the whole of creation. It is found in mountains and plains, in rivers and streams, in trees and flowers, in heaven and Earth, and, crucially, in human beings. Harnessing this vital energy harmoniously (with the correct balance of yin and yang) is the key to a long and ultimately happy life.

Harmony and balance

To achieve harmony, certain Taoist groups have developed elaborate rituals involving meditation, chanting, physical exercise, and natural medicine. The mere chanting of certain Taoist texts is believed to bring about a physical and mental change in a person, promoting the harmony of yin and yang that is the goal of religious Taoism. When these forces are not in harmony, things start to go wrong. An imbalance of yin and yang, for example, is believed to be at the root of some diseases that can only be cured when the balance is restored. Destructive energy, often in the form of an unquiet spirit, is thought to be a result of excess yin.

Above *It is common to see groups of people of all ages practicing* t'ai ch'i *in public places. This stylized series of exercises was originally a martial art and is practiced to harmonize the yin and yang forces in the human body, as well as to promote health and long life.*

Left *Taoist priests play an important role in Chinese communal worship. Their function is to perform the harmonizing rites that will ensure health and long life for the community.*

Achieving immortality

Whereas Confucians strive to become sages or wise people at the service of society, the Taoist strives to become an immortal (a *hsien*). Confucianism places greater emphasis on the organization of the ideal state than Taoism, which is more concerned with the individual and personal development. Some Taoists interpret the notion of immortality literally and go to great lengths to achieve it. In the past, stories circulated of secret rituals known only to a select group of devotees who drank herbal potions to become immortal. There were tales of supernatural feats of levitation where their bodies would rise up into the air by magic. Some of these Taoist societies still exist today.

Natural medicine

Most practicing Taoists do not go to such extremes. They believe the body is like the natural landscape, crisscrossed by invisible channels of vital energy that control bodily functions. At certain points along these channels, a little like floodgates along a canal, are points where the flow of energy can be interrupted and controlled in order to reestablish the correct combination of yin and yang. At these points, acupuncturists (traditional healers) insert fine needles to treat various ailments. Taoism says that nothing is fixed. Life is in constant flux and humanity should go with its flow.

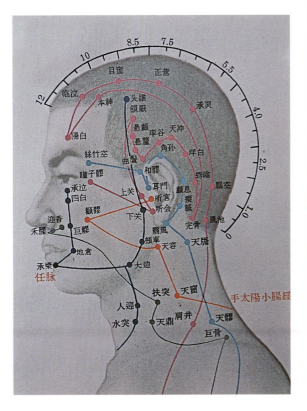

Right Just as people make maps of the landscape, so Taoists make maps of the human body detailing the channels of energy (ch'i) that control the body's functions.

REFORM AND REVOLUTION

The main religions in China have always influenced each other and people often practice a form of religion that contains elements of each. The religions themselves have also developed or altered over the centuries, producing schools of thought that some have followed and some rejected. For example, the Confucianism of Confucius and Mencius was reformed again in the A.D. 1100s and the 1400s by two Neo-Confucians—Zhu Xi and Wang Yangming (*see page 75*). Both agreed that wisdom and compassion were the main goals of life, but they disagreed on how best to achieve them. Zhu Xi founded the *li-hsueh* school of teaching, which argued that, to practice benevolence (*jen*) toward humanity, people had to go through a long process of self-development. Only after many years of refining one's understanding of the world, he believed, could one's own human nature be refined to the point where true benevolence and compassion were possible. The school of Wang Yangming—the *hsin hsueh*—disagreed with this gradual approach and taught that sudden enlightenment was possible if the mind was brought into harmony with the Tao. This fusion of Confucian and Taoist principle is typical of the direction Chinese religion has taken.

Above China's Communist Party disapproved of religion, but its leader from 1949, Mao Zedong, was venerated in a way that was almost religious. Here, his portrait hangs above a family shrine.

A single framework

In the 1500s, philosopher Lin Chao-en tried to bring Confucianism, Buddhism, and Taoism into a single framework. He combined the meditation and self-development practiced by Buddhist monks and Taoist masters with the selflessness and public service of the Confucians. Even today, many people borrow freely from each tradition.

Right During the seven-week festival of Da beiba, Taoist priests bless offerings made to the gods and pray for peace.

Religion under threat

The upheavals of the 1900s have had a great effect on the religious lives of ordinary people in China. Mao Zedong's Communist Party, which came to power in 1949, disapproved of religion. Communists have described religion as "the opium of the people"—a powerful but dangerous drug that prevents people from seeing the world as it really is and stops them from launching a revolutionary challenge to the forces of injustice in the world.

The Cultural Revolution of 1966 tried to rid the country of what it believed to be backward and conservative religious practices. Temples were destroyed, Confucius was denounced, believers were persecuted, and life for the faithful was made extremely difficult. Ironically, the cult of Chairman Mao had some of the marks of a religious movement. He was venerated in schools, factories, and farms, and his image, which appeared on signs and billboards in villages, towns, and cities, had the look of a religious icon portraying a savior of the people.

But religious belief is remarkably resilient and the authorities were eventually forced to accept it as a fact of life. Religious groups had to be registered with the state. In effect, this meant that religious believers could practice their faith in return for a degree of state control. The Chinese authorities have been very wary of foreign influence, and the Vatican in Rome has been allowed little formal control of Catholicism within China. Those Chinese people choosing to worship outside the supervision of the state formed underground groups that functioned in secret. Their members risked severe penalties if their activities were discovered, but many persisted, believing that religious freedom is a basic human right that should not be suppressed.

Below Colorful masks are worn to represent different gods in a long procession through the streets of Taipei in Taiwan. One of the largest religious events of the year, the festival celebrates the birthday of the god Chingshan Wang, and is held on the 22nd day of the 10th lunar month (usually November or December).

POPULAR RELIGIONS IN CHINA

Chinese popular, or folk, religion is not found in any specific religious text. Over the years, it has grown out of a mixture of superstition and established religious practices of the day.

Elemental worship

In ancient China, people lived close to nature and believed that heavenly spirits controlled the wind and the rain. They depended on the land for their livelihood. Extremes of heat, cold, or rain could destroy crops and threaten their survival. In times of need, they asked the heavenly spirits for help, and, in times of plenty, they gave them thanks. Local cults grew up that looked to a particular spirit (sometimes the spirit of a dead ancestor, who could intervene in heaven) to ensure that crops would be healthy and harvests bountiful.

Left A festival lion is paraded through the streets of Hong Kong to mark the New Year. Houses and stores are decorated with vegetables and red money packets and, when the lion dances by and takes these, it brings good luck.

Domestic gods

Believers might have a shrine to a particular god whom they would approach in a ritual way, bowing respectfully before asking for a favor and leaving an offering of food or flowers. The gods of happiness (Fu Hsing), of wealth (Tsai Shen), and of long life (Shou Hsing) are popular figures in Chinese folk religion and are often worshiped at family birthdays and the New Year. As well as appealing to the gods for help and good fortune, people also look to them for protection against evil spirits.

Above At this funeral, paper "money" is being ritually burned as an offering to the gods of the underworld.

Below The god of wealth, Tsai Chen, is a popular figure in Chinese folk religion and is often represented at festivals.

Helping the spirits

Funeral rites are treated with special attention because any failure to send a person to the heavenly realm in the proper way may result in that person's unquiet spirit remaining on Earth to bring misfortune to the family. Before the soul of the deceased arrives safely in heaven, it must first descend to the underworld, where it has to explain its actions in life. Those who have maintained good behavior during their lifetime are guaranteed a faster journey to heaven. It is believed that the soul of the dead person can be helped along its way by the living, who will offer up paper "money" to the gods of the underworld to bribe them into letting in their dead relatives. They may also build paper models of cars or planes to ensure transportation to heaven.

Spiritual powers

In folk religion, the gods (*shen*) symbolize order in the face of the chaos that is caused by evil spirits. Some of these gods are believed to cure common illnesses, and others, such as Tsou-chen, to control epidemics, such as smallpox.

Also popular is the practice of *feng shui* (wind and water). *Feng shui* involves the positioning of buildings, or objects in the home, or in other places such as the office, in a particular way that will be in harmony with the Earth's natural energy (*ch'i*). If sitings are correct, this is said to balance the yin and the yang in nature, and bring the person involved good fortune.

Above The smiling Chinese god of long life holds a staff and a peach from which a crane chick is hatching.

JUDAISM: AN INTRODUCTION

Judaism is the world's oldest monotheistic religion—that is to say, it is the first of the world's great faiths to accept as its central belief that there is only one god who created the world and who continues to rule over it. Judaism began with Abraham, who can properly be called the first Jew. God promised Abraham that, in return for his obedience, Abraham would become the patriarch (father) of a great nation. God commanded Abraham to leave his home (Ur of the Chaldees in present-day Iraq between the Tigris and Euphrates rivers) and to travel to a land that God had promised him—Israel. Abraham agreed, thus accepting the Covenant (agreement) that God had made with him and, by extension, with the people of Israel. As a sign of the Covenant, even today, every male Jew has to be circumcised.

Revelation on Mount Sinai

According to the Hebrew Bible, the word of God was revealed to Moses on Mount Sinai some 3,500 years ago. It is said that at that moment God handed over not only the Ten Commandments but also the first five books of scripture, known as the Torah.

The ancient Israelites are said to have chosen to accept the honor and responsibility of the Covenant at the same time that God is said to have chosen them. Hence, they and their descendants consider themselves to be "The Chosen People."

From tribe to nation

The "Israelites" began as a small family, forced into slavery in Egypt, then wandering in the desert before arriving in the Promised Land of Canaan, where King Saul, and then King David, built them into a nation.

Above This boy is carrying the Torah scrolls to a service, where they will focus the hearts and minds of the congregation on the word of God. On their thirteenth birthdays, boys are allowed to read from the Torah scrolls for the first time.

Left This Jewish Ethiopian boy is holding the scrolls. The Jews are not a race. They are best described as a people or a family from many different races and lands united by a shared sense of belief and tradition.

Around 950 B.C., David's son, Solomon, built a magnificent Temple. It was destroyed in 586 B.C. by the Babylonians, who took the Jews into captivity. A second Temple was built, but this was destroyed by the Romans in A.D. 70, leading to another great dispersal (*diaspora*) of the Jews throughout the Middle East and Europe.

Unity in adversity

Despite the fact that the Jews were spread far and wide, they tried—not always successfully—to stay true to God's law. Eventually, the interpretations of the law contained in the Torah were debated and written down by the rabbis (teachers) and gathered together into a collection of writings known as the Talmud. Study of the Talmud helped to give a unity to Jewish practice.

Death and regeneration

The biggest challenge to the Jewish people in the modern age came in the late 1930s, when the Nazis, under Adolf Hitler, began what they hoped would be the complete extermination of the Jews. More than six million Jews were murdered in what has come to be called the Holocaust. And yet, although comparatively few in number (today there are only some 12 million worldwide), the Jews have exerted a spiritual, ethical, and intellectual influence out of all proportion to their numbers. Their religious practices have been adapted to suit modern times, but the core of the Jewish faith recalls a pivotal event—when the ancient Israelites were said to have submitted themselves to the word of God and were inspired to lead their lives by it.

Right The Star of David was first used as a symbol of Jewish identity in the 1300s. It was originally used as a magical sign in the Middle East, where it was known as Solomon's Seal.

THE HISTORY OF JUDAISM

Above *The great rebellion against the Romans ended at Masada, a desert fortress by the Dead Sea. Rather than surrender, the entire camp committed suicide. Masada has since become a symbol of heroism and resistance.*

Judaism began with Abraham, who was uncomfortable with the many pagan gods of his homeland in Mesopotamia and responded to the call of the one true God to leave home. The story of his departure is contained in the first book of scripture (Genesis 12:1), where God says, "Leave your country, your people, and your father's household, and go to the land I will show you." Abraham's grandson Jacob (later named Israel by God) had 12 sons whose families became the 12 tribes of Israel. Several generations later, the twelve tribes were taken into slavery by the Egyptians. Eventually, they were led out of Egypt—in what is known as the Exodus—by Moses, who later received God's Ten Commandments on Mount Sinai. After 40 long years of wandering in the desert, the Israelites entered the "Promised Land" of Canaan—led not by Moses, who did not live to take them there, but by his brother Joshua. The Israelites grew in strength and, after rule by leaders known as Judges, looked for a king to govern.

A nation divided

The Bible describes the Israelites hope that this king, ritually blessed and anointed, would triumph over their enemies and establish a kingdom in which divine justice. prevailed. The succession of kings anointed in this way (beginning with Saul) symbolized the Jewish expectation that God's righteousness would eventually be a reality on Earth. King David made Jerusalem his capital. His son Solomon built the first Temple there. When Solomon died (*c.*930 B.C.), the nation was split into two by an internal rebellion. Jeroboam and ten of the 12 tribes established the Kingdom of Israel in the north, while the descendants of Rehoboam founded Judah in the south.

Left *The menorah (a candlestick with seven branches) was first used in the Tabernacle in the desert and later installed in Solomon's Temple, Jerusalem.*

There was great tension between the prophets and the kings. The prophets criticized their rulers for worshiping false idols and for straying from the path of God. The Kingdom of Judah (from which Judaism takes its name) outlived that of Israel, whose ten tribes vanished from history. But Judah was itself overrun by the Babylonians, who captured the Jews and destroyed the Temple in 586 B.C.

Above *According to scripture, David killed the giant Goliath, a warrior of the Philistines, with a single slingshot. David eventually became king of the Israelites and made Jerusalem his capital city.*

Exile and return

Fifty years later, the Babylonians were themselves captured by the Persians, who gave the Jews permission to return home. Some Jews did so and they began to rebuild the Temple. Others stayed in Babylon until around 458 B.C. when, under Jewish leaders Ezra and Nehemiah, they returned and put the law of the Torah and worship of God at the center of their religious and political lives.

In the next centuries, further invasions threatened to destroy Jewish identity with Greek philosophy and with pagan forms of worship. In 165 B.C., Judas Maccabaeus led a revolt against the Syrians and restored the Temple to its original purity. This victory is remembered each year in the festival of Chanukah (*see page 103*).

Below *Moses, a towering figure in Jewish history, leads his people out of slavery in Egypt. Behind the Israelites, Pharaoh's army drowns in the Red Sea.*

Dispersal

The country came under Roman control in 63 B.C. This was hard to accept and the Jews mounted a series of rebellions that ended in A.D. 135. In A.D. 70, the Romans had destroyed Jerusalem and its Temple and killed many of the inhabitants. Other Jews dispersed throughout the Middle East and Europe, and developed their own religious life, many hoping that one day they would return to their homeland. The State of Israel was finally founded in 1948.

THE DIASPORA

The destruction of the Temple by the Romans in A.D. 70 was a decisive event in the history of Judaism. At a stroke, Jews lost the unifying feature of their spiritual life—Temple worship—and were also in danger of losing their identity.

The rabbinic tradition

A decision by Johanan ben Zakkai to set up a religious academy on the Judean coast in Yavneh, however, provided a solution. The academy, staffed by rabbis or teachers, soon became a focus of learning and shared tradition within the Jewish world. Although it declined in importance after the failure of the last Jewish revolt against the Romans in A.D. 135, other academies in Galilee and Babylonia took its place and a sense of continuity was maintained.

The Golden Age

When the Roman Emperor Constantine converted to Christianity in A.D. 313, making it the state religion a decade later, life became hard for the Jews. By now, many had already dispersed, settling around the Mediterranean, especially in Spain. Persecution became commonplace and they would not know real stability until the middle of the A.D. 600s when Muslim Arab invasions transformed the map of Europe. The Jews flourished under the Moors to such an extent that the 900s and 1000s were known as Spain's "Golden Age," when philosophers and religious leaders from both Islam and Judaism shared each others' ideas and lived together in harmony.

Above This 14th-century illumination shows a service in a synagogue in northern Spain. Jews and Muslims lived together in harmony, and the influence of Islamic or Moorish art on the synagogue is clear.

Left The destruction of the Temple in A.D. 70 is depicted on the victory arch of Titus in Rome. Roman soldiers carry off the Temple menorah.

MAIMONIDES' 13 PRINCIPLES OF FAITH

1. God exists.
2. He is one.
3. He is unique and incorporeal (i.e., not made out of flesh and blood like humans).
4. He is eternal.
5. He alone should be worshiped.
6. The prophets spoke God's revealed word.
7. Moses was the greatest of the prophets.
8. God revealed himself to Moses and gave him the Torah.
9. Neither God nor the Torah will change.
10. God knows everything.
11. People will be rewarded for good deeds and punished for bad.
12. The Messiah will come to Earth.
13. The dead will be resurrected.

Sephardi and Ashkenazi

The *diaspora* (dispersal) of the Jews outside Israel produced two distinct traditions: the Sephardi Jews of Spain and the Mediterranean who spoke in a mixture of old Spanish and Hebrew known as Ladino, and the Ashkenazi Jews who settled in central Europe and Germany and who spoke in a mixture of German and Hebrew dialect known as Yiddish.

Philosophy and mysticism

Spain's Golden Age provided a period of stability that produced many outstanding Jewish scholars. One of these was Moses Maimonides (1135–1204), who is famous for the *Guide for the Perplexed*, a book that tries to show that the ancient Torah is compatible with modern philosophy. Maimonides also drew up the 13 principles of the faith, which are a cornerstone of Jewish belief even today.

Spain also produced the mystical tradition known as the Kabbalah, which tries to go beyond mere intellect in search of a personal, spiritual union with God. The main Kabbalist text is the *Zohar* (Book of Divine Splendor), finished by Rabbi Moses de Leon of Granada (1250–1305). It sees God as *Eyn Sof*, or The Infinite One, and attributes to God specific characteristics (the ten *Sefirot* or "emanations"): the supreme crown of the divine name; wisdom; intelligence; love; power; beauty; endurance; majesty; foundation, and kingdom.

Below Jews are herded from the Warsaw Ghetto in 1943 by German SS soldiers. It is estimated that six million Jews were murdered in the Holocaust.

Dispersal again

The Christian conquest of Muslim Spain ended in 1492 when the Jews were forced to convert to Christianity or leave the country. Another dispersal followed, taking the Jews all around the Mediterranean and beyond. For the best part of two centuries, Jewish communities attempted to reconstruct and maintain themselves, but kept alive the hope that the Messiah would free them from their enemies and create a better world.

THE TORAH

The Torah is the name given to the first five books of the Hebrew Bible—Genesis, Exodus, Leviticus, Numbers, and Deuteronomy. They are believed by traditional Jews to be the word of God as revealed to Moses on Mount Sinai. Progressive or liberal Jews believe that the word of God was not revealed at one particular time, but is part of a continuing process that successive generations work out under God's inspiration.

The Ten Commandments

As well as creation stories, Jewish history, poetry, and family sagas, the first five books also contain the Ten Commandments. These set out the basic principles that even non-Jewish societies should follow for their own good. In addition to this, they set down religious and moral codes that Jews should follow if they wish to do God's will.

Personal morality

The Ten Commandments are central to the Torah, but many other important rules are found within the five books. These are the basis of 613 *mitzvot* (commandments), which cover areas of personal morality, such as loving your neighbor as yourself, or treating people with respect. The *mitzvot* govern relationships between husband and wife, and between parents and children. They state what rituals Jews should carry out, what they should wear, how they should worship, how animals should be slaughtered, and what foods can and cannot be eaten.

Above The five Books of Moses are copied by hand onto parchment and made into scrolls brought out for weekly synagogue worship.

Right Studying the Torah is the work of a lifetime.

Left The study of the Torah is central to Jewish faith. Students are encouraged to read and re-read it in order to understand how God's law can be put into practice in everyday life.

The "Oral Torah"

As well as the five books known as the "Written Torah," Moses is also thought by traditional Jews to have received from God the "Oral Torah." This is the ongoing interpretation of the laws contained in the written Torah— laws debated and questioned by rabbis down the generations. It instructs Jews on how they are to live a life pleasing to God, as an example to the world.

> "I am the Lord your God ... You shall have no other gods before me."
>
> God to Moses on Mount Sinai, Exodus 20.2–3

A place of honor

As a reminder of how sacred it is to the Jewish people, a copy of the Torah, handwritten on special scrolls, is kept in a container called an ark in every synagogue. Rabbis argue over the exact meaning of the text. Traditional Jews believe that the Torah, being divinely inspired, is as valid today as it was in the ancient world. Those who take a more liberal view say that some of the strict rules have to be adapted for Jews to come to terms with the modern world.

Left Moses is traditionally said to have received the Ten Commandments directly from God on Mount Sinai. These established a framework of law on which a civilized society could be built.

THE TEN COMMANDMENTS

Exodus Chapter 20, verses 2–17

1. I am the Lord your God. You shall have no other gods before me.
2. You shall not make a graven image.
3. You shall not take the name of the Lord your God in vain.
4. Keep the Sabbath Day holy. Do not work on the Sabbath.
5. Honor your father and mother.
6. You shall not kill.
7. You shall not commit adultery.
8. You shall not steal.
9. You shall not bear false witness.
10. You shall not covet your neighbor's property.

PATRIARCHS, PROPHETS, AND KINGS

Throughout the 4,000 years of its history, Judaism has produced a number of powerful individuals who have made their mark on the faith and shaped it into what it is today.

Abraham, Isaac, and Jacob

The first of the patriarchs was Abraham, whose story is told in the Book of Genesis (which is partly an early tribal history of the people of Israel). Around 2000 B.C., Abraham left the city of Ur of the Chaldees to go where God chose to send him. Abraham was 75 years old, and although he and his wife Sarah had no children he was told that he would father a great nation. When Abraham was 100 years old, he and Sarah had their first child, Isaac, who was very precious to Abraham because he would be the next in line to carry out God's plan. According to the Hebrew Bible, Abraham was commanded to sacrifice Isaac as proof of his obedience to God. With a heavy heart Abraham agreed, but at the last moment God intervened and, praising Abraham for his faithfulness, spared Isaac and ordered Abraham to sacrifice a ram instead.

Isaac had twin sons—Jacob and Esau. Jacob had a dream one night in which he saw angels climbing a ladder into heaven and heard God promising him and his family the land on which they slept. Many years later Jacob met a stranger who challenged Jacob to wrestle with him through the night. The stranger revealed himself as another angel of God, and told Jacob that from now on he would be called Israel, which means "one who strives with God." The 12 tribes that formed the nation of Israel (*see page 88*) are said to have descended from Jacob's (Israel's) 12 sons.

Above As a sign of obedience, God commanded Abraham to sacrifice his son Isaac. At the last moment, when he was sure of Abraham's faithfulness, God intervened and spared Isaac.

Left Isaiah and the other prophets of the Hebrew Bible criticized immoral and ungodly behavior. They constantly challenged people—even those in power—to walk the path of righteousness.

> "Behold, I have set the land before you: go in and possess the land which the Lord swore unto your fathers, Abraham, Isaac, and Jacob."
>
> Deuteronomy 1:8

Moses and David

Moses is the next major figure to shape the ancient Israelite experience. According to the Torah, Moses led the Israelites out of slavery in Egypt, and following a unique experience with God, he handed on to the people enduring laws govering worship and daily life. Once in the Promised Land, the Israelites submitted themselves to the authority of anointed kings, whom they hoped would rule justly. Their first great king was David, a warrior and musician credited with writing some of the Psalms—the sacred hymns of the Hebrew Bible.

The prophets

Over the years, the kings and the people ignored God's teachings and were criticized for their bad behavior by the prophets. Isaiah was a prophet of Judah in the 700s B.C., at a time when many felt that some of the rich people

Above Jacob, who was later renamed Israel, had a dream of angels ascending a ladder to heaven. This painting is from the Christian Lambeth Bible (c.1140–50).

were lazy in their worship and unjust to the poor. Isaiah told them that God would punish Judah if they did not improve their ways. Jeremiah was a pessimistic prophet who foretold the destruction of Jerusalem. Other minor prophets spoke on similar themes: that faithfulness to God and a life of holiness are the most important things, and the consequences of sin and disobedience can be severe.

THE TEMPLE

After King David turned Jerusalem into a great city, his son Solomon built the first Temple and established Jerusalem as the geographical and spiritual capital of his kingdom.

At the back of the Temple there were steps that led to the Holy of Holies, where the Ark of the Covenant was kept.

The Ark of the Covenant

At the core of the Temple was the Holy of Holies, the sanctuary where the Ark of the Covenant, a chest containing the Ten Commandments, was placed. The chest was carried by the ancient Israelites as they wandered through the desert toward the Promised Land, and it was their most precious possession. The Temple gave it a permanent home. So sacred were the Ark and its contents that only the High Priest could enter the sanctuary, and only once a year, on the Day of Atonement, Yom Kippur.

Building the Temple

The construction of the Temple is described in detail in the Book of Kings. The wood is said to have come from the cedar trees of Lebanon, or from fir and olive groves, and it was carved with tiny flowers to form the floor, walls, and roof beams. The stone structure was, in fact, carved elsewhere and assembled on site so that the sound of hammers and chisels would not disturb the sacred place. Construction of the Temple ("house" in the Hebrew Bible) was proof that the Jews were serving God who, in return, would bless them. Precious stones and metals were used in the construction, and even the hinges of the door leading to the Holy of Holies were made from gold.

Before they were sacrificed, lambs were washed in wheeled basins of water.

Left This view of Jerusalem shows the Dome of the Rock and the Western (Wailing) Wall in the foreground.

Below The Temple, built by King Solomon, was the spiritual center of Jerusalem and of the kingdom. It was not just one building, but a series of buildings ringed by courtyards. The outer courtyard was open to everyone, including non-Jews (Gentiles), but the rest of the space was reserved for Jews only. The inner courtyard of the priests is shown here.

Temple worship

Temple worship was extremely ritualistic and involved sacrifice and elaborate rites performed by priests. Later, some of the priests were criticized by the prophets for putting the form of the ritual above the content of God's message. The prophets felt that no amount of sacrifice or incense would compensate for ungodly behavior; if people sinned against God or other people by lying, stealing, or killing, they felt God would punish them.

Above The largest remaining section of the Temple Mount is the Western Wall. Jews come here to say their prayers, facing the Wall and bowing ritually.

Destruction of the Temple

The Temple was destroyed in 586 B.C., rebuilt after the Babylonian exile, and extended under King Herod the Great, before its final destruction in A.D. 70. Today, the remaining Western Wall is the most sacred site in the Jewish world. Jews recite their prayers at the Wall or write them down on slips of paper that they insert into the cracks between the stones. The Western Wall is sometimes called the Wailing Wall because of the cries of devout Jews lamenting the destruction of the Temple. Traditionally, it is said that when the Messiah comes the Temple will be built again and that God's Kingdom of righteousness will come to Earth. When the Temple was finally destroyed, temple worship came to an end and local synagogues took its place.

Sacrificial lambs were slaughtered at the altar. To this day, a lamb shankbone is eaten on Passover in commemoration of this ritual sacrifice.

JEWISH WORSHIP

With the destruction of the Temple in A.D. 70, worship gradually centred on the synagogue, which originally meant "meeting-place." Worship, or *avodah* in Hebrew, implies service to the Creator and was referred to by the ancient rabbis as "the service of the heart," that is to say, something done willingly and joyfully to give thanks for the divine gift of life.

Synagogue worship

Devout Jews attend the synagogue three times a day, in the morning, afternoon, and evening—in a pattern that recalls the now vanished ritual of the Temple. In the morning and evening they recite the *Shema*. This is a group of three readings from the Torah, beginning with the words, "Hear O Israel, the Lord is our God, the Lord is One." The *Shema* is the basic affirmation of the Jewish faith.

For a full Orthodox service to take place, ten men need to be present—a minimum requirement for communal worship, known as a *minyan*. At the heart of the service is a series of blessings called the *Amidah*, which the congregation recites while standing. While Orthodox men and women sit separated by a balcony or other divider, non-Orthodox men, women, and children generally worship together.

Above *A child lights the candles of a* menorah, *a branched candlestick, used to celebrate Chanukah.*

The day of rest

The focal-point of the Jewish week is the Sabbath (*Shabbat*), the day of rest that the Ten Commandments decree should be kept holy. The Sabbath begins on Friday evening at sunset, and families frequently make a last-minute dash to prepare and cook the meal that ushers it in. Many Sabbath observances center on the home.

Right *The* Shabbat *meal has preserved Jewish identity. Here the blessing of wine and bread is made at the Sabbath table.*

An act of worship

The beginning of the Sabbath is traditionally marked by the lighting of candles, followed by a special meal. A blessing is made over the wine and bread, and the family sits down together to eat in commemoration of the creation of the world and the deliverance of the people of Israel out of slavery in Egypt. The family meal is an act of worship in itself—when the food is blessed, the table becomes an altar, emphasizing its importance as a spiritual focus. This domestic event has kept the Jewish identity intact in the most hostile circumstances.

The Torah gives practical instructions for observing the Sabbath, and the "Oral Torah" is even more explicit. No work is permitted, and the definition of work extends to activities such as driving and sewing—although an exception is made to all these rules if someone's life is in danger. For some Jews, simply switching on a light is considered work. However, many Jews do not consider these restrictions to be an inconvenience. Instead, they have devices such as time switches that allow electric appliances to come on automatically during the Sabbath, which liberate them from the working week and allow everyone in the family to spend more time in worship, study, or conversation.

Above *According to Jewish law, Jews must ritually wash their hands at certain times, such as before eating.*

Below *When praying in the synagogue, male Jews wear a* yarmulke, *or skullcap, as a sign of respect to God.*

STUDYING THE LAW

The Hebrew Bible is not a book like any other. Many Jews believe it contains the basis for all there is to know in order to live a godly life. In particular, they base their lives on the revealed word of God, said to have been handed down in the form of the Torah on Mount Sinai. The Torah, as we have seen, comprises the first five books of the Hebrew Bible and contains 613 commandments, or *mitzvot*, which pious Jews seek to study, to understand, and to follow.

The tradition of scholarship

Study of these texts, which has exercised the minds of the most brilliant scholars in Jewish history, is the work of a lifetime, but every Jew is expected to spend some time studying the Torah. From an early age children are taught what the commandments are and are shown, through study and example, how to carry them out. At first they learn from their parents in the home, then from their teachers at the synagogue. Boys may also go to a *yeshiva*, or religious academy, where they will study the scriptures into their early twenties. Although study and debate are intense, the atmosphere is relaxed and informal. Orthodox women are generally not expected to study the Torah. Their religious duty is primarily to care for the home and raise children. In the non-Orthodox world, women do study the Torah, and have the same expectations as men. Some become rabbis themselves—although women rabbis are not recognized by the Orthodox community.

Above *Elaborately decorated cases are used to house the Torah scrolls. The decoration does not include any human figures—in obedience of the commandment not to make a graven image.*

Oral tradition

Throughout Jewish history the Torah has been discussed endlessly, and from the earliest times interpretations have been handed down by word of mouth to the next generation. Around the A.D. 100s, Rabbi Judah ("the Prince") brought the oral traditions together in a written collection known as the *Mishnah*.

Left *This female rabbi is using a yad, or pointer, to read from the Torah. The text of the scrolls is never touched directly. The yad is used both to protect the Torah, and as a sign of its sanctity.*

> "Behold, I set before you this day a blessing and a curse. A blessing if you obey the commandments of the Lord your God and a curse if you will not obey the commandments."
>
> Deuteronomy 12:27–28
> Exodus 20:2–3

In parallel with this, another volume of commentary was being prepared. The *Midrash* is a collection of sermons, stories, and parables (*Aggadah*) told by rabbis to explain the Torah. Between A.D. 200 and 500, the *Mishnah* received its own commentary (known as the *Gemara*, or completion). Together these formed one huge collection—the Talmud, a comprehensive commentary on Jewish religious law (*Halakah*) that forms the backbone of a Jew's scholarly and religious life. It is said that in the hereafter Jews are rewarded with an eternity in the presence of Moses, discussing the finer points of the Torah.

Reverence for the Torah

While the Talmud and other commentaries are regarded as books like any others, the Torah scrolls are given a special religious status. When a service is over, the scrolls are carefully rolled up and replaced in a case, which is often richly decorated. Conditions of life have changed since the time of Moses, who could not have imagined a world of high technology, transplant surgery, genetic engineering, or space flight. But many Jews still believe that the basic laws of 3,000 years ago can be reinterpreted to apply to every circumstance today.

Left Scholarship is very important in the Jewish tradition. Study of the Talmud begins at an early age.

THE JEWISH CALENDAR

The Jewish New Year begins with Rosh Hashanah, a time to look back on mistakes made during the previous year and to resolve to do better in the year ahead. A ram's horn (a *shofar*) is blown, and this produces a raw, piercing sound that is meant to call sinners to repentance. The Rosh Hashanah festival also commemorates God's creation and it is a time to consider how the deeds of the past year will be judged. Traditionally, Jews eat apples dipped in honey and they wish each other a sweet New Year. The next ten days are then set aside for serious reflection and preparation for Yom Kippur—the most sacred Jewish holy day.

The Day of Atonement

Yom Kippur is the culmination of the ten days of self-examination that began at Rosh Hashanah. In ancient times, this was the one day in the year when the high priest made a sacrifice to atone for the sins of the people and entered the Holy of Holies in the Jerusalem Temple, where the Ten Commandments had been placed. Today, sacrifice is no longer carried out and, instead, the Day of Atonement is focused on the synagogue, where a day-long service is held, accompanied by a 25-hour fast. When the congregation has admitted its sins, prayers are said for forgiveness. Yom Kippur is regarded as an annual opportunity for spiritual renewal.

Above For the festival of Sukkot, these Jewish school children are building temporary shelters (tabernacles or booths) as a reminder of the years that the Israelites spent wandering in the desert with only tents for shelter.

Left A family lights the Chanukah candles recalling the re-dedication of the Temple in 165 B.C. after it had been desecrated by the Syrians.

102

The Feast of Tabernacles

Five days after Yom Kippur, the Feast of Tabernacles, or Sukkot, takes place, when Jews remember how God provided for the Children of Israel as they wandered in the desert for 40 years before arriving in the Promised Land. As a reminder of their time in the wilderness, when they had only tents to sleep in, Jews construct temporary shelters (tabernacles or booths) at home or in the synagogue. They may eat, study, and even sleep in them. At the end of Sukkot there is a synagogue service known as Simchat Torah, or Rejoicing in the Law. The scrolls are paraded around the synagogue, to the accompaniment of joyful singing and dancing.

> **"Love the Lord your God and keep . . . his laws and his commandments always."**
>
> Deuteronomy 11:1

Right A shofar, or ram's horn, is blown at Rosh Hashanah to call Jews to repentance.

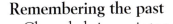

Remembering the past

Chanukah is a winter festival, but it celebrates more than just a seasonal cycle. It reminds Jews of the period in their history (165 B.C.) when they fought the Greek influences that threatened their identity and the purity of their Temple. Judas Maccabaeus, a member of the Hasmonean family, led a revolt against those who had desecrated the Temple. According to legend there was enough oil in the Temple lamp to last for one day, but miraculously it burned for eight days, at the end of which Judas Maccabaeus re-dedicated the Temple. In public and private ceremonies Jews celebrate the festival by lighting candles on an eight-branched *menorah*. A ninth branch holds the "servant candle" from which the rest are lit—one on the first day, two on the second, three on the third and so on, until the candlestick is ablaze with light.

THE FESTIVAL YEAR

Passover, or *Pesach* in Hebrew, recalls the story of the Exodus from Egypt. It takes its name from the last of the ten plagues that persuaded the pharaoh to set the Israelites free. First, the Nile River turned to blood, then there was a plague of frogs, a plague of gnats, and a plague of flies. Next, the Egyptians' cattle died, and the people were afflicted with boils. After hailstones and a plague of locusts, followed by a three-day period of darkness, the most devastating of the plagues descended. The Angel of Death "passed over" the children of Israel, but the first-born son of every Egyptian died. The pharaoh agreed to release the Israelites, who left in such a hurry that they were unable to let the bread they had prepared for their journey rise. As a result only unleavened bread (bread without yeast) can be eaten during the week of Passover. A ritual meal is prepared of foods that symbolize the flight from Egypt. Traditionally, the youngest child present asks, "Why is this night different from all other nights?", and the father tells the story of the Exodus.

Shavuot (originally a harvest festival) is celebrated 50 days after the second day of Passover and it recalls the handing over of the Torah to Moses on Mount Sinai. The Ten Commandments are read out in the synagogue, which is often decorated with flowers and fruit to celebrate the first fruits of the season.

Above Passover is as important today as it was in the time of Moses. The symbolism of the meal, here depicted in a 15th-century manuscript, has remained unchanged.

The Festival of Lots

Purim—the Festival of Lots—is a minor festival that precedes Passover. It marks the victory of Esther and her uncle Mordechai over Haman, a minister of the Persian Emperor who threatened to exterminate the Jewish people and cast lots (*purim*) to decide on which day he should carry out his threat.

THE SEDER MEAL

The ritual Passover meal is known as *seder*. Bitter herbs recall slavery, an egg and a lamb shankbone commemorate ritual sacrifice, saltwater symbolizes the tears of the Israelites, and a mixture of nuts, cinnamon, and wine represents the mortar they were forced to mix for the pharaoh's building. The unleavened bread—a dry cracker known as *matzo*—is the bread of affliction.

Right *A Jewish bride and groom celebrate their wedding under the* huppah*(canopy) which is a symbol of God's sheltering, protective power.*

Below *At the age of 13, a boy comes of age and becomes a* Bat Mitzvah, *or Son of the Commandment. During prayer, Orthodox Jews wear* tefillin *on their head and arms. These are small boxes containing scriptural texts.*

Rites of passage

As descendants of the patriarch Abraham, Jews belong to an ancient family, and it is as a family that they mark the great life cycle events. These begin shortly after birth, when boys are circumcised as a mark of God's covenant with Abraham. Girls receive a special blessing in a synagogue or at a service at home. Jewish boys come of age when they are 13, at a special service marking the transition into adulthood, when they become a *Bar Mitzvah*, or Son of the Commandment. Girls come of age when they are 12 and become a *Bat Mitzvah*, or Daughter of the Commandment.

Weddings are very festive occasions, with the whole community joining in the celebrations. Couples marry beneath a *huppah*, or canopy, a survival of the ancient bridal bower in which newlyweds used to be secluded after the ceremony. The groom breaks a glass beneath his foot—a reminder that life is fragile.

Jewish funerals usually take place within 24 hours of death. Relatives tear a garment as a mark of mourning and the deceased's children recite the *Kaddish*, a prayer which is a mark of mourning, but also an affirmation of life.

DIVISIONS IN JUDAISM

Throughout their long and often troubled history the Jews have tried to keep their identity as a people intact. However, being part of a family, they have sometimes had bitter family quarrels that have caused divisions among them. The principle theological divisions in our day are between Orthodox and non-Orthodox Jews.

Orthodox Judaism
Orthodox Judaism sees itself as the most authentic form of Jewish belief and practice, maintaining a tradition stretching back to Moses. Orthodox Jews cannot keep to all the 613 commandments because many relate to the era of the Temple, which has ceased to exist, but those they do keep have to be followed, however inconvenient this may be in the modern world.

At the end of the 1800s, a modern Orthodoxy emerged, encouraging Jews to break out of the ghetto (the section of a city to which Jews were restricted) and take part in the intellectual, political, and artistic life of the wider community while still remaining true to the Torah. It was now possible for a Jew to mix with mainstream society at school, university, or work and still be true to his or her Biblical inheritance.

One branch of Orthodoxy, known as Hasidism began in Poland and Germany in the 1700s. Even today, its members continue to follow the traditions and styles of dress of that era. They tend to live in close-knit communities centering on the home and synagogue. Their contact with modern Orthodox and non-Orthodox Jews may be limited. The best-known group is that of the Lubavitch, which thrives in New York.

Below Ethiopian Jews, or Falashas, airlifted to Israel in 1985, were thought by some to not be authentically Jewish. Many underwent "re-conversion" ceremonies to reaffirm their faith.

Reform Judaism

Also known as Progressive or Liberal Judaism, the Reform movement began in Germany early in the 1800s and spread in particular to the United States, where it is the dominant form of Judaism today. Followers do not believe that the Torah was "handed over" complete to Moses, but that it was written by humans with God's inspiration. For them, the attempt to work out God's will is an ongoing process.

Conservative Judaism

In the late 1800s, a new response to the challenges of modernity arose in the United States in the form of Conservative Judaism—which lies somewhere in between Orthodox and Progressive Judaism. The Conservative movement, and the Reconstructionist school that developed from it in the mid-1900s, observe most traditional laws and practices, and stress the community aspect of the faith.

Above The ultra-traditionalist community of Mea Sharim in Jerusalem keeps itself apart from mainstream society and retains its own distinct identity.

Zionism

Jerusalem was also known as the City of Zion, the name lent to the modern Zionist movement founded by an Austrian Jew, Theodor Herzl, in the late 1800s. He believed at first that Jews could flourish in any country, but changed his mind when he saw how deeply rooted anti-Semitism was. He therefore suggested establishing an independent homeland in Palestine. Some opposition came from Reform Jews, who felt that absorption into the wider society was healthier for Jewish culture, and also from some religious conservatives, who felt that no return to the land of Israel was possible until the Messiah had come. In 1948, the State of Israel came into being, but while its legitimacy is constantly being questioned by its Arab neighbors, it has offered Jews around the world a haven from persecution.

Right Modern Zionism championed the idea of an independent homeland for the Jews. These children carry the Israeli flag.

CHRISTIANITY: AN INTRODUCTION

T he founder of Christianity was Jesus, a Jewish teacher and healer who lived about 2,000 years ago in Palestine. His life, death, and resurrection became the basis for a religion practiced by almost a third of the world's population.

Early ministry

The details of Jesus' life and ministry are found in the four Gospels, in the New Testament of the Christian Bible. They accept the authority of the Hebrew Bible (known as the Old Testament), but believe it was superseded by a new covenant with God, of which Jesus was the living sign. Jesus himself said he had not come to alter the scriptures, but to fulfill them. He taught by example, living a simple and selfless life based on love. Christian love has two elements— love of God and love of other people. Despite the cruelty sometimes committed in the name of Christianity, this is the basis of the faith.

Below Jesus chose 12 apostles, or disciples, to help him spread the word of God (the gospel, or "good news"). They believed him to be the Messiah ("anointed one") foretold in the Hebrew scriptures. On the night before his death, Jesus ate a final meal with his disciples—"the Last Supper."

> ## "I and my Father are one."
> John 10:30

Life and death

In his day, Jesus' teachings were controversial and brought him into conflict not only with the Romans who occupied the country, but also with Jewish religious leaders. They considered him to be a false messiah who refused to accept the rulings of the religious authorities—an offense for which the penalty could be death. Jesus was thought to be a threat to the stability of the state, so he was handed over to the Romans and crucified—a death that involved nailing him to a cross and leaving him there to die.

Above The Eucharist, also known as Holy Communion, commemorates the Last Supper and is central to Christian worship.

Below From its origins in the Mediterranean, Christianity has spread all over the world. Here, Christians remember events leading up to Jesus' resurrection during the Festival of Holy Week in Peru.

Resurrection and salvation

The circumstances surrounding Jesus' death are of as much importance as his ministry. The Bible says that, three days after his crucifixion, Jesus rose from the dead and appeared again to his disciples. This miraculous resurrection was taken as proof that he was indeed the Son of God, and that his message of salvation was true.

Spreading the word

Christianity has always been a missionary religion, with the goal of converting people to its way of life and its message. During the last 2,000 years, missionary movements have spread it all over the world. One of the principal figures responsible for spreading Christianity after Christ's death was Paul of Tarsus, a Jew and a Roman citizen, who converted to Christianity after seeing a blinding flash of light on the road to Damascus. While some members of the newly formed sect saw Christianity as another branch of Judaism reserved for Jews only, Paul argued that it was a universal religion that should be taken to every corner of the world and freely offered to humankind.

THE DEVELOPMENT OF CHRISTIANITY

From its origins as a simple community of 12 disciples who owned few possessions and shared everything, Christianity has become a global religion of great complexity. The Church owns land, buildings, churches, cathedrals, and even television stations and satellites to further the Kingdom of God on Earth.

The Holy Spirit descends

The initial impulse to take the Gospel to every part of the world came at Pentecost and is described in the second chapter of the Acts of the Apostles. The disciples were sitting together planning how best to spread God's word now that Jesus was no longer with them, when suddenly the room was filled with "a rushing mighty wind and cloven tongues of fire." They were filled with the Holy Spirit, which enabled them to speak in other languages, and which prompted them to spread the faith far and wide.

The Holy Roman Empire

In his epistles (letters), Paul describes the community life of the early Christians, who were a minority religion persecuted by the Roman Empire. It was not until Emperor Constantine converted and made Christianity the state religion that their fortunes improved. However, official recognition was a mixed blessing because it became associated with powerful empires that used force to expand their territory.

Above Between A.D. 46 and 62, Paul traveled around the Mediterranean on missionary journeys. The black line shows his first journey (A.D. 46–48), the green line his second journey (A.D. 49–52), and the red line his third journey (A.D. 53–57). The blue line shows how Paul's fourth journey (A.D. 59–62) took him as far as Rome.

Below Peter the Hermit, riding on a donkey, addresses Crusaders on their way to recapture the Holy Land from Islamic occupation in A.D. 1096.

Right In the Orthodox tradition, icons, or devotional pictures of holy figures—here Mary and the baby Jesus—are important in worship. Some Western Catholics in the 1000s (and even some Christians today) viewed them with great suspicion, comparing their use to idol worship. This was one of the factors leading to the great split.

Below The medieval cathedrals are monuments to the intensity of Christian faith in the Middle Ages. This picture, by a French artist of the 1400s, shows the building of a cathedral.

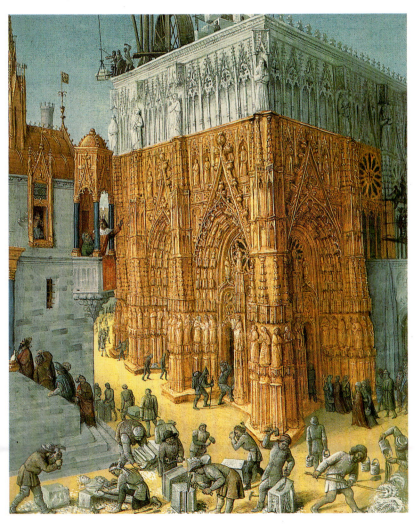

Division and dissent

As Christianity grew, so, too, did its divisions. The first major split was the "Great Schism" of 1054, which resulted in a division between the Western Catholic Church based in Rome and the Eastern Orthodox Church based in Constantinople (now Istanbul in Turkey). Fifty years later, a series of religious and military expeditions known as the Crusades was mounted. These were organized by Christian forces in an attempt to conquer the Holy Land and liberate the holy sites from Muslim control.

Although the Middle Ages, which lasted until the 1400s, produced magnificent Christian art and architecture, there was deep unrest. Abuse of religious power, immoral behavior by priests, bishops, and popes, and a general neglect of the essentials of the Christian faith were common. Reform was needed.

Change and reform

The most important of the reforming groups was led by the German theologian Martin Luther (1483–1546), who opposed the Church's sale of "indulgences." These were "pardons," which were handed over by the priests in exchange for cash. They were supposed to release people from their sins and so allow them to buy their way into heaven. Luther condemned this practice and went further still. He stressed "justification by faith" and argued that no amount of good deeds would save people from sin. Forgiveness came only through faith in Jesus. The Lutheran group and other similar movements are known collectively as the Reformation. They upset the power structures within the Church and split it in two—the Roman Catholic Church, and the breakaway Protestant Church, which itself divided into many different denominations.

THE LIFE OF JESUS

Despite the many divisions within Christianity, all believers try to live a life based on that of their founder, Jesus Christ. Accounts of the life of Jesus Christ were passed on by word of mouth, and it was not until some 35 years after his death that they were first written down in story form. The first account was in Mark's Gospel, on which the gospels of Matthew and Luke were partly based. These, known as the Synoptic Gospels (accounts describing Christ's ministry from the same general point of view), were joined by a fourth, John's Gospel, which is different in tone and concentrates less on the life than on the interpretation of the message.

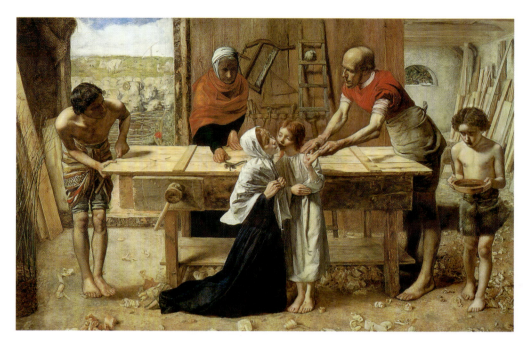

Above Christ in the House of His Parents, *painted in 1849–50 by Sir John Everett Millais, depicts Jesus' boyhood as a carpenter's son.*

The life of Christ

The Gospels say that Jesus was born of the Virgin Mary, who conceived him through the power of the Holy Spirit. He was born in Bethlehem and brought up by Mary and her husband Joseph, a carpenter, in Nazareth. When Jesus was about 30 years old, his ministry began with his baptism by John the Baptist in the Jordan River. After this, he went into the desert to fast and prepare himself spiritually for the work ahead. After 40 days in the wilderness, he was tempted by the devil, but resisted. His ministry lasted only three years, but in that time he became a charismatic teacher and healer, impressing people with his goodness, gentleness, and strength. Jesus was tolerant of people's failings and slow to condemn.

Left In this painting by Piero Della Francesca (c.1419–1492), John the Baptist baptizes Christ at the start of his ministry. The dove is the traditional sign of the Holy Spirit.

Above One of Jesus' most famous miracles was the feeding of the 5,000 (Matthew 14:13–21). A crowd of people had come to hear Jesus preach and were amply fed with only five loaves and two fishes.

"I am the door; by me, if any man enter in, he shall be saved."

John 10:9

Performing miracles

The Bible says that Jesus performed many miracles, such as turning water into wine at the wedding feast at Cana (John 2:1–11). Miracles are not magic tricks done to impress an audience—in Christian thinking they are spiritual signs that show a truth about God's kingdom. The wine is a symbol of the abundance of life that believers in Christ receive.

A friend to all

Jesus was frequently seen in the company of people rejected by society. In particular, he healed lepers, who were considered unclean by the Temple priests. Jesus appealed very much to ordinary people because he spoke in a way they could easily understand. His method was to use parables, simple stories that illustrate profound spiritual truths. Among the most famous are the parables of the Good Samaritan, the Unjust Judge, the Great Feast, and the Laborers in the Vineyard. Jesus' teachings were considered a threat by the Temple authorities, who began to consider how they could get rid of him. One of the last things Jesus did before his arrest was to eat a meal with his disciples. At the Last Supper, Jesus said that the bread and the wine would be a memorial to his body and his blood, and that the meal should be symbolically re-created by his followers in his memory. The Gospel of Matthew ends with Jesus' promise, "I am with you always, even unto the end of the world."

113

THE CRUCIFIXION

The crucifixion of Christ and his resurrection from the dead are at the core of Christian belief. Jesus' anguish as he approached death and his agony on the cross with nails through his hands and feet, as described in the Gospels, have come to be called the Passion.

The first covenant

The Old Testament Book of Genesis says that God created humans in the form of Adam and Eve and made an earthly paradise known as the Garden of Eden. But Adam and Eve rebelled and were cast out of paradise—a doctrine known as the Fall. From then on, the long process began to liberate people from sin and to restore God's kingdom on Earth. God's first attempt after the Fall involved a covenant with Noah. God promised that Noah and his family, plus two of every animal in creation, would be spared from a destructive flood by escaping on an ark (vast boat). But after the flood had subsided, humanity again returned to its wicked ways and worshiped false idols.

The second covenant

God's second covenant was with Abraham and the people of Israel (*see page 88*), but again the people sinned. Something urgent had to be done once and for all, so God decided to make what Christians believe is the ultimate sacrifice, to free creation from its wickedness: he sent his only son, Jesus, to Earth, knowing that he would die on the cross. With this supreme act of self-sacrifice, Jesus, the promised Messiah, would save humanity from sin.

With the crucifixion and the resurrection, Christians believe that God, through Christ, has ultimately broken the power of the devil and offered salvation to all those who want it.

Above In the top section, Judas, one of the disciples, betrays Christ with a kiss. He was so ashamed that he later committed suicide. In the bottom section, Jesus is brought before Pilate.

Left Christ was made to carry his own cross to Golgotha, and he was mocked by the people. In many parts of the world, this scene is reenacted every Easter.

Above Jesus was stripped naked, beaten, and crowned with thorns as a mocking reminder that he had claimed to be King of the Jews.

"And Jesus cried with a loud voice, and gave up the ghost."

Mark 15:37

The story of Christ's Passion
Jesus' claim to be the Messiah and his criticism of the Temple's rules and rituals angered the religious authorities. At one point, Jesus went into the Temple compound, overturned the moneychangers' tables, and announced that they were turning the house of God into a marketplace. The chief priests feared that Jesus would destroy their authority and decided to have him arrested. They made a deal with one of his disciples, Judas Iscariot. In exchange for 30 pieces of silver, Judas agreed to betray Jesus. Jesus knew this and said so (Mark 14:18–21) at the Last Supper. He went to the Garden of Gethsemane to pray and to ask God to release him from his fate, but finally realized that God's will, not his own, had to be done.

As Jesus was about to leave the Garden of Gethsemane, he and his disciples were surrounded by soldiers. Judas Iscariot stepped forward and kissed Jesus—this was a prearranged signal to let the soldiers know whom to arrest. Jesus was tried before Pontius Pilate, the Roman governor, who found him guilty of no crime. However, he agreed to the mob's wishes and had Jesus crucified on a hill called Golgotha (the place of the skull), between two criminals.

After some hours on the cross, Jesus died in agony with the words, "Father, into thy hands I commend my spirit" (Luke 23:46). Immediately, there was an earthquake, and part of the Temple was destroyed. Three days later, the Bible says Jesus rose from the dead and told his disciples that they should now spread the message of God's love for humankind and the hope of life after death.

THE TRINITY

Christians traditionally believe that Jesus Christ had a divine father (God) and an earthly mother (Mary). As a result, they believe Christ to be both human and divine.

The Incarnation

The doctrine of the Incarnation (Latin *caro*, meaning "flesh") is summed up in statements at the beginning of John's Gospel: "In the beginning was the Word, and the Word was with God, and the Word was God . . . and the Word was made flesh." Christians understand the "Word" to mean the divine plan underlying all Creation, a plan that is not separate from God himself. The divine plan was revealed to humanity in the flesh and blood of one man, Jesus, who similarly is not separate from God himself. Jesus is one with God. Father and son are one.

The Holy Spirit

After his ascension into heaven, Jesus was no longer visible in the world, but the Bible says he communicated with humanity through his Holy Spirit, which descended on the disciples at Pentecost. God, Christ, and the Holy Spirit are known as the Trinity, or three beings in one God—God the Father, God the Son, and God the Holy Spirit—rather than a collection of three gods. This complex theological idea has long been debated by Christians. A mainstream belief is that the Trinity represents three "persons" of God, or three ways of knowing more about God's nature and purpose.

Above This painting, The Descent of the Holy Ghost, *is by Sandro Botticelli (c.1441–1510). In Christian doctrine, the Trinity—Father, Son, and Holy Spirit (or Ghost)—is thought of as the three elements of one God.*

Left Masai women attend a Pentecostal service in Tanzania. Charismatic or Pentecostal Christians believe that the gifts of the Holy Spirit help them to heal the sick.

Above In Christian imagery, God often appears as a wise and powerful old man, a patriarch like Moses. This is how the artist Michelangelo portrayed God's creation of the first man on Earth, Adam.

Below The Lamb of God is a powerful symbol of Christian redemption. This picture of the lamb in heaven comes from a manuscript called the Lambeth Apocalypse (c. A.D. 1260).

Knowing the unknowable

Christians believe that God is infinite and eternal and, as such, beyond human understanding. However, certain things *can* be known about the Creator—that he is a father figure, for example, who cares for humanity as a father cares for his children, loving at all times, but also occasionally strict. But other Christians say this description is not sufficient. They point to other imagery in the Bible that stresses the feminine side of God's nature, and even refer to God as "Our Heavenly Father and Mother."

The Lamb of God

Through the second person of the Trinity, Jesus Christ, Christians believe that other aspects of God's nature have been revealed. An image often used is that of the lamb. This has its origins in the Jewish tradition of sacrificing a lamb at Passover (*see page 104*), but in Christian thinking it means that God so loved the world that he was prepared to pay the ultimate price—the sacrifice of his only son—to buy back (redeem) the world from the clutches of sin and death.

> **"There is one body and one spirit, one Lord, one faith, one baptism, one God and Father of all."**
>
> Ephesians IV:4–6

117

CHRISTIAN WORSHIP

Christian worship can take place anywhere and at any time, but it is usually carried out privately with prayers in the home, or publicly at church services attended by a congregation or community of believers. Worship takes many different forms. For example, it can be full of ceremony with priests and bishops dressed in colorful robes or vestments; or it can be a simple gathering of Christians meeting together for prayer at someone's house. There may be loud music with trumpets, organs, guitars, and choirs, or there may be quiet meditation in the silence of a plain room. Jesus said that all that was needed for Christian worship to begin was the presence of people gathered together in his name.

In practice, most Christians consider Sunday a special day to be set aside for worship in church. They meet to say prayers, sing hymns, and hear extracts of the Bible. The priest or minister will deliver a sermon—a short talk designed to explain an aspect of the Christian life. Before or after the service, there might be Bible study or Sunday school classes in the church hall.

Above *Christian prayer is essentially a conversation with God. Children are taught that, even though they cannot see him, Jesus is with them always.*

The five themes

Christian worship focuses on five principal themes—adoration, praise, thanksgiving, repentance, and petition. Adoration is the expression of the love that Christians believe is owed to God the Creator, who gave his only son to save the world. Praise is the passionate celebration of God's splendor, power, and majesty. Thanksgiving is the expression of gratitude for the gift of life. Repentance involves the confession of sin and the promise to be a better person, and petition is the equally human request for help in times of need.

Left *A young girl lighting candles at a Catholic church service in Lithuania. Candles have always been important in Christian worship as a symbol of the light that Jesus brought into the world.*

Below Singing hymns is a popular part of a Christian church service. The music is traditionally played on a organ and there is usually a choir to lead the congregration in singing.

The Lord's Prayer

The New Testament contains the prayer that Jesus taught his followers to say—the Lord's Prayer. It is central to Christian worship in that it provides a model of prayer and tells believers what Christ himself considered important about relationships with God and with one another. It is sometimes asked why, if God knows all of humanity's needs (Matthew 6:32), there is any need to pray at all. There are two answers to this. The first is simple: Christ prayed, so Christians should do so, too. The second answer is that God wants people to cooperate with him, rather than expecting him to do everything for them.

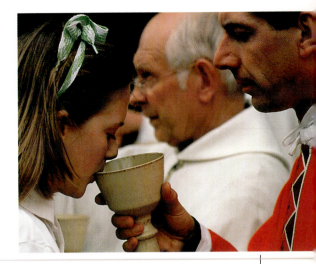

Above At Holy Communion, the priest or minister blesses the bread and wine and the worshipers receive them in memory of the body and blood of Christ.

Church worship

In some traditions, notably the Catholic, Episcopal, and Orthodox, there is a carefully prepared structure to most church worship, which is known as the liturgy. This sets out the form of the prayers, the order of service, and the choice of readings. For some, this structure has not changed for generations and people go to church knowing exactly what to expect. In some (now rare) Roman Catholic services, the entire service still takes place in Latin. In some Protestant and other churches (especially Evangelical), the whole service is more spontaneous and informal. Members of the congregation are encouraged to take part—either in the preparation of the reading or leading of prayers. But whatever form Christian worship takes, people are gathered together in friendship to offer praise and thanks to God.

THE SACRAMENTS

C hristian worship often focuses on scenes from Christ's earthly ministry and uses them symbolically to mark important turning points in people's lives.

The sacrament of baptism

A sacrament is defined as "an outward and visible sign of an inward and spiritual grace." The first of these is the sacrament of baptism. Baptism marks admission to the Christian Church and recalls the moment, at the beginning of Christ's ministry, when he was baptized by John the Baptist in the waters of the Jordan River. Today, there are two forms of this ritual—infant and adult baptism—and there is debate as to which form is preferable. Some say that admission to the Church should be delayed until people are old enough to make this commitment for themselves. Others argue that people should be welcomed into the community of believers as soon as possible, shortly after birth.

> **"You are all the children of God by faith in Christ Jesus."**
>
> Galatians III:26–8

In churches that baptize children, there is a font (ceremonial bowl) or pool set aside for baptism. Baptism with water has its origins in early purification rites, but in Christianity it is used as a visible sign that the child is being born again into a new life in Christ. Normally, the mother and father choose godparents, who take part in the ceremony and promise to encourage the child's spiritual development.

Adult baptism frequently involves total immersion in the water, which symbolizes purification from the sins of Adam and Eve and the beginning of a new life of obedience to Christ. The minister and helpers stand waist deep in the water and, after prayers, tip the person backward and totally immerse him or her for a second or two.

Above In some traditions, baptism is considered such an important rite of passage that only those who have made a mature decision to become a Christian may be baptized—usually by total immersion in the water.

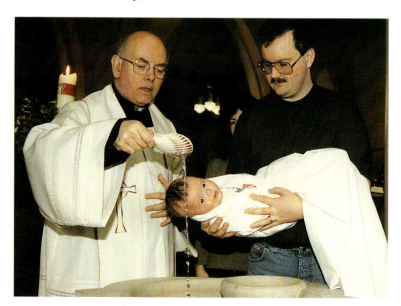

Right Children are baptized by a minister or priest, who welcomes them into the Christian Church by pouring water over their foreheads.

Confirmation

Adolescents or adults who have been baptized as infants often affirm or renew their commitment to Christianity once they have developed a more mature understanding of the faith. They are usually required to attend a series of classes conducted by a minister or priest, and then undergo a rite of confirmation carried out by a bishop or minister, in which they publicly affirm their baptismal vows.

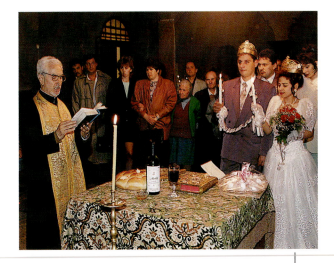

Above A marriage in church is both a joyful event and a solemn exchange of vows. Here, an Orthodox Christian wedding takes place in Sofia, Bulgaria.

The Eucharist

Also known as Holy Communion, the Lord's Supper, the Mass, and the Divine Liturgy, the Eucharist commemorates the Last Supper, when Christ told his disciples to eat bread (his body) and drink wine (his blood) in remembrance of him. In some traditions, Communion, during which the congregation is given a small piece of bread or a wafer (a host) and a sip of wine or juice, is reserved for those who are full members of the Church through baptism or confirmation. In the Roman Catholic tradition, it is believed that during this sacrament, the bread and the wine actually become the body and the blood of Christ—a doctrine known as transubstantiation.

Below Full members of the Church take Holy Communion in remembrance of the Last Supper. Here, Mass is being celebrated in Zimbabwe.

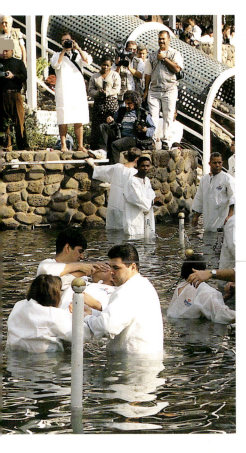

Holy matrimony

During the sacrament of holy matrimony, the bride and groom vow to remain faithful to each other until death. Marriages are happy occasions and call to mind the first of Jesus' miracles at the wedding feast in Cana, where he turned water into wine (*see page 113*). Marriage is also a symbol of Christ's union with his Church.

121

CHRISTMAS

Christmas is the time when Christians remember and celebrate the birth of Jesus Christ. It is a happy time when people give presents in memory of the joy God brought to the world in the form of his only son.

"Lighten our darkness"

In the early days of Christianity, Easter was the central Christian festival, and it was not until 400 years after the birth of Christ that Christmas became an official Christian observance. Before that time, there were many folk or pagan midwinter festivals, when people celebrated the fact that the worst of winter was over and warmer weather and longer days were not far away. The early Church modified these existing festivals for its own purpose and gave them a Christian significance. They became an opportunity to celebrate the birth of Christ as "the Light of the World."

Preparing for Christmas

Preparations begin four Sundays before Christmas Day at the start of Advent, which means "coming." During this time, Christians think about what the arrival of Christ means to them personally, as well as to the whole human race. Children are often given an Advent calendar so they can count down to Christmas Day.

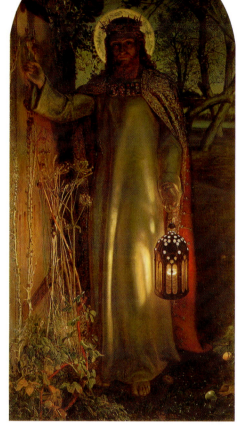

Above *Many artists have portrayed Christ as a light coming into the darkness of the world. This painting, entitled* The Light of the World, *is by William Holman Hunt (1827–1910).*

THE NATIVITY

Only two of the New Testament Gospels, Matthew and Luke, tell the story of Christ's birth, or Nativity. The stories are not the same, but some of the details overlap. The traditional picture that Christians have is a mixture of the two accounts. The baby Jesus was born in a stable surrounded by farm animals and laid in a manger or feeding trough. His parents, Mary and Joseph, had been turned away from the inn where they intended to stay because there was no room for them. To mark the event, Three Wise Men, or Magi, were guided by a star to the manger. They laid gifts of gold, frankincense, and myrrh at the infant's feet. Children frequently reenact the scene in Nativity plays.

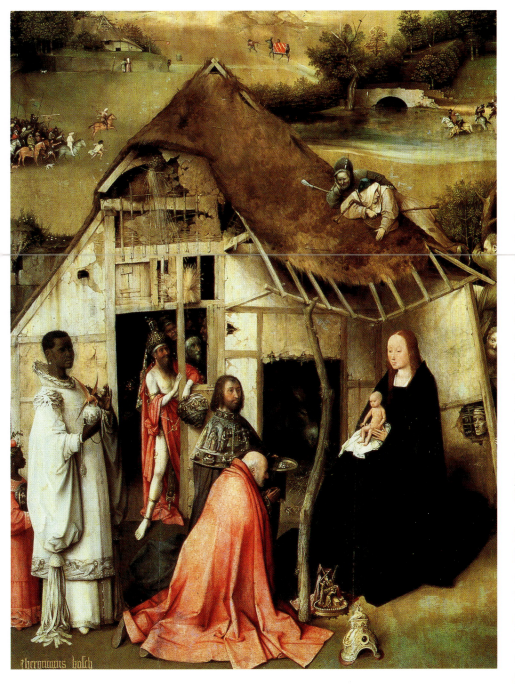

Above *The presents brought by the Magi are symbolic. The gold suggests Christ's majesty as a king and Messiah. Frankincense and myrrh are sweet-smelling resins from the bark of certain trees. They also have healing properties, which make them useful for embalming (preserving) dead bodies.*

"Magi came from the East to Jerusalem and asked, 'Where is the one who has been born King of the Jews?'"

(Matthew 2:1-2)

In most Christian traditions, Christmas Day is celebrated on December 25—though the Orthodox Christmas is on January 6. Homes are decorated with holly and ivy—plants that symbolize Christ's eternal presence in the world. Christmas carols that tell of Christ's birth are sung, and in some churches, Mass is held at midnight on Christmas Eve so that worshipers can enter into the joy of Christmas from the beginning of Christmas Day.

Christmas in the West has become very commercialized, but even some of the secular elements have religious roots. Santa Claus is based on the patron saint of children, St. Nicholas, who is traditionally associated with the giving of presents. Despite the pressure to spend money and to "eat, drink, and be merry," many people still catch a glimpse of the pure joy that Christ's birth is believed to have brought to the world.

The Three Wise Men

The Festival of Epiphany in early January celebrates the arrival of the Three Wise Men, who were the first Gentiles (non-Jews) to see Christ. This shows that Christ's message—peace on Earth and goodwill to all humanity—is a universal one, and that salvation is open to anyone who believes in him.

CELEBRATING EASTER

The Easter season is the most important time of year for Christian believers and a time of both sadness and joy. On Good Friday, they remember the Crucifixion, when Jesus Christ was put to death on the cross. On Easter Sunday, they remember the Resurrection—the day he rose from the dead.

The 40 days before Easter is a special time for Christian prayer and contemplation. The period is known as "Lent," and some people deny themselves pleasures such as candy. The story of Easter is told in the New Testament. Jesus claimed to be the son of God and was considered a threat by the Jewish and Roman authorities. On Good Friday, he was crucified on a hill outside Jerusalem on the order of Pontius Pilate. Later that day, his followers took his body and buried it in a tomb—a cave sealed with a stone. On the third day, celebrated now as Easter Sunday, women followers went to visit the tomb. They discovered that the stone had been rolled away. The body of Jesus had gone and in its place were two angels who said, "Why do you look for the living among the dead? He is not here, but has risen."

Above *Jesus Christ rises from the dead and steps out of the tomb on Easter Day. Although this Italian painting is more than 500 years old, the scene is still central to Christian belief.*

Above *In many faiths, the egg is a symbol of life. This Easter egg, studded with jewels, was made for the Russian Czar Nicholas II.*

Right *On the night before Easter every year, Christians at the Church of the Holy Sepulchre in Jerusalem celebrate the ceremony of "new light" with candles. The church is a blaze of light as flares are passed from hand to hand.*

Left This egg is divided into 48 triangles in a design often referred to—incorrectly—as the "Forty Days of Lent."

Above Fish symbols, often associated with Christ, decorate this Ukrainian Easter egg.

"Fear not . . . I know that you seek Jesus who was crucified. He is not here. For he has risen . . ."

Matthew 28:5–6

Traditionally, to mark the joy of this event, Christians break their Lenten fast on Easter Sunday and celebrate with a feast. Holy Week and Easter have always been celebrated by Christians as a time to remember that God loves people so much that he sent his son, Jesus, to die for the world. As a result, Easter has always been a special time for the baptism of new Christians.

Even before Christian times, many people celebrated spring in a special way. It is the season when trees sprout leaves again, when nature is "reborn" after the deadness of winter—just as Jesus rose from the dead. People held spring festivals, and many of their traditions carried over into the Christian Easter. The giving of Easter eggs, for example, goes back to pre-Christian times. The egg, from which a chick will be born, is a sign of fertility, a reminder that older generations die, but that younger ones will eventually take their place.

THE HISTORY OF EASTER BREAD

Special breads are eaten at Easter. The hot cross bun (*below left*) bears the sign of the cross on which Jesus was crucified. The fruit and spices that are used to make the bun are a reminder of the happiness that his resurrection brings. For centuries, the people living in Frankfurt, Germany, ate pretzels (*far right*) at their very popular Easter fairs.

125

THE RELIGIOUS LIFE

I n every religion, there are individuals who feel drawn to a more intense form of spiritual experience. As a result, some may feel a vocation (calling) to religious life and to an extra degree of Christian commitment.

The ordained ministry

To become ministers or priests, candidates must undergo several years of training, during which time they learn about the history and traditions of the church, study the Bible and other books of Christian theology, and learn about the practical requirements of being a church leader. (In the Roman Catholic and Orthodox churches, they must be men.) If, at the end of the training, they still believe they have been called to the ministry, and the Church is satisfied that their calling is genuine and that they are temperamentally and intellectually suitable, they are ordained. He or she may then be assigned to a church, or a church may invite them to serve as its minister.

Monks and nuns

Some people feel called to take up the religious life as monks or nuns in monasteries and convents. They take three vows—of poverty, chastity, and obedience—and live a very disciplined life, deliberately set apart from the outside world. There are many religious groups, or orders. Among the best known are the Dominicans, the Franciscans, the Benedictines, the Carmelites, the Cistercians, and the Trappists. Some of these are enclosed, contemplative orders in which monks and nuns devote themselves to prayer and reflection in a community that is completely cut off from the outside world. Other orders have considerable contact with the world and work with people who need their help.

Above *St. Francis lived a life of self-denial and was said to be very close to nature. Birds and animals felt safe in his presence, and it is even said that they came to hear him preach.*

Right *Pilgrims were a familiar sight on the roads of Europe in the 1400s. Here, they are making their way to the cathedral at Santiago de Compostela in northern Spain.*

The first monasteries

The pattern of Western monasticism was set by an Italian, St. Benedict (*c.* A.D. 480–550) At the age of 14, he became a hermit, and his devotion to Christ's austere way of life attracted many followers. In the mid-500s, he established a monastery at Monte Casino, between Rome and Naples, and drew up what is known as the Rule of St. Benedict. This involves a strict timetable of study, prayer, and manual work within the community, which is headed by an abbot. During the Middle Ages, the monasteries became great centers of learning, and they preserved many ancient manuscripts.

Saints and martyrs

Perhaps the most popular saint of all is St. Francis (*c.* A.D. 1181–1226), who was born into a rich Italian family, but renounced his wealth when he felt God calling him to a life of service. One night while he was praying, an angel is said to have appeared to him and given him the *stigmata*—wounds to his hands, feet, and side in imitation of Christ's wounds on the cross.

Over the years, many men and women have been persecuted for their faith, and put to death for it, or martyred. The first Christian martyr was St. Stephen, who was charged with blasphemy (speaking disrespectfully about God) by the Jewish authorities and stoned to death in Jerusalem around A.D. 35.

Many martyrs became holy figures venerated by the Church. St. Catherine of Alexandria was a 4th-century saint and martyr who opposed Roman persecution and was strapped to a spiked wheel and tortured to death. The Catherine wheel gives its name to a firework that spins around when lit. The Roman Catholic Church uses a process known as "canonization" to declare someone a saint, and requires evidence of great devotion and a miraculous event associated with their life. However, many people who have led saintly lives have not been declared saints.

Above *Many Christian men and women dedicate their lives through missionary work, setting up churches, schools, and medical clinics in developing countries.*

DIVISIONS IN CHRISTIANITY

Many Christians find it sad that the community that Jesus Christ founded as a unified family of believers is deeply divided. Divisions emerged shortly after Christ's death, when early Christians disagreed over the exact detail of his teaching and how it should be put into practice. The first major split, or schism, was in A.D. 1054, when the Church divided into two branches—Eastern and Western.

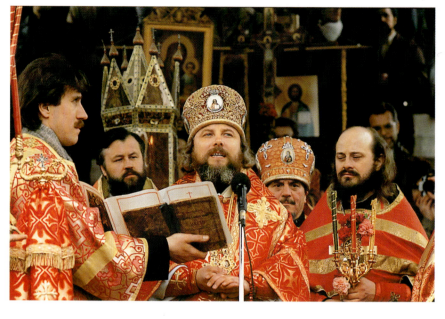

Above The traditions of the Eastern Orthodox Church have remained unchanged for centuries.

The Eastern or Orthodox tradition
This grew out of the Byzantine Empire (the eastern part of the Roman Empire), of which Constantinople was the capital. Its influence spread to Greece, central Europe, and Russia, and the most important groups today are the Russian, Greek, Armenian, Serbian, and Romanian Orthodox Churches that put great emphasis on tradition.

The Western or Roman Catholic tradition
This is a Church based on the authority of the Bishop of Rome, who is in direct succession to the apostle Simon (later called Peter). The pope, or head of the Roman Catholic Church, is held to be infallible—in other words his opinion on theological matters cannot be wrong and must be followed by Roman Catholics everywhere. The refusal by the Orthodox Church to accept papal authority was one reason for the "Great Schism" in the 1300s. Today Roman Catholics are the largest group of Christians, with 890 million adherents. Outside Europe, South America has the most Roman Catholics.

Below Barbara Harris was the first female bishop of the Episcopal Church of the United States. The role of women in the ordained ministry of the Christian Church is a source of deep theological division.

The Protestants

The Reformation began in the 1300s when people like Jan Hus, a preacher in Prague, attacked the Roman Catholic Church for its excessive wealth and its departure from the simple teaching of Christ. But most people date the Reformation from 1517, when the German theologian Martin Luther nailed 95 criticisms ("theses") of the Church to the door of the cathedral in Wittenberg. He argued that people did not need priests and the pope to mediate between themselves and God. He stressed a personal relationship with Christ and a close study of the Bible as a way toward salvation. Because of their protest, his followers became known as Protestants.

Above Evangelical or Charismatic worship is informal and spontaneous. These people are praying at a religious service in Newport Beach, California.

Many denominations

Despite internal tensions, the Roman Catholic Church continues to be a unified body, but Protestantism has fragmented into many different denominations—Episcopalianism, Lutheranism, Methodism, Presbyterianism, and many others that share the core beliefs about Jesus Christ and his ministry, but worship in different ways. A modern phenomenon in the West is the House Church Movement, which has abandoned the traditional institutions of the church and worships in an informal style. Members tend to belong to the Evangelical or Charismatic wing of Christianity; that is to say, they put great emphasis on the gifts of the spirit and on a personal encounter with Jesus Christ. There are some theological disagreements between the liberal wing of the Church and those Evangelicals who interpret the Bible in a more literal way, but all Christians are trying to wrestle with the challenges contained in the Gospel and to make the faith a living reality in their lives.

Below Pope John Paul II gives First Communion to Roman Catholic children in Trondheim, Norway. The pope is the head of the Roman Catholic Church.

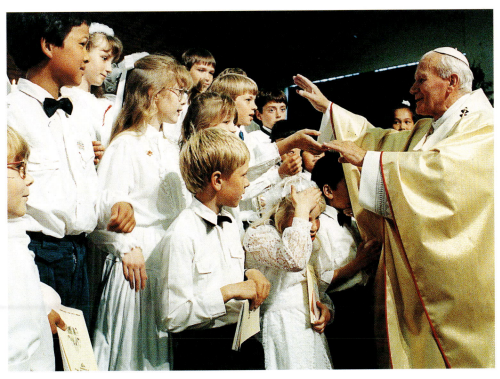

ISLAM: AN INTRODUCTION

Islam, which means "submission" to one God, is the religion practiced by almost a billion Muslims around the world. It is based on the teachings of the Prophet Muhammad, believed by Muslims to have received the word of Allah (God) about 1,400 years ago in Mecca (present-day Saudi Arabia).

The final revelation

Muslims believe that part of the divine message to humanity was revealed to earlier prophets, including Noah, Moses, and Jesus, but that Muhammad was the last of the prophets to bring Allah's final message to the world. The message is contained in the Koran, Islam's holy book, which cannot be changed or added to. Such is the reverence for Muhammad that whenever the faithful speak his name, they respectfully say "Peace be upon him," after it.

Islam teaches that the message of Allah was revealed to Muhammad by the chief angel Jibril, or Gabriel. Christians believe that Gabriel, who is also mentioned in the Koran, appeared to the Virgin Mary to foretell Jesus' birth. The revelations of Jibril were not given all at once, but over a period of years. They were brought together in the Koran. It contains basic Muslim beliefs and outlines religious practices, which Muslims everywhere are required to follow.

A way of life

Islam is a whole way of life with guidelines for the moral, spiritual, and political organization of society. In Islam, nothing is regarded as secular (nonreligious) and every action or thought must be guided by the will of Allah. Indeed, this total submission to God's will requires Muslims to see themselves as God's creatures, here to serve God and humanity.

Above Muslims submit themselves to the will of God by prostrating themselves in worship. They can pray alone or, as here, with their fellow Muslims in a public display of devotion that is very impressive.

Left The hilal, *or crescent moon and star, is the symbol of Islam. In the Koran, it says that Allah created the stars to guide people to their destination. The moon is a reminder that the Islamic year is governed by the lunar calendar.*

Above This 16th-century Persian engraving shows pupils studying the Holy Book at the feet of their teacher.

Below Children are expected to study the Koran and to be able to recite large parts of it by heart.

A revolutionary message

Islam emerged at a time when Judaism, Christianity, and polytheism (worship of many gods) coexisted on the Arabian Peninsula. Many people worshiped idols, so Muhammad's message of the "One Creator God" was revolutionary and led to his persecution. And yet, within 30 years, Islam became a powerful religion and later the basis for an influential Islamic empire. Islam teaches that Allah the Merciful will judge people's actions when they die. If they have done what is good and lawful (*halal*), they will be rewarded; if they have done what is not permitted (*haram*), they will be punished.

Islam is sometimes misunderstood in the West, and the term "Muslim fundamentalist" is frequently used as an insult. It is also misleading—Muslims take their faith seriously, so it is natural for them to follow "fundamental" principles. An increasingly secular West sometimes finds such devotion hard to understand.

THE DEVELOPMENT OF ISLAM

Islam first emerged in Mecca, the birthplace of the Prophet Muhammad, and later in Medina. Mecca was situated on one of the Middle East's principal trade routes, and was an important religious center because of its shrine, the Kaaba. Merchants and visitors drawn to its annual fairs carried the news of the new prophet to distant lands.

Early beginnings

At first, Islam was just a local religion with a few followers led by Muhammad, who believed Allah was revealing his message to him. This belief brought Muhammad and his followers into conflict with the traders of Mecca, who did not want an important (and profitable) place of pilgrimage for Arabs with pagan beliefs threatened by the message that there was only one God. Muhammad was persecuted and eventually forced to leave. In 1622, he and his followers moved north to Yathrib (later named Medina), in a migration that became known as the *hijra*. It marks the start of the Muslim calendar and of Islam as an organized religion.

Above The influence of local architectural styles can be seen in this mosque in Mali, West Africa. The mosque is made of mud.

Medina

In Medina, Muhammad continued to receive divine revelations, including rules of law that he applied to the growing community of believers. By now, Mecca was hostile to Medina and launched a series of unsuccessful raids on the city. Muhammad was a skilled military leader who resisted attack, and led an armed force of his own on Mecca in A.D. 630 to cleanse the city of its pagan worshipers.

ART AT THE TIME OF SÜLEYMAN THE MAGNIFICENT

In the reign of the Ottoman sultan Süleyman the Magnificent (A.D. 1520–1566), Islamic art and science flourished. At its height, the Ottoman Empire was one of the most influential in world history. The empire lasted until the end of World War I. Its capital, Constantinople (now Istanbul), was the center of Islamic thought, and produced a culture that embraced everything from ceramics and calligraphy to architecture and astronomy. This mosque lamp of the period is characteristically ornate and comes from one of the numerous mosques that were constructed during Süleyman the Magnificent's reign.

Muhammad's army met little resistance and he took Mecca practically without bloodshed. Many people who were initially hostile to Islam now embraced it, and became Muslims themselves. One of the Prophet Muhammad's first tasks was to cleanse the Kaaba of its idols and to return it to its original purity as a focal point for worship of the one God. To this day, it remains Islam's holiest site.

Expansion

When the Prophet died in A.D. 632, there was disagreement over who should succeed him— a disagreement that later resulted in the division between the Sunni and Shia branches of Islam (*see page 146*). Muhammad's successor was his father-in-law, Abu Bakr, who became the caliph (*khalifa*), or head of state. Under the first four caliphs, Islam expanded at a colossal rate into present-day Egypt, Syria, Iraq, and Iran.

After the caliphs, the Umayyad dynasty (A.D. 661–750) took the faith west as far as Spain and Morocco and east as far as India. Their successors, the Abbasids (A.D. 750–1258), made Baghdad (in present-day Iraq) their capital and extended their territory

Above This battle scene is from the 16th-century Book of Conquests *by Süleyman. All Muslims are expected to defend Islam against outside threat by means of* jihad, *or holy war. This also refers to a person's inner struggle against sin and temptation.*

still farther into central Asia. In 1258, the Mongols took control of Baghdad and became Muslims themselves. In 1453, Constantinople (the Christian capital of the Byzantine Empire) fell to the Ottoman Turks and was eventually renamed Istanbul. Islam experienced another period of renewal in 1979, when the Iranian Revolution deposed the ruling monarch, the Shah of Iran, and introduced an Islamic state under the leadership of Ayatollah Khomeini.

THE LIFE OF THE PROPHET

Muhammad was born in A.D. 570 in the Arabian city of Mecca. Orphaned at the age of six, he was raised first by his grandfather, then by his uncle, with whom he traveled on trade missions to Syria.

Early life

When Muhammad was a young man, he worked as a trade agent for a rich widow named Khadija. The city of Mecca was home to the Kaaba, the "sacred house," said to have been built by Abraham and his son Ishmael. In Muhammad's time, it was filled with pagan idols worshiped by Arabs visiting Mecca on pilgrimages. This arrangement suited the traders because the pilgrims were a source of income. When he was 25, Muhammad married Khadija and had several children by her. He became rich and highly respected in the city, but was uncomfortable with the pagan worship around him and sought solitude in the deserts and mountains.

Above *The Dome of the Rock in Jerusalem houses the rock from which Muhammad is said to have ascended into heaven.*

The message from God

At the age of 40, Muhammad was meditating in a cave outside Mecca when the Angel Jibril appeared to him. Jibril ordered Muhammad to read, but when he replied that he could not, Jibril squeezed him tightly and insisted. "Read," he said, "read in the name of your Lord who created you from a drop of blood." This was the first message that he received directly from Allah.

Left *The Prophet's cave at Jebel Nur in present-day Saudi Arabia. Some Muslims believe this is where Adam, the first man created by Allah, appeared on Earth.*

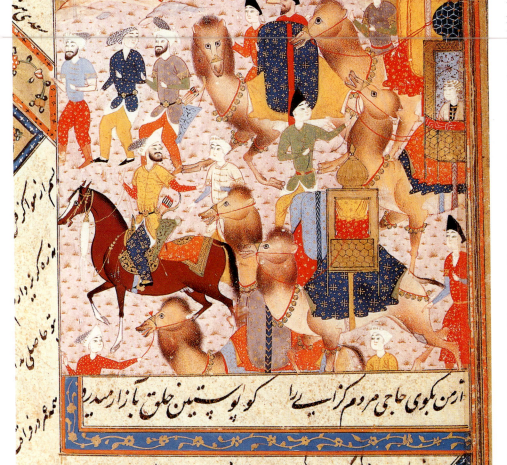

Above This print shows a caravan of pilgrims on the road to Mecca. In the past, Muslims from all over the world traveled by foot, on horseback, or camel. The journey could take years, so the pilgrims met many people along the way. Today, modern air travel means that Mecca is only hours away.

"Be steadfast in prayer. Practice regular charity and bow down your heads with those who bow down in worship."

The Koran 2:43

The Night Journey
In about the tenth year of his ministry, Muhammad is said to have undergone a miraculous experience. In what has come to be called the Night Journey, Muslims believe he was taken up into the sky in the company of the angels. From Mecca he was taken to Jerusalem, where he prayed with earlier prophets including Abraham and Jesus. He then ascended to heaven (from a rock now contained in the Dome of the Rock in Jerusalem), where he received God's instruction to institute prayers five times a day.

The message spreads
After being forced out of Mecca because of persecution, Muhammad became the ruler of Medina, which was the target of hostilities by the people of Mecca. When Muhammad took Mecca in A.D. 630, he behaved with such generosity and tolerance that many of his former enemies became Muslims themselves. Two years after cleansing the Kaaba of its pagan worship and restoring it to the worship of one God, Muhammad gave his last sermon, asking his followers to obey God and treat each other with justice and kindness. His aim in life was now complete—he had delivered the word of Allah, which would remain true for all time. Muhammad died at the age of 63 in Medina, where he was buried.

THE KORAN

The Koran is the holy book of the Muslim world. The word means "reading" and is taken from the instruction the Angel Jibril gave Muhammad (*see page 134*), that he should read the word of God.

Learning by heart

Because the revelation was made in Arabic, Muslims have always studied the Koran in its original language. Very often, for boys and girls starting to study it, this means that they recite the words while not fully understanding what they mean. However, since the words are believed to be the actual words of Allah, merely reciting them is seen as an act of worship in itself. Students are encouraged to learn as much of the Koran as they can by heart, and in 1998, a six-year-old Muslim girl in South Africa became the youngest girl ever to have memorized the whole text in Arabic—114 *suras* (chapters) in all, divided into verses.

Reverence for the holy book

The text is treated with great care and touched only by those who have ritually cleansed themselves beforehand. It is often wrapped in ornate cloth and kept in a special place in the home or mosque. Unlike the Ten Commandments, the Koran was not handed over at one single time, but over a period of 23 years. As a result, it contains different styles of writing that deal with all aspects of life. There are instructions on how to pray, how to organize society, and how to apply the law. It lists rules for the structure of family life, the duty of individuals to behave well, and penalties for sinners on Judgment Day. Above all, it stresses the "Oneness" of Allah and the need to obey him.

Above As an act of personal devotion, Muslim calligraphers (scribes who practice the art of handwriting) try to produce the most beautiful and ornate versions of the text by hand. This script with floral illuminations was written by Ismail Al-Zuhdi in 1802.

Left This boy is studying the Koran in Arabic. In the Indian and Pakistani tradition, pupils sit around the edge of the classroom, not in rows behind each other. This is because it is considered disrespectful to have one's back to the holy book.

Other sources of guidance

Because Muhammad is believed to have led an exemplary life, his actions and sayings are also considered important by Muslims. Stories of the Prophet's life are taken as practical examples of how devout Muslims should try to lead their own lives. Therefore, the traditional customs and practices of the Prophet (the *Sunna*) and his words and sayings (*hadith*) are consulted alongside the Koran. Together, they provide the faithful with a complete guide book to a godly life.

Although there are divisions within Islam, and scholars from different traditions around the world may interpret the text in different ways, all Muslims accept the ultimate authority of the Koran over their lives and try to live by its rules.

> "This is the Book. In it is guidance sure, without doubt to those who fear God."
>
> The Koran 2:2

Below Some Muslims believe that the original version of the Koran has existed since the beginning of time on tablets stored in heaven. The text is venerated as the complete revelation of Allah's holy word.

MECCA AND THE FIVE PILLARS OF ISLAM

Mecca, the birthplace of the Prophet Muhammad, is a holy city and a place of pilgrimage for over two million Muslims every year. The pilgrimage, which all healthy Muslim men and women are expected to make at least once in a lifetime, is known as the *Hajj*, and is the fifth of the "Pillars of Islam." Just as the pillars in a mosque support the building that rises above them, so the Pillars of Islam support the beliefs and practices of the Islamic faith. The pilgrimage brings together Muslims of diverse cultures and races who seek spiritual purity, and to pray alongside one another in the Kaaba.

Below *At the center of the holy city of Mecca is the Kaaba, a cube-shaped shrine covered in black and gold velvet. When Muslim pilgrims visit the Kaaba, they walk counterclockwise around it seven times, reciting prayers to Allah.*

Left Regular prayer is central to Islamic practice. The women and children worship separately from the men.

The *shahada*

The first pillar is the statement of faith— the *shahada*. It says, "There is no god but Allah and Muhammad is the Messenger of Allah." In reciting these words of faith, devout Muslims proclaim their belief in one God and their conviction that God's teaching has been revealed to Muhammad. This simple statement is the basis of all Muslim belief. It is the first thing whispered into a child's ear when he or she is born, and the last thing a Muslim hopes to utter at the moment of death.

Salat and *zakat*

The second pillar, *salat*, is daily worship—the prayers recited at dawn, midday, afternoon, evening, and night. Muslims stop what they are doing to bow down in worship in the direction of Mecca. The third pillar is *zakat*, or charitable giving. This is meant to emulate the generosity that Allah shows toward his people. It also shows kindness to those less fortunate in a practical way.

> "I bear witness that there is no God but Allah, and I bear witness that Muhammad is the messenger of Allah."
>
> Words from the *shahada*

Sawm

The fourth pillar is fasting, or *sawm*, which involves going

without food and drink during daylight hours throughout the holy month of Ramadan. For people with jobs, and children going to school, total abstinence is not easy, but it does bring spiritual reward. The end of Ramadan is celebrated with the festival of Id al-Fitr.

Left The religious duties of which the Five Pillars are the core are taught to Muslims like this Algerian girl, at an early age.

ISLAMIC LAW AND SCIENCE

The system of Islamic law known as *Shari'a* comes from the Arabic word describing a track leading camels to a watering hole—a description implying a pathway that, if followed by humanity, will lead to Allah.

Sources of the law

The Koran and the *Sunna* (customs and practices of the Prophet) are the two principal sources of the law in Islam. There are five categories of actions: what Allah has decreed, what Allah has forbidden, what Allah has recommended but not insisted on, what Allah has disapproved of but not expressly forbidden, and what Allah has remained silent about. For example, visiting a sick person is recommended whereas seeking treatment for an illness is required. Not all issues are so clearly explained. Alcohol is forbidden, but tobacco is different. Some scholars have argued that it is not covered in the Koran, although they suspect it is a gray area that, while not expressly forbidden, is disapproved of. These differences have given rise to different opinions about many social issues.

Above *Islamic law deals with all aspects of family life. A man may have more than one wife, provided he can look after them equally—an arrangement that is increasingly rare in the West.*

Interpreting the law

Shari'a deals with every aspect of human society including family life, property, crime, punishment, business, and morality. Since the Koran is silent on many specific issues of modern life, scholars constantly interpret the law, and their findings also become a basis for lawmaking. Experts able to rule on points of law are known as *muftis*. Shiite Muslims also accept the rulings of their highest religious leaders, the ayatollahs. Interpretation of Islamic law may vary, but its fundamentals always apply.

Right Young women working in a laboratory in Egypt continue the centuries-old tradition of scholarship and science.

> "It is God who sends the winds and they raise the clouds. Then does he spread them in the sky as he wills."
>
> The Koran 30:48

Muslim scholarship

Throughout the Dark Ages of Europe (c. A.D. 500–1100) the flame of scholarship was kept alive by writers, philosophers, and mathematicians from the Islamic world, who translated many of the classical texts of ancient Greece into Arabic. The Western system of numerals is of Arabic origin. By superseding Roman numerals, they made modern mathematics possible. Muslim mathematicians also gave the world algebra.

Astronomical exploration

Islamic scientists founded observatories from which they plotted the positions of the stars. They used and refined a special instrument known as an astrolabe, which enabled them to carry out a scientific function (measuring the angle of the stars and plotting distances and directions on the ground) and a religious function (establishing the direction of Mecca—the *qibla*—for their daily prayers). Astrolabes were important for navigation and mapmaking, and led to many discoveries. Islam encourages scholarship and has produced eminent philosophers, doctors, and scientists, but it also teaches that Allah alone is the source of all knowledge and all creation.

Above This painting shows astronomers at work in the 16th-century observatory in Istanbul. Globes, maps, astrolabes, telescopes, and compasses have all been refined by Muslim scientists.

WORSHIP AND FESTIVALS

Muslims believe that humans were created to worship Allah and the purpose of life itself is total submission to his will. Everyday life is organized around *salat*, the five daily prayers that are recited in the direction of Mecca. Muslims will often have a special prayer rug, or *sajjada*, for use at home or when they are traveling. This allows them to create a ritually pure and holy space from which to direct their thoughts to Allah. At home and in the mosque, shoes are removed as a sign of reverence.

The festival year

Just as prayers punctuate the day, so festivals punctuate the Islamic year, which has 12 lunar months, or 354 days. In some Islamic traditions, the calendar begins with the celebration of the *hijra*, the Prophet's migration from Mecca to Medina in A.D. 622. This is followed two months later by a festival marking his birth in 570.

The ninth month, Ramadan, is the most significant of the year and is marked by a complete abstinence from food and drink during daylight hours. Muhammad is thought to have received Allah's first revelation during Ramadan and, as a result, Muslims recite the holy book throughout this month. Fasting is a physical and spiritual discipline designed to focus attention on Allah in a concentrated way. It is a duty that every fit and healthy adult is expected to perform. Children are not expected to fast, but many do, in imitation of their parents' devotion to Allah.

Above Five times a day, Muslims stop whatever they are doing, face the direction of Mecca, and prostrate themselves in prayer.

Left These children have a homemade Id card. The end of Ramadan is associated with blessings and joy, and people often exchange presents.

Above Ramadan ends with the joyful festival of Id al-Fitr when families and friends break their month-long fast.

> "People, adore your Guardian–Lord who created you."
>
> The Koran 2:21

Daily routine in Ramadan

In many households, the day begins before dawn with prayers and a reading from the Koran. People then set off for work or school knowing that they will not be able to eat or drink anything until the sun sets. Attendance at the mosque increases during Ramadan, particularly toward the end of the month when people gather to commemorate *Lailat al-Qadr*, the Night of Power, believed to be the night that Allah first revealed the Koran to the Prophet Muhammad. Muslims try to stay awake all night and may stay in the mosque praying or reciting from the Koran. The fast concentrates mind, body, and spirit on Allah and demonstrates the important of resisting temptation. It is also thought to be a way for the rich to experience the hardship of the poor.

Fasting for a feast

Ramadan ends as soon as the new moon is sighted—in some Muslim countries, this is signaled by the sound of a cannon. The fasting stops and Muslims prepare for the joyful festival of Id al-Fitr, when they sit down to enjoy their first meal during daylight for a month. Wealthy families are expected to give food to the poor so that everyone can mark the day happily. Presents are often exchanged, as a sign of sharing with others what God has given.

Left Children in Singapore celebrate the end of Ramadan. People put on their best clothes to celebrate the day in style.

143

THE MOSQUE

The word "mosque" comes from an Arabic word that means "place of prostration." It is the house of prayer where Muslims gather together to worship Allah. There are many different styles of mosque, and they reflect the traditional architecture of the countries in which they are found. However, all of them share common design features.

Pointers to Allah

Perhaps the most distinctive element of a mosque is its minaret, the tall, slender tower designed to be seen from a distance as a reminder of Allah's presence. As a person's gaze goes up the minaret to the top, they are symbolically looking up toward heaven, where Allah is supreme. Similarly, the dome of the mosque symbolizes the roof of the sky where Allah reigns in splendor and majesty.

The harmony of creation

Although mosques are often richly decorated, the decorations are always abstract and geometrical, symbolizing divine harmony. Because Muslims are careful to avoid the sin of idolatry (worshiping anything other than the one God), there are never any pictures of people or animals that might accidentally distract the worshiper from Allah alone.

House of prayer

The mosque is usually full at midday on Friday, which is an important day for communal worship. Unlike Judaism and Christianity, Islam does not have the concept of the Sabbath. Since Allah never stops working, Muslims believe that they should not stop working either.

Left Traditionally, the muezzin (or proclaimer) calls the faithful to prayer from the minaret, or tower of the mosque. In most Islamic countries, the task is now carried out electronically through a loudspeaker system.

The mihrab is a niche in the wall that marks the direction of Mecca.

The minbar is a pulpit from which the Imam delivers his sermon on Fridays.

The minarets have balconies from which the call to prayer is given by the muezzin.

Left The Blue Mosque in Istanbul is one of the most beautiful religious buildings in the world. It was built between A.D. 1609 and 1616 on the orders of Sultan Ahmet I.

Once they have said Friday prayers, they resume their working day. Prayer is led by a religious leader (*Imam*) or by a preacher (*khatib*). When praying, Muslims always face Mecca—the direction is indicated by an empty niche or alcove known as the *mihrab*. Because prayer involves ritual movements of standing, kneeling, and bowing, the space in the main prayer hall has no seating of any kind. Instead, carpets cover the floor, marking it out as holy ground. Although some mosques have a separate area for women to worship, praying in a mosque is usually an all-male activity. Worshipers leave their shoes at the door and proceed to a small room— usually a communal space with low seats in front of individual faucets—where they rinse their hands, face, nostrils, mouth, arms, and feet in ritual purification.

Above Men congregate for prayer at the Prophet's Mosque in Medina, Saudi Arabia. They kneel on carpets and face Mecca.

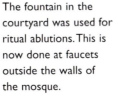

The fountain in the courtyard was used for ritual ablutions. This is now done at faucets outside the walls of the mosque.

Equality in the sight of Allah

In the prayer hall, the worshipers line up together—young, old, rich, and poor occupying the same space to show that all are equal in the sight of Allah. Next to the *mihrab* is the *minbar*, which looks like a small staircase, from which the preacher delivers his sermon, or *khutba*. Mosque worship is based on the word of Allah so there is no singing or music of any kind. Muslims believe that group worship is more pleasing to Allah than individual prayer, so they make a special effort to attend.

DIVISION AND DIVERSITY

The Koran describes Muhammad as "the Seal of the Prophets," that is, with him, the line of the prophets (beginning with Adam and continuing through Abraham, Moses, and Jesus) has been sealed for all time. Muhammad is the last and no other will follow him.

After the Prophet
Problems arose after the Prophet's death when there was disagreement about who should lead the Muslim community. Two branches, Sunni and Shiite, emerged. The Sunnis took their name from the *Sunna*, or traditions of the Prophet. They argued that as no one could ever equal Muhammad in wisdom and goodness, his chosen successor had to be the person judged most suitable by the community. The Prophet's first successor was Abu Bakr, who became the first of the four caliphs who ruled the (as yet) undivided *umma*, or community of believers.

The decisive split
The group that eventually became the Shiites was unhappy with this arrangement and argued that only Muhammad's nearest relative, his cousin and son-in-law Ali, was fit to follow in the Prophet's footsteps. Becoming known as the "followers of the party of Ali" or *shi'at Ali* (Shia for short), they believed that Ali had inherited some of the qualities and authority of their founder, qualities that made him especially suitable to become their religious leader, or *imam*. The decisive split between Sunnis and Shiites came in A.D. 680, when Ali's son Hussain was killed by Muslim rivals at the Battle of Karbala. His tomb in what is now southern Iraq is still regarded as one of the holiest shrines in the Shiite Islamic world.

Above From 1979–89, the influence of Ayatollah Khomeini was important in defining the character of Shiite Islam. The revolution he inspired in Iran, and his insistence on a particular type of Islamic purity, brought him into direct conflict with countries in the West.

Right These Chinese children reciting parts of the Koran in Arabic show how far Islam has traveled since its beginnings on the Arabian Peninsula.

Above Islamic dress should be modest at all times, but different countries interpret modesty differently. These Afghan women wear a very conservative style of dress that leaves only the eyes visible, and these are also sometimes covered by a veil.

Shiites and Sunnis

Shiism itself soon divided, this time into three groups. The majority Imami, or Twelver, group, found mainly in Iran, Iraq, and Lebanon, believed in 12 principal *Imams*, the twelfth of whom is said to have disappeared, but will return at the end of time. The Ismailis, or Sevener, group supported a man named Ismail as the seventh *Imam* in his claim to be the head of Shiism. The Zaydis, the third group, are found mostly in Yemen. Sunni Muslims account for about 80 percent of the world's Islamic population. A principal center of Sunni Islam is Saudi Arabia, which is also guardian of the most important religious shrine in Mecca. Shiite Muslims, most of whom live in Iran, account for the remaining 20 percent.

> "When you recite the Koran, seek refuge in God from accursed Satan."
>
> The Koran 16:98

THE WAY OF THE SUFI

The Sufis are not a separate branch of Islam. They can be drawn from both the Sunni and the Shiite groups and are defined by their mystical approach to the faith. Taking their name from the *suf*—the simple woollen robe they used to wear (*suf* means "wool")—they search for a closer, personal relationship with Allah. Sufism was influenced by the ascetic practices (giving up material possessions) of Christian monks and hermits. Like them, Sufis turned their back on the world and took vows of poverty.

The mystical tradition

During a service known as a *dhikr*, Sufis use song, dance, and drumming to focus all their attention on Allah. In this state of heightened concentration on the divine presence, they hope to completely release themselves from worldly attachments in order to have a clear and enlightened mind to experience God's presence.

The Sufi tradition produced the most famous female mystic in Islam's history: Rabi'a al-Adawiyya (721–801) was a freed slave who devoted her life entirely to Allah.

Closer communion with God

In the 1100s, a number of Sufi orders, or brotherhoods (*tariqas*), sprang up and were based in enclosed communities set aside for study and prayer. Perhaps the best known of the Sufi groups that came out of the *tariqas* are the Dervishes, whose name comes from the Turkish and Persian words meaning "beggar." They, too, took vows of poverty and devoted their lives to love and experiencing God's presence. Following the guidance of a religious teacher (a *shaykh* or *pir*), they practice rituals that induce an almost hypnotic or trancelike state in which they hope to experience the divine.

Left *This woman uses prayer beads to aid her devotion. They are a physical way of helping the mind focus on Allah.*

Above Whirling Dervishes of the
Turkish Sufi sect spin around to induce
a trancelike state that is believed to bring
them into a closer relationship with Allah.

The Whirling Dervishes

Unlike other Muslim groups, the Sufis use ritual music in their
devotions. The group popularly known as Whirling Dervishes
rotate around and around to the accompaniment of a repetitive
beat, seeking a higher level of consciousness that they hope will
ultimately bring them into direct experience of Allah. The whirling
is said to imitate the rotation of the planets around the sun and
that of the whole of Creation around Allah. Some Muslims consider
music ungodly because it can lead to temptation, but for Sufis it
is often used as an aid to devotion. Sufi mysticism appeals as
much to the heart as to the head, and at its center is the
simple but all-consuming love of Allah.

MODERN-DAY BELIEFS

Religious beliefs are not carved in stone. They develop constantly as men and women of every generation seek new answers to some of life's old questions. Dissatisfied with the religions they see around them, some may invent new religious movements, while others will look to existing religions, borrow elements from them, and add new ones of their own.

The Church of Jesus Christ of Latter-day Saints
Members of this church are known as Mormons. This name derives from one of their central scriptures, *The Book of Mormon*, which their founder Joseph Smith (1805–44), is said to have translated under divine guidance. It is believed to be another Testament to be studied along with the Old and New Testaments of the Bible.

Mormons believe that Jesus Christ visited what is now known as America, and that their Church is a restoration on Earth of Christ's Church. They believe Jesus will come again and institute a thousand-year reign, after which Satan and the forces of evil will be defeated. This doctrine is known as millenarianism, and is shared by other groups influenced by their reading of Christianity. With more than 10 million members worldwide, the Church is growing fast. It has no paid clergy, but young men and women are expected to complete a period of missionary service abroad to spread the gospel.

Mormons lead a disciplined life, avoiding intoxicants such as alcohol and tobacco, and they have a strong self-help philosophy.

Above The Church of Jesus Christ of Latter-day Saints (Mormons) reenact the Long March of 1847, when Mormon pioneers trekked across the plains from their winter quarters to the valley of the Great Salt Lake.

Left Although some modern-day Druids claim to be in a tradition stretching back to Celtic Druids, the modern order was only founded about 300 years ago. Their rituals center on the elements of air, fire, and water, and on a reverence for the Earth.

150

Other Christian-influenced groups

Seventh-day Adventists also have a millenarian philosophy and believe that the second coming of Christ is not far off. They observe Saturday as the Sabbath, or day of rest.

Jehovah's Witnesses spread their message through door-to-door evangelism, but reject much of traditional Christian doctrine. For example, they deny the idea of the Trinity (God as Father, Son, and Holy Spirit) and they forbid their members from having blood transfusions.

Baha'i

The Baha'i faith was originally an offshoot of Islam and was founded by Mirza Husayn Ali Nuri in A.D. 1863. At first, he had been a follower of a man known as "the Bab," who preached that Muhammad was not the last of the prophets, but that a messenger of God was still to come. Nuri took the name Baha'u'lla (Glory of God) and taught that all religions are basically one and that people should strive for world peace and harmony between the world's faiths.

Hare Krishna

One of the most distinctive of the Hindu-inspired groups is the Hare Krishna movement. Devotees put the god Krishna at the center of their worship and they chant a *mantra* (a short repetitive phrase) based on his name. Yoga, meditation, and daily readings from their scriptures are part of their devotions.

Right The International Society for Krishna Consciousness (ISKON) was founded in 1966. Hare Krishna devotees worship the Hindu god Krishna.

Finding a way

In every generation, there are those whose spiritual longings are not satisfied by existing religions and who decide to establish religious movements of their own. In our own age, countless new beliefs have emerged. Only time will tell whether they will flourish or wither away.

Rastafarians

Rastafarianism, which is practiced largely in Jamaica and the Caribbean, has at its heart devotion to the late Emperor Haile Selassie, born Tafari Makonnen, of Ethiopia (1892–1975). Its followers consider him (also known as Prince, or "Ras" Tafari) a savior who will lead black people to their sacred homeland of Africa and deliver them from what is seen as the oppression of white people.

Followers of Rastafarianism look to the Hebrew Bible to define their identity and believe that they are the descendants of the 12 tribes of Israel (*see page 88*). In particular, they believe that they are fulfilling Psalm 68, which tells of God's liberation of the oppressed. Using the name contained in verse 4 of that psalm, they refer to God as "Jah." Perhaps the most famous Rastafarian of modern times was the singer Bob Marley (1945–81) who, through his music, brought the culture of Rastafarianism to a mass audience.

The New Age Movement

This term is used to describe a number of different groups that, while they have no creeds or structured belief system, have certain elements in common. Typically, New Age believers in the West borrow from Eastern religions and focus particularly on healing and the environment.

Above *Members of the Unification Church (the "Moonies") take part in a mass wedding. The movement was founded in Korea in 1954 by the Reverend Sun Myung Moon. His controversial teachings blend elements of Christianity and Taoism.*

Left *Although based on traditional Christianity, televangelism has developed a character of its own by reinterpreting an old message in a new way and using modern mass communication to spread the Gospel.*

Many believe that the Earth contains unseen energies that can be channeled to promote good health and a sense of well-being. These energies are believed to be found in places (prehistoric sites associated with worship, myth, magic, or legend), or things (crystals, perfumes, or colors). The movement also includes modern pagan worshipers, who look to the Earth as a source of fertility and power.

> **"There is only one religion, though there are a hundred versions of it."**
>
> George Bernard Shaw

Good or bad?

Some of those people who feel the need to form a new religion are well-meaning with a real concern to share what they see as the truth of existence. But some are motivated by power or money and want to found a religion just to control other people's lives. As a result, alongside those new religious movements that are harmless and beneficial, there are some dangerous cults that demand absolute obedience and have, in extreme instances, forced their members to harm themselves. The intentions of such new religions will become clear over time.

Throughout history, people have often had to suffer for their beliefs—sometimes being made fun of, being punished, or even being killed. People who have clung to their beliefs, regardless of the price, have shown how powerful religions can be. Having embarked on the great adventure of faith, they continue to trust that, though the cost may be great, the reward will be greater still.

Left Rastas are distinguished by their dreadlocks, a symbolic refusal to conform to the expectations of white people. This style is said to be inspired by the biblical description of the mane of the Lion of Judah.

153

GLOSSARY

Adi Granth The Sikh holy book, which is treated as if it were a revered teacher, hence its other name, the *Guru Granth Sahib*.

Ahimsa In Hinduism, Buddhism, and Jainism, the respect for all living things and principle of nonviolence.

Ahura Mazda The creator and god of Zoroastrianism.

Ancestor worship In Chinese and Shinto belief, and in native religions, the practice of venerating dead relatives.

Ascetic A person who practices extreme self-discipline in order to develop spiritually.

Avatar In Hinduism, one of ten earthly manifestations of the creator god, Vishnu.

Baptism The Christian rite that involves the ceremonial use of water and signifies formal admission to the Church.

Conversion A change in one's religious direction by adopting a new belief.

Covenant A bargain or agreement, especially the one between God and the Israelites.

Creed An agreed set of beliefs.

Dharma In Hinduism, the eternal law of the universe. In Buddhism, the teachings of the Buddha.

Dreamtime In the Aboriginal tradition, the period of creation when ancestral beings roamed the Earth and formed the landscape.

Druids Ancient Celtic priests.

Eucharist Also known as Holy Communion, eucharist is the Christian sacrament that commemorates, with bread and wine, Jesus Christ's last meal with his disciples before his death and resurrection.

Fasting Abstaining from food as part of a spiritual discipline.

Five Pillars of Islam The principal duties every Muslim must carry out: the profession of faith in the one God, daily prayer, charitable giving, fasting during the month of Ramadan, and pilgrimage to Mecca.

Gospels The first four books of the New Testament of the Bible that describe the life and teachings of Jesus Christ.

Guru In Hinduism, a spiritual teacher, and in Sikhism, one of the ten early leaders of the faith.

Hadith In Islam, the collection of sayings and traditions of the Prophet Muhammad.

Halakah Jewish religious law.

Heaven In many religious traditions, the home of God or the gods and the place where the good will go when they die.

Hell A place or state of eternal torment reserved for the wicked.

Incarnation The Christian doctrine stating that God took human form in the person of Jesus Christ.

Jihad A holy war in defense of Islam and the personal struggle within oneself to lead a godly life.

Kami In Shinto, unseen spirits which live in the natural landscape.

Karma In Hinduism and Buddhism, the eternal law of cause and effect. In Jainism, the invisible matter that attaches itself to the soul and prevents it from progressing.

Khalsa The community of pure, fully initiated Sikhs.

Lent The 40-day period of spiritual discipline preceding the Christian festival of Easter.

Lama A spiritual teacher in Tibetan Buddhism.

Libation The pouring out of a drink in honor of a god.

Mantra In Buddhism and Hinduism, a word or syllable repeated as part of meditation and believed to possess a spiritual power of its own.

Messiah In Judaism, the deliverer of the Jewish people as foretold in the Hebrew Bible. In the Christian tradition, Jesus Christ himself, whom Christians believe to be the Savior of humankind.

Moksha In Hinduism and Jainism, achieving liberation from the ongoing cycle of birth, death, and rebirth.

Monasticism The religious tradition of withdrawing from the world to devote oneself to prayer and meditation.

Monotheism The doctrine that there is only one God.

New Age A loose collection of religious movements dating from the 1960s, that mixes Eastern and Western spiritual traditions, and focuses on the healing energies of the natural world.

Night Journey The Prophet Muhammad's supernatural journey across the sky from Mecca to Jerusalem from where he ascended into heaven and into the presence of Allah.

Nirvana In Buddhism, the release from all suffering and all desire into a state of perfect spiritual enlightenment.

Passover The Jewish festival that commemorates the Exodus of the Jews from Egypt.

Pilgrimage A journey to a sacred place.

Polytheism Belief in many gods.

Rabbi A religious teacher in the Jewish tradition.

Ragnarok In the Norse tradition, the end of the world and the beginning of a new heaven and a new Earth.

Ramadan The Islamic holy month during which the Prophet Muhammad received God's revelation.

Reincarnation Rebirth into a new body.

Repentance Turning away from wrongdoing, expressing sorrow for sins, and resolving to do good.

Resurrection The return of Jesus Christ from the dead after his crucifixion.

Samsara Hinduism's continual cycle of birth, death, and rebirth.

Shaman In traditional religion, a person believed to be capable of direct contact with the spirit world. Also known as a medicine man or witch doctor.

Sharia Islamic religious law.

Sin The breaking of holy laws.

Torah The first five books of the Hebrew Bible, which contain God's laws.

Trickster gods In native religions, mischievous gods who change shape and appearance to show that the world can be a surprising and unpredictable place.

Trinity The Christian doctrine stating that in God there are three persons: God the Father, God the Son, and God the Holy Spirit.

Umma The community of Muslim believers.

Voodoo A mixture of native African religion and Roman Catholicism practiced on the Caribbean island of Haiti.

Yin and Yang Equal and opposite forces in Taoism. Yin: feminine, dark, and passive. Yang: masculine, bright, and active.

Yom Kippur The most solemn day of the Jewish calendar. Also known as the Day of Atonement, it is a time for repentance.

INDEX

ACKNOWLEDGMENTS

3 Magnum Photos/Bruno Barbey.
4 Impact/Michael Mirecki, TL; Michael Freeman, TR; Bridgeman Art Library/Victoria & Albert Museum, BL; Bridgeman Art Library, BR. 5 Hutchison Library/Liba Taylor, TL; Peter Sanders, MR; Sonia Halliday, B. 6 Magnum Photos/Steve McCurry, TR; Magnum Photos/Abbas, BR. 7 Magnum Photos/Jean Gaumy, TL; Trip, B. 8 Tim Slade, B. 9 Robert Harding, TL. 10 Werner Forman Archive/National Museum, Copenhagen, BL; 10-11 AKG, B; 11 Robert Harding, TL; AKG/Erich Lessing, BR. 12 Hutchison Library/Jeremy A. Horner, BL; 12–13 Michael Holford/British Museum, T. 13 Bridgeman Art Library/Oriental Museum, Durham University, TR; Robert Harding, BL. 14 Roger Hutchins, TR; 14–15 Roger Hutchins, B; 15 Trip/R. Cracknell, TR. 16 Bridgeman Art Library/The De Morgan Foundation, London, TR; 16–17 Bridgeman Art Library/Louvre, Paris. 17 Bridgeman Art Library, TL; Michael Holford, MR. 18 E.T. Archive, TR; Collections/Michael Diggin, BL. 19 Bridgeman Art Library/Royal Library, Copenhagen, TL. 20 Bridgeman Art Library, TR; Ancient Art and Architecture Collection, BM. 21 Ann and Bury Peerless, T; Magnum Photos/Bruno Barbey, BL. 22 Bridgeman Art Library, TR; Werner Forman, BR. 23 Trip, TR; Impact/Michael Mirecki, BL. 24 Michael Holford, BL. 24–25 Trip/T. Bognar, M. 25 Bridgeman Art Library/National Library of Australia, TR. 26 Bridgeman Art Library/Corbally Stourton Contemporary Art, London, TR; Werner Forman, BL. 27 Bridgeman Art Library, TL; Bridgeman Art Library, BL. 28 Bridgeman Art Library/Royal Ontario Museum, BM. 28–29 E.T. Archive. 29 Bridgeman Art Library, BM. 30 Trip, TR; Still Pictures, BL; 31 Trip/C. Treppe, TL; Bridgeman Art Library, TR. 32–33 Peter Sanders, T; Robert Harding, B. 33 Claire Pullinger, BR. 34 Bridgeman Art Library/National Museum of India, BL. 34–35 Roger Hutchins, M. 35 C.M. Dixon, TR. 36–37 Magnum Photos/Steve McCurry. 37 Bridgeman Art Library, TM; Bridgeman Art Library, BR. 38 Bridgeman Art Library, ML. 38–39 India Office Library. 40 Bridgeman Art Library/British Library, TR; Frank Spooner, ML; Bridgeman Art Library/Oriental Museum, Durham University, BR. 41 Bridgeman Art Library/Victoria &

Albert Museum. 42 Hutchison Library/Liba Taylor, TR; Tony Stone/Mark Lewis, B. 43 Hutchison Library, TL; Still Pictures/Sarvottam Rajkoomar, BL. 44 British Library, Oriental and India Office, TR; Robert Harding, BL. 45 Hutchison Library/K. Rodgers, TL. 46 Trip/H. Rogers, BM. 46–47 Trip/Dinodia. 47 Trip/Dinodia, TR. 48 Robert Harding, ML; Hutchison Library/J. Horner, BR. 49 Hutchison Library. 50 Trip/H. Rogers, TR; Robert Harding, BL. 51 Bank of India. 52 Trip/H. Rogers, TR; Robert Harding, BM. 53 Michael Freeman, T; Magnum Photos/Raghu Rai, BL. 54 Magnum Photos/Raghu Rai, BL; 54–55 Michael Freeman. 55 Robert Harding/Jeremy Bright, TR; Format/Judy Harrison, BR. 56 Format/Judy Harrison, BL. 56–57 Panos/Liba Taylor, T. 57 Michael Freeman, BR. 58 Michael Freeman, B. 59 Michael Freeman, TL; Bridgeman Art Library/Christie's, BR. 60 Michael Freeman, TM; Michael Freeman, MR. 61 Bridgeman Art Library/Oriental Museum, Durham University. 62 Bridgeman Art Library/Osaka Museum of Fine Arts, BL; E.T. Archive/British Library, TR. 63 Sygma, T. 64 Trip/B. Vikander, BL. 64–65 Magnum Photos/Raghu Rai, T. 65 Magnum Photos/Ferdinando Scianna, TR; Network/E. Grames/Bildenberg, BL. 66 Michael Freeman, TR; 66–67 Mitchell Beazley. 67 Michael Freeman, TL; Michael Freeman, BR. 68 Michael Freeman, TR; "Fuji Above the Lightning", from the series 36 Views of Mount Fuji by Hokusai/Bridgeman Art Library/Fitzwilliam Museum, BL. 69 E.T. Archive, T; Tim Slade, BL. 70 Michael Freeman, TR; Michael Freeman, B. 71 Trip/P.Rauter, TL; Michael Freeman, BL; Network/Gideon Mendel, TR. 72 E.T. Archive, TR; Still Pictures, BL. 73 E.T. Archive/British Museum, TL; Bridgeman Art Library/British Museum, BR. 74 Bridgeman Art Library/Bibliotheque Nationale, BL; Bridgeman Art Library, TR. 75 E.T. Archive/British Museum, B. 76 Robert Harding, TR, Hutchison Library/Ian Lloyd, BR. 77 Bridgeman Art Library, T. 78 Bridgeman Art Library, BL. 78–79 Hutchison Library/John Hatt, T. 79 Bridgeman Art Library/Oriental Museum, Durham University, BR. 80 Magnum Photos/Fred Mayer, BL. 80–81 Hutchison Library/Robert Francis. 81 Magnum Photos/Bruno Barbey, BR. 82 Robert Harding, TR; Magnum Photos/Fred Mayer, BR.

83 Trip/A. Tovy. 84 Trip/A. Tovy, BM; 84–85 Hutchison Library, T. 85 Impact/Simon Shepheard, BL; Bridgeman Art Library/Oriental Museum, Durham University, MR. 86 Format/Raissa Page, BL. 86–87 Network/Gideon Mendel, T. 88 Robert Harding/E. Simanor, BL. 88–89 Michael Freeman, T. 89 Sonia Halliday, TR; Bridgeman Art Library, BL. 90 Bridgeman Art Library/British Library, TR; E.T. Archive, BL. 91 Keystone/Sygma, BL. 92 Format/Brenda Prince, ML; Rex Features, BR. 92–93 Magnum Photos/Fred Mayer, T. 93 E.T. Archive, BM. 94 Bridgeman Art Library/Musee Conde, Chantilly, TR. E.T. Archive, BL. 95 Bridgeman Art Library/Lambeth Palace Library, London. 96 Sonia Halliday, BL. 96–97 Roger Hutchins, T. 97 Sygma/Jamel Balhi, TR. 98 Trip/H.Rogers, TR; Magnum Photos/Fred Mayer, BR. 99 Trip/ E. James, TL; Hutchison Library/Liba Taylor, B. 100 Format/Brenda Prince, BL. 100–101 Sygma/J.P. Laffont, T; Sygma/Daniel Mordzinski, B. 102 Hutchison Library/Liba Taylor, BL. 102–103 Trip/H.Rogers, T. 103 Hutchison Library/Liba Taylor, BR. 104 E.T. Archive/Bibliotheque de l'Arsenal, Paris, TR; Trip/H. Rogers, BM. 105 Sonia Halliday/Barry Searle, BL; Sygma/Daniel Mordzinski, TR. 106 Format/Meryl Levin, BR. 106–107 Network/Barry Lewis, T. 107 Robert Harding/ASAP/Aliza Auerbach, BR. 108 Bridgeman Art Library/Giraudon/Louvre, Paris, B. 109 Hutchison Library, TL; Magnum Photos/Stuart Franklin, BL. 110 Tim Slade, TR; E.T.Archive/Bibliotheque de l'Arsenal, Paris, B. 111 Michael Holford, TR; Bridgeman Art Library/Bibliotheque Nationale, Paris, BL. 112 *Christ in the House of His Parents* by Millais/Tate Gallery, TR; *Baptism of Christ* by Piero della Francesca/Bridgeman Art Library/National Gallery, London. 113 *The Feeding of the Five Thousand* by Hendrik de Clerck/ Bridgeman Art Library/Kunsthistorisches Museum, Vienna, TL. 114 Bridgeman Art Library/Musee Conde, Chantilly, TR; Sygma/E. Pasquier, BM. 115 *Christ Mocked; the Crowning with Thorns* by Hieronymus Bosch/E.T. Archive/National Gallery, London, TL. 116 Trip/D. Butcher, BL; *The Descent of the Holy Ghost* by Sandro Botticelli/Bridgeman Art Library/Birmingham Museum and Art Gallery, TR. 117 *The Creation of Adam* by Michelangelo/Robert Harding/Roy Rainford, T; *Lambeth Apocalypse*/Bridgeman Art Library/

Lambeth Palace Library, BL. 118 Robert Harding TR; Trip/A. Tjagny-Rjadno, BL; 119 Collections/Geoff Howard, TR; Sonia Halliday, BL. 120 Robert Harding, BR. 120–121 Robert Harding/E. Simanor, T; Hutchison Library/Lesley McIntyre, B. 121 Hutchison Library/Melanie Friend, TR. 122 John Walmsley, BL; *The Light of the World* by William Holman Hunt/Bridgeman Art Library/Keble College, Oxford, TR. 123 *The Adoration of the Magi* by Hieronymus Bosch/Bridgeman Art Library/Prado, Madrid, TL. 124 *The Resurrection* by Piero della Francesca/Bridgeman Art Library/Pinacoteca, Sansepolcro, ML; Bridgeman Art Library, TR; Magnum/Fred Mayer, BM. 124–125 Altamont Press Inc. U.S.A., T. 125 Roy Williams, BM. 126 *St. Francis Preaching to the Birds* by Giotto/Bridgeman Art Library/San Francesco, Assisi, TR; 126–127 Robin Carter/Wildlife Art, B. 127 Hutchison Library/Lesley McIntyre, BR. 128 Sygma/Ira Wyman, BM; Sygma, TR. 129 Trip/S. Grant, TL; Topham Picturepoint, BL. 130 Peter Sanders, TR. 131 Sygma/S. Elbaz, BL; Bridgeman Art Library/British Museum, T. 132 Hutchison Library/Mary Jelliffe, TR; Michael Holford, BL. 133 Sonia Halliday/Topkapi Palace Museum, Istanbul. 134 Sygma/A.Gyori, TR; Peter Sanders, BL. 135 Bridgeman Art Library/British Library, L. 136 Bridgeman Art Library, TR; Peter Sanders, BL. 137 Bridgeman Art Library/Musee Conde, Chantilly, B. 138–139 Peter Sanders, M. 139 Magnum Photos/Abbas, TL; Frank Spooner, BM. 140 Peter Sanders, TR; Magnum Photos/Abbas, BR. 141 Sonia Halliday, Istanbul University Library, L. 142 Format/Impact, TR; Trip/H. Rogers, BL. 143 Trip/H. Rogers, TL; Trip, BL. 144 Hutchison Library/Isabella Tree, BL; 144–145 Roger Hutchins, M. 145 Peter Sanders, TR. 146 Sygma/Alain Dejean, TR; Impact/Mark Henley, BR. 147 Magnum Photos/Abbas, T. 148 Peter Sanders, BL. 148–149 Robert Harding, T. 150 Magnum Photos/Steve McCurry, BL. 150–151 Network/Gideon Mendel, T. 151 Sally Greenhill, BR. 152 Network/Homer Sykes, BM. 152–153 Sygma/Les Stone, T. 153 Sygma, BR.

Front cover: Hutchison/Liba Taylor, TL; Collections, TM; Tony Stone, TR; Michael Freeman, B.
Back cover: Bridgeman Art Library/Victoria & Albert Museum.

HV
6250.4
.C34
D43
1993

Death and celebrity.

$14.95

TRUE CRIME

Death
and Celebrity

BY
THE EDITORS OF
TIME-LIFE BOOKS
Alexandria, Virginia

Death and
Celebrity

COVER: DOROTHY STRATTEN

Fame's Deadly Undertow

Celebrity confers burdens as well as blessings on those it touches, but often the two are indistinguishable. The trappings of celebrity—the relentless exposure, vast wealth, devoted admirers, a license to outrage—can have a dark side, providing a fertile ground for the obsessions, greed, and envy that sometimes drag the famous, and those around them, down to murder.

Thus, the rising star of *Playboy* Playmate Dorothy Stratten becomes too bright for her husband, Paul Snider, to endure, and he destroys them both. The rare musical talent in singer Marvin Gaye spawns such fear and envy in his father that the parent guns down his child. Cheryl Crane, the daughter of film legend Lana Turner, shunted aside to make room for a procession of male admirers, kills to protect her mother. The great Marlon Brando's eldest son, Christian, groping for his father's approval, commits murder. And star-crossed punk rockers Sid Vicious and Nancy Spungen, made briefly famous, spin through a haze of music and drugs toward their lonely doom. In each case, the powerful magnet of celebrity drew the players together as if on a stage; in the last act, violence shattered their seemingly privileged lives, and tragedy unfolded.

The facade of wealth and privilege shattered for actor Marlon Brando in 1990, when his 32-year-old son, Christian, killed Dag Drollet, boyfriend of Christian's half sister Cheyenne, at Brando's Beverly Hills home *(background)*.

I had planned originally to work at getting my degree in law, and I'll go back and do that. I'm not going to go jump off the *H* in Hollywood.

DOROTHY STRATTEN

1

L.A. Story

Paul Leslie Snider was going through a kind of seamy renaissance in January 1978. His 30th birthday was just three years down the line, and the way he saw it, his life still hadn't settled into the style for which it so clearly had been intended. A slender five-feet-eight-inches in height, Snider kept himself looking good—he worked out with weights and wore his dark hair carefully styled, with well-trimmed sideburns and a thin mustache framing the clear brown eyes and broad white smile of the born hustler. He was slick; many women found him irresistible. He dressed like a tango dancer or a pimp. His wardrobe ran to gold chains and lizardskin boots, tight pants, and the fur coat and broadbrimmed hat often favored by men who trade in women.

Yet, as life constantly reminded Snider, looks and hustle were not enough. A tireless promoter of one get-rich-quick scheme after another, he had begun staging automobile shows, in his hometown of Vancouver and down in the States. But on his last venture, five months earlier in Los Angeles, Snider had lost most of the $100,000 a family friend had put into two of his automotive extravaganzas: the California Truckin' & Cycle Show at the Convention Center in June, and the Motorcycle U.S.A. Show at the Long Beach Arena in July. Sometimes the shows made big money, but these had not done well. The Long Beach gathering had been sabotaged, Snider said, by a competing airshow, totally unexpected. To Snider, the fiasco repeated a familiar pattern in his life: He would set something up, something perfect, and then some unexpected event would come flapping out of nowhere and mess it up. It was as if the world had been designed to thwart Paul Snider.

There was never any shortage of great ideas, however. Snider claimed to have invented the wet-T-shirt contest that debuted at a bar down in a seedy area of Gastown, Vancouver's oldest section. It didn't make any money, but that was the owner's fault for not promoting it correctly. The metal art Snider had copied from a Canadian sculptor had sold pretty well; he opened a boutique in the city's tony West End, and the Sheraton Hotel had displayed one of the pieces in its lobby. Unfortunately, Snider had been forced to take money out of his sculpture business to cover a debt, and the shop folded.

Nothing ever quite worked out, and he was terrible with money besides. One day he'd have five, ten thousand dollars tucked in his pants and a stunningly beautiful woman on each arm, and a day later he'd be broke and alone. There was talk of his being a pimp, and before he'd gone down to Los Angeles this last time, the Vancouver police had thought enough of the rumors to put him under a few months' surveillance. But Snider's women wouldn't testify against him, so no charges were brought.

To many who knew him, Paul Snider was just the small-time sleaze he seemed to be, a young drone willing to live off the sexual revenues of women, a promoter of trivial events, an eternal adolescent about cars, a mere tadpole in the quiet pond of Vancouver's nether world. To know him was to loathe him.

But Snider was also something more. He was a handsome man, streetwise, imaginative in a small way, often funny. His ineptitude with money came partly from his wish to strut as a big spender but also from a grand generosity—he genuinely enjoyed sharing what he had. He could build almost anything out of wood or metal and would labor like a donkey when he had to. Snider wasn't afraid of hard work—it was just that on a nine-to-five routine he might miss that sudden, life-reviving opportunity, that main chance, in which he so resolutely believed. As his father, David, put it, "He wasn't the working type, he was too ambitious for that."

As for his dealings with women, much of Paul Snider's manipulative power flowed from the fact that he possessed a generous heart and the palpable vulnerability of the youthful loser. He was capable of falling in love and would do astonishing things in order to help a girlfriend. His women may also have liked a kind of courage that he displayed. Although Snider would flee from the prospect of physical

CALIFORNIA TRUCKIN' & CYCLE SHOW
L.A. CONVENTION CENTER
JUNE 3, 4, 5

MOTORCYCLE U.S.A. SHOW
LONG BEACH ARENA
JULY 22, 23, 24

pain, he was slow to back down. In any confrontation, Snider always quickly escalated to the brink — but only to the brink. He seldom let matters fly out of his control. "Paul wasn't much of a fighter on the street," one old friend observed. "He was scared of being hurt physically and he would turn tail when he felt someone was going to punch or hurt him. He really had a big heart but the way he carried himself, most guys just hated him."

So did Paul Snider. His greatest internal contradiction may have been that he, perhaps more keenly than anyone else, perceived the sleaze, the pimp, the chronic small-timer he had become. He aspired to something better than showing off in Vancouver's nightspots or persuading women to turn tricks or to take off their clothes in a rough bar. He yearned to escape to the more respectable world of money and fame he'd seen reflected in such magazines as *Playboy* — to Snider, getting a woman into *Playboy*'s centerfold was hitting the big time.

Snider found his future waiting for him one night in January 1978, in an unexpected form, in an unlikely place. The form was a 17-year-old waitress named Dorothy Ruth Hoogstraten; the place was the Dairy Queen restaurant at East Hastings Street and Lakewood Drive. He and a woman were out driving along East Hastings, where Vancouver shades from the eateries and nightspots of Hornby Street into fast-food restaurants and muffler shops in the city's shabby-genteel East End. In the mood for something sweet, Snider pulled into the Dairy Queen parking lot and the pair got out; he wore a thick fur overcoat against the cold, damp wind. This particular franchise was an odd and possibly

With a poster promoting a couple of his less successful automotive shows as a backdrop, Paul Snider models his preferred uniform: fur-lined leather overcoat, open shirt, skin-tight bell-bottoms, and massive costume jewelry.

provocative choice: It was owned by a bearlike biker named Dave Redlick, who'd known and despised Snider for years. He wouldn't have wanted Snider in his restaurant. But Redlick wasn't around that night. Instead, a tall blond girl took their order.

No one knows if Paul Snider looked at this dazzling young woman, who would soon be modestly famous as Dorothy Stratten, and saw his fate, or detected the stunning luminosity she reportedly possessed, or experienced a leap of the heart. According to all reports, the alluring, fresh-faced Dutch blonde in the shapeless red Dairy Queen uniform was then almost pathologically shy and devoid of confidence—part of her beauty, in fact, was her utter ignorance of it. She believed herself to be outsized at five-feet-nine, skinny, a bit coarse and clumsy, uninteresting. But Snider flirted—he was always flirting. "What's *your* name?" he asked. She told him. He ordered a Strawberry Sundae Supreme. There was no magic, no music, no hint that their fates were linked.

But the latent beauty behind the counter and the little man in fur had much in common. In a way, they were made for each other. Both longed to be someone, and somewhere, else. Snider may have feared that the currents of life were taking him nowhere. Stratten, who'd worked in Redlick's Dairy Queen since she was 14 years old, fretted that she was forever trapped in the life of a child, like a lovely genie in a jar. There is no evidence that they took overt note of such similarities. Nevertheless, with that first meeting, their fates may have been sealed. Each would offer the other that most precious of emotional commodities: hope. Within a few weeks they would be lovers. In 16 months they would marry, and Snider would boast that they were on a rocket ship to the moon. Sadly, they never made it. Dorothy did not see 21, and Paul, as things turned out, needn't have worried about hitting 30. In August 1980 they were found dead in a West Los Angeles bedroom spattered with brain and blood, casualties of the terrible breaking of Paul Snider's heart.

The interplay of entrepreneurial energy, disappointment, and sudden death had largely defined Paul Snider's boyhood universe. His parents, David and Evelyn, had met in Winnipeg, the prairie capital of Manitoba province, in 1938, when both were just 15. They married while David Snider was serving with the Royal Canadian Air Force dur-

ing World War II. After the war ended in 1945, Snider's father-in-law arranged a year's training in industrial design for him in New York, then took the young man into the family apparel business. The couple's first child, Penny, was born in 1948. Paul followed on April 15, 1951. Several years later a second son, Randy, arrived. The Sniders had a large house in the north end of Winnipeg, and their life seemed tranquil and productive. While the father learned the manufacturer's trade, the family appeared to flourish.

In the summer of 1953 the parents were just 30, and Paul was a toddler. He shared a room with his adored sister, who had just turned five and was the light of the Snider household. Then, on the evening of August 13, that light was suddenly extinguished. "I remember every incident that night," Evelyn Snider recalled later. "Paul was just a little boy, and getting supper off the table. And David and his brother were talking." The uncle had given little Penny a dime. She was excited and wanted to go with a little girlfriend to get an ice-cream cone. The two girls hurried to the street corner together.

"Penny ran across," her mother said. "I guess she was terribly anxious. And this big gravel truck—I only saw her little birthday shoes on her feet, pink and blue they were, under the tires. I couldn't go any further then, when I saw the tires—they were gigantic as the mountains here. And I just saw her little feet and I started to scream and faint and scream and scream. Paul was at the door when I came in after the accident—oh, can you imagine a child hearing his mother screaming like that. And I kept screaming, 'Penny, Penny, Penny is gone.'" Paul stood there, watching his mother, until the gathering neighbors took him outside. "I think I might have said, 'Take him away for awhile.' I didn't want him to hear me scream. Well, all our lives changed from the death of that child."

Paul was sent to live with a paternal aunt for a week—to a little boy, a bewildering exile. "When he was 19 years old," his mother remembered, "we were driving in the car and he said, 'You know, Mum, I've always missed Penny, because I remember her. But when something happened, I thought I did it.' He thought that he was being punished."

Under the pall of Penny's accident, the family slowly began to fracture. They moved to Vancouver that same year. The crossroads port city offered David Snider more possibilities than Winnipeg; he could have his own business and make his own way. And it was more than a thousand miles from where the gravel truck had killed his daughter. The Sniders moved into a house on West 35th Avenue in Vancouver's Quilchena district and resumed their placid routine. The father entered a successful partnership as a shirt manufacturer, a position that commanded virtually all of his attention. But life was good—he joined the country club, drove a company car, took good, if frugal, care of his family. Soon after there was an omen of life: Their last child, Jeffrey, was born.

Outwardly, the Sniders' lives proceeded much as they had back in Winnipeg. But the marriage could not shake the ghost of Penny's death. Paul's mother, unnerved by her daughter's accident, watched with rising dread every time her eldest son crossed the railroad tracks on his way to or from school. The bonds that linked the parents weakened, triggering a collapse that would take an agonizing decade and a half to complete.

In retrospect, an observer might see this structural failure reflected in Paul Snider's behavior. Some found him a bit too aggressive on the playground, and his temper flared explosively when he didn't get his way. On the other hand, his mother remembers that he "liked nice things. He loved to serve the table, he liked to be busy in the kitchen, he liked to bake cookies once in a while."

He also liked to hustle. "Paul made a little show when he was very young, under the house, and he was selling tickets," his mother recalled. "He promoted the whole thing. And if you won, he had little prizes. Maybe that's where some of my jewelry went, to the other kids." She added, "He was always selling and buying, he was busy. Anything okay that would make a dollar." His father remembered that during this period Paul "always had money. He was always working with his dad. I made sure that he earned the money. From the time he was 12 or 13 years old he used to come and sweep my factory after school."

In the early 1960s David Snider abandoned Vancouver, first for Bellevue, Washington, then for the rolling hill country north of Los Angeles. The move was another watershed for Paul.

At first, the California teachers thought it would be good for the touchingly lonely boy to have a position of authority, and they made him a monitor. "Paul was put in charge," his mother said. "They make little officers in school. He was about 14 and he managed well, but then he got a little bit too pushy. I guess somebody didn't answer right or some-

thing, I don't know." California was the boy's last brush with school, and he evidently never looked back. "He never had much of a little boy's life," his mother said. "He had to be a man very early in life."

"He wanted to be like his dad," offered David Snider, who also made his way on native wit. But Paul wanted something special, according to his mother: "Paul said to me, 'I have a goal, Mum, it's right up there as high as the sky. The star. That's where I'm going to go.'"

By 1964 it had become clear that neither father nor son would find his star in California. David Snider's business lost money, and the family returned to Winnipeg. Defeated by grief and the elusiveness of success, Snider and his wife arrived at the bitter dregs of their marriage. Evelyn Snider found herself seeing less and less of her hardworking mate; the pair had never fought openly, but the rancorous silence between them deepened.

Chilled by this parental cold war, the family returned to Vancouver around 1969, and Snider successfully stepped back into the apparel trade. But his wife's suffocation was irreversible. A year later, taking only what she could carry, Evelyn Snider fled to a neighbor's house, never to return. The boys stayed with their father for a time. Paul worked in the elder Snider's factory as a leather cutter and took care of his younger brothers—teenager Jeffrey was eventually sent to live in a foster home. Paul also helped his mother, who was by now in a paralysis of despair and always in tears. The couple divorced in 1971.

The next year, their eldest son turned 21 and went looking for a life of his own. His search took him into the nightspots of Hornby Street and Gastown, where Vancouver's underworld was concentrated. Paul Snider liked the big Lincoln pimpmobiles and their drivers' flashy costumes—some called Snider, who was Jewish, the Jewish Pimp for a jeweled Star of David he wore on a gold chain around his neck.

"He used to strut around to all these nightclubs with a girl hanging on his arm," remembered one old friend, a former bouncer in Vancouver clubs. "He had a black book and somewhere between 150 and 200 phone numbers of girls. It was an out-and-out ego thing with Paul. Anyplace, anywhere he went he would hit on girls, he would get their phone numbers. He didn't care if their boyfriends were there." Snider evidently considered himself an irresistible force. "When he met a girl, he would phone her a hundred times to get a date with her. It wouldn't matter what the girl said to him, how she put him down. He would keep phoning. He would enter her name in this book. It wasn't a matter of turning the girls into prostitutes. He had an ego. He would want to pick the girl up, get the girl to doll all up and he would strut her through every club in Vancouver."

About this time Snider met Dave Redlick, who would later run the East Hastings Dairy Queen, and tried to join the Trojans, a club of tough bikers. "They wouldn't let him in," Redlick said. "We didn't need the heat. Because all he was after was the accessibility to certain things that we were involved in at the time." Redlick has declined to say what those things were. As for Snider, "He was a sly, little seedy bastard, looking for a free ride."

But Snider had other irons in the fire. He was developing his auto shows and had opened his metal-sculpture boutique in the city's tony West End. He'd also taken aim at his highest aspiration. In 1974 he took a pretty blond stripper named Judy to see Vancouver photographer Uwe Meyer. "His big plan," according to Meyer, "had been to get a girl into *Playboy* and be her manager and make money." That effort, too, came to nothing.

In 1976 Vancouver police, suspecting Snider of running prostitutes, put him under surveillance. "When I started surveilling him," said one retired officer, "he was living in North Vancouver with three young girls, all suspected prostitutes. They worked the clubs on Hornby Street. Snider used to drive them downtown, drop them off at a club and then pick them up later. Snider had some beautiful girls working for him; he hit pay dirt with those girls." The closest police came to bringing charges was when they learned that a former prostitute who'd moved to Kelowna, about 300 miles away, was willing to testify against Snider. The city wouldn't pay police travel expenses, however, and the matter was dropped. "My partner at the time," the officer mused, "always said Dorothy Stratten would be alive today if only they'd allowed us to go to Kelowna."

Among the women he consorted with, Paul Snider had a steady girl known by the nickname Bon Amie and remembered by the ex-bouncer as a stripper who also turned tricks. "Paul lived with Bon Amie on and off for a few years. She had a job and he had a job. Her job was to go dancing and turn the odd trick. It wasn't a matter of Paul," the friend insisted. "He never put girls out there to work and took money from them. He was a pretty good money hustler himself. He probably spent more money on them than they ever put to him. When she had the money she would pay. When he had the money he would pay. She was a very nice girl. She was totally in love with him. Even when he was going out with Dorothy."

Such devotion perhaps grew out of the extraordinary generosity Snider sometimes exhibited. "Paul was starting to date a girl named Sam," the same man remembered. "This girl had screwed some guy out of $50,000 worth of drugs or something. She was really a nice girl. Not far off from Dorothy Stratten herself." But the man she'd cheated wanted his revenge. "He grabbed her and put her in the Hyatt Regency in Vancouver." His idea, according to the ex-bouncer, was to sell the young woman for sex "and he was going to deduct $25 off until his 50 grand was back.

"Paul knew this guy had grabbed the girl and had her in the room. Like I say, this guy was nobody to play with. When the girl refused to turn tricks, two guys held her out the window of the Hyatt Regency by her ankles. After they did that, she started turning tricks for the guy. Paul said 'I want to get her out of this.' So the guy said 'you give me $50,000 and she's yours.' " Snider took the money out of his metal-sculpture business to pay the young woman's debt and installed her in a furnished apartment. She left him not long after. "He took her leaving with a grain of salt," his friend recalled. "He didn't have a lot of respect for money."

Nelly Hoogstraten, born Peternella Füchs in the Netherlands in 1935, must have nervously watched her much-loved Dorothy during those first weeks after Paul Snider strode into the Dairy Queen, and into her life. When the mother met Snider a few weeks later, she was not impressed by the qualities that had captivated her daughter—to Nelly, Snider was just a flashy little hustler. Besides, she knew the disappointments men could bring, and she wanted better for her Dorothy.

In 1940, when she was only five years old, Peternella had been placed in an orphanage by Dutch authorities because her mother worked and couldn't take care of a child. She'd grown up an orphan, lonely, uncertain of her own worth, hungry for affection—and determined. She'd leaped at a chance to become a dental assistant—and to leave the orphanage. Not long afterward, in 1954, she married a carpenter named Simon Hoogstraten and set out with him for Vancouver, British Columbia. Hoogstraten was soon building houses in their adopted land, where his wife shortened

The doomed relationship between Paul Snider and Dorothy Ruth Hoogstraten—later Stratten— began in 1978 at this east Vancouver Dairy Queen, where 17-year-old Dorothy had worked as a waitress since 1974.

her name to Nelly—Peternella was unwieldy in North America, where things seemed to happen with greater speed than they had at home.

For five years, Simon built houses, but not a family—he and Nelly remained childless. Then, in 1959, she traveled to Holland and spent two weeks touring her homeland. She was also reunited with her mother. The pilgrimage changed something in Nelly, and she became pregnant soon after her return. Her husband, practical as ever, bought four lots on an East End slope and built four homes, two to sell, one to rent, and one to live in.

In February 1960 the new mother brought her firstborn, Dorothy Ruth, home from the Salvation Army Hospital. Two years later a son, John, arrived. But the third Hoogstraten baby was stillborn; Nelly discovered that she was Rh negative—her blood and her baby's could be mortal enemies. Nelly and her two small children made a reviving visit to Holland in 1963; Simon stayed behind in Vancouver. Before the year was out, and evidently without prelude, the hardworking carpenter left his wife of nine years for an-

other woman, and Nelly Hoogstraten found herself alone.

Determined to survive on her own, she and the children moved to an upstairs apartment in a poor part of Vancouver's East End, and she took any job she could find. Barely three years passed before she met another man who was to betray her. Working as a housekeeper, Nelly Hoogstraten fell in love with her employer and was soon carrying his child. But when she told him of her pregnancy, he angrily turned away from her. At first, the hapless woman decided to have an abortion, a legal option because of her negative Rh factor. But when she felt the fetus move, she lost her resolve. A second daughter, Louise, was delivered in 1968 and survived the replacement of her incompatible blood.

The little family moved often—one year they moved six times—always keeping to the East End except for one terrible year in a mountain cabin. Finally, the mother's tenacity paid off. She secured a pleasant little house in Coquitlam, a suburb about 15 miles east of central Vancouver.

In 1974, to help meet expenses, 14-year-old Dorothy had found her first job, a part-time spot at Dave Redlick's Dairy

Queen. He remembered her as "a tall little skinny girl that did her job and never said much. She kept to herself." The bearish owner made sure Dorothy's mother knew her daughter had safely caught the bus home from work; often, he rode her home on the back of his bike. Redlick and his wife lived out toward Coquitlam, and on nights when she didn't work Dorothy often baby-sat their children.

The young woman's last two years of education were spent at Coquitlam's Centennial School, where Dorothy Stratten is remembered as a good student, rather shy, and pretty. "If anything I would think of her as a slightly quieter and shyer person than a lot of other kids in the class," recalled Paul Odermatt, her 11th-grade English teacher. She already possessed the latent beauty that would soon turn heads whenever she entered a room, he said, "but she never, to my way of thinking, really did an awful lot to enhance those qualities in the eyes of other people." He remembered that once, when Dorothy dropped off an essay for him, one of the boys in the back of the room gave a spirited wolf whistle. Dorothy blushed and quickly left. Perhaps she

thought the whistle mocked an ugly duckling; in fact, it saluted an emerging swan. Later, when the prospect of fame impelled her to begin writing an autobiography, she opened her story there, in 1977, when, it could be argued, Dorothy Stratten's life really began.

It was during her junior year that Dorothy met Steve Mirkovich, a thin youngster who was about a year older than she. The two dated, but although he was good to her, there were things about him that she disliked. Still, she didn't leave him. In August 1977 the pair drove down to California in Mirkovich's old truck for a three-week vacation. It was one of the few times Dorothy had ventured outside British Columbia, and Mirkovich, while imperfect, was her first lover; he represented the sum of her experience. But the couple did not stay together long after their holiday. That winter, skiing on Whistler Mountain northeast of Vancouver, Mirkovich became so furiously jealous of a young man named Craig that he destroyed a ruby ring that Dorothy had given him for Christmas—one that she'd paid for a little at a time from her meager earnings. Although

they remained in occasional contact, Mirkovich and Dorothy Hoogstraten went their separate ways. She was dating Craig in January 1978 when she first met Paul Snider.

The smooth young operator had run true to form. After his first encounter with Dorothy Hoogstraten in the Dairy Queen, Snider began to call. When Dorothy's co-worker wouldn't give him her home number, he left his and a message for her to call him. Nelly Hoogstraten advised her not to—reason enough, perhaps, for the daughter to make the call. After he explained who he was—the guy for whom she'd made a towering Strawberry Sundae Supreme—he asked her out. Dorothy was sick and declined. But Snider persevered and finally she accepted.

When Snider drove up to her house in his black Datsun 240Z, he wore the usual sharp outfit beneath a leather over-coat trimmed with fur, and he sported two impressive diamond rings and a gold bracelet with the initials PLS written in gems. His date was wearing gray slacks and a black top. He told her she looked nice, but she sensed that he was disappointed to find her so casually dressed. In the car she shyly watched Vancouver whirl by; Snider did all the talking. He touched her hand now and then, a gentle promise of things to come.

They went to Snider's place on West 15th Avenue at Granville, the top apartment in a three-story building. The compact bachelor pad was full of plants, the floor covered with big fur rugs. It had a large platform bed, closets with full-length mirrors, and a balcony. The apartment perfectly reflected its occupant's tastes. But to Dorothy Hoogstraten it was something from another stratum—a world in which people had money and fame and power.

Snider cooked dinner for them and serenaded her with his guitar and songs he claimed to have written himself. He explained that he was a big-time promoter of car shows in Vancouver and down in the States. Although puzzled that such an important man would want to go out with a Dairy Queen waitress, Dorothy was entranced by his glibness. Like a deer caught in headlights, she watched bashfully as he deftly drew her into his sphere.

The next evening, a somewhat conscience-stricken Dorothy went out with Craig and resolved not to see Snider again. But when Snider phoned a day later, asking to pick her up before she went to work, she reluctantly agreed. She also let him pick her up after work. When she explained her

problem, Snider gave her a good-night kiss and left, and that seemed to be the end of it. But the next night he was back, wanting to go for a drive and have a talk. Snider drove out to little Como Lake in Coquitlam and parked the car. If she liked him, he said, she should see him, whether she also saw Craig or not. Happiness didn't come from the brain, he told her, but from the heart: Let your heart take you where it wants you to go. The next time she saw Craig was the last time. Her heart had taken her to Paul.

On February 28, 1978, Dorothy Hoogstraten turned 18. Without being quite aware of it, she had begun to flower spectacularly, not least through the ministrations of Paul Snider. It was not in him to make her classy, but he could make her glow with his affection; and that seemed to bring forth her special luminosity, the evanescent quality that made her beauty so striking. Snider gave her a diamond ring for her birthday, but she wasn't the only woman in his life—Bon Amie was still there if he needed her, and he continued to enjoy the occasional prowl. In fact, he initially treated Dorothy as he had all the others, strutting her through his Gastown and Hornby Street haunts, showing off to the world the big, beautiful young woman Paul Snider had brought under his control. He also began teaching Dorothy the ways of his world. For example, Snider was appalled by the way she let even her younger sister walk over her, and he began to coach his new acquisition in the art of taking stands—his specialty.

Dorothy waited nervously for his calls and was depressed if none came. She was hurt by her family's derision of him—the more they saw of Snider, the more they thought he was a crook. And when Dave Redlick found Snider waiting for Dorothy at the Dairy Queen, he threw the rascal out. Dorothy resigned soon afterward.

In March Snider put on one of his World of Wheels spectaculars at the city's Pacific Northern Exhibition grounds and asked his new girl to work with him on it over the weekend. During those three days they talked intimately of their lives and feelings and aspirations. Dorothy realized that she was in love, but she fretted with characteristically low self-confidence that she might not be enough for him—she might be nothing more than a new toy for a man of his experience.

There is no trace of what Snider really thought about his new toy. Perhaps he reciprocated her feelings. According to Dorothy's memoirs, he told her what she most wanted to hear: that she was pretty, well-built, intelligent, that she made him feel good. He bought her gifts and pampered her when she was ill. He helped her find the kind of dresses a beautiful woman should wear.

While he was molding the young waitress into a statuesque beauty, Snider was also exploring the world of photography. He asked Uwe Meyer to take some bodybuilding shots of him with his shirt off, apparently for his own pleasure. Snider had also run into Vancouver photographer Ken Honey, who'd placed several Canadian women in *Playboy* magazine. "I first met him at a club where there were dancers," Honey recalled. "The owner of the club said, 'I'd like you to meet Paul Snider. Paul Snider thinks he has a girl that would be good for *Playboy*.'" But Honey didn't meet Dorothy then. "Dorothy was just going out the door," he remembered. "I couldn't really see her because of the dark light in the club. I never thought anything about it. I gave him a card and that was it."

Snider's sudden interest in photographers may have sprung from what, to him, would have looked like a chance to escape smallness forever. On March 27, 1978, *Playboy* editor Hugh Hefner opened a nationwide search for the magazine's 25th Anniversary Playmate. "For appearing as the centerfold in the magazine's gala January 1979 Silver Anniversary Issue" a subsequent *Playboy* press release read, "this very lovely, very special lady will receive $25,000." After her appearance in the January issue, it went on, "the Playmate will continue to represent *Playboy* at all functions related to the magazine's yearlong anniversary celebration, as well as at numerous charity, sports and other major pub-

Radiating the innocent beauty for which she became noted, Dorothy Ruth Hoogstraten sits for her senior photograph in Centennial School's 1978 yearbook. By now attached to the most sophisticated man she'd ever met—Paul Snider—the girl felt that her real life was just beginning.

lic events throughout 1979." To Paul Snider, the contest was a stairway to the stars.

Dorothy Hoogstraten celebrated her approaching high-school graduation at the senior prom on May 25, wearing a low-cut white dress that Snider had selected and bought for her. He picked her up early for the dance and drove over to Meyer's studio, where Dorothy posed for her first formal portrait. Soon after that, the new graduate went to work as a secretary for BC TEL, the provincial communications giant. It was Dorothy's first good job, and she was proud that her skills had found her a place there.

That summer Nelly Hoogstraten went to Europe on vacation, and Louise went off to camp, while Dorothy and her brother, John, stayed in the Coquitlam house. Dorothy spent most of the time with Snider, however, going home now and then to see how John was faring. It was during this interlude that Snider first broached the matter of her becoming the Silver Anniversary Playmate, an idea that must have appealed to Dorothy as well—$25,000 was more than three years' salary at BC TEL.

Snider tried to reach Ken Honey, only to find that the photographer was out of town in Winnipeg, visiting his dying mother. But Uwe Meyer, who'd taken Dorothy's graduation portrait, was willing to take some photos for a chance at *Playboy*'s $1,000 finder's fee. Meyer and the couple met at Snider's apartment in late June for a different kind of photograph—shy, pretty Dorothy, in the nude. She took it in stride. "Dorothy was very much a part of the whole thing," Meyer said later. "There was no kind of force really. I've photographed nude people before and it's usually a compliment to be photographed in a glamorous way. It's a pleasant experience. She was very cooperative." During the first session, Snider was always present, as he had been when Meyer photographed Judy four years earlier. "He had quite a good eye," Meyer commented. "He was actually helping me."

But Snider was not satisfied with the photographs, and he called Ken Honey, who'd returned to Vancouver, about photographing Dorothy. Honey agreed to look at her, but he had some reservations about working with Snider. "I didn't like him," the photographer remembered. "I think most people, 90 percent of people, would meet him and didn't like him at first sight. He would never smile. It was sort of a sneer."

There was a bigger problem, however. The girl was under 21; a parent would have to sign a release before Honey could proceed. Nelly Hoogstraten was away, and she almost certainly would not have permitted Dorothy to pose nude. But Snider, ever resourceful, managed to produce a release bearing what he said was the mother's signature.

Ken Honey met Dorothy on Tuesday, August 8, and immediately saw that she was extraordinary. "She had a combination of face, figure, and innocence about her," he said. "Maybe it was her naiveté that made her special, I don't know." Preferring to work in natural light, he arranged to photograph her the following day in Snider's small apartment. At 4:30 p.m., a tired Dorothy hurried home from her BC TEL job, bathed, made up, and began posing for Honey's camera.

She liked her compact, balding photographer, but the session was difficult. Dorothy was fatigued from working all day, and, because Snider had run an ad to sell one of his cars, the telephone rang constantly. But she made it work. "A very, very charming girl," Ken Honey mused later. "Perfect personality, but very withdrawn, still very, very naive. You've got to remember her age." The photographer added, "She was such a nice girl. She never talked about what she would do with the money. It was what she could do for her mother or her sister or for Paul. Everything was for somebody else."

Two days later, Honey expressed a dozen of his photographs of Dorothy to *Playboy* in Los Angeles, along with a standard Playmate biographical form. Under career ambitions, Dorothy had written: "I would like to become a star of sorts." That weekend she and one of her girlfriends were working as cashiers at Snider's latest automotive show out at the Kerrisdale Arena. They were there on Friday night when Ken Honey dropped by. He'd heard from the magazine, he told Dorothy. They wanted her to fly down to Los Angeles for more test pictures—right away. The magazine

Approached by a broad circular drive around an ornate fountain, the stately *Playboy* Mansion West nestles among tall pines and a grove of redwood trees on the magazine empire's lavish estate in the posh Holmby Hills section of Los Angeles.

had booked only one round-trip flight, which meant that Snider would have to stay behind in Vancouver, a slight that he resented but endured. The important thing was that Dorothy was on her way to stardom.

Marilyn Grabowski, a *Playboy* vice president and West Coast photo editor, thought the Canadian beauty might very well be a contender for the 25th Anniversary Playmate. According to one former centerfold, Grabowski, along with Hefner, was the creator of the modern Playmate—"the look that would satisfy the *Playboy* image for the men and make it so that women didn't go nuts." Grabowski "set up a really wonderful, safe place in which to take your clothes off and get photographed," the former Playmate continued, "surrounded by really bright, really interesting women." Looking at Dorothy's pictures, the empathetic editor had immediately discerned the rare, deeper beauty that lay behind the pretty Dutch face.

That Sunday morning, Grabowski and Hoogstraten arrived simultaneously at the *Playboy* building on Sunset Boulevard. Dorothy was breathless from her first remembered flight in an airplane, from being met by the *Playboy* limousine, from being suddenly swept away to Hollywood; but she tried to conceal it. "Dorothy was very blonde and very tall," Grabowski recalled of that first encounter. "She wore a simple but quite smashing black jump suit. My first impression, as she got out of the limousine, was that this was not an unusual experience for her. As I walked up to her and introduced myself, I realized I was wrong. I remember thinking: Here is a very young woman playing grownup. Her vulnerability drew an immediate, protective response from me."

The two were joined in Grabowski's office by Mario Casilli, a fatherly veteran of centerfold photography. After a half-hour meeting, Casilli drove Dorothy to his Glendale studio and began to make this shy young woman famous. "She enjoyed it as a kid would a new experience," he remembered years later. "It was that kind of an enjoyment. It wasn't anything other than that except she was just having fun. Now, of course, I know a lot more than I did then but I think she was just so sheltered that this was like a coming out time for her and she was excited about the idea of being in *Playboy*."

Casilli found his new subject strangely mature, but also childlike. "A woman-child," the photographer said. "You were looking at a woman but every once in a while a child would come through. You forgot that she was so young. She carried herself very well and she was mature in her looks. Also, in a way, she handled herself well with people. But there were things that would happen during a shooting or during a conversation that just made you realize she was still a child."

It was the child who, escorted by Marilyn Grabowski, arrived at the *Playboy* Mansion West guesthouse, which Dorothy would share with three other Playmates, late that Sunday afternoon. Spread across 5.3 acres in the posh Holmby Hills neighborhood, the enclave was a fairyland of fountains, statuary, gardens, fields, forests, and even a gothic castle—an internationally recognized symbol of the affluent, sexually liberated good life extolled by the magazine. Like all proper castles, the place teemed with the great and the famous, present to share one of the Mansion's many customs, the Sunday buffet and film.

Grabowski introduced Dorothy to Joni Mattis, Hefner's social secretary, a former Playmate who had been with the organization for 20 years. Then Dorothy met her host, the man who had sown the seeds of the *Playboy* empire in 1953. Hefner was dressed in his adopted uniform—silk pajamas—and carried a bottle of Pepsi and a pipe, his trademark props. Standing in his presence, Dorothy felt her knees go weak: She had never met anyone so famous, so rich, or so powerful.

Unable to stay with Dorothy because of a prior dinner engagement, Marilyn Grabowski put her shy charge with a trusted friend, Patrick Curtis, a producer who'd once been married to actress Raquel Welch. Curtis took Dorothy in hand and saw her through the buffet line and introduced her to people as famous as her host. Later, one of the guests showed her around the property and once tried to kiss her, but she refused, reminding him that this wasn't why she had come to California. After watching part of the night's feature film, she walked back to her room and soon fell asleep.

Early Monday morning Dorothy awoke to the cheerful clamor of her housemates, who roamed the guest quarters naked; the newcomer demurely put on a robe. At breakfast, it took her a while to work up the courage to ask the butler for something to eat. The rest of the day was spent posing for Casilli's camera. But these shoots were only preliminary. Principal photography for the magazine would take at least two weeks; she'd be needed back in Los Angeles.

For Paul Snider, the two days Dorothy was gone had been a nightmare. He could not conceal his envy of her experience, his impatience with her palpable excitement, or his worry—perhaps he'd felt the first cold touch of what his life would be without her.

"From the very moment that she left he was pacing back and forth," recalled Ken Honey, to whom the task of calming Snider had fallen. "He would phone me several times during the day. 'Have you heard from *Playboy?*'" To pacify him, Honey appealed to the young man's considerable interest in himself. "He wanted to be in the limelight so I went along with it," said Honey. "I shot a bunch of pictures for him, which made him happy."

The day after she returned from Los Angeles, Dorothy Hoogstraten made her last pilgrimage to BC TEL. She'd asked a friend to tell her supervisor that she'd be absent on Monday because of out-of-town family problems. Now, apologizing for the sudden absence, she said that her family problems continued and asked if she could have two weeks off. One week was the best BC TEL could do; she would have to resign and reapply upon her return to Vancouver. The separation was not very wrenching, however. Dorothy wasn't the same 18-year-old who'd taken such pride in being hired there barely six weeks earlier. She was a young woman who could possibly earn big money by taking off her clothes for the camera.

No one was more aware of that difference than Paul Snider. He bitterly watched his companion, his ticket to the stars, get back on the airplane to Los Angeles. Then, jittery and angry, Snider got on the phone.

For the next three weeks, Dorothy Hoogstraten lived at the *Playboy* Mansion in Holmby Hills, working with Mario Casilli on her photographs. The shoots went well, but the centerfold, which was shot on a large-format 8-by-10-inch view camera, was taking longer than the model had expected. The *Playboy* limo would bring her home to the Mansion after a day under Casilli's lights, and she would usually eat and go to bed, although now and then she mingled with the guests who roamed the place at all hours. She attended the customary Friday and Sunday buffets and movies, and she danced some of the nights away. But mainly hers was a quiet, hardworking life.

Dorothy was changing, however. With Casilli especially she'd become bolder and more open, quick to laugh. Even

Whatever I'm doing for Dorothy, we have a pact. We have a love pact.

PAUL SNIDER

when the work made her tired and cranky, she behaved like a trouper. "Dorothy was never late," Casilli said admiringly. "She was very punctual and very professional for a girl who had never been involved in anything like that. I was quite impressed."

Paul Snider provided an unnerving counterpoint to her success. Each day, her continued absence amplified his apprehension. He called Ken Honey constantly, berating him for having no news of her. "He referred to Mr. Hefner as the King," said Honey. " 'She's down there with the King and she's not answering my phone calls.' " Trying to keep Snider from derailing the project, Honey took more photographs of him. But the calls continued: to Casilli, wanting to know what was going on, whom Dorothy was with; to Marilyn Grabowski; to the Mansion three or four times a day. No amount of telephoning could quell his central fear: They were luring Dorothy away from him; they were driving her out of his life in a *Playboy* limousine. As always, something unexpected was about to intercede in one of his grand schemes—and cheat him out of that trip to the stars he believed the world owed him.

In a way, Dorothy shared his fears. As she moved among the scores of guests who frequented the Mansion, she met a lot of men—powerful, wealthy, famous men, with one thing very much in common: They wanted her. Their gravitation, and Snider's, had begun to tear her apart. She sensed a widening gap between her life and that of the man who, she believed, had created the lovely creature who so charmed the denizens of the *Playboy* Mansion. She owed him everything. Her spirits descended; many nights she cried. Toward the end of this Los Angeles interlude she spent some of her nights at the Beverly Hills home of Patrick Curtis, who'd become her platonic guardian and guide.

Late August 1978 brought a pivotal event. *Playboy* threw a huge slumber party to which hundreds came wearing pajamas and robes. Dorothy danced and drank and played the night away. She woke up the next morning with a crashing hangover and the certain knowledge that her life had begun to slide. When Snider made his midmorning call, she told him how much she needed to see him. She picked him up at the airport late that afternoon, and they spent the weekend together in a hotel. But even with Snider lying at her side, she could feel the abyss widening between them.

The next month, Mario Casilli took Dorothy back to Vancouver for location photography on her home ground,

with Ken Honey helping out. Snider met the entourage with a limousine. His message seemed to be: You don't have to be Hugh Hefner to travel in style. When Casilli and his aides moved to enter the big sedan, Snider said, "The limousine is for Dorothy and me." The pair rode into Vancouver alone; Casilli and his two assistants rode with Ken Honey.

Once photography began, Snider wanted to stay close to Dorothy, even when on location. "He wanted to sit around," Casilli recalled, "and Ken kind of warned me. I don't have people around watching. It's not a sideshow, it's a job." Honey's job was to give Snider the message and keep him off the shoot. When the photography was over, Casilli and his people went back to Los Angeles. Her job finished, Dorothy lingered in Vancouver, waiting to hear whether she was going to be the Silver Anniversary Playmate.

Word came in mid-September. From thousands of contestants, it had come down to two women, Dorothy Hoogstraten and Candy Loving, one an 18-year-old Canadian with little experience of the world, the other a senior in public relations at the University of Oklahoma. The title went to Loving, who, the *Playboy* organization believed, had the promotional know-how that the 25th Anniversary Playmate would need. But Dorothy would be Miss August in 1979, which brought with it a $10,000 fee, and she had an excellent crack at the 1980 Playmate of the Year title. As her mother had shortened her first name to Nelly years before, Dorothy altered her surname: Her star would rise as Dorothy Stratten.

Paul Snider wanted his star to rise at her side, and he produced a large diamond ring to prove it. They should get married, he told her. Not yet, she countered. They became engaged. Snider kept clear of making any kind of formal management contract with his protégée, although friends and relatives urged him to protect his interests. "He said to me," Evelyn Snider recalled, " 'Mum, it's between Dorothy and me. This is like a friendship. Whatever I'm doing for Dorothy, we have a pact. We have a love pact.' "

Snider believed that fortune awaited them in Los Angeles, with *Playboy*. In fact, he considered L.A. his town. He'd spent a good deal of time there and had made a few friends. He liked to hang around George Barris, one of the city's preeminent car customizers and a genius with automotive special effects—the orignal Batmobile was among his credits. Snider had also gotten to know Max Baer, Jr., who had become a producer and promoter after playing the youthful lout Jethro in television's long-running "Beverly Hillbillies." Snider had telephoned Baer when Dorothy first came south to Los Angeles, asking him to look out for her, which Baer agreed to do.

In October, Stratten called Patrick Curtis and asked if she and her fiancé could live with him for a time. They wanted to come back to Los Angeles, and they were broke. Curtis let them have a spare bedroom and prepared to welcome this Paul he'd heard so much about. He wasn't prepared for the provincial hustler who strode into his home.

While they lived with Patrick Curtis, Snider's mind teemed with ideas for promoting his woman and himself. Actor-photographer John Derek, whose photography had won fame for his wife, Bo, should do the same for Dorothy; there should be a Dorothy book, a Dorothy poster. Snider saw lines of Dorothy perfumes and Dorothy cosmetics. He pestered his host for tips on crashing Hollywood. Although Curtis began spending more and more time away from home—partly for business reasons, partly to escape his oily guest—he helped Stratten find an agent as well as an acting teacher, Richard Brander. Curtis enjoyed their visit most when Snider made brief forays back to Vancouver on business and he was left alone with Stratten, whose choice of companions had begun to worry him.

Patrick Curtis was not alone in his concern for Stratten. When the couple arrived in California, Snider had taken her to meet Max Baer, Jr., at his home in Van Nuys. "She seemed like she just got off the farm," Baer said, recalling an evening when they got together at a Beverly Hills spot called PIP. "She really was Joe Square, and for some reason I think she retained that all the time." Later he talked to Snider alone. "I said, 'Look, get her the hell out of here.' He said, 'No, I really love her.' I said, 'Okay, fine, get her out of here because there's nobody that gets out of here with their marbles.' "

Both Stratten and Snider enrolled in Brander's twice-weekly class of 10 students in nearby Sherman Oaks. Brander thought Dorothy had a star quality that evoked the late Marilyn Monroe—an honest innocence radiated from her, and she was as trusting as a child. Snider also seemed to have acting talent, but he wasn't interested. He came to class only to watch over Dorothy's career.

In fact, Snider hated revealing his emotional core. Once, in a scene taken from *Love with the Proper Stranger*, the female character told him, "Your eyes are dead," and held up a mirror for him to see. Snider's line was "My eyes may be dead, but I do feel things and I really love you." The exchange overcame him; his mouth worked, his eyes gleamed. "I don't want to go on," he said.

"Don't worry about it," Brander coached. "Let it all out, go with it, don't stop."

"No," said Snider. "Those kinds of things only get you in trouble."

Acting classes also bridged the doldrums that separated the strenuous camera sessions and Stratten's appearance as a Playmate. Her August 1979 centerfold and the swirl of promotional activity that would accompany it were still almost a year away, and in the meantime, she had only her *Playboy* fee to sustain them. Paul Snider didn't look for a job—he was a visiting Canadian without a work permit, and besides, he was too busy imagining the trajectory of Dorothy's career. Had she been in Los Angeles on her own, Stratten could have lived at the *Playboy* Mansion guesthouse; as it was, she had free access to the enclave's parties, movies, and tables of free food. She was allowed to bring her fiancé with her; Snider was even permitted to visit the Mansion alone.

A fashion standout among Vancouver pimps, Snider was a sleazy embarrassment in Holmby Hills. To the Mansion, Snider brought a style that had flourished briefly in Los Angeles perhaps a decade earlier. He favored spandex pants in iridescent colors, short lizardskin boots, a colored silk shirt, jewelry, a flashy coat. Dorothy took her garish consort to the Mansion's Halloween party that year. She was costumed as an angel in white satin. Snider wore his former Hornby Street uniform, a broadbrimmed hat and fur coat—he went as a pimp. When Hefner later said as much to Stratten, she laughed it off. It had been a disguise, she protested, not the real Paul.

Although Dorothy was not aware of it yet, Paul Snider was not the only important man in her life. A few days before the Halloween party she'd met noted film director Peter Bogdanovich, just back from location in Singapore and coming off a highly publicized eight-year relationship with actress Cybill Shepherd. At 39, according to the director's own account, he was at loose ends and inclined to run with the pack at the Mansion, about a mile from his own Bel Air estate at 212 Copa de Oro Drive. Evidently taken by Dorothy's stunning beauty, Bogdanovich had signaled his interest with what he later called the oldest line in

Posing in 1978 for Ken Honey, the Vancouver photographer who sent her pictures to *Playboy*, Dorothy Stratten *(left)* models nautical togs and a pensive mood, while Paul Snider *(above)*, dressed to kill, playfully shoots the photographer with an extended index finger.

the world: He was putting together a new film; would she like to read for a part? He wrote his name and phone number on a piece of *Playboy* notepaper. Stratten didn't call.

But that brief chance encounter was a beginning, not an end. Like the first brush with Paul Snider in the Dairy Queen not quite a year before, it would reverberate through Dorothy Stratten's short life to the end.

Although Dorothy Stratten and Paul Snider had attained Los Angeles, these were not exactly their salad days. Her $10,000 Playmate fee had been paid almost immediately, in September 1978, a rare departure from the *Playboy* policy of keeping something back in the interest of its models. Snider had spent much of it on engagement and wedding rings, partly out of his charming but foolish extravagance but also as a way of sustaining his pressure to get married. The cage of marriage, he believed, might be strong enough to hold his rare bird.

In November, Dorothy accepted a part-time job as a door bunny at the Century City *Playboy* Club, spending most of her evenings in a rabbit-eared, fluffy-tailed costume cut low in front and high in the rear. As a Canadian citizen in the United States for *Playboy,* she could work nowhere else without obtaining a work permit — a green card. Snider had picked up a white four-door Cadillac for his use; Dorothy drove a rusting 1967 green Mercury Cougar. They moved from Curtis's house to a furnished one-bedroom place off Barham Boulevard, where the sullen glitter of Hollywood gives way to the fabled ordinariness of Burbank.

The couple met a young woman in acting school, Molly Basler, who began driving out to the apartment to rehearse a scene that she and Dorothy were doing for Richard Brander's class. "Everyone was just so naive," she remembered. "I met these two people, whom I hardly knew. The next thing I knew they asked me to move in and I said okay." Later, Snider told Basler that he'd picked her out to be Dorothy's friend. "That's how controlling he was," she said. The trio found a one-bedroom-and-loft apartment in Westwood.

According to Basler, none of them had very strong identities. "We were all trying to be actors and make it in the big city and everyone was probably pretty scared but didn't really recognize that. Dorothy didn't even know if she was in love with him, and yet she was with him because she felt like she had nothing else to go back to." She added, "Paul and Dorothy both were desperate, in a way. Yes, they paint her as beautiful, nice, and so on, but she was desperate and clinging to something. And he was clinging to her."

During these months, Stratten struggled to keep their new life going. By day she went out on auditions, by night she

Film director Peter Bogdanovich reflects beside the grotto pool at the *Playboy* Mansion a few months before his fatal affair with Dorothy Stratten began.

A sextet of male strippers, one of Paul Snider's many get-rich-quick promotions, flaunts it for William LaChasse's lens at Culver City's Chippendale's in 1979.

put on her bunny costume and greeted customers at the *Playboy* Club, returning late, exhausted, often in tears.

Snider, too, was busy. His schemes multiplied apace. Just as he'd introduced the wet-T-shirt contest to Gastown, he brought his newest brainstorm—male strippers—to the Victorian interior of Chippendale's, a nightspot down near Culver City. He was having a local photographer named William LaChasse shoot some of his dancers, with a view to placing the young men in a *Playgirl* centerfold. He was working on a wet-shorts competition, a contest for handsomest L.A. male, and yet another leap by battered motorcycle daredevil Evel Knievel. Snider also envisioned a two-stage epic called "Battle of the Male Exotic Dancers," an endless competition among G-stringed male dancers from across the country. He thought there must be a movie—*For Women Only,* he called it—in the Paul Snider story, which became more compelling by the day. And, of course, there was always Dorothy to mold, to train, to dress, the Stratten career to manage. Still, despite this busy schedule, he often spent his days sleeping behind drawn blinds.

At first, Molly Basler was not sure what to make of him. "I knew he was slimy and kind of weird," she remembered, "but he was also kind of funny and nice." Then, "There was a sweetness about Paul that would draw you in."

But Basler also detected the disquiet in her companions' strained relationship. "I never thought they seemed in love," she said. "She wouldn't really say, 'Oh, I've got to get away from Paul.' She'd just say, 'Let's go up to the Mansion and swim and goof around.'" Sometimes the two women sneaked out to have coffee, which Snider forbade—it would stain Dorothy's teeth—or smoke or eat something fattening at the nearby Westward Ho market. Their best times together were when Snider went off on his Vancouver forays.

That summer should have evaporated any tensions, for there was a sharp smell of success in the smoggy Los Angeles air. For Stratten, it came from the suddenly rising tempo of her new career—the *Playboy* promotional machinery was cranking up for her August centerfold, and she and Snider were working with LaChasse on a Dorothy Stratten roller-skating poster. For Snider, success wore a different fragrance: Dorothy had agreed to marry him.

Nobody thought much of the marriage idea. Molly Basler believed that her friend's acquiescence reflected the low self-esteem of the chronic victim. To Stratten's many protectors, it was as if light had volunteered to be swallowed up by darkness. "It was during a session that she blurted out the fact that she was going to get married," Mario Casilli recalled later. "And I said, 'Why would you want to do that?' I didn't put the onus on him, it was more her age and things were happening. I said, 'Why don't you just wait a while?'"

Stratten told Marilyn Grabowski the good news at a health club called Ruffage, where they worked out from time to time. "She told me she was thinking of marrying him," Grabowski recalls. "She owed him, he had done a lot for her. I said I wouldn't do that if I were you. I would live with him, I wouldn't marry him. I just think that so much is going to be offered to you and you're going to grow so much that this doesn't seem to be the best thing for you." Hugh Hefner was more succinct: "Paul has the personality of a pimp."

On June 1, 1979, Snider and Stratten were married in the Silver Bell Wedding Chapel in Las Vegas, in a $65 ceremony. After a three-day honeymoon in a Vegas hotel, the couple returned to Los Angeles and a reception at Max Baer's Van Nuys residence. "It was strange," remembered Molly Basler. "Paul was a strange guy. He was always sort of stiff and self-conscious and the party felt that way." Only 1978 Playmate of the Year Debra Jo Fondren attended from *Playboy*. David Snider was there, but no one came from the Hoogstraten family. Not until weeks later was Dorothy able to tell her mother that she'd married Paul.

The tie that bound must have strangled something in Dor-

Masking their tensions, Snider and Stratten *(above)* smile for their wedding portrait and a traditional threshold crossing *(above, right)* after their 1979 wedding in Las Vegas, where their marriage certificate *(right)* was issued. At a subsequent reception in a friend's Los Angeles home *(left, clockwise from lower right),* Dorothy chats with father-in-law David; bride and groom pose with auto customizer George Barris; Dorothy feeds Paul the obligatory first slice of wedding cake; the newlyweds go cheek to cheek.

MAILING ADDRESS: 3208 CAHUENGA BLVD. W., HOLLYWOOD, CALIFORNA 90068 #13

BOOK 568 **Marriage Certificate** 002411

State of Nevada } ss. No. B 205679
County of Clark, }

This is to Certify that the undersigned James G. Whitehead
did on the 1st day of June A.D. 19 79
at Silver Bell Wedding Chapel 607 Las Vegas Blvd. So., Las Vegas Nevada
(Address or Church) (City)
join in lawful Wedlock PAUL LESLIE SNIDER
of LOS ANGELES State of CALIFORNIA
and DOROTHY RUTH HOOGSTRATEN
of LOS ANGELES State of CALIFORNIA
with their mutual consent, in the presence of JAKE MASTRAN
who was a witness with GLENN McMICHAEL

Recorded in Book of Marriages,
Clark County Nevada Records,
Joan L. Swift, Recorder.
Date JUN 19 1979 James Gee Whitehead
Fee $3.00 B. V. Deputy MINISTER: Church of Christ
(Sign this in official capacity.)

TO BE GIVEN TO THE RECORDER

othy Stratten's feelings for her groom. "After they got married, she couldn't sleep with him," revealed Basler. "Obviously she knew intuitively that something was wrong and she didn't love him."

Increasingly, the dark side of their life intruded. As Dorothy's career accelerated, Basler and Snider found themselves often left alone together. Snider made occasional unsuccessful passes at her and suggested that she pose for *Playboy* so he could have the finder's fee. Once, she provoked him enough to see a brief flash of the violence he kept pent up within.

"I didn't agree with the whole *Playboy* scene," Basler said. "I think it's degrading to women, and I started to verbalize that more and more. Paul didn't like it and we got in an argument." Basler told Paul off in rather graphic terms. "I'll never forget Dorothy's face. She turned totally white. And he said, 'What did you say?' and I kept saying it. And then he came at me and kicked over the kitchen table. He literally freaked out because I showed disrespect. And then I was terrified. He didn't touch me, but I knew that he could have. He could have been pushed over that edge. And that's when I chose to leave."

In Vancouver to promote her appearance as *Playboy*'s August 1979 centerfold *(opposite)*, Dorothy Stratten enjoys a reunion with her family *(right):* 18-year-old brother John, mother Nelly Hoogstraten, 11-year-old sister Louise, and Dorothy.

Molly Basler moved out that summer, but she remained close to Stratten. She remembers talking with some other aspiring actresses about Dorothy, who had often accompanied them to Ruffage for a workout and to Nate 'n Al's afterward for breakfast. "It was so strange," she observed, describing the group's view of Dorothy Stratten. "It was almost like she wasn't of this world, in a weird way. I always look at them sort of as a metaphor, like Paul was evil and Dorothy was good. And they were put on this earth to fight it out. And no one won."

Such metaphorical battles were the least of Dorothy Stratten's concerns that summer of 1979. The 19-year-old's career was suddenly spinning like a turbine and it was all she could do to keep up. Snider arranged for her to pose for the LaChasse cameras at Chippendale's, still hoping to market a million Dorothy Stratten roller-skating posters. In July she set out on a transcontinental odyssey of publicity as the August Playmate, one of the rare Canadian beauties to be featured on the *Playboy* centerfold. The magazine sent her to Montreal to meet the woman who would guide her through an unfamiliar, often hostile world of strobe lights and interviews: Elizabeth Norris, the magazine's Chicago-based publicity manager.

"I met her just as she was becoming a Playmate of the Month," said Norris. "She was kind of an ugly duckling. She was big and gangly and she didn't shave her legs. Her nail polish was chipped. She was a little girl who had never been anywhere or done anything. I worked with her for a month. We went across Canada, we started in Montreal and went west. And, if you look at the videotapes of the interviews she did at the beginning of that month and the interviews she did at the end, you wouldn't believe the difference." Between Quebec and British Columbia, the ugly duckling became a swan.

The journey was more than a publicity tour for Dorothy Stratten—it was her triumphant return to a city where she'd grown up poor, where she'd worked as a waitress in the Dairy Queen, where she'd been morbidly shy and hadn't known that she was beautiful. On the road, Norris remembers, Stratten talked about her brother, John, her sister, Louise, and Nelly, the persevering mother who'd taken care of them all; about life, men—about everything except Paul Snider.

Stratten had fretted over her mother's reaction to her

Playboy nudes and was delighted to discover that Nelly Hoogstraten was proud of her famous daughter. Stratten and Norris stayed in the Westin Bayshore on Burrard Inlet, where Dorothy and Louise would do cartwheels on the broad green lawn. One night they all took the tram to the top of Burnaby Mountain, which looms over Vancouver's East End; the Hoogstraten kids had played there as children. In a way that it had not been in her childhood, Vancouver had become Dorothy Stratten's town.

Only one cloud marred Stratten's return. Toward the end of a long interview with BCTV's Mike McCardell, the reporter callously asked Stratten to take off her clothes. "Dorothy looked so horrified," recalled freelance publicist Joy Metcalfe, who helped arrange media events for the new celebrity. "She was just coming back to show her friends that she had money and had clothes, that she was glamorous and the world was wonderful. When McCardell told her to take her clothes off she was just so shocked. She said, 'Why on earth would you ask me to do that?' And he said something to the effect that, 'Well, you did it for hundreds of thousands of men in this magazine, why can't you do it for us?' He was rather persistent. She finally ran off crying."

When they finished the Playmate promotional tour, Norris returned to Chicago, and Stratten went back to Los Angeles. "I still can't believe I'm home," Dorothy wrote her new friend. "It's a good thing our good-byes were short and sweet at the airport. I think otherwise we would have flooded the place in tears."

Stratten had little time to miss Elizabeth Norris, however. While the new Playmate had toured Canada, her film and modeling career coalesced. On her return to Los Angeles she did a bit part in a film called *Americathon,* with actor John Ritter, and another feature, *Skatetown, U.S.A.* Columbia Pictures wanted her to do a television episode of "Fantasy Island." She went to Winnipeg to begin shooting her first film lead in a low-budget Canadian production called *Autumn Born,* the story of a young woman captured by a mind-control organization whose members use rape, beatings, isolation, and other means to brainwash her into submission. If Stratten detected any echoes of her own life, she kept them to herself.

Her August 9 letter to Norris from Winnipeg contained a poignant request. "I wanted to ask you, that when you write to me, if you could send it to the Sunset Building in c/o *Playboy* Models. Paul reads my mail and I'd at least like to read it before he does." Then, "September 8th is also the big 'Playmate Reunion.' Think you could make it?"

Norris could not, but 136 Playmates of the Month, including Dorothy Stratten, were at the Silver Anniversary reunion that September. The Playmates each received a jeweled rabbit pendant to mark the event. A *Washington Post* reporter who interviewed Stratten at the reunion was impressed by her beauty—and by the odd contrast it offered to the slick young man at her side, who quietly prompted her on how to answer the correspondent's questions. Stratten and Snider also ran into June 1979 Playmate Louann Fernald, whom Dorothy knew from the year before, and her boyfriend Jefferson Wortham Clark, Jr.—Chip—a surfing pro from New Smyrna Beach, Florida.

"The Playmate reunion was so much fun," Stratten wrote Elizabeth Norris on October 3. "I met a lot of playmates— new and old. It was so exciting to see them all. Press was there from all over the world. It lasted all day and night." Then, "I thought maybe you would be at the reunion. I was sorry you weren't."

The letter also brought news of Stratten's improving situation. "My husband and I moved out of our apartment," she wrote. "We now live in a two story house in West Los Angeles. Two bedroom, two bath, 2 car garage. It's brand new—we're the first tenants. We had to buy furniture. We bought a living room set, kitchen set, bedroom set (waterbed), decorations for the walls. We also have a real fireplace. And last but not least we got a loan and this week we're buying a Mercedes 450SE 1974. It looks brand new —It just had a $2,400 paint job done to it. So, once again I'm broke—but it sure feels good to own some things."

Paul Snider, who was cashing most of the checks David Wilder, Dorothy's agent, wrote to her, thought so too. "We're on a rocket ship," he told anyone who would listen. "To the moon."

The new house at 10881 West Clarkson Road had been erected in the shadow of the Santa Monica Freeway, a mighty east-west river of traffic that bisects Los Angeles and, in a sense, defines it. North of this artery the neighborhoods climb toward Hollywood, Beverly Hills, Holmby Hills, and Bel Air, toward the *Playboy* Mansion and the Bogdanovich estate, the "Tonight Show," the studios. To the south, the city descends as a carpet of stunted pastel cottages and low commercial buildings toward Venice by the Sea, Culver City, and the airport. South of the Santa Monica Freeway was Paul Snider's natural habitat; going north he became increasingly the alien, although to go north was his greatest aspiration. Dorothy Stratten, on the other hand, had begun to sense that she might find a comfortable adoptive home there.

The couple shared the Clarkson Road place with Steve Cushner, a young physician who'd met Dorothy at the *Playboy* Club. Cushner was moving his practice from Long Beach to Beverly Hills and needed some minimal accommodations for himself, his German shepherd, and his Rolls Royce. The house offered him a fenced yard for the dog and half of a two-car garage for the Rolls. Besides, he had been quite taken by Dorothy and often almost liked Paul. Cushner got the upstairs bedroom and bath, Snider and Stratten the downstairs suite adjoining the garage. The living room, kitchen area, and a deck overlooking the freeway were shared by the occupants. It was an ideal arrangement for all concerned, since Cushner spent much of his time at his girlfriend's or building his practice.

Chip Clark and Louann Fernald moved to Los Angeles from Florida late in October. Soon after they arrived, Snider dropped by to pick up Fernald, who had a *Playboy* promotion to do with Dorothy, then returned to Clark's place, and the two men went out to take a closer look at Los Angeles. "When I first met him, he just wanted to show me all around and he was a real friendly character," recalled Clark. "It was entertaining because he knew everyone everywhere, and could get in anywhere, just about. I guess people knew him out there. They let him in everywhere we went and we just would park right at front doors and stuff. I was impressed."

It is from Clark that one gets some sense of what Paul Snider was like now that he'd become a lunar rocketeer. "This guy would go out and he would be worth a hundred grand in what he was wearing in jewelry and clothes," Clark said. "It was like, someone will kill you for what you are wearing, buddy. His wardrobe was unbelievable, $150 shirts and $1,000 suits. He was a real boot fanatic, had every kind of boot you could imagine, $200-$300 boots. The jewelry he wore was second to none. I mean, huge diamonds and giant watches, tons and tons of gold. What he wore wasn't gaudy as much as it was just huge, so you knew it was expensive. Not a ton of chains, just one heavy chain. And not a lot of diamonds, but one five-carat diamond, just hanging there." A Vancouver friend notes, however, that Snider's gems were fake.

If Snider feared anyone, he kept it well concealed. "He was one of those guys that gets a rise out of being able to see how far he can push you," said Clark. "If somebody said something wise to him, he could come back pretty fast and he didn't seem to be intimidated by anybody. He wasn't a real big guy, but he had an intimidating aura about him. He was just one of those guys that would turn the heat up faster than you probably would and that's kind of intimidating. I never saw him get in a fight. I just saw him back people down."

Clark detected the same good qualities in Snider that had confused Molly Basler and attracted Dorothy Stratten. "This guy was amazing. He was a very talented speaker. He was a very talented musician. He could do all kinds of custom work with metal and leathers and upholstery. The guy was so talented in so many different ways. Super good promoter. He was just destined to make money. Dorothy was a perfect example of his promotional skills."

Snider was as protective of his other creations as he was of Dorothy. One night he and Clark walked into Chippendale's, where a master of ceremonies was giving a lackluster performance to a female audience. "Paul was just getting bent out of shape," said Clark. "So finally he got up and took the mike from the D.J., and got him off the stage in a forceful way the crowd would think was part of the show. He took that show over and it was something for somebody to see. I would never have believed, coming from the East, you could get a pack of women that wild."

But even in his natural element, Snider remained a loner. "Everyone treated him with respect and gave him a lot of leeway," Clark observed, "but they didn't actually hang with him." Clark liked Snider enough to lend him a .38 revolver for protection.

Chip Clark was around as Snider's precarious grip on success began to slip. The Evel Knievel jump, the male stripathon, the Paul Snider story shuddered and died. His promotions seemed invariably to poise on the brink of success, then peel off into failure. An argument with Chippendale's manager severed Snider from his profitable male strip show

there. Bar owners, always open to new Paul Snider concepts, would sometimes take the idea, share a little with Snider, and then appropriate it for themselves. He clung to the Dorothy Stratten poster like a drowning man to a log. Everything was going wrong, again—and Dorothy was changing, although the jittery Snider could not have said precisely how, or why.

In late October 1979 the *Playboy* Mansion mounted one of its revels for ABC television cameras. The show, the *Playboy* Roller-Disco and Pajama Party, was a three-day weekend shoot and offered Dorothy Stratten a small comedy bit to do. Among the guests was Peter Bogdanovich, whom she'd met a year earlier. They renewed their acquaintance in the buffet line.

At the end of the evening, Bogdanovich told Stratten that he'd been working on a script for a new film, a comedy called *They All Laughed*. He hoped she would read for a part. Ten days later, on Thursday, November 1, Dorothy Stratten and her agent, David Wilder, pulled up at the gate telephone at 212 Copa de Oro Drive. They announced themselves and watched the wrought-iron gate swing open to reveal the Bogdanovich estate, a stucco-and-tile Spanish colonial. In his memoir, the director remembers Stratten entering in a frilly white cotton dress and floppy hat, evoking an earlier time. They read the few scenes written for her character, an efficient secretary named Amy who was secretly in love with her boss. Bogdanovich was impressed. "It didn't take more than a few minutes," he wrote later, "for me to realize she was a natural actress with a fine ear for nuance and a wry, simple delivery that always rang true."

But something would have to be done about her stage name—another actress had registered with the Screen Actors Guild as Dorothy Stratton, with an *o*. Snider had been pushing another name, Kristen Shields. Bogdanovich suggested the initials of Dorothy Ruth: D. R. Stratten. D. R. became his pet name for her; it appears on her gravestone.

With the prospect of a major film shimmering on her horizon, Stratten learned in late November—unofficially, so that Mario Casilli could begin the necessary photography— that she would be the 1980 Playmate of the Year, a title that would bring her $25,000 in cash and about $175,000 in expensive gifts. *Playboy* also planned to begin shooting a special Stratten feature, in which she would portray such epic blondes as Jean Harlow, Betty Grable, Marilyn Monroe, and Marlene Dietrich.

As his wife's star ascended, Paul Snider frantically shored up his dwindling options, as if he sensed that she would soon be lost to him. He began to draw another pretty female under his wing: 17-year-old Patti Laurman, whom he met in November at an auto show. "It wasn't a real romantic relationship," Chip Clark recalled. "I think it was a wounded, just hang-out-with-me-and-make-me-feel-good kind of thing." If Snider slept with Laurman, Clark conjectured, he did it "out of a grudge kind of deal, and not enjoying it because it wasn't Dorothy. He was fixated on Dorothy."

Snider was tightening his suffocating grip on his wife. So that people would know that they were somebody special, he ordered new vanity plates for their cars: GAL-X-INA for Stratten's Mercury, after the title of a film he wanted her to do; for the Mercedes, which he drove, he chose STAR 80. On December 7, when she returned to the Bogdanovich house for a second reading, Paul waited for her in the Mercedes for two hours, no doubt fuming with impotence—*he* was supposed to be with her, coaching her, shaping her, controlling her.

Stratten was worried about doing the science-fiction farce *Galaxina*—her character was a blond android—and she turned to Bogdanovich, going alone to his home for advice. The director counseled her, then, according to the director, the talk turned to Paul.

The pair talked about Snider's latest strategy. Paul had begun to push for a contract that would assure him half of Dorothy's income and property for life, whether or not they stayed together. Managers typically received only 15 percent of a client's income. According to Bogdanovich, Stratten smelled Snider's lack of trust and was wounded by it—and frightened.

"She had the demeanor of someone who had been hit and hit often," recalled Rosanne Katon, a Playmate who had known Dorothy from those first days at *Playboy*. "It wasn't so much what she said. It was the way she acted. She acted like she was scared of him. I always thought he beat her. I think she recognized a streak of violence in him that she kind of took for granted. It was almost like she thought that's how guys are. And Peter was a revelation for her."

Stratten sent Bogdanovich a grateful Christmas card and, on December 23, went by to see him. He reciprocated with a piano serenade. Her adoring younger sister, Louise, came down from Vancouver for a visit, and Dorothy gave her a tour of the *Playboy* Mansion and introduced her to Bogdanovich and his daughters. A new decade was dawning, and it looked as if it might belong to the film director and the budding star.

Shooting on *Galaxina* began in January 1980 on a ranch in the hills above Malibu, about 15 miles west of the couple's Clarkson Road house. Many mornings Paul made the drive with Dorothy, often hanging out on the set or returning to spend the lunch break with her, then back again to pick her up at night. When he wasn't on the set he was telephoning her. Often she was crying when she put down the receiver.

Stratten's low spirits began to mar her photography sessions for the Playmate of the Year and famous blondes pictorials. "She cried almost daily," said Marilyn Grabowski. "She'd get phone calls from him. She wouldn't cry in front of us, but her eyes would be all red. They'd fight a lot." Alarmed, Grabowski stepped in and packed Stratten off for three days at La Costa, a health spa about 35 miles north of San Diego. "I was surprised because she didn't talk about him whatsoever in a negative way. Instead she asked if I thought that Hef would loan them some money so she could get Paul a ranch, a farm out in the country, and get him out of Los Angeles. I was totally floored when she asked because as far as I could see all he did was make her life very uncomfortable."

The brief respite from Paul's pressure calmed Dorothy. To keep her spirits rising, Grabowski picked up a puppy for her, a little Shih Tzu. Delighted, Stratten named it Marston, Hefner's middle name. A week later, Marston was dead. "She told me a couple of days after that Paul was jealous of the dog," Grabowski said. "I was convinced that he killed the dog." Stratten reportedly told her *Galaxina* makeup aide that Snider had poisoned it.

On February 3 Peter Bogdanovich called from New York. He and Dorothy had continued to circle each other warily; but on January 20, walking on a deserted beach near Los Angeles, they had finally stepped into each other's arms. He'd offered her a part in *They All Laughed*, which had coalesced into a major film starring Audrey Hepburn and Ben Gazzara. Now, evidently distressed that his emotions would be seen as ruling his mind, Bogdanovich called to tell her that they must let their love go until she broke free of Paul Snider. Stratten took the call during a Marlene Dietrich shoot for Mario Casilli. For years afterward, the pho-

Tucked behind a wrought-iron gate and wall of trees, the Spanish colonial Bel Air estate of Peter Bogdanovich was Stratten's home in the summer of 1980.

As a beautiful android in her fourth motion picture, *Galaxina,* a stoic, silver-clad Dorothy Stratten prepares to zap somebody with her ray gun.

tographer believed her tears had been caused by another ugly call from Snider.

A few days later, Bogdanovich telephoned to apologize for the tone he'd taken. The day after Valentine's Day, he was back in Los Angeles and the two made up, steeling themselves for a month of separation before Stratten joined him in New York to shoot *They All Laughed.* Yet her domestic life proceeded, sometimes with haunting foreshadowings of things to come. In February, Chip Clark remembers, he and Louann Fernald and Dorothy and Paul were sitting around in the kitchen of the Clarkson Road house when the conversation turned to the issue of spouses leaving spouses. "Dorothy said, 'Oh, I would never leave Paul,' " Clark recalls, "and Louann said something like, 'Well, why not?' and she said, 'Well, Paul would kill me, he would literally kill me.' And Paul said, 'Yeah, I would kill you.' And it was kind of serious."

One night the foursome went out to see *All That Jazz,* a new film by Bob Fosse. "We came out and we were driving home," Clark said. "It was a foggy Londony night. And he pulls down this alley and there is this little cemetery wedged in between a bunch of buildings. He pulls up, turns the headlights of the Mercedes on this little mausoleum, and we all get out. We walk up and it's Marilyn Monroe's grave. And Dorothy looks at it, and she says, 'Wow.' Around that area there were a couple of empty spots, and she asks, 'I wonder who's going to be buried there?' "

Clark saw the Stratten-Snider relationship enter a kind of Hollywood eclipse, of a type he had seen many times before. "I watched every couple that became our friends go through the exact same scenario," he said. "Basically, a lot of the Playmates stuck together out there, so you'd get to meet their boyfriends or husbands and you'd watch the things that went down in the relationships as the girls started moving through the industry: the photo industry, the film business, all the agents, all the BS that goes down, the pressures and what not. And you watched how it affected the quality of the attention they'd get, the money they're making, and typically they were outshining the guys they were with."

In fact, Stratten shone with special brilliance then. Provided an entrée by an older admirer at the Mansion, she was able to hire a business-management firm with a number of celebrity clients to shepherd her finances. Robert Houston, the junior partner, was assigned her case. "It had just been announced that she was about to come out as Playmate of

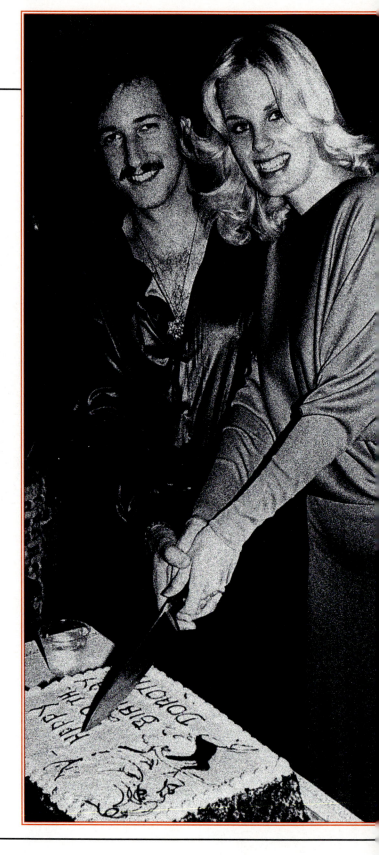

Snider and Stratten grin and bear it for Dorothy's 20th birthday *(left)*. Below, Paul *(right)* leans on guest Ken Russell, backed up by roommate Steve Cushner and his girlfriend, Catherine Apstein, beside Snider's STAR 80 Mercedes.

the Year," Houston recalled, "and she was dealt this money and all these stupid gifts—the brass bathtub and stereo equipment and lingerie. She had done a couple of films. So we set up this corporation and we took her on as a normal client. We signed the checks and we set up a corporation so the money would come in there."

Stratten and Houston's firm could draw money from the corporation, but Paul Snider could not. "So we had this every other day visitor," Houston remembered, "Paul com-

ing to visit us and lobbying his case." He was full of money-raising schemes, all of them vintage Snider. "He wanted to take out a full-page ad in the L.A. *Times* that would read something to the effect: Send in $35 and we'll mail you the secrets of becoming a millionaire. All it needed was for x number of people to respond and then Dorothy would mail them an envelope that says: Take out an ad in the news-

paper and tell people to send in $35 and we'll mail you the secret of becoming a millionaire. He said that this was okay and would be a great deal. I'm sitting here with important things to do trying to give him a lecture on good citizenship and responsible behavior."

Cut off from Stratten's income, the high-rolling Snider was forced to hard labor, although it was not in him to find a straight job. Chip Clark was running a Nautilus club at Wilshire and Bundy, in an era before fitness centers were on every corner and when few people built weightlifting gear. Snider immediately smelled money in making weight benches. "He had a full metal shop at the house," Clark said. "He could build a car if he wanted to. He says, 'Man we can crank these things out and sell them for $400 or $500 and they cost about $60 in parts and labor and maybe an hour and a half of time.' And so we went over and started making a few." They offered the benches in a paper called the *Recycler,* verified the market, and went into production. "Pretty soon it was a full-time deal," Clark said. "We were working nine to five so that we could build the benches. And they were high-quality products."

One day, cruising down Santa Monica Boulevard, Snider suddenly whipped the Mercedes to the curb. "I've got to show you this place," he told Clark. The pair entered an intriguing emporium called The Pleasure Chest. "It's a three-story sex novelty store," Clark said. "Not a little perverted, kinky shop, but a full-blown department store with just every wild thing you can imagine. This one area had these bondage machines that sold for $600 or $700. Paul looks at them and says, 'You know, we throw scraps away that would make these things.'"

Days later, Snider showed Clark his prototype bondage bench, replete with adjustable surfaces and Velcro straps. He'd built it in 15 minutes, he said. Snider talked to The Pleasure Chest and was told they'd buy one if it were of

Playboy publisher Hugh Hefner and new Playmate of the Year Dorothy Stratten meet the press
at the Los Angeles Mansion in April 1980.

better quality and cost them about $350.
Clark opted out of the deal and Snider
didn't pursue it on his own. "The only person that I ever knew that got in that thing
was me, just to see if it worked. And it
worked—I was pretty helpless. He put it in
the corner of his room and it sat there for
months and months and months."

By that time Snider had another, ruling
preoccupation. He could feel Dorothy slip-
ping away from his love, his care, his control, and taking her income with her. He
badly wanted to go with her to New York
for the filming of *They All Laughed*. Stratten, until then a compliant mate, told him
she was going alone.

On March 22 Stratten headed for New
York. The lunar rocket ship had lifted off at
last, and Paul Snider wasn't on it. Dorothy
was gone, and, Snider may have sensed,
gone forever.

In New York, Dorothy Stratten's life
started over, as it had in Vancouver
just two years before. As the Dairy Queen
girl had been turned into a famous naked
beauty, the Playmate was transformed into
a lovely actress with knowledge of the great
cities and restaurants and hotels of the
world, a woman who read Hemingway
and the great Russians. The interlude was,
according to Peter Bogdanovich's account,
an idyll of rides through a snowy Central
Park in a hansom cab, quiet dinners at
Nicola's, and private moments in his pent-
house suite in the Plaza Hotel. The day after her arrival, he wrote, they made love for
the first time.

The days were spent on a busy shooting
schedule, in the hope of bringing in *They
All Laughed* on budget and on time. Suspect at first, Stratten soon captured the
hearts of her colleagues with her rare combination of innocence, beauty, and a kind
of good-hearted grit. She had a room at the

Wyndham Hotel on 58th Street but, increasingly, found herself in Bogdanovich's Plaza suite. Their affair, handled with vast discretion, was an open secret among the cast and crew; but no one thought of breaking it to outsiders.

Stratten's absence terrified Snider, trapped without her love or money in Los Angeles. He called incessantly, each time yelling at her, then calling back to make up, then exploding again. In Los Angeles, he'd tethered her with talk of conspiracies, of how "they" were going to steal her away from him, take advantage of her. That strategy didn't work once she got to New York, where she would sometimes take his calls, sometimes not, and finally she refused to speak with him at all.

In April, during a break in production, Stratten returned to Los Angeles to begin a new round of *Playboy* promotions, this time to celebrate her ascension to 1980 Playmate of the Year. Elizabeth Norris, the Chicago publicist, flew in to help, and the Playmate bandwagon geared up for a number of events, including a guest spot on Johnny Carson's "Tonight Show" and another trans-Canadian tour. This one would reach Vancouver in time for Nelly Hoogstraten's second marriage, to a Coquitlam man named Burl Eldridge.

Snider wanted to join Dorothy in her dressing room at the "Tonight Show," but she refused, with a little help from her mentor. "It was my territory," explained Norris, "it wasn't his territory, and I'm the boss. 'Paul, you can't come in, she doesn't want you in here.' So he didn't." At the Playmate of the Year press conference and luncheon, Snider hovered humbly at Stratten's side, but his wife of not quite a year ignored him.

The Playmate publicity tour rescued Stratten from him, for a time. On their last trip across Canada, Norris and Stratten had scarcely talked of Paul Snider. On this one, they talked of little else. "She wanted to be away from him," recalled Norris, "and she didn't want to hurt him. He would call, and call, and call, all the time."

One weekend, Norris remembered, Stratten traveled to New York for a rendezvous with an unnamed man. When she returned, all her demons had flown. "She came in and did a backwards somersault on the bed. And she said when she got to New York that she knocked on the door of his hotel room. He came to the door, and took her in his arms and just held her for the longest time, standing in the doorway. She thought that was just the ultimate. Then the phone rang and I picked it up, and I said, 'I don't know who you are, but thank you for making Dorothy so happy.'"

The next day Norris learned that the mystery man was Peter Bogdanovich. "I think they were probably perfect for

Hours after being named 1980 Playmate of the
Year, Stratten chats with host Johnny Carson on
the set of television's "Tonight Show."

each other," she said. "Because he was sensitive and the artist in him would have attracted the sensitivity in her, the poet in her. I'm sure that he tapped her feelings, appreciated the depth of her. The last time I saw her she was reading Dostoevsky—*The Idiot.*"

Between them, the two women drafted a letter to Snider. It used a poetic metaphor of a caged bird to urge him to give her more room, to let her test her wings alone. They sent it by courier, then Stratten waited nervously for Snider's response. "When he got it," Norris said, "he exploded over the phone. He went into a rage. Then either he hung up or she hung up on him and she was very shaken. Then he called back a few minutes later and he was completely calm." But Snider's sudden tranquility masked a new tactic. He would meet Dorothy in Vancouver, he said. He was going to be an uninvited guest at her mother's wedding.

Although exhausted by Snider, Stratten was evidently buoyed by the proximity of friends and family, and by the exhilarating affair with Bogdanovich. She trouped through the usual tourist stops in Vancouver—to Gastown and the steam-powered clock and the statue of Gassy Jack, proprietor of the city's first saloon. The press loved her. "She was very sweet," wrote one Vancouver columnist, "and I don't think she particularly liked the odd little beat of fear or something like it that she inspired in the men whose heads she turned, though she was canny about it."

Snider skulked around the sidelines of his wife's confident celebrity. "There was Paul trailing in the background," remembered publicist Joy Metcalfe, "always trailing, always being kind of shut out in some way. There would be Dorothy, Elizabeth, and myself in this huge seven-passenger limo and he'd come running out and Elizabeth would stick her head out the window and say 'it's full in here, take a cab or stay back in the hotel room.'" Dorothy Stratten had become very professional—she'd begun to listen, as Metcalfe put it, to her own press releases.

"She'd just changed," said Metcalfe, "and I felt kind of sad. All of a sudden it was different. And there was poor old Paul dragging in the dust. He would take a cab and he would turn up and he would sit on one side of the room. He would say things like, 'She's only going to do this for a short time and then we're going to start making movies together. I've got so many plans for her. We're together and Dorothy really doesn't like this anymore, she really wants to get away from it. She's not really happy. She's just

doing this so we can make money so we can get away and do things on our own.' In my mind I was thinking, Paul, you're a dreamer."

Snider moved back to center stage only once. After the wedding he took Dorothy to Gastown and Hornby Street, where he'd made a deal to show her off at nightspots—for a fee. Then Snider returned to Los Angeles, where he had weight benches to build. Stratten went back to New York to resume filming *They All Laughed,* which would keep her there well into July.

Left on his own, Snider began a series of unsuccessful assaults on Stratten's closely guarded assets. Even as the Playmate of the Year pictorial appeared in *Playboy,* Snider was visiting the bank with a blonde or a brunette in tow claiming to be Dorothy Stratten, trying to cash a $2,000 check. He blustered into Bob Houston's office, hoping to siphon off some funds for one of his schemes. And his anxious calls to New York drew fewer and fewer responses.

In June 1980 a letter arrived from Stratten expressing her wish to live separately. "He came over with a Dear John letter," remembered Max Baer, Jr., "and said, 'What should I do?' I said, 'Hey, I told you, man, you treat her like crap and you bring her here and I said you're going to blow it. I told you to take her back to Goddamn Vancouver.' He said, 'What am I going to do?' I said, 'Hey, buster, I have no idea, you're the one that blew it.' And he read me the letter. He was sitting on the sofa crying."

At about the same time, Snider took two corrective steps. First, he hired a private investigator named Marc Goldstein to find out what Dorothy was doing. Then he moved Patti Laurman into a makeshift first-floor bedroom next to his on Clarkson Road. With a little work on her thighs, he told himself, she could be the new Dorothy Stratten—although, in his heart, Paul Snider knew there could be only one.

In July, Snider telephoned his mother. "'Mum, I'm coming to Vancouver,'" she remembered him saying. "'I've got to sew up a few things. I'm going to come and take you to dinner.' He took me, it was the last supper, at Harbor Center." When he came to her apartment, she said, he brooded over photographs of him that she had displayed, hating them, hating himself. "I'd plastered the wall, very neatly, with beautiful pictures that he'd sent, professionally done and gorgeous. He was handsome, so handsome, I can't tell you. Even when he was growing. He went up to the wall and shook his head as if to say: I hate you. That's how they

Stratten rejected this prototype poster by Los Angeles photographers William and Susan La-Chasse—Snider's last chance to profit from his wife's new fame.

made him feel. He hated himself." He had become, she said, childlike. On the way back they passed a cemetery. "He looked at me in silence," she said, "and it was sort of a last good-bye. You could see it in his eyes. He looked over at the cemetery at night, riding by, and he looked into my eyes, and you know something, I felt death right there."

Dorothy Stratten's career seemed buoyant beyond anyone's dreams. With the filming of *They All Laughed* nearing completion, she had begun to think of a modeling career when her *Playboy* contract expired in June 1981. But her interest in the Dorothy Stratten poster still being developed by William and Susan LaChasse may have waned: Someone who'd played opposite Audrey Hepburn needn't appear as a roller skater.

Meanwhile, the LaChasses had doggedly pursued the poster project until they found an interested company. According to testimony given later by Su-

PLAYMATE OF THE YEAR - DOROTHY STRATTEN

Oblivious to a passing photographer in July 1980, Stratten and Bogdanovich have eyes only for each other on the New York set of *They All Laughed.*

san LaChasse, she called Stratten at home to tell her the good news and got a curt response from Snider: The poster project, he said, was off; forget the poster. He told her that he didn't know what had happened. Dorothy had gone to New York, and he couldn't find her or get in touch with her or even talk to her. Seeing their project unraveling, the LaChasses got Stratten's number at the Wyndham Hotel and tried to call her there. Unable to reach her, they decided to fly to New York.

The couple arrived in time for the last day's filming on *They All Laughed,* but they found no trace of Dorothy Stratten. "She wasn't at the hotel they claimed she was at, so I called the production office," Susan LaChasse reported. "I said I'm trying to find my friend Dorothy, could you please tell me where she is shooting. She has been abducted or something. It was kind of a joke." The man on the other end of the line told LaChasse that Dorothy was with Peter Bogdanovich and gave her the couple's room number at the Plaza Hotel. The LaChasses waited for hours in the Plaza's lobby with their transparencies, poster design, and a contract for Stratten to sign. Finally, they went up to the Bogdanovich suite.

"We took the Do Not Disturb sign off and knocked on the door," Susan LaChasse testified later in a deposition. "Dorothy comes— she was just probably woken up, because her eyes were all red and she had a man's bathrobe on, and she says, 'What are you guys doing here?'" She couldn't ask them in, there were others in the room, but she talked to them in the hall for a minute. "She was kind of scared," said LaChasse. "We all sat in the hall on the floor talking and we showed her the picture." According to LaChasse, Stratten liked the poster shot but asked if she could take it inside for a moment. "At first she thought it was wonderful," said LaChasse, but each time Dorothy went back into the room, she came out a little less certain. The impromptu meeting seemed to be ending on

a positive note, however, when Stratten voiced her confusion about signing the contract. She wanted to talk to her lawyer, she said.

The LaChasses returned to Los Angeles and found several messages from Stratten on their answering machine. They tried to reach her at the Plaza, where, according to Susan LaChasse, the production unit denied all knowledge of Dorothy Stratten. Their quarry had slipped away again. Finally, a call came from Wayne Alexander, Stratten's lawyer: Dorothy was not going to do their poster. Period.

When she tried to call Alexander back, Susan LaChasse released a bit of tragic mischief into the world that could never be retrieved. She'd written Paul Snider's telephone number on the same slip of paper bearing Wayne Alexander's number. She dialed and, when a man answered, lashed into him. "I am very angry at you," she remembered saying, "for putting us through all of this and telling us that Dorothy doesn't want to do the poster—or that she is off with Peter Bogdanovich and she was saying a bunch of stuff to him. I don't understand why you are doing this and what you have done to Dorothy. I don't appreciate it." Suddenly, in the midst of her tirade, "this person goes, 'What, what, she is with Peter Bogdanovich?' I said, 'Hello, who is this?' He says, 'Who do you think this is, this is Paul.'"

Stratten had told Paul she was going to London with her friend and costar Colleen Camp. Now Snider knew that in this latter part of July, while he bent beneath the burden of Marc Goldstein's reports (an operative had reportedly shadowed Stratten in New York) and letters of separation and the need to build weight benches for a living, *she* was in some grand hotel in London. Elizabeth Norris learned of the trip from Paul Snider. When she called the house for Dorothy, he told her in a low, even voice: "She went to London with Bogdanovich."

Paul Snider desperately tried to arrest his accelerating slide. He hired a divorce lawyer, J. Michael Kelly, to help him hang on to some of the Stratten wealth. He began organizing women weightlifter shows and was pushing Patti Laurman at the Mansion, to which, improbably, Snider still had some access. He met Lynn Hayes, a Loyola Marymount College student, at a Beverly Hills disco called Max 151 and let her take him out.

According to Chip Clark, such dates were a buffer against the concern of friends. "This wasn't a closed-door relationship. He was a watched love triangle out in Los Angeles.

And this was humiliating publicly. We'd go places and people would talk to him about it. And he'd get bent." Bent to the breaking point.

Even Marilyn Grabowski, who'd spent two years avoiding Snider, in whom she sensed something evil, was moved by the man's plight. One night at the Mansion, when Snider had lined up for the buffet dinner, she asked him to eat with her. "I felt guilty because everyone was on Dorothy's bandwagon," she recalls. But Snider immediately launched into his tirade: *They* had drugged her, *they* were holding her against her will, *they* wouldn't let her take his calls, *they* wouldn't let him see her. "Paul was going beyond any rational behavior that night," Grabowski said. "Without saying I knew anything of what Dorothy was doing with Peter, I said she's probably very busy, she doesn't want the disruption. You've had a lot of fights, haven't gotten along very well, and it's time you put some positive energy into your own life."

Snider didn't listen. "He just kept carrying on like that, mildly delusional. He didn't raise his voice. I recognized that there was something more; because I had come from an abusive family situation my first thought was that she'd see him and he'd hit her or he'd start working her mind and upset her. He certainly would not take things lightly. I was very concerned about it." Later, Grabowski tried to communicate her fears to Stratten. "I described everything I could in great detail so she *knew*—but she didn't want to. It was that kind of fairy-tale existence. I don't think she dealt with reality very well."

Still, Snider's friends began to sense that he had taken hold. "He actually seemed like he was coming around," said Chip Clark. "The last two weeks I was out in L.A. he really seemed like he was getting a grip. He was working pretty good with Patti and was moving along."

So was Clark. "I was moving back to Florida," he said, "and I was taking a couple of my guns with me and I wanted to leave one of them with Louann. And that was obviously the .38 I had lent him as a result of three attempted break-ins at his house." Clark went over to Snider's house to collect the revolver. "He hands me the gun," Clark recalled, "and I check it out. Then he takes it for a second, walks back out in the front yard, aims at the freeway, and fires a round off." But when Snider handed the pistol back and Clark checked the cylinder, he saw that three rounds had been fired. When questioned, Snider confessed that he'd

gone to Bogdanovich's house with the pistol and waited for someone to appear. When no one did, Snider said, he'd fired twice at the house and driven off.

On August 7, Clark left Los Angeles. The loss of his best—perhaps his only—friend saddened Snider. "He was choked up," Clark said. Then came some bad news from *Playboy*. He learned that he was no longer welcome at the Mansion without Dorothy. Snider's spirits curdled.

The object of his growing anxiety had been busy since her return from London on July 30. Back in Los Angeles, Stratten avoided the Clarkson Road house. For appearance' sake she would use the Beverly Hills address of Bogdanovich's secretary, Linda MacEwen; but she'd be living at 212 Copa de Oro. In early August, Stratten made a publicity swing to Dallas and Houston for *Playboy*, traveling with her good friend, Elizabeth Norris. Dorothy was very excited, Norris recalled, and with reason: Back in Los Angeles, Peter Bogdanovich had just told Hugh Hefner that they were in love and that it was serious. But Stratten's deepening relationship with Bogdanovich gave special urgency to her settling her other, fractured life with Snider. Steeling herself, she called him from Houston. They arranged to have lunch at the Clarkson Road house on Friday, August 8.

On the advice of his attorney, Snider tried to show Dorothy a new Paul. It was their first meeting since the Vancouver trip in May. The Queen was coming back, he told everyone. The luncheon had to be just right. Patti Laurman cleaned the house for them, and Snider bought flowers, chilled a bottle of champagne, and put on a fawn-colored three-piece suit. The idea was to remind her how comfortable life with him could be. He imagined how she would dress up for him, and how they would work their way toward a reconciliation. Dorothy arrived in casual clothes, however, and ignored the champagne—and Paul. Their meeting was merely civil. Over lunch she told him that it was time they reached a settlement. When she left she didn't bother to take his flowers. Snider was baffled, according to Laurman. He'd done what his lawyer had told him to do, and it hadn't worked.

Two
days later, Dorothy,
with little sister Louise, went into
the Mojave Desert on a two-day shoot for a sun-
glasses ad. Snider, now barred from the bashes at the *Playboy* Mansion, decided to have a party of his own and staged
a grim barbecue at his house. Marc Goldstein was there,
and Lynn Hayes, Patti Laurman, the LaChasses, and a
handful of others. "We stayed about four hours," Susan
LaChasse recalled later. "Everyone had left and we stayed
because Paul was—was so on edge."

That morning a man named Michael Tuck had dropped
by to see Snider but had missed him. Tuck had run an ad
in the *Recycler*, the paper where Chip Clark and Paul had
first offered their weight benches, and Snider had called

about it. Tuck
was selling a short-barreled
12-gauge Mossberg pump-action shotgun
and this was the only way a nonresident alien could buy
one. The morning after his barbecue, Monday, August 11,
Snider tried to find Tuck's house in the San Fernando Valley
but got lost and gave it up. He arranged to meet the gun
owner two days later, on Wednesday, the 13th. The two
men met at a derelict construction site. Tuck showed Snider,
who had no experience with guns, how to load and fire the
Mossberg and let himself be talked down from the $150
asking price to $125. Even at this juncture, Snider could not
pass up a round of bargaining.

Meanwhile, Stratten was back from the desert, happy and
in love. She and Louise Hoogstraten were Marilyn
Grabowski's luncheon guests at Le Dome in Beverly Hills
on August 13, and the editor found Stratten especially lu-
minous that day. Things were going well: The famous
blondes pictorial had been laid out, and Stratten liked it. She

was going to see Bob Houston the next day to talk about reaching a settlement with Paul, and she thought, she told Grabowski, that they would be able to part friends. On Friday she was supposed to meet with the producer of another film, *The Last Desperado,* and she was scheduled to appear as a guest on the "Merv Griffin Show." Her new life beckoned. But Dorothy Stratten said nothing about another appointment that she'd made by telephone from Mojave: She'd agreed to meet Paul at the house on Clarkson Road the next day, August 14.

Snider talked to J. Michael Kelly, his attorney, on that Wednesday, and among other things, they discussed a $185,000 North Hollywood house that Snider wanted Dorothy to buy. Later Snider called Houston, urging him to remind Dorothy about the house when he met with her the next day. He also sent Patti Laurman over to the LaChasses to be photographed. "We shot Patti," Susan LaChasse remembered, "and through the whole time we were shooting Paul was calling, letting us know where he was. He said he was home, then he was out shopping, and I always talked to him, and I said calm down, Paul, it's okay, she's doing pretty good, it looks pretty good, everything is fine. He says that's wonderful and he sounded very different, very strange. He sounded like—like a big burden and pressure had been lifted off him. He was very, very happy, very excited."

That night about 11 p.m., Snider came over with Lynn Hayes to look at Patti's proofs. He seemed very happy, according to LaChasse, and stayed until after one in the morning. But the conversation took an odd turn. "I just remember that he was being really morbid about Playmates dying before they got their big chance and what *Playboy* does when it happens," LaChasse said. "Like *Playboy*

> *I just remember that he was being really morbid about Playmates dying before they got their big chance.*
>
> SUSAN LACHASSE

usually takes the pictures out of the magazines if they can pull it in time."

Snider also talked to his bouncer friend in Vancouver. It looked like the end for Dorothy and him, he said, he might never see her again, they were splitting up. "He never mentioned anything about guns or anything like that," the friend said. "It was never in his heart."

August 13, 1980, was an important anniversary for Paul Snider, although he seems not to have been aware of it. It was the second anniversary of Dorothy Stratten's first sitting for Mario Casilli's camera. And it marked the day of another playmate's death. Twenty-seven years earlier, little Penny Snider had run beneath the wheels of a gravel truck in Winnipeg.

Everyone had told Dorothy Stratten that her husband was a dangerous man, rendered explosively unstable by his declining fortunes, by his failure to achieve, by his loss of the only woman he seemed to love. Back in 1978, when Snider had first entered Stratten's life, a girlfriend had warned that they'd find Dorothy dead in an alley. Fellow Playmate Rosanne Katon said he was capable of killing Dorothy and himself—"He has no life value." Marilyn Grabowski warned her. Nelly Hoogstraten Eldridge, according to the Bogdanovich account, woke up on Thursday, August 14, with a terrible premonition and called to talk to Dorothy. Perhaps that was why, when she left the Copa de Oro house about 9:30 that morning, everyone but Louise knew of only two meetings: one with Bob Houston, then on to more famous-blondes poses for Mario Casilli. Louise alone knew that, between Houston and Casilli, Dorothy would be with Paul.

Stratten drove the couple of miles from Bel Air to Century City in her battered Mercury with the GAL-X-INA plates for her 10 a.m. appointment with Houston. He remembers her as being terribly uncertain about what she should do. "She just said that she was one unhappy, confused young lady," he recalled, as though she was not convinced that leaping from one intense relationship directly into another was right for her.

While they were talking, Paul Snider called. "It was a very strange conversation," Houston said. Snider asked if Stratten was there, and whether she'd discussed the matter of the house. "One of his projects was finding them a house outside the city where there would be some horses and kind of a retreat." This was the ranch, perhaps, that Stratten had mentioned to Marilyn Grabowski. She seemed to believe that buying Snider a house would also buy her freedom, from him and from her own nagging sense of obligation. "I think everybody, Peter and I and her mother and everybody, was saying that was absurd," said Houston. "You don't owe him anything. You don't even owe him the courtesy the way he's been behaving." She didn't need to see Snider, Houston advised—he could be handled with money and help in acquiring a green card.

Over in the noisy shadow of the Santa Monica Freeway, the morning had been less tranquil. Snider had called his Vancouver friend twice since 8 a.m. "I said to him, Paul, why don't you just come back where you know people," his friend recalled. "Sell whatever you've got down there—he said he didn't have any money—and come back here." In between calls, Snider tried to focus on the approaching meeting—really, the confrontation—with Dorothy. He listed what he needed to work out with her: a green card, money, the ranch. Lynn Hayes and Patti Laurman went roller-skating in Venice about 11 o'clock; he promised to meet them no later than 2:30. He called Houston to talk about the house. After Dorothy telephoned to say she was on her way, Snider checked back with Houston: Had he mentioned the house? He had not.

Stratten stopped at her bank and withdrew $1,000, apparently for Snider, then continued south, away from the promised land of Bel Air and *Playboy,* down to Snider's turf. A little after noon she parked her Cougar next to the Mercedes at 10881 West Clarkson Road. She got out, this tall, beautiful 20-year-old in flats and slacks, carrying a big zippered handbag, and entered the house. At 12:30, Marc Goldstein called from his car phone. Snider answered and said everything was going fine. After that no one answered when the phone rang.

Hayes and Laurman came home about 5 p.m. and saw the two cars parked outside. Entering, they noted that the door to the downstairs bedroom was closed; they supposed that Snider and Stratten wanted their privacy. In the upstairs living room, they found Dorothy's big purse; later, the police would find Paul's list of necessities in it. Hayes and Laurman watched the evening news, then, about 6:30, they went out to eat. Snider's telephone rang and rang, but no one answered.

Steve Cushner, Snider's roommate, came home about an hour later. His German shepherd was jittery and whining in the backyard. The intermittent ringing of the phone worried Cushner. At about 8 p.m., Lynn Hayes dropped Patti off at the house and told her to call when Snider and Stratten emerged. She couldn't bear the sight of her more-favored rival, whose old Mercury still sat outside. Still later, at about 11 o'clock, Marc Goldstein called Cushner on his direct line. They'd been in there a long time, Goldstein told him; maybe he should go down and take a look. Goldstein waited on the phone.

"I knocked a couple of times," Cushner remembered. "Once I had the door open and was convinced it wasn't a bad dream I really don't think that I ever crossed the door jamb because I could see. He was in the foreground and it was very obvious. You don't have to be a doctor to know what brain material looks like." And there was brain material everywhere.

No one knows all of what transpired in the hour that Stratten and Snider spent together on that last afternoon. They must have talked, for Stratten's purse and his list were found upstairs. They must have fought, for police found bits of blond hair in Snider's fists. They had what appeared to have been a brutal round of sex, for they were both naked and there were signs that Snider's bondage apparatus had finally been used—Stratten had been painfully anchored to it not by the usual straps, but by medical tape.

At some point, Snider had brought out the shotgun. Police found two cartridges on the floor, one expended, one live, and surmised that the gun had been used to force Dorothy to undress for the sex that she had largely abandoned on their wedding day. To the experienced eye of detective Richard de Anda, the unexpended shotgun cartridge evoked a nervous killer new to guns, cocking the gun menacingly and ejecting a live round onto the floor. The empty walls had been sprayed with blood and brain. An expended round remained in the gun's breech.

As the police pieced the events together, at about 1 p.m., Snider put the muzzle of the 12-gauge Mossberg against the fine curve of Dorothy Stratten's left cheek as she sat on the corner of their waterbed. She must have started and brought up her left hand to shield her face. But it was too late. He pulled the trigger, destroying her index finger and half of her face. She'd fallen back on the heaving surface of the bed, then slumped forward, her face resting on the floor, her knees bent. There were bloody hand prints on her buttocks

Snider purchased a 12-gauge pump-action Mossberg similar to this one on August 13, only a day before he used it to murder Stratten and himself.

L.A. investigators stand in the illuminated door of the Clarkson Road house more than 12 hours after the mid-day deaths of Snider and Stratten. The bodies were found in a bedroom next to the garage.

A live shotgun round, possibly ejected inadvertently before the killing began, lies on the blood-flecked carpet
near what appears to be a Velcro strap on Paul Snider's
prototype bondage-sex apparatus.

and thighs, but he evidently hadn't moved her, and there was no evidence of postmortem sex.

About 30 minutes later, Snider made his own act of contrition. Having seen for the first time what a shotgun could do to a human head, he nevertheless pointed the Mossberg at his own right temple and blew his skull away. He fell forward with the gun beneath him; his body would show a pale imprint of it.

Dorothy Stratten was buried in that little Westwood cemetery, near the plots she'd wondered about a few yards from Marilyn Monroe's grave. Her epitaph was selected by Peter Bogdanovich from Ernest Hemingway's *A Farewell to Arms*:

"...If people bring so much courage to this world the world has to kill them to break them, so of course it kills them.... It kills the very good and the very gentle and the very brave impartially. If you are none of these you can be sure that it will kill you too but there will be no special hurry."

It ended with "We love you, D. R."

Those who knew Dorothy reacted in various ways to her murder. Mario Casilli shot no more nude centerfolds. Peter Bogdanovich nearly bankrupted himself trying to distribute *They All Laughed*, which became his memorial to Dorothy; in 1988 he married her younger sister, Louise.

Paul Snider was buried in Vancouver's Schara Tzedeck cemetery; his grave bears no fine prose. Speculation about why he killed Dorothy abounds, but his motives are eternally unclear. Some believe he killed Dorothy for revenge, and to sabotage *Playboy* and his rival's new film. "Sometimes Playmates die," he had said. Some say he merely feared the loss of a good meal ticket, or returning to Vancouver a bum. But those who knew him best believe that Snider had plumbed the awful abyss of despair, and that those blasts of shot were the sound of a cracking heart.

"Dorothy's death was kind of a flame-out of that era," observed Rosanne Katon, whose words might be an epitaph for an era. "It seemed that the year after people started disappearing and gay guys started dying, and I kind of associated Dorothy's death with the end of that kind of carefreeness. I know a lot of people felt that way, especially among the *Playboy* crowd. I think that the fact that she was killed saved a lot of young girls a lot of heartache. It was a real loss of innocence." ◆

DOROTHY STRATTEN

28, 1960 — AUGUST 14, 1980

NG SO MUCH COURAGE TO THIS WORLD

HAS TO KILL THEM TO BREAK THEM. SO

KILLS THEM... IT KILLS THE VERY GOOD

NTLE AND THE VERY BRAVE IMPARTIALLY.

E OF THESE YOU CAN BE SURE THAT IT

BUT THERE WILL BE NO SPECIAL HURRY

WE LOVE YOU. D.R.

W here I come
from, even to
raise your hand
to your father
is an invitation for
him to kill you.

MARVIN GAYE

2

Prince and Pauper

Marvin Gaye may or may not have been insane just before he died. Without question, he was a very sick man. On the day prior to his 45th birthday, the great soul singer and entertainer, the charming Prince of Motown, the creator of 51 hits and winner of two Grammy Awards lay on a rumpled king-size bed upstairs in his parents' house in the black middle-class Crenshaw district of Los Angeles. He huddled in the same maroon bathrobe that he had worn for days. The once-handsome face was puffy, the intelligent, almond-shaped eyes bleary and unfocused. His sister-in-law brought his meals to him, and his beloved 71-year-old mother, Alberta Gay—Marvin had added an *e* to his surname when he began recording—came to his room to read him Bible verses.

Behind the closed door, Marvin Gaye did massive doses of cocaine and watched porn videos on the TV across the room. On the wall nearby hung a picture of Jesus Christ; he stared at it when he wasn't staring at the action on the screen. From time to time, his hand went to the pocket of his robe. There was a pistol in the pocket, one of a number of firearms friends had brought to him at his insistence; another was under the bed. He gripped the pistol tightly—Marvin Gaye was convinced, with the paranoid certainty of longtime drug abuse, that someone meant to kill him.

Who that someone might be Gaye never said during the seven months that he'd been hiding out in his mother's house. But his terror was real enough. "He was a scared little boy," said his mother. "Pitifully scared."

In fact, no one at all was plotting against Marvin Gaye's life on that warm Sunday morning of April 1, 1984. Quite the contrary; legions of friends and business associates were trying to help him. Yet no one could get through the enveloping fear and misery.

Gaye was entitled to some anxiety; there were real troubles aplenty—perhaps sufficient to churn a mind already out of touch with reality. His artistic powers were still intact; that amazing three-octave voice had not deserted him. But his career was in decline—a shambles really. Not per-forming or recording and always a spendthrift, Gaye was broke and in debt to the extent of more than $5 million; the Internal Revenue Service, the state of California, a host of creditors, an ex-wife from the second of two calamitous marriages—everyone was hounding him for money.

But the most oppressive force in his life was much closer to the disintegrating singer's emotional center. Down the hall, in a room adjacent to Alberta's bedroom, swigging vodka, dwelled his nemesis: Marvin Gay, Sr., his 69-year-old father, a one-time Pentecostal minister who'd focused a bleak hatred on his oldest son since the boy's birth. The father had beaten Marvin junior unmercifully when he was little, had subsequently ignored his son's every success while resentfully living off the proceeds, had maltreated the mother—and had on occasion threatened to kill Marvin junior if he so much as raised a hand against him. Perhaps it was the awareness of this destructive parent—this perverse mirror image of himself—only a few feet away that fixed Marvin Gaye's troubled mind on the idea that someone was bent on murder. Perhaps Gaye sensed in this other ruined man the death he had courted for years.

The senior Gay had been born into a large family—some said a violently feuding family—of Kentucky sharecroppers. As a youth, he had joined a Pentecostal sect known as the House of God and had gone on the road to preach its curious mixture of Judaism and Christianity, of Old Testament and New. In time, he had become a minister and moved to Washington, D.C., where he met and married Marvin junior's mother in July 1935. She had a son from an earlier relationship, but Gay wanted nothing to do with the boy, and he was sent away to live with an aunt. Over the next eight years, the couple had four children of their own: two girls, Jeanne, the oldest child, and Zeola, the youngest; and two boys, Marvin junior, born on April 2, 1939, followed three years later by Frankie. All were brought up as rigorous Pentecostals, well outside the mainstream of the capital's large black commmunity.

Most of their Washington neighbors regarded the Pentecostals as distinctly odd. While the followers believed in Jesus Christ, they ignored Christmas and Easter, adorned their pulpits with the Star of David, and celebrated the Sabbath on Saturday, not Sunday. They ate unleavened bread on Passover and otherwise observed Old Testament dietary laws; pork was forbidden, as was shellfish. Young people were held to onerous rules: no movies or television, no music and no dancing outside of church. The girls found it especially difficult to forgo sleeveless dresses, open-toed shoes, nylon stockings, and lipstick; a woman could not even show her hair on the Sabbath but had to cover it with a white headdress.

That was what seemed so strange about Marvin Gay, Sr., a bishop — or high-ranking minister — in the church. A slender, delicate, even effeminate-looking man of about five-feet eight-inches and 170 pounds, he made a point of flaunting his religion's dress code for women. He went through periods of wearing his hair long and curled under; occasionally, he donned a wig. And sometimes he matched the hair with women's clothes; Alberta Gay acknowledged that her husband enjoyed wearing her gowns, shoes, nylons, even her underthings. His quirkiness, if that is all it was, made

him the butt of jokes that humiliated his children, particularly Marvin junior.

"I wanted to smash their faces and cut their throats," Gaye later said of those who taunted him about his father. "But I was afraid. I suppose I was afraid that I was just like him — that I was too much of a woman to fight back. Instead of taking my blows like a man, I ran." Among his main memories of childhood was a constant running away; it would become a complex characteristic of the man. There was one adversary, however, that Gaye was never able to

Marvin Gay, Jr., attended Randall Junior High School *(left)* in southwest
Washington, D.C., where he was photographed with classmates in 1954 *(inset)*.

elude: Father, as Marvin senior was called by his children.

Father was severe with all his kids, scourging them often and well with his leather belt or a switch. But he seemed to have a special grudge against Marvin junior. A distant cousin suggested that Gay "had expectations which were too high for a little boy to reach." Alberta Gay may have been closer to the truth, however, when she told an interviewer, "My husband never wanted Marvin. And he never liked him. He used to say that he didn't think he was really his child. I told him that was nonsense. He *knew* Marvin was his. But for some reason, he didn't love Marvin and, what's worse, he didn't want *me* to love Marvin either. Marvin wasn't very old before he understood that."

When young Marvin wet his bed, his father would whip him so savagely that his mother and older sister got down on their knees to pray for God's intervention. "By the time I was 12," Gaye recalled later, "there wasn't an inch of my body that hadn't been bruised and beaten by him." Father could be particularly cruel about it, too. "You see, he's a man with a subtle mind," the singer continued. "He understood that if you're interested in inflicting pain, prolonging the process adds to the excitement. He'd say, 'Boy, you're going to get a whipping.' Then he'd tell me to take off my clothes and send me to the bedroom." Father liked mind games, his son went on. "He'd make me wait an hour, or even more, all the while jangling his belt buckle loud enough so I could hear."

When he was not whopping the daylights out of his son, Marvin Gay tended to ignore him. He rarely gave the boy a word of encouragement or an approving look. Provocation became young Marvin's currency in this sad, bereft relationship. If he could not win his father's love, he could rivet the old man's attention by challenging him. Over and over again, according to his sister Jeanne, Marvin junior would disappear on Saturday morning when it was time for church, wander off after school and come home late, or commit the domestic sin of borrowing, but not cleaning, his father's hairbrush. The beatings would follow.

As mothers paired with harsh fathers are wont to do, Alberta Gay tried to make up for her son's loss of affection. She spoiled the boy outrageously—so much that he would grow up fixated on women and expecting too much of them. The mother who loved him also kept the roof over everyone's head. Father was as lazy as a man could be, so Alberta rose at dawn each morning and rode the bus out to the white Maryland and Virginia suburbs where she worked as a domestic. "I didn't have any choice. I had to bring in the food, and I did," she said. "I'm proud of myself. I kept my family alive." In his daydreams, her son fantasized himself robbing banks to save his mother from "cleaning rich people's toilets for slave wages."

But his fortune lay in music, not in crime. If the House of God's doctrine was rigid and ascetic, its music was old-time gospel, wild, free, and ecstatic, the voices calling and responding, feet dancing in the aisles, hands clapping time, all of it backed with organ, piano, trumpet, saxophone, and tambourine. The idea was to make a joyful noise, and Marvin Gaye discovered his clear, sweet soprano voice while he was still in short pants. "He sang 'Precious Lord' with such beautiful feeling that there could be no doubt of the boy's spiritual gift," said a family friend.

Father occasionally took young Marvin along to outside gospel meetings. But then the parent would grow fiercely jealous of his son's gifts. "When I pleased all the women, he'd look at me like I'd done something very bad," Gaye remembered. "He hated it when my singing won more praise than his sermons."

Neither one was long for the church at any event. In the late 1940s, the House of God split into rival factions: Marvin senior chose the weaker side and soon found himself without a congregation to lead. By 1949 he had returned to the main church and was named to the Board of Apostles, but he turned bitter when he failed to become chief bishop. By the mid-1950s, he was drawing away, into a secluded, alcohol-washed world of his own, where he remained for the rest of his days.

Marvin junior meanwhile was becoming a brilliant musician. Without lessons, entirely by ear, he learned to play the organ, piano, guitar, and drums. But singing was always the big thing. In defiance of his father, Gaye began singing outside of church. At Randall Junior High School, he and a couple of friends crooned soft, sweet romantic melodies in the hallways, empty classrooms, everywhere. "I still believed in Jesus," he later recalled, "but by then so many sorts of music were buzzing in my ear. Other musical voices were stronger."

Gaye loved music so much that some of the kids called him Strange Marvin. The boys would tease him about the music he'd sing, and "he'd smile a strange smile," remembered one acquaintance. "He paid no attention." The girls

Chester Simmons   Reese Palmer   James Nolan   Marvin Gaye   Charles Barksdale

In 1959 singer-impresario Harvey Fuqua *(kneeling)* replaced the talent in his group, the Moonglows, with four young D.C. crooners—*(from left)* Chester Simmons, Reese Palmer, James Nolan, and Marvin Gaye—plus second bass Chuck Barksdale *(far right)*.

went crazy over the love songs of Marvin junior and his friends. For the first time, Gaye began to realize his own great sexuality and the overriding power of his voice.

Father Gay of course denounced his son's singing. "You're running around with bums and you're going to wind up a bum," he raged, punctuating his words with beatings. Marvin junior had grown taller and stronger than his father, but he never struck back. "Where I come from, even to raise your hand to your father is an invitation for him to kill you," he later told his friend and biographer David Ritz. For now, Marvin junior's defiant retaliation was to keep on singing.

He was a bright kid, a lot brighter than average, and he made the honor society in junior high school. But when he moved up to Cardozo High School, he began to look around at his all-black school in a city whose neighborhoods divided along color lines, and he angrily rebelled at the burdens of his race. "School was jail," he remembered. "Learning all the supposedly wonderful lessons of American history, and knowing deep inside that they're lies."

Gaye and his friends skipped class, formed a group called the D.C. Tones and, for all their ire, sang sweet songs of innocent, teenage love. At 17, within a year of graduation, Marvin dropped out of school—and did something altogether amazing for a young man at odds with the establishment. On a sudden impulse, he marched into a recruiting office and joined the U.S. Air Force. "I suppose I thought I was being bold," he recalled. "I fancied myself a flyer—like Errol Flynn with an ascot tied around his neck." But the air force put him to work washing planes and peeling potatoes, and he didn't like that at all. He was a civilian again inside of eight months, with a discharge presciently stating that "Marvin Gay cannot adjust to regimentation and authority."

The most interesting part of the experience for the young man was an encounter with a prostitute, who impatiently relieved him of his virginity. He found that sort of sex—"love for sale," he called it—crude and frightening. "But I also found it exciting"—and ever after, he would turn to such women in moments of distress. "I need prostitutes," he once told a magazine interviewer. "Prostitutes protect me from passion."

Back in Washington and feeling a failure, Marvin could not bear to live under the same roof with Father. He stayed with friends, sneaking home to grab some food and accept a little money from his mother; he avoided even seeing his dad if he could help it. "Mother believed in my singing," he said. "Father was waiting for me to fall on my ass." For a while, it looked as if Father had it right.

Marvin Gaye hated Washington: The government city was deadly for a black musician in those years. There were few big-time places to perform, no recording studios, no one to promote or distribute music. He listened enviously to crooners such as Johnny Mathis, Frank Sinatra, and Nat King Cole, and he joined some friends in a group called the Marquees to sing at school dances and local theaters. But nothing was happening.

The man who broke Gaye out in 1958 was Harvey Fuqua, who would remain an important part of his life forever after. At 30, Fuqua was not only a rising black singer but a songwriter of note and a musical innovator as well. For his group, called the Moonglows, he and Alan Freed, a white disc jockey, had written a string of hits, among them "Sincerely" and "Most of All." The Moonglows were known for what Fuqua called blow harmony, a vocal technique he developed that infused a song's lyrics with a rich, breathy, romantic quality.

Marvin Gaye loved the sound and copied it. Fuqua in turn was taken by Gaye and the Marquees when he heard them sing in Washington. He asked the group to audition and on the spot decided to replace his current singers with these strong new talents. Marvin Gaye was more than ready. "Harvey's world was filled with cool times and hot women," he recalled. "I was ready for a taste of the big time. I saw myself singing before thousands of women, making them swoon, choosing any one of them for the mere asking. That was my destiny, and the sooner the better."

It would all happen, if not immediately, then soon enough. Yet the funny thing was that Marvin Gaye, the great showman and sex symbol, would develop a terrible fear of performing that would at times reach paralyzing proportions. All through his career, he would be happiest away from the crowds and oblivious to the screams, working in the recording studio, where as he put it, "there are only six inches between my mouth and the microphone."

Leaving Washington in late 1958 for Fuqua's base in Chicago, 19-year-old Marvin junior assured his mother that he was not deserting her; he would never do that. He and his father just stood and looked at each other.

Marvin Gaye envisioned himself as the coolest of cats—the black Frank Sinatra, or perhaps Perry Como. "I never wanted to shake my ass. Never wanted to sweat," he once said. "I wanted to sit on a stool and sing soft love songs." What he got from Fuqua was voice-developing hard work, iron-handed discipline, and a succession of exhausting Moonglow tours singing the complex harmonics of what was called doo-wop. The show-biz glamour wore off mighty fast—"just one raunchy club and dirty dance hall after another," as Gaye remembered it.

He met a young woman in the touring group, a dancer who went by the descriptive name of Titty Tassel Toni. Fuqua felt that he needed something besides five-part harmony to focus the audience's ardent attention. For her part, Toni focused on handsome Marvin Gaye. But it was a brief romance. The two fought a lot, to the point where she once bit him so severely on the chest that he wound up in a hospital emergency room in Hollywood, Florida, for stitches and a tetanus shot.

Whether it was Toni who taught Gaye to do drugs is not known. The stuff was part of every musical scene, and the young singer was an easy convert. "I started because I hated drinking," he once said, possibly thinking of his father. "And if you want to be hip what else is there? Slowly, you see the world through this fascinating filter, and slowly you decide you'd rather live your life stoned than straight." Eventually, not a single day went by without a toke or a snort of some kind.

Nothing Gaye put up his nose affected his voice, however. He was gifted with three distinct ranges: "a silky natural, a soaring falsetto, and an urgent growl," as one music critic put it. Promoter Fuqua knew how great the young man could become. When doo-wop started to fade, he broke up the Moonglows in late 1959 and hustled Gaye off to Detroit, where a fabulous black musical empire was aborning.

This was Motown, the creation of a certifiable genius named Berry Gordy, Jr. Only 10 years older than Gaye, Gordy had a vision of where black music ought to go and what it ought to sound like. He wanted to take black music out of the ghetto. He wanted it to sound great over every car radio and hi-fi in America. The Motown sound that evolved was a fusion of rock and rhythm-and-blues, with a swinging dance beat amplified by a heavy bass and insistent drumming. It spoke to the country's teenage condition—black, white, and all shades in between. Berry Gordy called it "The Sound of Young America" and made that his corporate slogan. Motown was perfect for performers as well as recording artists, flexible enough for everyone to develop an individual personality.

Stars were born in galaxies: Stevie Wonder, Mary Wells, Kim Weston, Tammi Terrell, the Four Tops, Gladys Knight and the Pips, Smokey Robinson, the Temptations, Diana Ross and the Supremes—and Marvin Gaye. The sound would turn Detroit-based Motown into a more successful commercial enterprise than all 165 of the music firms housed in Manhattan's famed Brill Building. And it would make Berry Gordy a millionaire many times over.

If Marvin Gaye had been impressed by Harvey Fuqua, he regarded Berry Gordy with the awe reserved for a deity. "BG—that's what we called him—was also the coolest dude I'd ever met," Marvin told biographer Ritz. "Had women like you wouldn't believe. Beautiful world-class women. In his time, Berry's gone with Miss Universe herself. Combine that with a talent for making millions—all in the music business—and you get some idea of the impact this guy had on me. Harvey was terrific, but Berry had a wider worldview. This cat was serious."

Fuqua connected with Gordy as a producer in Detroit and eventually became a member of the family by marrying Gordy's sister Gwen. Meantime, he sold the maestro his contract with Gaye, thus commencing a relationship that would endure for more than two decades. Gaye started out not so much as a featured singer, but as a drummer and piano player, occasionally helping with the song writing.

In 1960 a very important woman entered his life: Anna Gordy, one of Berry's four sisters, 17 years Marvin's senior, good-looking, worldly-wise, and an ambitious power at Motown. "She knew she wanted me and she got me," Gaye said. "But I also knew what I wanted; I wanted her to help me cut into that long line in front of the recording studio." That Anna Gordy swiftly did. Gaye made his first album for Motown in June 1961 and did it his way—as a collection of Sinatra-style jazz-pop ballads, not the thudding rhythm-and-blues that was making Motown's name.

The Soulful Moods of Marvin Gaye went nowhere with the disc jockeys and record stores. Sinatra, Cole, Como, and the other top crooners all sang "Witchcraft" and "My Funny Valentine" with more emotional and musical oomph than 22-year-old Gaye. With Anna's loyal backing, he cut two more singles during the next year, but neither of them were much of a success.

Gaye would never stop thinking of himself as a balladeer, and he might have triumphed one day. But Motown was about hits, not art, and even though Marvin was living with Anna Gordy in late 1961, he had to produce. "Without a hit, even if you were going with the boss's sister," he said, "your ass would be out of there in no time."

Marvin Gaye's hit was "Stubborn Kind of Fellow" and it was no love song. Anna, who had married Gaye in January 1962, had been telling him what a stubborn character he was. The idea floated around in Gaye's head until one day he and a fellow songwriter started fooling with it in the Motown studios. At that point, Berry Gordy happened to come by; he listened for a minute or two, then sat down at the piano and banged out some chords. "How 'bout trying these chords?" he said. "I think you'll sell some records." Observed Gaye, "That was Berry's genius. Just a few chords and I was gone."

Gaye was gone into a kind of music that had little to do with the ballads he'd been singing. "Stubborn Kind of Fellow" was a rhythm-and-blues tune rendered authentic by Gaye's autobiographical lyrics, delivered with streetwise authority. Released in October 1962, the song quickly broke into the Top Ten on the R&B charts. That same month, Marvin Gaye went on the road with the first Motortown Revue, his name up there in lights along with Stevie Wonder, Martha and the Vandellas, the Marvelettes, the Miracles, and the Contours.

He was on a roll. By then Gaye had cowritten the Marvelettes' hit "Beechwood 4-5789" and another big winner for himself, "Hitch Hike," about a quest for a lost girlfriend. That June, "Pride and Joy," a paean to his love for his wife, rocketed to the Top Ten of the pop charts, the first Gaye song to cross over from the largely black audience of rhythm-and-blues.

Finally in the money, Gaye moved his parents out of their Washington, D.C., project housing into a big house on tree-lined 15th Street, N.W. At long last, Alberta Gay could say good-bye to cleaning other people's homes. Her Marvin was on his way. White kids were dancing to his music now.

MARVIN GAYE
amla Recording Artist

Personal Management
Berry Gordy Jr. Enterprises, Inc.
Detroit 8, Mich.

Pensive balladeer Marvin Gaye gazes from an early 1960s publicity photo made for Berry Gordy junior's fledgling Detroit music company, Tamla, named for his favorite Debbie Reynolds film, *Tammy*. By mid-decade, Tamla had become the motor city's preeminent label, Motown, and Gaye had abandoned crooning for the rhythm-and-blues that would make him famous.

He started appearing on Dick Clark's "American Bandstand" television show. He was competing good-naturedly with the Four Tops, and conceded that Stevie Wonder's "superior musical intelligence" kept him on his toes. At his best, said the *New York Times,* Marvin Gaye "combined the soulful directness of gospel music, the sweetness of soft-soul and pop, and the vocal musicianship of a jazz singer." With a good marriage, his new success, and the sense of finding a large talent, he was enjoying himself. But he was still Marvin the Rebel when it came to authority.

Berry Gordy worked all the Motown artists hard, 18 hours a day if they could stand it. They wrote, rehearsed, recorded, went on tour to promote what they had recorded. Motown was slick, bouncy music aimed not just for hip young blacks but for the crossover white audience with money to spend on records. To go with it, Gordy devised a kind of charm school where his artists learned to dress, speak, dance, do interviews graciously, and perform in clubs—the Supremes with top hats and canes, the Temptations dressed up as riverboat gamblers for a gig at New York's Copacabana.

Gaye nixed the classes in a hurry. "Soon as I had a couple of hits, I said 'No, I don't want no charm school. I don't need no charm school and no one's going to make me go.'"

Being married to Gordy's sister, he got away with it. Yet the truth was that Marvin Gaye did not really need lessons in grace or manners. He had a natural poise and bearing—even a touch of the aristocratic—that led people to call him The Prince. Onstage, he was an absolute knockout, letting that superb voice make love to each and every woman in the audience. Sometimes, he would take out a handkerchief, mop his brow, and toss the damp cloth to his fans, then watch, smiling, as they fought over it.

But to listen to Gaye talk was to hear the voice of stage fright and self-doubt. "I'm just extremely nervous about singing," he told an interviewer. "I want to be liked so much, and I've got such a tremendous ego. If it's deflated or punctured or hurt at all, I'll withdraw into my own little pain." He did just that one night in the mid-1960s when he was due to perform at a Detroit club called the 20 Grand Lounge. His nerve suddenly gone, Gaye refused to go on. Berry Gordy, who was out in the audience and ready to blow his top, came backstage and restored the singer's nerve with a hard slap across the mouth. In a few minutes, Gaye was performing with his usual brilliance.

Some time later, however, Berry Gordy was not there to slap Gaye back to responsibility. Flying to an engagement in New York, the singer suffered an attack of the self-doubt blues, got off, boarded another plane, and flew back to Detroit. "Watching Marvin," a friend said, "I got the feeling that he was this incredibly talented man who just didn't like himself."

In November 1964, after the Beatles had stormed the United States, Gaye and his entourage invaded Great Britain for a six-day tour. "I was enthralled," he said. "The English people and I shared an immediate rapport. There was a very soulful thing between us."

Back home, the Prince of Motown remained humble enough to bless his food before eating, as he had from childhood, and he wore a simple, quarter-inch rubber band around his wrist to remind himself that "material things aren't all that important." Still, the garage held three snazzy cars: a Rolls-Royce, an Excalibur, and a Cadillac. The Gayes were enthusiastic partygoers, and Anna was known as one of Detroit's dazzling dressers. A baby boy made the fan-magazine picture complete; unable to have children, in 1965 they had adopted an infant and named him Marvin III. By 1967 the rising star was able to maintain a big house—albeit one handed down from brother-in-law Berry Gordy when BG bought himself a virtual palace.

But beneath the surface corrosive poisons had begun to eat away at the marriage. Shouting had turned into throwing things, and throwing things had escalated to slaps and punches. Both partners were routinely unfaithful. Gaye never could accept Anna's deep love for her brother Berry, and she was increasingly jealous of Marvin's sex-god image—not to mention his singing partners.

Gaye had been performing and recording in duet, initially with Motown's Mary Wells, then later with Kim Weston. But these were mere preludes to his duets with singer Tammi Terrell. "Ain't No Mountain High Enough," recorded in 1967, was a smash hit. They clicked together perfectly, doing what a singing duet should: creating characters who sang their love. Onstage with Terrell, Gaye was the model of romantic young black manhood. Nine tunes from the three albums they recorded together shot up the charts. Though he and his partner never had an intimate relationship, Gaye said, when they sang, they were in love.

One summer evening in 1967, when Gaye and Terrell were performing at Virginia's Hampden-Sydney College,

Marvin Gaye and his wife, Anna Gordy *(right)*, one of Motown president Berry Gordy's sisters, say their farewells at Detroit's Metropolitan Airport in November of 1964 as Gaye sets off on his first London tour. Below, an ebullient Gaye performs with two unidentified backup dancers.

Terrell suddenly looked stricken and fell silent. Gaye caught her as she slumped to the floor and carried her offstage. He never really knew what the diagnosis was, though he was aware that she suffered excruciating headaches—caused, some said, by the fists of a jealous boyfriend. Others laid her collapse to a brain tumor. She was just 21, and Gaye's heartache was huge as she commenced a lengthy series of hospitalizations and brain operations that would end with her death in 1970.

By the late 1960s, Marvin Gaye had acquired another, more dangerous, partner: cocaine. The experimenting with marijuana that had begun on the road with the Moonglows had escalated since Gaye joined Motown until there were occasions, he admitted, "when I snorted up so much toot I was convinced I'd be dead within minutes. I rather liked the idea of there being nothing left of me but my music." In spite of his success, suicide, in fact, was much on Gaye's mind; in 1968, he decided to do something about it. He got a pistol, holed up

in a Detroit apartment, and announced to anyone who came near that he was about to kill himself. His father-in-law, Pops Gordy, patriarch of the Gordy clan and a man for whom Gaye had a great fondness, finally went to the apartment. As Gaye remembered it: "I was sitting with a loaded gun in my hand and he came over and said, 'Now Marvin, why do you want to go acting the fool like this? Give me that gun, boy, before you hurt yourself.' And I did. No questions asked. Pops Gordy saved my life."

Almost in spite of himself, Gaye's career now entered a blazing new phase. Gone was the shmaltzy romantic Motown image of life. He was almost 30 years old and angry at just about everything. His songs were searing, filled with the pain and rage of the betrayals he and Anna Gaye were still in-

A publicity portrait pairs Gaye with Tammi Terrell, with whom he sang his most popular duets. In 1967 Terrell was stricken by neurological problems that led to her death in 1970, at 24.

flicting upon each other. "I Heard It through the Grapevine" told how a man learns that his lover has chosen someone else. Gaye had not written "Grapevine," but he explored it, wrote rock critic Dave Marsh, "as if the song were a lost continent of music and emotion, as if the plotters in the song were his true and personal demons, had in fact scorched his identity all but out of existence. In those three-and-a-quarter minutes, Marvin Gaye earned his independence from the Motown mill."

Released in November 1968 as a single, "Grapevine" sold nearly 4,000,000 records. It became Gaye's first No. 1 hit across the boards, and the biggest Motown smash ever.

That year, Gaye took a little of his money and bought his father a Cadillac. But if the old misanthrope felt grateful, he failed to show it. The singer considered asking his father to come visit him, then rejected the idea. "I really didn't want him around," said Gaye unhappily. "He knew that, and that made him angrier. It was a vicious cycle."

So was Gaye's life. In his grief and cocaine-colored confusion, Marvin Gaye was not performing and scarcely recording; he hid out for weeks without letting anyone know his whereabouts. Like many performers, he was loose with his money. The royalties from "Grapevine" were going for cocaine and whatever else he fancied.

As before with old Pops Gordy, friends came to his rescue. Always a sports fan and blessed with an athlete's body, Gaye was friendly with Lem Barney and Mel Farr, pro football players with the Detroit Lions. They talked him into working out with them. It got him out of the house. His health improved. He ran three to five miles a day, pumped iron, quit smoking and doing drugs. He felt so much better after five months of training that, with his usual bravado and delusions of grandeur, the six-foot, 195-pound singer decided that he could start for the Lions at offensive end. The Lions' management reacted in horror to the thought of the famous Marvin Gaye being injured in a scrimmage. "I've never seen anyone so disappointed in my life," recalled Farr, who had to break the bad news. But at least Gaye had his head back together—and he was about to assert the artistic independence he had earned with "Grapevine."

Since 1962, Gaye had recorded a dozen hit singles for Motown. Despite his problems, he was one of the company's most dependable moneymakers. But nobody, not even Berry Gordy, thought much of his 1971 album,

What's Going On. It was as far from the usual Motown product as carbolic acid from molasses, and while "Grapevine" expressed Marvin Gaye's anguish over a shattered personal relationship, *What's Going On* bespoke his despair for a whole society.

Gaye's younger brother, Frankie, had been in Vietnam and had brought home the horror of that war. Marvin himself could see how veterans were treated back in the States, and he had wept over the student deaths from National Guard bullets at Kent State University. He also knew how audio technology was improving; fantastic things could be done in the studio. All this came together as Gaye gave America a hard, appraising look in a style that bridged rhythm-and-blues and jazz. The album's ethereal sound was a cry from the heart about the bitter realities of war, racism, poverty, pollution. It was a black man's urgent plea for peace and justice.

Advances in dubbing technology allowed Gaye to use his extraordinary range to harmonize with himself. His Detroit Lion friends, Barney, Farr, and others, provided backup singing and chatter. Musically, as one writer said, the album was "a vast, melodically deft symphonic pop suite in which Latin beats, soft soul and white pop, and occasionally scat and Hollywood schmaltz, yield effortlessly to each other." *Rolling Stone* ranked it as one of the best albums ever made.

But Motown Records hated it, at first anyway. "They didn't like it, didn't understand it, and didn't trust it," Gaye told his friend David Ritz. "Management said the songs were too long, too formless, and would get lost on a public looking for easy three-minute stories. For months they wouldn't release it."

When it finally came out in May 1971, Gaye was artistically, personally, and financially redeemed. The album was the biggest smash in his recorded history: over the next 10 months, three of the LP's nine tracks—"Mercy Mercy Me," "Inner City Blues," and "What's Going On"—made *Billboard* magazine's Top Ten on both the pop and the soul charts. The album itself sold two million copies.

Billboard named Gaye the Trendsetter of the Year and the NAACP gave him their fifth annual Image Award. However, Lou Rawls won the 1971 R&B Grammy for "A Natural Man," an award that both baffled and angered Gaye. "I felt like I was swindled," he said. The performer was still living in Detroit, while much of the music scene—including Berry Gordy and Motown—had moved out west

Marvin Gaye *(center)* escorts his mother, Alberta, and father, Marvin Gay, Sr., past the District of Columbia government office building on May 1, 1972, declared Marvin Gaye Day by D.C. Mayor Walter Washington.

to Los Angeles. Gaye blamed the Grammy loss on favoritism and Hollywood politics. Realizing that he needed to be closer to the action, he decided to take a small apartment in West Los Angeles.

Gaye also began performing live again, starting in May 1972 at the Kennedy Center for the Performing Arts in his hometown of Washington, D.C. He ruefully reported: "I got through it, but I was a wreck." At Cardozo High School they asked Marvin, the role model for kids, to say a few words about drug abuse. "I went along, but I really can't remember what I said," he confessed to Ritz. "I'm sure I was a little stoned."

These were heady days for black performers who appealed to a wide audience. Music was hotter than ever, and "blaxploitation" films such as *Shaft* and *Superfly* had appeared, creating what seemed to be a new film genre and a rich market for gifted musicians such as Isaac Hayes and Curtis Mayfield. Later that year, Gaye wrote the score for the movie *Trouble Man,* his only foray into the Hollywood music business. Every song was his alone. Much of the score was bluesy, instrumental jazz, but the title song became a kind of personal anthem that, later, would be seen as eerily prophetic. Only three things in life are certain, he declared: taxes, death, and trouble. He repeated the word "trouble" many times, and the last sound on the album is a gunshot. The album *Trouble Man* became a hit.

Although Marvin and Anna Gaye were in desperate marital straits, they still had not formally separated. They continued to depend on each other: He needed her drive, advice, and influence with her brother; and she enjoyed the status lent by his name. In 1973 they purchased a white ranch house in the Hollywood Hills and he bought his parents the big green-and-white house at 2101 South Gramercy Place in Crenshaw, a block north of the Santa Monica Freeway.

From then on, whenever life became unbearable, the Gramercy house was where Marvin went to hide—unpleasant as the household was. The elder Gays were no happier than Marvin and Anna. Father had begun using profanity for the first time in his life, shocking Mother. He abandoned sex with her and kept more and more to himself, brooding over his vodka.

The whole family, in fact, was in Los Angeles, drawn west by the pull of Gaye's wealth. Most of them lived off the singer. "He was so sick of them using him," his lawyer

Curtis Shaw said. But Marvin never found a way to say no or to limit their dependency. It was the same with friends and hangers-on.

Two years had passed since *What's Going On* and a year since *Trouble Man*. At Motown, it was always "What have you done for me today?" Impatient for product—a term Gaye had come to detest—Gordy talked him into cutting a duet album with Diana Ross, whose career also needed a boost. Ross, pregnant and in a difficult marriage to a white man, was preoccupied and tense. Gaye, however, was up for the gig. He entered the studio for a session with a joint in one hand and glass of wine in the other, and "sang circles around her," the recording engineer remembered. "She just couldn't keep up." The two ended by recording their parts separately. When the album appeared, sales were only average.

While the Ross project dragged along, Marvin Gaye was working on an album of his own entitled *Let's Get It On.* That music went slowly, too. He was doing more cocaine than usual, even for his high-octane habit, and depression was settling in again. Then something very good happened.

Her name was Janis Hunter. She was the daughter of Slim Gaillard, a well-known

black jazzman, and an attractive white woman named Barbara Hunter. The melding of genes had produced the girl of Gaye's dreams. She was 17 years old, making her 17 years Marvin Gaye's junior, as Anna was 17 years his senior. When she and her mother turned up in the studio as guests of Gaye's collaborator, Ed Townsend, the singer could not tear his eyes away from her. "That's the finest woman I've ever seen," he said.

Suddenly, *Let's Get It On* swelled with lusty life. Some listeners swore they could hear Gaye's love for Hunter in the music he made. "There's nothing wrong with me loving you," he sang. "And giving yourself to me can never be wrong if the love is true." Motown's slickness had been wearing thin with some fans, as the guttier southern soul of Wilson Pickett, Aretha Franklin, and Otis Redding gained popularity. These artists influenced Gaye, and so did the sexual revolution, which was well under way. With shouts, purrs, growls, and his own transporting falsetto, Gaye powerfully married carnal ecstacy to the spiritual.

The new album came out in August 1973, sprang to the top of every chart, and became the biggest record of Gaye's career. One initial reorder for the single alone amounted to 350,000 records; a Motown executive estimated that total sales might top 4,000,000. Marvin was renegotiating his contract with Gordy at the time. He was so exhilarated and the record was making so much money that he demanded Gordy personally write him a $1 million check. Gordy did it. Gaye was flying. He was certain that he'd win the Grammy this time.

A hit record traditionally meant a big concert tour, consolidating the artist's success, piling up profits, and creating loyal fans for the next album. But instead of going on the road, Gaye and his "gift of God," as he called Janis Hunter, retreated into the mountains, to a rustic lodge in Topanga Canyon, northwest of Los Angeles.

"It was the most wonderful place I'd ever seen," Gaye said. "If I wanted company, I'd have to meet them at a gas station on the highway and lead them up the hill around all these twisty unpaved roads. The air was clear and the clean smell of the country was everywhere. I had two Great Danes to protect me from intruders, a little phonograph, an old piano, a wood-burning stove, and a righteous woman. What more did I need?"

Gaye remained on the mountaintop with his lover for more than a year. Fans clamored to see him, Motown was

Back on stage in 1974 after a long
absence, Gaye adopted a new look:
silver jump boots, studded tunic, and
silver-threaded knit cap.

Motown leading lady Diana Ross joins Gaye in a 1973 duet intended to boost both singers' careers.

incessantly on the phone, and Anna was beside herself with fury, but Gaye didn't care. "I felt above the world," he said. "Our happiness was all that counted."

Only two things marred that joy: Marvin Gaye lost the 1973 Grammy to Stevie Wonder, and despite that million-dollar check from Motown, he still needed money. He had a big family and a massive retinue to support. And he began to see that leaving Anna was going to be a very expensive proposition.

His deteriorating financial situation led Gaye to come down from Topanga for a concert at the Oakland Coliseum in January 1974. He sang well, and when he did "Distant Lover," Ritz wrote, "the powerful pain in his voice brought down the house." He ornamented his performance with carefully choreographed sexy moves. Onstage, he felt, his "theatrical obligation" was to "drive the women wild," Ritz observed. And he did that with ease.

Starting in August 1974, he was on the road again with a major tour: 20 dates in 20 cities. Gaye included his mother in his entourage. "If Mother hadn't traveled with me," he said, "I'd never have the nerve to do live performances." Janis Hunter stayed in Los Angeles, where on September 4, she gave birth to their daughter, Nona Aisha.

Ebony magazine reported that the August concert take alone amounted to more than $1.5 million, with Gaye playing to huge crowds in places like Atlanta's Braves Stadium. But expenses were monumental for the 20-piece orchestra and all the dancers bopping around. Added to that, Gaye spent lavishly for a five-acre estate in Hidden Hills, a fancy enclave in the San Fernando Valley. The spread included a stable, bridle paths, swimming pool, and several hot tubs. Gaye put in a cobblestone driveway leading up to the huge, Spanish-style mansion; the driveway alone cost $30,000. Marvin and Janis took up residence early in 1975. By November, the couple had a second child, a son, named Frankie Christian Gaye.

Janis Hunter, on the telephone in this 1970s snapshot, met Gaye in 1973, when she was 17. Marvin introduced her to the world in a song called "Jan," recorded for his 1974 *Marvin Gaye Live* album.

Shortly after buying the mansion, Gaye treated himself to something he had wanted for years: his own personal recording facility. Located on Sunset Boulevard in the heart of Hollywood, the Marvin Gaye Recording Studio was a model of extravagance: two reception areas, a state-of-the-art control room, and a studio big enough for the singer's 18-piece orchestra, all done in rich wood paneling and carpets. The control-room walls were hung with paintings of a Christlike Marvin surrounded by children and doves. Behind a heavy upstairs door Gaye had a loft apartment, with a small kitchen, a bath, a huge jacuzzi, and a custom-made emperor-size waterbed. A long, one-way window looked down into the studio below.

Together, the estate and the studio cost Gaye more than $1 million—just as the break with his wife reached its inevitable conclusion. Anna Gaye won a divorce at the end of June 1975, although the terms of the separation would not become final for another two years. The court ordered Marvin to pay Anna $5,000 a month in alimony, $500 a month to help support Marvin III, and $25,000 in legal fees.

Gaye was still recording for Motown at this point, and in 1976, he released *I Want You,* which his devoted fans swarmed to buy. He thought it ranked among his greatest

work, but critics trashed the album—with its background effects of ecstatically gasping women—as a knock-off of Barry White's bedroom disco-soul. The Grammy for 1976 once again went to Stevie Wonder.

The money kept rolling in—and right out again. By now, Gaye had collected at least 14 automobiles and had purchased another house, this one in Arizona. The studio soaked up money, particularly since he stubbornly refused to rent it to Motown for its overflow business. And Gaye blew hundreds of thousands of dollars on cocaine and the Sunset Strip prostitutes he invited up to his studio loft.

As always, Gaye let his finances deteriorate to the point of screaming emergency, then he went on tour. This time, he allowed a British promoter, Jeffrey Kruger, to plan a European concert trip. A longtime fan of Gaye's and a seasoned showman, Kruger found his new artist exceedingly difficult. "No, Marvin was not difficult to negotiate with," he told an interviewer. "He was impossible to negotiate with. You couldn't negotiate with him." Kruger saw part of the problem. "He'd been screwed royally, if you'll excuse the expression, by American promoters, agents, by his family, by Berry—in his head anyway." Nevertheless, Kruger managed to get the trip organized. The Royal Albert Hall and the London Palladium sold out within days of the announcement. That no doubt pleased Gaye and brought back fond memories of his first trip abroad in 1964. But it also scared him; the old stage fright returned and he almost immediately started trying to back out. Britain was enduring a drought, he said earnestly, it would not be proper for him to add to the problem by drinking English water.

When he finally performed, Gaye was received with a frenzy of enthusiasm. "Marvin Gaye swayed, immaculate in electric blue suit and red velvet waistcoat and bow tie, like the Cary Grant of soul, and just as relaxed," wrote one dazzled critic. "It was an entirely young audience of both white and black, whose enthusiasm almost threatened to stop the show at at least one point."

Jeffrey Kruger was not surprised. The performance, the promoter said, was "what all of us who were fans of Marvin had been waiting for, for countless years." Gaye, however, because of his own carelessness and the enormous waste by his hangers-on, went home with far less than the $100,000 he earned.

And back home, alas, trouble was brewing with 20-year-old Janis Hunter. As had happened to him and Anna, Marvin Gaye could not maintain a stable relationship with his new love. "If Marvin found happiness," his mother once said mournfully, "he always found a way to lose it."

The initial issue was one of artistic conceit. The young woman had a nice voice and she desperately wanted to sing. From the start, she'd been hanging around the studio. Gaye resented it. "I tried to make it clear," he told his friend Ritz, "that there was room for only one singer in our family." But she refused to take no for an answer. Now, returned from Europe and putting the finishing touches on *Live at the London Palladium,* Gaye was coming up short for a four-sided album. "Motown was screaming disco at me," he said. "Disco, disco, disco, disco!" So they filled up the last 11:48 of the fourth side with a long disco number called "Got to Give It Up." Hunter finally got her chance to sing background for the track. But Gaye never allowed her to record with him again.

The other woman in Gaye's life saw her divorce become final in March 1977. Anna Gaye had been demanding $1,000,000 as the price of a final settlement, and the singer's lawyer, Curtis Shaw, thought they should try to work out a compromise. All the depositions and quarrelsome hearings were tearing Marvin Gaye apart.

Shaw suggested a creative way out: Pay Anna off in music. The lawyer's idea was to offer $600,000—Marvin's advance of $305,000 for his next album, and the balance to come from royalties. That album, *Here, My Dear,* related in music Gaye's angry, self-justifying version of his and Anna's blighted marriage. When it finally was released, one uncomfortable reviewer wrote that it "made many feel they were listening to pus running from speakers. Its emotional range was too great, its bitterness too close to the surface." Other critics were less charitable. "A soap opera set to music," sniffed *Stereo Review,* and London's prestigious *Melody Maker* dismissed the album as "banal meanderings." The LP's sales were poor.

In any case, the marriage to Anna was history. The deal was finalized and Gaye wed Janis Hunter in October of 1977 in New Orleans; she was 21, he 38. As he had sung to, for, and about Anna, he sang to, for, and about Janis. His first album was a collection of ballads, the kind of songs he'd always yearned to sing. He'd studied them for years, had them arranged to his taste, and finally, in early 1979, he went into the studio and sang them all in one night. Berry Gordy refused to issue the LP. Gaye was enraged, but he was also unnerved—he needed a hit to calm his maelstrom of financial woes.

The debts had been mounting. In addition to the cash drain of the divorce settlement, in December 1977 a Los Angeles superior court judge had awarded $196,800 to four musicians whom Gaye hadn't paid for a year—and a one-time friend told the show-biz paper *Variety* that Gaye had stiffed more than 30 musicians in one way or another since 1973. In January of 1978 the swirl of debts finally carried him under: He filed for bankruptcy, listing more than $3.8 million in liabilities and only $1,270,000 in assets; in actuality, his debts totaled closer to $7 million. Both the recording studio and the Hidden Hills mansion were later sold to pay back taxes.

Again, Berry Gordy came to Gaye's aid. In September 1978 he signed the singer to a sweetheart of a deal: a seven-year contract promising $600,000 each for the first two albums and $1,000,000 for every album thereafter. All Gaye had to do was deliver.

But that was precisely what he couldn't do. Gaye had no hits in 1978, and none in 1979. He toured a little, traveling in a luxuriously appointed bus to still his fear of flying, but the engagements did not make the kind of money a smash

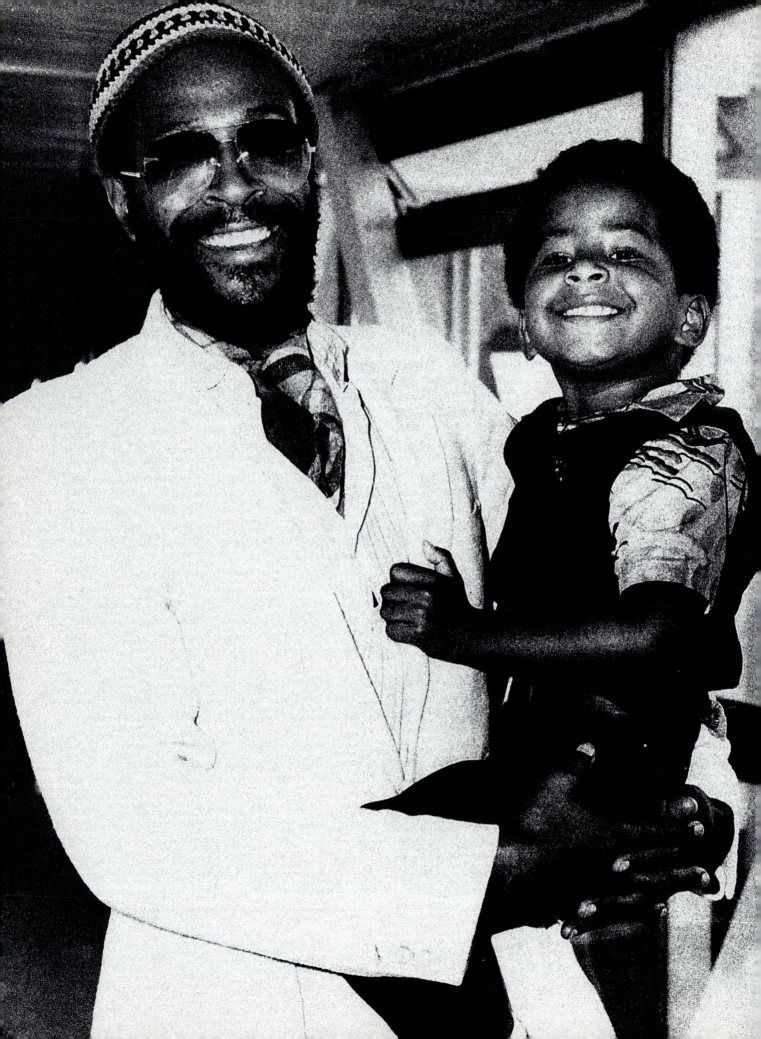

Marvin Gaye and his son
Frankie Christian—called
Bubby—grin for cameras
at London's Heathrow
Airport at the start of a
third, disastrous, British
tour in 1980.

album brings in. His mind was not on performing, anyway.

Anguished thoughts of his wife filled his days and nights. Marriage had not smoothed the disagreements and fights, and Janis Gaye had taken the kids and moved back to her mother's house in Hermosa Beach. When Marvin returned from the road and went to visit, Janis feared that he meant to kidnap the children and called the police. The cops ordered him to leave, but he refused, and a brawl ensued; Gaye wound up with bruises and a black eye.

Mother came to the hospital to take him home. "Whenever he felt hurt, he'd go home to his mother," Curtis Shaw said. In Marvin Gaye's head, she was the only one who would never betray him; but he saw betrayal as a certainty where anyone else was concerned. He tortured both himself and his wife with his obsessive fear of treachery. Often, Janis came back to him, but he drove her away again by insisting that she have sex with other men and then tell him all the excruciating details.

"Marvin just didn't ask Jan to fool around," said his older sister Jeanne. "He'd become angry at her when she'd refuse to obey and wouldn't tell him the stories of the affairs he wanted her to have." Alberta Gay knew it well. "He wanted Jan to go with other men," she said, sorrowfully. "Then he'd suffer with the consequences. He wanted to suffer."

Eventually, Janis Gaye had an affair with the young singer Rick James, who infuriatingly called Gaye "Uncle Marvin"—and, worse, was scoring *Billboard* hits when Gaye was coming up dry. Before long, Gaye could agonize that he was right again about his wife. In September 1979, she filed for divorce and went traveling with Teddy Pendergrass, a singer with a powerful, opera-quality voice who posed a considerable threat to Gaye's eminence. "Suddenly," he told a friend, "I was left without my wife, my kids, my career, or my house."

After a tour to Hawaii and Japan in November, Gaye decided to return to the islands and simply hang out there. He pleaded with Janis to visit him, and she did, bringing both children. "All we did was fight and scream and scratch at each other," said Gaye. At one point, he came close to killing her. "I had a knife so close to her heart that I thought I was dreaming," he said. Janis Gaye fled home again but left their four-year-old son with his father.

Gaye adored the boy and called him Bubby. Yet having Bubby around didn't deter him from one day snorting up almost a gram of pure cocaine within an hour, then phoning his mother to inform her that he was dead, or would be soon. "But God wasn't ready to take me. I was saved that day, only to suffer the next," said Gaye, full of self-pity.

His mother hurried out to Hawaii, bringing two diamonds to hock for her son. "That's how broke he was," she said. "Marvin had tried to borrow money from some of his celebrity friends like Smokey, Little Stevie, and Famous Amos. But they turned him down. Motown wouldn't give him anything because he hadn't finished his record. Some members of his fan club and a few women who used to work for him were sweet enough to send checks for $200 or $300. But it was still a sad, sad time."

Janis Gaye continued with her divorce. Gaye phoned her, begged her, threatened her, wept, but she was determined to have her freedom. "The more I loved her, the more I hated her," Gaye told Ritz. "And the more she loved me, the more I harmed myself."

By January 1980, when Jeffrey Kruger arrived in Hawaii hoping to set up another European tour, Gaye, his son, and Fleecy Joe James, a gofer from the studio days, were living on the beach in Maui. They had found an old bread-delivery van and were using that for shelter, while existing mainly on pineapples and bananas. Gaye, of course, was doing cocaine whenever he could scrape together the money and smoking dope; he'd also experimented with hallucinogenic psilocybin mushrooms.

"He was living in filth," Kruger recalled. "I mean, I've never seen anybody look so ill. Very thin, incoherent. It was quite obvious he couldn't do a tour. He couldn't stand. If he wasn't in the hospital soon, he'd be dead."

Kruger, with the help of Alberta Gay and Jewel Price, an older woman friend of the mother and son, finally induced Gaye to end his exile. They got him back into some sort of shape and persuaded him to try another tour of Europe in the summer of 1980. Even at this point, Kruger believes, Gaye could have recouped his finances and saved himself. Unfortunately, it didn't work out that way.

Alberta Gay, Jewel Price, and Bubby accompanied Gaye to London, Geneva, Amsterdam, Rotterdam, Montreux, and back to London. But the singer was still depressed and hated the pressure of constant travel and performing. He dragged his feet, fought with Kruger, as he always did with anyone in authority, and consumed alarming quantities of drugs. He was spending thousands for the stuff, Kruger said, paying more than the going rate. However, without the drugs, he probably would have collapsed; the drugs made it possible—usually—to deal with him.

"When Marvin was high, he was charm personified and very rational and one was able to talk to him," says Kruger. "When he came down to earth he was like Jekyll and Hyde—this was the side the public never see: a sullen, obstinate, stubborn man who had no regard for any propriety or human kindness."

The grand finale of the tour was to be a royal gala charity show, at the Lakeside Country Club, about an hour's drive outside of London. According to *Variety,* "some 850 people paid between $235 and $1,000 per table for the charity." Gaye was to have supper with Princess Margaret at 8:15, then perform at 9:45.

The princess counted herself a devoted fan of Gaye's, and Kruger was tremendously pleased. "It was a great personal honor and he was representing not only black music but also the American people," the producer told Gaye. "He should be very proud." Possibly no remark was better suited to arouse Gaye's resentment. He snapped back that he didn't want to be a "representative" for anyone. "Why would the princess want to have this nigger perform in front of her?" he asked bitterly.

When dinnertime arrived on July 8, Gaye was lying on his London hotel bed, stark naked and stoned to the eyeballs—and anything but charming. Cancel the show, he snarled when Kruger found him. An evening of testy negotiations followed, with his mother, Jewel Price, and a palace lady-in-waiting acting delicately as intermediaries between Princess Margaret and the Prince of Motown. The Prince, however, was incoherent. By phone, Motown offered him $50,000 to show up at the dinner. The night wore on, then finally wore out. The royal party left the hall. By the time Gaye arrived and began to play the piano for a handful of stragglers, the angry cleaning crew brought down the curtain on his abortive performance. Kruger told Gaye that the two of them were through.

"Soul Singer Snubs Royalty!" gasped the Fleet Street press next morning. Gaye refused to apologize. "Why should a prince have to apologize to a princess?" he asked airily.

When his plane left for the United States, Gaye was not aboard. Too many problems back home. Besides, he had no plane tickets; Kruger had canceled the airfares for the whole retinue, including a dozen musicians. Gaye, his mother, Bubby, and the musicians all moved into a small apartment in London's West End. Alberta Gay had a mattress on the floor and cooked for the group. After a couple of weeks she went home, and eventually Motown sent money for the musicians to fly back. Gaye remained in London, blowing the $60,000 he netted from the tour on drugs and women.

Fall turned into winter and a cold New Year for Marvin Gaye. His divorce from Janis became final on January 26, obligating him to pay her $2,500 per month plus $1,000 for each child. He ignored the court order—he couldn't have met the payments even if he had wanted to. Longtime pals Smokey Robinson and Stevie Wonder supplied some heartfelt advice but no cash. Harvey Fuqua, his old mentor and ex-brother-in-law, gave Gaye a few thousand dollars. However, Motown was reluctant to advance even a penny because Gaye had not completed a promised album called *In Our Lifetime?*

The theme was pure Gaye—philosophical and politically conscious, a plea for the sanity to avoid nuclear holocaust. "Is the world coming to an end in our lifetime?" he asked. A lot of it already was on tape, and he recorded from time to time in studios around London. In early 1981 the people at Motown decided to go with what they had, made some changes without consulting the singer, and released *In Our Lifetime*—without bothering to include the question mark.

Gaye was enraged. Yet another betrayal. "How dare they second-guess my artistic decisions," he told Ritz. "Can you imagine saying to an artist, say Picasso, 'Okay, Pablo, you've been fooling with this picture long enough. We'll take your unfinished canvas and add a leg here, an arm there.'" Then and there, Gaye made up his mind never to record again for Motown.

The question was: Would he ever record again for anyone? He was 41 years old and doing his best to destroy himself. "He was stoned out of his mind and could hardly get out of bed," recalled Jeff Wald, a Hollywood agent who visited Gaye. "The apartment was filled with these dirty-dog women. Drug dealers were running through and God knows who else. Marvin's little boy was asleep in the next bedroom." Wald shoved a wad of cash into Gaye's hands and somberly departed.

Again, there was a rescuer. In the spring of 1981, Marvin met a Belgian promoter named Freddy Cousaert who, like Kruger, was an admirer of American black music and of Marvin Gaye in particular. Cousaert talked Gaye into making another effort to recapture his health, sanity, and career

Shown here in a sparring helmet,
Gaye took up boxing as part of a
health regimen while under the care
of Belgian promoter Freddy Cousaert
(below, right) in Ostend in 1981.

and invited him to come live in Ostend, on the North Sea. Gaye agreed. Cousaert gave him money and an apartment, flattered his ego, and encouraged him to jog and bicycle up and down the coast. For the first time since his Detroit Lions pals shaped him up years earlier, Marvin Gaye accepted discipline.

Cousaert and his wife helped look after Gaye's son Bubby. His drug use dropped off. Cousaert started talking to him about resuming his professional life. Gaye's lawyer Curtis Shaw put the singer in touch with Larkin Arnold, who ran black music for CBS records, and together they began to extricate Gaye from his Motown contract.

In June and July 1981, the able Freddy Cousaert took Marvin Gaye on another European tour, but the singer was still a little shaky and his performance was uneven. He was nervous and not sleeping well because Janis was coming to visit and he prayed for a reconciliation. Yet when she arrived, hope was quickly demolished. They fought again, and she left, taking Bubby with her.

Now Gaye was alone. But he was kicking free of Motown, which had settled for $1,500,000; CBS was glad to

pay it and signed Marvin to a contract that would give him $600,000 for an album every nine months. He needed the CBS deal badly. He owed the IRS, his ex-wives, and his children. He had to support his various dependents. Physically, his condition had deteriorated shockingly. On a visit to Ostend, David Ritz found Gaye flabby, with lines of worry etched into his forehead and puffy eyes bulging out of a thin, drawn face. Gaye's apartment was filled with pornographic magazines, many of them featuring sadomasochistic themes. He had not completely given up drugs, and even in press interviews with strangers he often revealed his mental state. He seemed, wrote one reporter, "a man full of doubts, despair and regrets."

One day in the apartment, Ritz noticed the abundance of porn and suggested that what Marvin needed was "sexual healing." Bingo! It was as if a mammoth light bulb had suddenly flashed on. The phrase galvanized Gaye. In a few weeks, with Ritz helping on the lyrics, he had completed a song to go with the title and delivered a demo tape to Larkin Arnold in Brussels. Arnold was impressed. Marvin Gaye's comeback was under way.

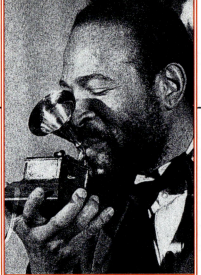

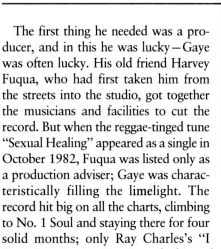

Planting a kiss on the miniature golden phonograph, Marvin Gaye accepts one of the two Grammy awards he received for "Sexual Healing" in February 1983.

The first thing he needed was a producer, and in this he was lucky—Gaye was often lucky. His old friend Harvey Fuqua, who had first taken him from the streets into the studio, got together the musicians and facilities to cut the record. But when the reggae-tinged tune "Sexual Healing" appeared as a single in October 1982, Fuqua was listed only as a production adviser; Gaye was characteristically filling the limelight. The record hit big on all the charts, climbing to No. 1 Soul and staying there for four solid months; only Ray Charles's "I Can't Stop Loving You" matched it and that was in 1962, two decades before. Gaye's follow-on album, "Midnight Love," sold more than 2,000,000 copies.

Gaye, however, was not behaving like a confident man. He dumped Freddy Cousaert, who arguably had saved his life, and then got into a bitter wrangle with David Ritz, not wishing to give his friend any credit for "Sexual Healing"; years later, Ritz's name would finally appear among the song's authors.

More trouble arrived when Gaye's beloved mother developed a kidney condition and underwent a serious operation. Gaye had been living in Europe for nearly three years, but he hurried home to his convalescing mom. He was furious with his father, who'd moved back to Washington, D.C., only a month before the operation and hadn't returned to his wife's side. Marvin told his mother that she should have divorced his father years ago.

Though his career was on the upbeat, Gaye himself seemed to be sliding backward. Others saw it clearly. Curtis Shaw thought he never should have left Belgium. There, the slow pace of life and Freddy Cousaert's good-hearted vigilance had kept the singer's self-destructive impulses under some control. But Cousaert was gone, and in his place came a swarm of sycophantic promoters and flunkies whose main function was to propitiate the Prince. From tour promoters, Gaye accepted cash advances he did not need, thus obligating himself unnecessarily and adding to the pressures. He quarreled over money with Harvey Fuqua, who was still trying to help him. He continued to pursue Janis, haplessly suffering rejection after rejection. Gaye had rented houses in Bel Air and Palm Springs, but he lived mostly with his mother at South Gramercy Place—where with Marvin senior gone he was at long last the man of the house.

That good feeling evaporated in January 1983, when the old man returned and reclaimed his seniority. He had sold the Gays' place in Washington—purchased for them by their son—but refused to give his wife her share. That greatly angered Marvin junior, and the atmosphere of jealous hostility thickened until it became palpable. The house was big, but it was not big enough for father and son. "I sensed the trouble and wanted no part of it," Marvin's older sister, Jeanne, said, and she moved out.

Marvin Gaye got it together on February 13, when he sang "The Star Spangled Banner" for the National Basketball Association's All Star game at the Fabulous Forum in Los Angeles. Conservatively dressed in a dark business suit, he walked to center court, and to a drum pattern slightly reminiscent of "Sexual Healing," delivered a magnificently soulful rendition of the national anthem, with nuances from Mahalia Jackson and echoes of his own deep, tangled feelings about America. The crowd went wild.

Ten days later, another triumph was his at the 25th Annual Grammy Awards. Finally, Marvin Gaye won a Grammy—two of them, in fact, for "Sexual Healing"—best male vocal and best instrumental. His acceptance remarks were sincere and graceful, and he even kissed the two little statuettes. But he blew the performance of his own song because he was "too high."

The Grammys were among the last good things that happened to Marvin Gaye. All the drugs, all the personal problems, all the fears and hatreds and delusions simply overwhelmed the man from then on. He undertook a long concert tour from April to August, and it became a rending parody of his earlier performances. Filled with self-loathing, he told interviewers that he was peddling sex for a living. Onstage, he wore a mock-military outfit ornamented with gold braid and epaulets. At first, audiences were glad to see him in person after so long an absence, but attendance fell off midway in the tour. A panicky Gaye began stripping down to his bikini underpants—something he'd vowed never to do only a few months earlier—as he sweated through

Breaking his vow never to strip for his audience, an exhausted Marvin Gaye stands almost naked at the end of a 1983 tour rendition of "Sexual Healing."

his "Sexual Healing" finale. He writhed and twisted his hips, whispering I-love-you-baby to women in the audience. Backstage, he kept a preacher in one room, a stash of drugs in another and bounced desperately back and forth in search of salvation.

He told his musicians that he was being stalked by murderers. He wore a bulletproof vest, stationed bodyguards onstage and outside his hotel room at night. Somebody was going to shoot him to death with a pistol, he said. Guns had become an obsession; his flunkies went around armed.

Janis Gaye visited him on the road. They fought as usual and she left. He quarreled with CBS as he had with Motown. He phoned the soul-disco songwriter Barry White and asked him to arrange his next album, told reporters that White would do so, then never called White again. He was hospitalized for exhaustion in Florida and had to cancel dates in Tennessee.

When he finally returned to Los Angeles, his mother said that she'd never seen him in such bad shape. In another fight with Janis, he lost all control and slapped her around. Her stepfather, Earl Hunter, was justifiably angry and afraid for Janis, and he said so. Gaye spoke darkly about how they would have to shoot it out with pistols. Hunter promised Gaye's brother Frankie to stay away from Marvin so as not to provoke him.

That would be easy, because Gaye seldom left the house at South Gramercy Place. He lay in the room next to his mother's, doing drugs. The dealers came and went. Women came and went. Infuriated by their presence or his own inadequacies, he sometimes hit them. One woman filed a police complaint. He talked about enemies, suicide, and the angry presence down the hall.

Marvin Gaye "was turning into a monster," his mother confessed. "He just stayed in that room, looking at that gun. Guns were always on his mind." She begged him to get rid of the pistol, and then someone brought him a submachine gun. Alberta Gay pleaded desperately, and her son angrily hurled it through the closed window. A passerby snatched it up and sprinted off. Dave Simmons, a loyal friend from the Detroit days, watched him throw a telephone through the same window.

"I can't describe how terrible he looked," said his sister-in-law, Irene Gay, Frankie's wife, who lived next door. "He'd gone completely crazy. He couldn't even put on his clothes, and when he did, he dressed like a bum." In March, Gaye left the house and threw himself in front of a speeding car; the car swerved away and Gaye managed to escape with just a few bruises. Curtis Shaw again urged him to return to Belgium, where he had been relatively healthy. Gaye promised to think about it, but he only stayed in his

3

Looking for Mr. Wrong

To Lana Turner, Hollywood's reigning sex goddess in the epoch between the 1930s' Jean Harlow and the 1950s' Marilyn Monroe, the world visible from her dressing room at Universal Studios in 1957 must have seemed a nightmare of change. Not that she fretted over the deepening Cold War between East and West, or the use of federal troops to integrate the racially segregated schools of Little Rock, Arkansas. Her world was smaller than that: a life with her daughter, Cheryl, and her mother, Mildred; the husband or lover of the moment; the film at hand. But in her more compact world, the changes she detected that spring smelled like impending collapse.

The studio system that had ruled the film industry and its players was dying; the contractual grip on actors had begun to slip. But this new freedom was a mixed blessing—the studios' clenched fists had also offered security, insulation from fans, and a shield against the glare of bad publicity. A year earlier, Metro Goldwyn Mayer, which had held Turner's contract for 18 years, dropped the fading star as an impossibly expensive luxury, given her continuing lack of success. The last flop had been a 1956 release called *Diane*. In fact, she'd become something of a dinosaur at MGM—the other members of Metro's family of contract stars had already jumped ship to become free agents.

Suddenly on her own after nearly two decades in the cocoonlike embrace of MGM, Turner had tried to start her own production company, without success. Then Universal had picked her up for the film she was shooting now, *The Lady Takes a Flyer,* in which she played a pilot-turned-housewife to actor Jeff Chandler's aviator. Compared with the old days at Metro, however, it felt like an eddy in an industry backwater; and compared with being forever in demand, it felt like obscurity. Where had the Turner screen magic gone?

But a faltering career was only the most visible part of her troubles. Although the petite blond beauty had never exactly had what could be called a calm or normal personal life, things had been especially unquiet on the home front recently. In the past two months she'd had to cope first with another miscarriage—her fourth—and then with yet another failed marriage—her fifth. Her parade of lovers had flown, or married, or died. Worse, a terrible pattern was emerging in her romances—a pattern of wild and impulsive love, followed by a period of gradual disillusionment as she confronted financial, or physical, or sexual betrayal. Her determined, lifelong search for Mr. Right kept turning up Mr. Wrongs. The last husband may have been the worst—the marriage ended when the Baby, as Turner still called 13-year-old Cheryl, reported that for years she'd been the victim of her stepfather's sexual abuse.

The pungent odors of such change pervaded Lana Turner's life, and rendered her fragile. Then, like a sign, there had come a signal of renewed adulation. First there'd been the barrage of phone calls from someone named John Steele; she had not accepted them—one could feel lonely and unloved and still not chitchat with total strangers. Yet there was something about the dogged quality of these attentions that Turner couldn't ignore. One day she asked her makeup man and longtime friend, Del Armstrong, to find out what Steele wanted. "All he wants is to send you some flowers," Armstrong reported back. "I told him there wouldn't be anything wrong with that."

In fact, whatever the mysterious Mr. Steele's other attributes, he was a world-class sender of flowers. Bouquets had arrived in splendid armadas. They were everywhere Lana Turner turned her famous blue eyes. Flowers of magnificent variety, flowers in all sizes and colors, burst from vases that had been crowded into every available space in the dressing room, then spilled out the door and down the hallway. Many were yellow roses, her favorite bloom. How had he known?

Flowers hadn't been enough for Mr. Steele. He'd also sent record albums offering the lilting, melodic music that Turner found so relaxing between takes. How had he known her taste in music? As she had so often before, Turner felt the gravitational tug of an interesting male still unexplored. She

In the title role of MGM'S 1956 swashbuckling flop, *Diane*, Lana Turner *(far right)* crosses swords with young British actor Roger Moore. According to her publicists, she was the first woman to fence with a man on the big screen.

took another look at the little card with his name and number — and picked up the telephone.

The man who answered sounded pleasant enough — a baritone, unaffected, rather charming in fact. He and Turner chatted, she warily friendly as he attempted to establish some common ground between them. They had a mutual friend, he said: actress Ava Gardner, then living in England. Finally: Could he meet Turner, for dinner, lunch, a drink, anything at all? She declined, citing her heavy work schedule and a policy of privacy.

After a few days and another barrage of flowers and music from Mr. Steele, however, Turner called again. This time, when pressed for a rendezvous, she was less resolute. Perhaps, she finally suggested, he could drop by for a drink at her apartment that evening after work. But he should call first, to let her know he was coming. He didn't bother; his black Lincoln Continental was parked outside her building when she arrived in her gray Cadillac, and he caught up with her before she got to the entrance.

"Mr. Steele?" Lana Turner used the sharp edge of her renowned little voice. She liked what she saw, however: a darkly handsome, broad-shouldered man not quite six feet tall, muscular, calm, solicitous to a fault. His steady gallantry soon cleared the air. By the time he left that evening, Turner had agreed to see him again — provided Mr. Steele remembered to call in advance.

Steele did better than that. He not only called, but when Turner suggested a lunch date in her own home, where she could avoid the prying eyes of the public, he insisted that he bring the food. Turner was flattered by his clairvoyant choice of a lunch entrée — vermicelli with white clam sauce, one of her favorite dishes. She also liked the little appetizer he'd sent over in advance — a gold bracelet sprinkled with diamonds. Within a few days, the bracelet was followed by a brooch, another bracelet, and a ring, all in a matching design of little gold leaves inset with diamonds. By this time Turner was more than flattered — her heart was tipping; she was falling in love.

"Do you have a money tree?" she asked John Steele.

The ardent fan smiled, deflecting Turner's curiosity with his easy charm. A money tree? "No," he replied. "Just the leaves."

But the man traveling under the bland, anglicized surname of Steele did have a money tree, of sorts. Under his real name of John Stompanato, he could draw upon the resources of his friend and employer, Mickey Cohen, the man who ruled the Mafia in Los Angeles; Cohen's empire included a Sunset Boulevard flower shop, source of the flowers crowding Lana Turner's dressing room. Working as a bagman, front, and bodyguard for Cohen, Stompanato was part of a very different Los Angeles from the stars' — a subterranean universe of crooked fiefdoms fueled by rackets, overseen by migrant gangsters from the East and easily corrupted officials. There, Johnny Stompanato was in his natural element as hustler, gigolo, mobster, and shakedown artist. He was a true serpent in the Hollywood garden, deft at seducing rich women who'd found their box-office receipts dwindling, their mirrors less than kind, their confidence cracked. He was the blustering, climbing small-timer in every Raymond Chandler mystery, the kind of man who kept a secret stash of compromising photographs of women he had known. How had he known her taste in flowers, music, jewelry, and food? He had made it his business — to hunt, you had to know your prey.

Johnny Stompanato, many have argued, was the quintessential Mr. Wrong, the man for whom Lana Turner had searched ever since her own hustling, card-sharking, womanizing — and altogether charming — father had followed his destiny to San Francisco years before. But the same applied to Stompanato. He had long been a hunter and lover of older women, predatory but also searching for something — a kind of respectability, perhaps — that he discovered in the person and aura of Lana Turner. In a sense, they had come down the years toward each other like marionettes on intersecting wires, doomed to collide.

But there was also a third, fateful player in their short, increasingly unhappy tableau: Cheryl — the Baby. Stompanato may have been looking for Cheryl, too: a female he could charm but could not bully, an accidental angel of death. The trio converged like three characters in search of a movie.

In fact, Lana Turner's life had been very like a film, a composite of hardship, desertion, affection, and outlandishly improbable good fortune. Born on February 8, 1921, Julia Jean was the only child of John Virgil Turner and his teenage bride, Mildred. They had met one night in a little roof-garden restaurant in Picher, Oklahoma, and fell in love instantly while on the dance floor. Mildred, whose mother had died in childbirth, was only 15 at the time and

traveling with her father, a mining engineer on an inspection tour. Virgil was a slightly more worldly 24, and he dazzled the young Mildred with his thick Alabama drawl and the many medals he'd earned as an infantry platoon sergeant in World War I.

Mildred's father was less dazzled, but when he tried to snuff their budding romance, the young couple, as if following a scenario, promptly executed another B-movie plot twist. They eloped, heading for the little Idaho mining town of Wallace. Their daughter, Julia Jean, was born there about a year later and commenced upon her dreary childhood.

After a brief interlude in which he tried but failed to launch a dry-cleaning business in Wallace, Turner returned to the grimy, dirt-poor life of an intinerant miner. Although the family was often without money or a secure home, Lana Turner would later recall bright moments: gay evenings when her father, weary and still grimy from a day in the mines, would crank up a phonograph and dance his pretty little daughter around their squalid home. She evidently inherited his blue eyes and pert nose, and his broad-shouldered, narrow-hipped build.

Virgil Turner had other, less winning traits too, including card playing and bootlegging. By the time he moved with his wife and daughter to San Francisco in 1927, any semblance of normal family unity had dissolved in this other life of his. Finally, the beloved father left his wife and six-year-old daughter and wandered off to pursue a gambler's life on his own.

Turner's departure made hard times that much harder for Mildred and Julia Jean. The mother first took a job in a beauty parlor in San Francisco, moved to a better position in Sacramento, and then returned to San Francisco. But money and food both remained so scarce that she eventually found a home for her daughter with a family named Hislop, in Stockton. There the girl slaved at household chores, except on Sundays, when young Julia Jean accompanied the Hislop family to Catholic church services—a ritual that she found so enthralling she decided to convert.

Throughout this time Virgil Turner continued to pay his daughter occasional visits and even bought her presents when he could afford it. Lana Turner would later remember how on one such outing her father bought her a pair of patent-leather pumps she had coveted, only to have her mother later insist that the "snappy" shoes be exchanged for something more sensible. On another visit, when Julia Jean begged her father for a bicycle, he promised he'd try to buy her one.

But there would be no bicycle from her father. Only a few days after that visit, nine-year-old Julia Jean was summoned with her mother to San Francisco to attend Virgil Turner's funeral—one with military honors. As the girl stood beside her mother and watched uniformed soldiers fire a salute to her father, the one-time war hero, she didn't know that her father had been bludgeoned to death in the street minutes after walking away as the big winner from a craps game in the basement of the San Francisco *Chronicle* building, or that he'd been found the next morning, slumped against a wall, his left foot bare. The shoe in which he'd kept his winnings was gone.

After her father's death Turner spent almost another year with the Hislop family, until one weekend when Mildred Turner came to visit her daughter and found her black-and-blue with bruises. Julia Jean confessed that Mrs. Hislop had flown into a rage over some unfinished household chores and beaten her with a stick of kindling. The girl left with her mother that day, only to be placed nearby in another foster home, with a large Italian family. Eventually, however, Mildred Turner found quarters for herself and her daughter with a family named Meadows, and Julia Jean began what would be a relatively stable and happy segment of her childhood. Enrolled at San Francisco's Presidio Junior High School, she was an average student who struggled with math but enjoyed history, English, and all languages. And she began to bloom.

Perhaps Mildred Turner noticed what a fine-looking young woman her daughter, Julia, was becoming and decided to take her to the land of golden opportunities a few hundred miles to the south—or perhaps she merely sought a drier climate. In any case, in 1936 mother and daughter packed their belongings on a borrowed car driven by a friend and headed for Los Angeles, then the urban heart of a loose constellation of such towns as Hollywood and Glendale, Santa Monica and Pasadena—the metropolis had not yet coalesced into a single sprawling entity.

It was a rainy trip, and along the way their car skidded and flipped. But eventually the wayfaring Turners arrived—their vehicle muddy and clunking, themselves bandaged and battered—in the glamour capital of the world. By chance, they got out at the corner of Sunset Boulevard and Highland Avenue, in front of a large new building that dazzled the newcomers with its broad white facade—Hollywood High School, an incubator for a generation of contract screen talent, and the site of Lana Turner's famous discovery.

Popular legend has it that Turner was sipping a malted at Schwab's drugstore at Sunset and Laurel when a Hollywood agent spotted her and decided to make her a star. In fact, she was sipping a Coca-Cola at the Top Hat Malt Shop, right across the street from Hollywood High, when she caught the eye of a newspaper publisher named William R. Wilkerson, who was having his afternoon coffee. Turner had been a student at Hollywood High for less than a month, but she was already cutting class—typing class to be exact. She and a host of others have recounted the unfolding of that famous day. "There's a gentleman who wants to meet you," said the young man behind the counter. "He's all right. He works down the street and eats here all the time. Do you mind if he speaks to you?"

After Turner had given her approval, Billy Wilkerson introduced himself and delivered the line: "Would you like to be in the movies?"

"I don't know," the surprised teen reportedly replied. "I'd have to ask my mother."

The rest, as they say, is history. Wilkerson turned out to be the publisher of the *Hollywood Reporter,* an influential motion-picture trade paper. Through him Turner was introduced to a series of agents and—after nine months of auditions and one job as a crowd-scene extra in the prophetically titled *A Star Is Born*—to Mervyn LeRoy, the Warner Brothers producer who would launch her career.

"She was so nervous her hands were shaking," LeRoy recalled of his first meeting with Turner. "She wasn't wearing any makeup, and she was so shy she could hardly look me in the face. Yet there was something so endearing about her that I knew she was the right girl. She had tremendous appeal, which I knew the audience would feel."

The part LeRoy had in mind for Turner wasn't much: a schoolgirl who gets raped and then murdered after delivering 18 lines early in the script. Still, only a few days after her 16th birthday, Turner had signed a contract that promised her a salary of $50 a week—twice what her mother was earning at a beauty shop. In addition to her salary, Julia Jean was given a new name—Lana, Spanish for wool and Mexican slang for money. The Warner wardrobe department chose an outfit that would become almost a uniform for the budding actress—a tight skirt, a patent-leather belt, high-heeled pumps, a tam, and a blue silk bra worn beneath a tight sweater of azure wool. Her director's instructions: "Just walk."

The 1937 film was called *They Won't Forget*—and they didn't. Audiences in movie theaters across the country were struck by the vision of Lana Turner sashaying down a street in her tight sweater. By the tender age of 17, Turner had been dubbed the Sweater Girl and fan mail was pouring in from across the country.

Soon Turner was driving her very own car—an old Willys Knight she bought for $50—to and from the sets where she

Flaunting the outfit and the figure that made her America's Sweater Girl in the 1937 motion picture *They Won't Forget,* Lana Turner strikes a publicity pose atop a cotton bale.

was racking up a series of back-to-back film credits. By February of 1938, when she left Warner and moved with LeRoy to MGM, Turner's salary had been bumped to $100 a week, and she was scheduled to begin shooting *Love Finds Andy Hardy,* which costarred Mickey Rooney and Judy Garland. By then Turner had also rented the first of many homes she would provide for her mother and herself—a three-bedroom house in Laurel Canyon. And the Willys Knight had been replaced by a new, fire-engine-red Chrysler coupe.

But Turner was also learning about being studio property. The working hours during filming were long—the workday sometimes lasted from 6 a.m. to 3 a.m.—and Lana and the other "children" were meant to squeeze studies and homework into the 15-minute breaks between takes. And she'd been forced to sacrifice a literal piece of herself. During the shooting of 1938's *Adventures of Marco Polo,* Turner's real eyebrows had been shaved off every day and replaced with fake black ones; after three weeks of this abuse, the real items never grew back.

Not content with directing their behavior on set, the studios had very strict ideas about how budding young stars should conduct their private lives. Turner was developing a taste for a fast-paced, nightclubbing, see-and-be-seen style of living, and she was reprimanded frequently during this period—by her mother, by LeRoy, by the Hollywood columnists, and once even by studio head Louis B. Mayer himself. But Turner was blessed with a Tinseltown variant of the golden touch: Her personal indiscretions served only to increase her public appeal. Fans loved this beautiful, sexy, fun-loving girl. The Beverly Hills Tropics Club named a cocktail for her: Untamed. "We had youth," Turner wrote later, "we had beauty, we had money, we had doors open to us."

They had everything but experience. "Let's face it," Turner brassily confessed to a reporter, "it's the physical that attracts me first. If you get to know a man's heart and soul, that's icing on the cake." At the time, she'd had her first few dates with men. Now, she began to work her way through a long list of attractive, sometimes famous Hollywood males—George Raft and Robert Hutton among them. Then, near the end of 1938, Lana Turner fell in love.

The object of the young star's first romance was Greg Bautzer, a big, tanned Los Angeles lawyer in his thirties. In a pattern that would repeat itself again and again throughout her life, Turner blindly followed the love-struck lead of her heart. She viewed everything Bautzer did through her special love lenses. When Bautzer gave her a little diamond ring, she assumed it was an engagement ring and that the two of them would be married. When Bautzer graciously accepted the fact that Turner's heavy work schedule left her very few free evenings, it didn't occur to her that he might spend that time in the company of other women—notably, it turned out, actress Joan Crawford. For something over a year, Turner protected herself from the increasingly obvious fact of Bautzer's infidelity by throwing herself into her work. But on February 12, 1940, after Bautzer broke a date

Budding superstar Lana Turner and jazz bandleader Artie Shaw gaze adoringly into each other's eyes after their February 1940 elopement to Las Vegas. Before the year was out, she was seeking her first divorce.

with her at the last minute, something in the young woman snapped. She decided to show her inattentive boyfriend—and the world—just how capricious a scorned screen goddess could be.

With a teenage contempt for good sense, Turner accepted a date with bandleader Artie Shaw, with whom she'd costarred several months earlier in a film called *Dancing Co-ed*. But she wasn't just dating. That night, after spending a few hours riding with him in his open convertible through a moonlit Southern California night, gabbing about the pressures of show business and the appeal of marriage and family, she jumped on an airplane with Shaw, flew to Las Vegas, and married him. "GOT MARRIED IN LAS VEGAS. CALL YOU LATER. LOVE, LANA," Turner wired her mother that night. Oddly, she forgot to mention whom she'd married.

The divorce took longer. When she'd first met him on *Dancing Co-ed*, Turner had been irritated by Shaw's arrogance and bad temper and had even aired her dislikes publicly to reporters. But the man was even less likable as a husband. Turner later recounted Shaw's efforts to transform his movie-star mate into a plainly dressed, subservient housewife who read such philosophers as Nietzsche and Schopenhauer on the side. When she failed to fulfill this vision, Shaw became surly, bullying, sometimes violent. According to Turner it was after Shaw kicked down a door one day, in a fury over whether or not she would take his shoes to be shined, that something inside her snapped again. This time she picked up the telephone and called Greg Bautzer—"the only lawyer I knew I could trust," she noted without irony—and set about filing for divorce.

During all of this personal turmoil Turner had been soldiering away on the set, churning out films, the most recent

of which was *We Who Are Young*—a story in which she played a young newlywed with many problems. When news of Turner's divorce from the demanding Shaw first broke, it was no doubt welcomed by the studio officials, who preferred to keep their valuable properties to themselves. But a few weeks after filing for divorce, while on vacation in Waikiki, Turner discovered that the failed relationship had become more complicated than ever: She was pregnant.

"So what?" was Shaw's gallant response to news of her pregnancy, according to Turner. There could be no reconciliation with such a man, and the studios had a strict taboo against children out of wedlock. With her career on the line, she chose abortion.

The year of Artie Shaw, 1940, was also the year of Turner's pivotal role in a lavish production called *Ziegfeld Girl*. The film catapulted the pretty teen from Wallace, Idaho, to stardom. But it did something more. The tale of a young woman discovered and groomed for theatrical success even as her personal life falls apart, *Ziegfeld Girl* signaled the onset of a strange transformation. The real person who'd been born Julia Jean Turner was becoming the blond screen image known as Lana Turner, until it seemed impossible to say whether Turner's real life reflected her screen roles, or vice versa.

After Turner had demonstrated her true star quality in *Ziegfeld Girl*, MGM started casting her in its major productions with the leading men of the day—Spencer Tracy, Clark Gable, and Robert Taylor, to name a few. Lana was considered a dangerous presence by these stars' wives and lovers, often with reason. Gossip columnists also followed her appearances with offscreen celebrity escorts—tycoon Howard Hughes, drummer Gene Krupa, singer Tony Martin, actor-playboy Robert Stack. By the middle of 1941 Turner had run through a platoon of real and alleged lovers, made 15 movies, and raised her MGM wage to $1,500 a week; she had been once married and divorced, had gone through an illegal abortion, and had bought her own house in Westwood, near Hollywood. She was 20 years old.

And, as she often was, Lana was about to fall in love. One evening in the summer of 1942, she met a young man named Joseph Stephan Crane III in the new, exotic Club Macombo on Sunset Boulevard. Crane evoked her father. He was good-looking and charming, loved to play cards, and had moved to California from the Midwest. Turner didn't ask questions. She simply fell in love on the Macombo dance floor, as her parents had two decades earlier in Picher, Oklahoma.

In July, three weeks after they met, Crane and Turner eloped to Las Vegas and were married. But, as she had with Artie Shaw, Turner neglected to nail down a few basic facts about her beloved before the wedding. In Crane's case, Turner had no idea what he did for a living beyond a vague reference to his family's "tobacco business" and a sense that money meant very little to him. In fact, the Crane tobacco business was a combination cigar shop and pool hall in the little town of Crawfordsville, Indiana.

Born Josef Stephenson Crane in 1917, Crane had been a restless young man who'd eventually recast his name in 1939 and headed west in a yellow Buick convertible to seek his fortune in Hollywood. Not long after arriving he had reinvented his face too, with cosmetic surgery to his nose and chin—an overhaul that he evidently paid for with a loan from his friend Virginia "Sugar" Hill, moll of famed Hollywood mobster Benjamin "Bugsy" Siegel. Siegel's successor as mob chieftain, Mickey Cohen, threw a champagne breakfast for the newlywed couple at his restaurant, Streets of Paris.

Turner absorbed Crane's modest duplicities without flinching. Then, after they'd been married about five months, he came to her with a more disturbing confession: He'd married her, he said, before his divorce from another woman had become final; their elopement amounted to bigamy. For Turner, who had also discovered she was carrying Crane's child, this news was unthinkable. She ordered him out of the house.

An annulment was granted. But Crane, once legally divorced, begged Turner to remarry him. Turner resisted, de-

spite compelling melodrama. Crane crashed his car outside her house in what was written up as a suicide attempt; a few days later, he wound up in the hospital from an overdose of sleeping pills. The suicide scenes didn't play to much effect with Turner; she was more susceptible to another cliché. Offstage, in the larger world, another great war was raging. Early in 1943, Stephan Crane's draft number came up. That Valentine's Day, the pair drove to the Mexican border town of Tijuana and, on a side street in the crushing heat with an anonymous passerby as their witness, were remarried. Five months later Cheryl Christina Crane—the Baby—was born.

The year of Cheryl Crane's birth, 1943, was the year that 17-year-old John R. Stompanato, Jr., finished high school and joined the Marines. Born on October 19, 1925, in the Illinois prairie town of Woodstock, about 60 miles northwest of Chicago, young Johnny had spent his boyhood pining for bigger, better, greater, and faster things. He was the youngest of four children, the son of a prosperous barber and successful dabbler in real estate; his mother had died soon after bearing him. Perhaps her absence left a bottomless pit in his spirit; or perhaps the difference he felt between himself and others was that his family was one of the few, in the predominantly Irish setting of Woodstock, with Italian roots. Reared by his father and a stepmother named Verena, Johnny seemed to want for nothing material; he had other yearnings.

After his freshman year at Woodstock High School, the boy was sent to venerable Kemper Military School in Boonville, Missouri, a magnet for well-off young men seeking discipline and an introduction to the military life. Stompanato was a mediocre student, noted for being above average in intelligence but below average in application. He excelled on the varsity football, baseball, and wrestling teams, but now and then he exhibited his fatal flaw: an explosive temper. One of his former classmates, actor Hugh O'Brian, remembered the cocky young Stompanato as a supreme opportunist, shirking his class assignments and his military duties. He also seemed to have powerful friends—O'Brian thought Stompanato's connections, even then, were with the mob. Years later, Lana Turner would be warned by another Kemper alumnus, who remembered Stompanato as bad news—a thief, and a man to be watched.

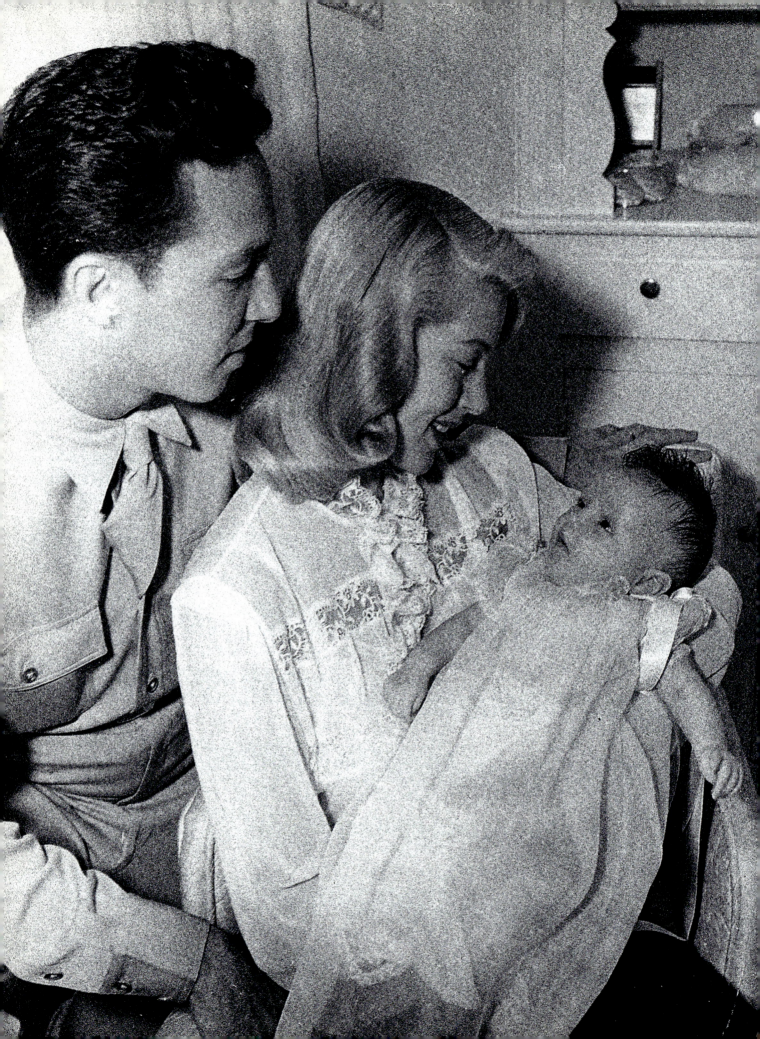

Stephan Crane looks over a beaming Turner's shoulder at daughter Cheryl—called "the Baby" by Lana until the girl was 14. Crane had been called up for World War II military service just months before the July 25, 1943, birth.

Despite his less-than-stellar record, Stompanato in June 1943 was graduated from Kemper, 83d in a class of 113. He did what many upstanding young men his age were doing. He enlisted in the Marine Corps. Classmate Hugh O'Brian, a drill instructor at Camp Pendleton when Stompanato arrived for boot camp, recalled that even here the barber's son seemed privileged: His black mane had been spared the usual scalping, and he was immediately able to go on liberty while other trainees had to stay on the base. O'Brian didn't serve with Stompanato in combat, but he sensed that his schoolmate would not have been much of a Marine. "In combat I can picture this guy hiding in a trunk if he heard any bullets," said O'Brian. "If he didn't have some kind of advantage, he wouldn't have gotten in a fight." Still, Stompanato served in the South Pacific, fighting in the Peleliu and the Okinawa campaigns. He was discharged in China in 1946.

It was during his postwar sojourn in China that John Stompanato's history acquired the slipperiness of the man himself. According to his first wife, a Turkish woman named Sara Utush who worked in a Tientsin dress shop, Stompanato claimed to be a civilian employee of the American government in Tientsin, but he actually ran a string of nightclubs. "He didn't tell me the truth," Utush told a reporter years later. "He said he was 25 when we met but he was only 20. He had a good heart, you know, but he never grew up." A decade later, the Johnny Stompanato story would play just the opposite way: Widely believed to have gone broke operating nightclubs in China, he had actually served as a minor U.S. government bureaucrat in Tientsin.

What is certain is that Stompanato was not in China for very long. In 1946 he returned with his Turkish bride to Woodstock, where his son, John R. Stompanato III, was born. For some this might have seemed the time and place to settle down. But

Johnny Stompanato, with his rugged good looks and his dreams of greater glory, was restless. In 1947, as Virgil Turner had 20 years earlier, John Stompanato deserted his family and headed west, to California. Cheryl Crane had just turned four.

The relationship between Lana Turner and the Baby had been problematic from the very start. Turner's Rh-negative blood produced a near-fatal reaction in her child's Rh-positive blood, almost killing the little seven-pound-fourteen-ounce girl at birth. For two months afterward Cheryl remained in the hospital, her tiny frame subjected to massive transfusions every four hours. Turner had been left severely anemic and weakened by the birth herself and was restricted to another hospital three blocks away from her daughter for the first nine days after giving birth.

It had not been the most auspicious launch for a mother-daughter relationship that was destined to be plagued by absence, inaccessibility, and a seeming dearth of love. Cheryl's father, Stephan Crane, had not done much better at her birth. After growing restless during his wife's long, 18-hour, labor, Crane had left to go watch a boxing match. When he returned to the hospital he arrived bearing gifts for the baby boy he hoped would now be awaiting him—a football, a catcher's mitt, a baseball bat.

Before Cheryl was a year old her parents had broken up for the second and final time. "Mother was not one to get herself involved in diapers and feedings," Cheryl Crane would later comment. "After she and Dad had settled the dire matter of who would have custody of me, they hurried back to their moviemaking and nightclubbing with hardly a backward glance at the nursery." Turner's movie career was stronger than ever at the time—she rated the best bungalow on the Metro lot and a weekly salary of $4,000. And any residual doubts about her screen presence were about to

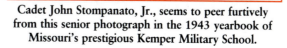

Cadet John Stompanato, Jr., seems to peer furtively from this senior photograph in the 1943 yearbook of Missouri's prestigious Kemper Military School.

Flanked by the proud groom and four-year-old flower girl Cheryl Crane, Lana Turner has her first and only fairy-tale wedding in 1948, to tin-plate millionaire Robert Topping.

be dispelled by her steamy role in 1946's *The Postman Always Rings Twice*—one that just squeaked by the censors.

As for Stephan Crane, after a couple of halfhearted attempts at acting himself, he'd gone back to his more promising talents as a charming nightclub regular and dedicated cardplayer—one of his fellow gamblers would be a rough chap from Illinois named John Stompanato. Cheryl Crane, meanwhile, was abandoned to the care of her Scottish nanny and her grandmother, Mildred Turner.

Before her divorce papers from Crane were final, Lana Turner had become involved with a Turkish actor named Turhan Bey, one of a long string of lovers and husbands who would become, for a little while at least, Cheryl's uncles. After Uncle Turhan left the scene, Tyrone Power strode onto the Turner stage in 1947; Power was the only man, according to the actress's memoir, she ever really loved—Uncle Tyrone was the alleged father of a child Turner was carrying. His advice, according to Turner: "Get rid of it." She did.

While the actress's personal life sputtered along, her career soared. With a salary of $226,000 a year Turner ranked as one of the 10 best-paid women in the country—but she had to earn her money. Motion pictures once shot on studio lots and sound stages were now being filmed on locations around the world. When she wasn't on location, Turner was often on vacation in such spas as Palm Springs and Acapulco, recovering from the rigors of filming. Even when Turner was home, Cheryl remembered that she used to stare at her mother's closed door "as if across a moat. I was forbidden to knock or listen or make sounds that might wake her. When I sometimes managed to steal away from Nana, I lingered outside and pondered for long solemn moments, yearning for the castle keep to yield my fairy princess. To my child's mind, she was the perfect dream of golden beauty, unattainable, beyond reach, everything delicate and soft and feminine that one day I wanted to. . . *what?* To be? To possess?"

The perfect dream of golden beauty had not, however, lost her penchant for doomed romance. An Uncle Bob—millionaire socialite Bob Topping—met Lana Turner in New York and proposed to her by dropping a 15-carat diamond engagement ring into her martini. "But I don't love you, Bob," Turner reported telling him. Topping's cool reply: "You will."

The wedding took place in Los Angeles on April 26,

1948, at the enormous home of Billy Wilkerson, the publisher who'd discovered Turner at the Top Hat Malt Shop. Four-year-old Cheryl was done up as a flower girl in a gown of 19th-century lace and turquoise satin; she watched, nervous and bewildered, as the press mobbed the wedding to report on its excesses, to note the ease with which Lana Turner moved from man to man, and to report that the 27-year-old goddess looked plump. The Baby also spent months at a time with her nanny and grandmother as Turner and Topping traveled breathlessly about the world.

In 1949 Turner set about the business of establishing a proper movie-star mansion home for her little family. The house she bought sat on four acres in exclusive Holmby Hills and had 24 rooms, a swimming pool, a tennis court, kennels, and a greenhouse. Turner named it Mapletop. For little Cheryl, life at Mapletop was a strictly regimented, severely lonely imprisonment. Crane's beloved grandmother, Mildred Turner, had been sent to live elsewhere—a result of growing friction between Lana and her mother, due largely to Mildred's closeness to Cheryl. After a kidnapping scare, Lana Turner increased her daughter's isolation even more. Until she was in her teens, Crane wrote later, she was not allowed past the eight-foot chain-link fence that encircled Mapletop.

The girl's isolation only deepened—everyone seemed to be droppping out of her sparsely populated life. Her grandmother now lived in a separate house, and her father, Stephan Crane, had moved to Europe for a few years. Her mother and new stepfather were often away, and they were rarely accessible to her when they were home. Then, in 1950, came perhaps the cruelest blow. Her beloved Scottish Nana left. She was nearly 80 and it was time for her to retire to Scotland. The turnover rate for Cheryl's governesses during the next few years would rival that of her mother's male friends.

Lana Turner had suffered two miscarriages during her marriage to Topping and, by 1951, found herself saddled with all their expenses as well—the one problem Turner hadn't expected this time around. She'd had some problems with the IRS, and in the past she'd often found herself paying bills for her man of the moment. But Topping was a millionaire, an heir to a tin-plate fortune, a man of inexhaustible wealth—or so she'd believed. Now it became clear that Topping had in fact exhausted his wealth, and he was buffering his decline with alcohol. He was an ugly

drunk. After the second drink, Topping could begin breaking things, and there were increasing signs that he was seeing other women.

Turner evidently tried to keep the marriage together, but not without melodrama. When she found out that Topping was leaving her for a figure skater from Sun Valley, the star attempted suicide. "It turned out that Mother had swallowed sleeping pills and slashed two tendons in her wrist with a razor in a feeble attempt to kill herself," Crane caustically recalled. Turner herself dismissed reporters' questions about suicide, saying, "I'm not the type." The same reporters noted that the monogram *LTT* on the side of her car door had been reduced to a simple *LT*. Lana Turner was on the loose again.

And, again, the Turner career took another leap. In 1952 she appeared in one of her few critical successes, *The Bad and the Beautiful*, as an inept, alcoholic star dominated by a tyrannical producer, played by Kirk Douglas. "You acted badly," Douglas sneers at Turner, "you moved clumsily, but the point is every eye in the audience was on you." It might have been an epitaph.

Turner's next "gentleman friend" was Uncle Fernando—Fernando Lamas, an Argentine film star who was her leading man in a remake of *The Merry Widow*. It was Uncle Fernando, according to Crane, who introduced the little girl to the unclothed male form when he swam naked in the Mapletop pool. As to making love, he was quoted: "We grab a girl around the neck, grasp her arms until they are black and blue, and shred her clothing." Evidently Lamas expressed his jealousy with a similar fervor, for after watching Turner flirt on the dance floor with a handsome new movie Tarzan named Lex Barker, he flew into a rage that, before the night was out, had erupted into spousal combat. It was *adios* for Uncle Fernando.

Lamas's physical violence may have been out of line, but the instincts that sparked his jealousy turned out to be exactly on target. Before long Lana Turner and Lex Barker were a Hollywood item. By September of 1953 they were man and wife—as were Lamas and Arlene Dahl, the former Mrs. Barker.

"Lex Barker, it turned out, was a strange man whose affability concealed cruel self-interest," Cheryl Crane would write with amazing understatement in her autobiography. There she reported that from the ages of 10 to 12 she was raped on a regular basis by her stepfather. According to

Crane, Barker threatened her into silence about his attacks, saying that she would be imprisoned in Juvenile Hall forever, never to see her loved ones again, if she told anyone. She kept her silence for three years, through what she described as a score of such attacks.

By Christmas of 1956, however, on vacation with Turner and Barker in Acapulco, Crane had begun to notice the familiar signs that her mother's marriages typically displayed in their final stages. After a particularly brutal attack by Barker the following February, Crane summoned the nerve to tell her grandmother about him. Mildred Turner summoned Lana.

As Crane recounted it, Turner returned to Mapletop late that night after hearing Cheryl's disturbing news, crept into the house, and stood over the sleeping Barker with a gun from the nightstand, poised for murder. Then she balked. Was "this rat" worth the rest of her life in prison, worth her career, worth ruining everybody's life? According to Crane, Turner lowered the gun and left the room; the next morning she told Barker to get out. Then she took her daughter to a doctor to be examined. Years later Crane would retrieve a copy of that doctor's report and note that in describing her vaginal opening, he had written: "Marital." Turner made no mention of Barker's sexual abuse of Cheryl in her own autobiography.

Perhaps the alleged brush with Barker had strengthened Cheryl, or perhaps the girl she now became was merely a neglected adolescent. But, clearly, trouble was brewing between mother and daughter. In May 1957, on her way back to boarding school after a Palm Springs weekend with her mother, Cheryl suddenly jumped out of the taxi and ran off into one of the sleazier sections of downtown Los Angeles. "The incident was my first real sign that my marital problems were hurting Cheryl," Turner gasped in her autobiography. "How I had tried to hide them and protect her!"

Cheryl told quite a different tale. At the last minute, she wrote, her mother had invited 22-year-old Michael Dante to join them for the weekend. By midday on Sunday, Crane remembered, her mother had consumed a few Bloody Marys and "was seething about something." Finally, according to Crane, Turner cornered her daughter, accused her of flirting with Dante, and intimated that she'd also flirted with Barker. Then she slapped the Baby hard across the face. For Crane, who has claimed that she'd long since felt the stirrings of a lifelong sexual preference for women,

Lana Turner swings into the Hollywood night on the arm of new screen Tarzan Lex Barker, whom she married in 1953 and divorced four years later, after allegations that he'd abused Cheryl sexually.

Turner's accusations must have seemed the cruelest injustice. The atmosphere between mother and daughter grew charged; tensions floated on the air.

It was that April, between the departure of Lex Barker and Cheryl's short-lived disappearance into a seedy Los Angeles hotel in May, that the flowers had begun to arrive at Lana Turner's Universal dressing room. They were from a mystery man who called himself John Steele—the first gentleman friend whom Cheryl would not call uncle.

Johnny Stompanato's westward pilgrimage from Illinois 10 years earlier had taken him into the underworld—even in Woodstock, on the rural fringe of that domain, he'd felt and coveted the mob's privilege and raw power. By the time he passed through Chicago, Stompanato had struck up an acquaintance with a wealthy Englishman named Sir Charles Hubbard. Exactly what their relationship was remains unclear, but Hubbard and Stompanato traveled together to California, where over the course of the next two years Hubbard would give Stompanato $85,000. When questioned by the IRS, Stompanato would claim that he'd borrowed the money; some officials thought that blackmail was a more probable explanation.

Not long after arriving in California, Stompanato had encountered mob boss Mickey Cohen. The rackets czar had moved his bookmaking operation from a paint store on Beverly Boulevard to Michael's Exclusive Haberdashery on Sunset Boulevard, a strip of nightspots frequented by stars. One of his neighbors was budding restaurateur Stephan Crane, who'd just opened The Luau, a swanky Polynesian hangout for celebrities.

Stompanato claimed at one point that he'd known Cohen in the Marine Corps. Later Stompanato explained to police, "I got to know Cohen because I went to his store to buy clothes." Cheryl Crane wrote that Stompanato "met mob boss Mickey Cohen while working as a greeter-bouncer in one of Cohen's clubs." It may be that Johnny had come to town with a letter of introduction from Cohen's colleagues in Chicago.

In any case, the newcomer had soon gone to work for Cohen as a bodyguard, then as a bagman, collecting profits from Cohen's gambling and extortion rackets. According to Cohen's memoir, Johnny was like a kid brother to him and destined for great things in his organization. But he was not a brute. "There was no get up about Johnny being a bodyguard at all," Cohen wrote. "He didn't have the vicious makeup whatsoever for those kinds of things. In fact, although he was a Marine hero, when it come to violence or gun activities outside a war situation, Johnny would shy away completely." Indeed, Stompanato was a Hollywood rarity—he seldom smoked or drank.

As a Cohen aide, Stompanato developed a certain reputation with the Los Angeles police. In 1949 they'd arrested Stompanato on a vagrancy charge; the prosecuting attorney described Stompanato as an associate of "Mickey Cohen and his 40 thieves," charging that the defendant had been seen "54 times in the presence of thieves" before his arrest. Stompanato was found guilty, but when he appealed the case and was granted a retrial the charges were dropped. A subsequent armed-robbery charge was also dropped.

Although the gritty life of the mob seemed at first glance to be the very antithesis of Hollywood glitter, the shadow world of crime held a curious fascination for the pampered denizens of filmdom. Stars not only portrayed mobsters on the big screen, they rubbed shoulders with the genuine items in real life—at parties, in drug deals, in paying to keep the Hollywood wheels greased or to retrieve compromising photographs. The actors might be the big shots on the bright white screen, but people like Cohen ruled the real world. In fact, there was a strange congruence between the realms of film fantasy and real crime. Stompanato was quick to learn that his good looks and racketeering talents could be profitably applied in a world where glamour and romance were highly prized commodities—and where people would pay well to keep their private lives private.

Stompanato discovered he could run a pretty brisk business as a gigolo who catered to older, lonely, wealthy women. Often Stompanato would use aliases—Jay Hubbard, John Holliday, John Truppa, John Valentine, John Steele—and claim to be older than he was to keep his victims comfortable. A cache of sexually explicit photographs discovered later suggested that Stompanato augmented his take with a bit of blackmail.

On at least two occasions Stompanato married his older woman of the moment. In 1949 he'd been married for three months to actress Helen Gilbert, eight years his senior. She'd played Andy's teacher in the Andy Hardy series and appeared in such films as *The Secret of Dr. Kildare* and *Thief of Damascus.* "Johnny had no means," Gilbert later testified. "I did what I could to support him." In 1953 Stom-

panato secretly married another, lesser-known, actress who was also older than he, Helene Stanley, who'd appeared in *All the King's Men* and *Snows of Kilimanjaro*. In the divorce proceedings that followed two years later, Stanley claimed that Stompanato had tried to strangle her mother after she mislaid his handkerchiefs. Stompanato would often stay out all night, Stanley testified, and then would tell her: "I don't take you anyplace because you bore me." Handsome Johnny was a charmer, but never for very long. Besides, he had higher aspirations. He'd dated actresses Janet Leigh and Ava Gardner. And in the spring of 1957, he had Lana Turner—*Lana Turner,* just divorced, abandoned by her studio—in his sights.

From the viewpoint of 13-year-old Cheryl Crane, this new gentleman friend of her mother's—this Johnny Stompanato—seemed different. He didn't gush; in fact, he was so brusque and almost distant that Cheryl wondered if her mother had told him about Barker's alleged trespasses. "He was handsome in an oily kind of way," Crane wrote of Stompanato. "He had the B-picture good looks that were not unremarkable in a town where almost every waiter had a star's profile. Thick-set, powerfully built, and soft-spoken, he talked in short sentences to cover a poor grasp of grammar. He seldom smiled or laughed out loud but seemed always coiled, holding himself in. His watchful hooded eyes took in more than he wanted anyone to notice, I think, and he had that heavy quiet about him that made you wonder what he was thinking. I seldom wondered, however. He was just Mother's new one." She called him Johnny.

But for Crane, the most important thing about Johnny Stompanato was that he had a horse, an Arabian mare named Rowena. Cheryl loved horses. She loved riding fast—indeed, she loved velocity in general. Stompanato not only let Cheryl ride Rowena as much as she liked and as fast as she liked over the next few months, he often went riding with her. The two of them would race at breakneck speed through hills that overlooked the fields where the chariot races for the movie *Ben Hur* had once been staged.

While the equestrians charged across the hills, Lana Turner began to turn up disturbing discoveries about her new lover. She learned, for instance, that he had lied to her about his name, that it was not the cool Steele who'd signed all those romantic cards—it was just a name he went by and, curiously, the name on his U.S. passport. His real name was

Right at home in Hollywood, 25-year-old Johnny Stompanato *(near right)* sits at the right hand of his friend, mentor, and employer, mob boss Mickey Cohen, during a 1950 court hearing.

John Stompanato, and friends had informed her that he had connections with various nefarious characters in the L.A. underworld. She could forgive the name thing, of course, and the shady contacts. Many other fine and upstanding people had links with the shady side of the law. Anyway, it was too late. Turner was already involved with Stompanato, in her characteristic head-over-heels approach to love.

Inevitably, as the year unfolded, Turner's interest in Stompanato began to wane—the idea of Lana Turner being tied, publicly, to a thug was more than her courage allowed. When she tried to stop seeing him, however, he quickly showed her how difficult he was going to be to dislodge. "By the glow of a small night-light I saw a shadow coming toward me," she wrote of one ambush. "With a jump he was on the bed, shoving a pillow over my face. At just the moment when I was beginning to black out, he took away the pillow. Holding my arms pinned to my sides, he straddled me and held my legs tight with his feet. I shrieked at him while he tried to kiss me, using every foul word I could think of." The attack was terrifying, but also somehow exciting. She didn't call the police. "Call it forbidden fruit or whatever," Turner explained, "but this attraction was very deep—maybe something sick within me—and my dangerous captivation went far beyond lovemaking."

Stompanato also seemed to have soared beyond his usual predatory affairs, and he claimed to be genuinely in love with Lana Turner. "I didn't really believe that he would fall as strongly in love with Lana Turner," said Mickey Cohen, "because I had known Johnny when he was with Ava Gardner and Janet Leigh. Johnny was a funny guy with girls. He took them as they came, like they were nothing." Cohen liked to kid Stompanato about his women. "So I said, 'Johnny, what in the hell ya doin' with that broad? For Christ's sake, she's old enough to be your mother.' Johnny went on to tell me, 'No, I'm really stuck for her.' I quickly said, 'Goddam, that's pretty goddam good, are ya kidding?' See, I didn't want to hurt no feelings. And he says, 'No, I'm really in love with her.'"

Turner was scheduled to travel to London, to star in *Another Time, Another Place*. Although Stompanato pleaded to come with her, she turned him down. But once in London, she wrote him, often with passionate affection. "My beloved love," the actress breathed in one letter, "just this morning

Looking tanned and happy, Lana Turner and Johnny Stompanato frolic like honeymooners during a two-month Acapulco winter holiday in 1958. She later claimed he kept her a virtual prisoner on the trip.

your precious exciting letter arrived. Every line warms me and makes me ache and miss you each tiny moment. It's beautiful—yet terrible. . . ."

In another, after talking to Stompanato on the telephone: "God, it was so wonderful to hear your voice again, Darling Daddy!" A dozen letters, later made public by Mickey Cohen, were peppered with the endearments of mutually obsessed lovers. Throughout them Turner addresses Stompanato as Daddy, Papito, and Papi; she signs her letters Mummy, Mom, Lanita. Neither seems to have heard, in these endearments, the sad quest for a lost parent.

Before long Turner had bought Stompanato a one-way ticket to London, and the two were interacting with the dangerous blend of passion and violence they seemed to find irresistible. Increasingly at issue was Turner's reluctance to be seen in public with Stompanato. When she steadfastly refused to let him visit her on the set, Turner recounted, Stompanato countered with "preposterous accusations" until finally, one Friday night shortly before Christmas, she told him to pack his bags and go home. When Stompanato refused, Turner threatened to call the police.

"I reached for the phone," she said, "but he knocked it away and lunged for my throat." She managed to get off a final scream that attracted her maid, who intervened. But Turner's vocal cords had been damaged so badly that it was almost three weeks before she could speak normally.

Cheryl Crane's account of these London fights suggested that one of the "preposterous accusations" had to do with a budding romance between Turner and her costar, actor Sean Connery. At one point Stompanato stormed onto the set and "waved a gun at Connery," Crane wrote. "Unperturbed, the soon-to-be James Bond flattened John with a right to the nose." Whatever its stimulus, Stompanato's behavior was sufficiently upsetting to Turner that, with the help of friends she'd confided in, she contacted Scotland Yard and had Stompanato deported from the country. He was physically escorted to an airplane and sent home.

Within a month, even this wound had healed. By January of 1958 Stompanato was suggesting that they should meet again, and Turner's letters back to him seemed to second the emotion: "Oh oh oh! How lonely it all is—hearing the music we played together!" Turner gushed. "Plus your last gift of records—Darling they bring happy aches. . . . But it's only a few more days and then OURS!!!"

According to Turner's memoir, Stompanato intercepted her in the Copenhagen airport and accompanied her uninvited to Acapulco. But whether it was by invitation or ambush, Stompanato spent the next eight weeks in Mexico with the actress. "Mother recalls life inside their hideaway as 'a sort of armed truce, marred by a few violent arguments,'" Cheryl Crane wrote of that interlude. "He smashed a door, slapped her around, and held a gun to her head, mainly because she refused to sleep with him. Instead, she preferred to get drunk and blot everything out."

Yet, despite such dramatic happenings, the pair retained the outward trappings of lovers on a holiday. Photographs taken on fishing and sailing trips show Turner and Stompanato smiling happily. In a letter he wrote to his stepmother in Woodstock, Stompanato described the good times he was having and noted that "Lana's as brown as a berry." Stompanato and Cheryl Crane even exchanged chatty notes, with Cheryl signing hers "Love ya & miss ya loads." Turner brooded, according to her memoir, over being caught up with a man like Stompanato, and being too weak to break his grip on her.

Then, resolve arrived in the form of unexpected, but very good, news. Her agent phoned to tell Turner that for the first time in her long career she'd been nominated for an Academy Award: best actress, for her portrayal of the mother of a troubled teenage daughter in *Peyton Place*. As always, it was difficult to tell where the movie ended and the real world began.

On March 24, 1958, the night of the 30th annual Academy Awards ceremony, Cheryl Crane watched her mother prepare with mixed admiration and apprehension. After 22 years and 40 movies, Lana Turner was a contender in the category of best actress. Turner had decided it was too important an evening for her to appear with John Stompanato hanging on her arm.

Getting dressed that night had been rather nerve-racking—during the entire time Stompanato had hung around Turner, pleading with her to take him and threatening her if she didn't. But she held fast. She was going with her mother, Mildred Turner, and her daughter, and that was that. And she was going to show the crowd at Hollywood Boulevard's old Pantages Theater that even at 37 she was still a knockout. For this most amazing night of her life she squeezed herself into a most amazing gown. Her strapless white lace gown hugged her famous figure down to the

knees, where it flared out into several tiers of stiffened lace. The outfit was set off with a constellation of diamonds.

But Turner was not the only family member dressed to kill. Cheryl was turned out for the first time in what she called a grown-up dress, in contrast to the child's clothing usually given her to wear. It was more than a fashion statement, however. Until quite recently, this five-foot-ten, 145-pound 14-year-old had been forbidden to watch any grown-up movies—including those that featured her mother. Now the Baby was suddenly a young woman, socializing with all the biggest stars, whom she recognized because she'd met them in her home. As she wobbled down the Pantages aisle in satin high heels and a halter-top chiffon gown colored "the lurid green of Prell shampoo," Crane felt for the first time that she was stepping out into the real world with a certain style all her own.

Lana Turner didn't win the best actress award that night—it went to Joanne Woodward for her performance in *The Three Faces of Eve*—but Cheryl and Turner thought the event was a smashing success nevertheless. As it turned out, taking Cheryl with her had been just the right touch. Now that the film world had honored her portrayal of a mother of a troubled teenage daughter, Turner seemed to have warmed to the role of mature mother. Cheryl noticed the slight shift in Turner's maternal tactics herself—a tendency to imitate the mother-daughter scenes in *Peyton Place*. On that Oscar night it really felt as if a new closeness might be developing between them. Turner had even invited Crane to spend the night with her in the Bel Air Hotel bungalow she was renting.

The darkness around them was thick with the scent of night-blooming jasmine, Crane remembered, as she and her mother tiptoed barefoot down the garden path to the bungalow later that night. Their feet were dying from hours of dancing in high-heeled shoes, and their heads were just a little light from champagne—Cheryl had managed to sneak a few sips. They were suffering a slight case of the giggles. The pair settled down for a rare mother-daughter chat.

They talked about Crane's teenage preoccupations of horses, school, the heart, and about whether Turner would take her latest film offer—a role starring opposite Jimmy Stewart in an Otto Preminger film entitled *Anatomy of a Murder,* which Turner later declined. They shared their impressions of the party that night, and then, just before they retired to their respective bedrooms, Turner announced that she'd rented a new house on Bel Air's North Bedford Drive. For the first time in years, Crane would share a home with her mother, a prospect that both attracted and repelled the girl—she wanted to be with Turner, but she would miss the freedom of boarding school and the occasional weekend with her grandmother.

Still, the evening had seemed so magical, so promising that Cheryl offered no resistance, even when Turner said she'd have Stompanato drive over to Mildred Turner's apartment to pack up Crane's belongings. That night, according to her memoir, as she shed her first grown-up gown for a girlish nightie and crawled into bed at 3 a.m., Cheryl Crane allowed herself to hope that her life was about to get better. She was dead wrong.

Moments later the bungalow shook with the sound of an angry man shouting in her mother's bedroom. It was Stompanato. "You bitch!" Crane recalled hearing. "How dare you tell me to leave? You think you're such a big star!" Crane was confused. The John Stompanato she knew had always spoken in quiet, careful tones. "This John was crude," she wrote, "with a cold, ragged edge to his voice."

Just back in Los Angeles from Acapulco, John Stompanato gets a warm welcome at the airport from Cheryl Crane while publicity-shy Turner reluctantly chats with a reporter.

The angry exchange was followed by crashes and smashes and the sound of glass shattering, punctuated by long silences. Then the fight continued in waves, escalating to a piercing scream from Turner, then another silence; this time Turner crept into her daughter's room. But Crane had withdrawn. She'd seen this drama before: It meant that Johnny Stompanato was about to be history, another of her mother's ex-men. When Turner whispered to Crane, the girl pretended to be asleep.

"John had slapped me around before but this was a full-scale beating, and I was in fear for my life," Turner would write of that same fight. "He punched and slapped me again and again. He finally slammed me against the closet door, and the back of my head hit the door good and hard." The damage she suffered from his blows was compounded, Turner said, by the fact that she was wearing heavy diamond earrings that dug into her neck and scraped her face.

According to Turner, shame at her abused condition kept her from going to the police or friends with her troubles. But there were other reasons, she said, for keeping quiet: Stompanato had threatened to hurt her by hurting her mother or Cheryl. He could have the girl kidnapped or have them both killed. Certainly, the use of such threats was in his nature. Hugh O'Brian recalled that, when he refused to lend his Kemper classmate money after Stompanato had reneged on an earlier loan, Johnny warned him how easy he would be to hurt. "Do you know what it would cost to get somebody to break your legs or throw some acid on your face?"

Dazzling in a strapless lace dress and diamonds, Lana Turner attends the 1958 Academy Awards banquet with 14-year-old Cheryl, whose youthful beauty is reminiscent of her mother as a starlet.

O'Brian quoted. "Well," he added, "I knew some important people too, and they told him to back off and he did."

The morning after the Academy Awards ceremony Crane noticed that her mother's hands were trembling and that she had applied the all-concealing orange pancake makeup used in Technicolor photography. But Crane said nothing about this, or about the shouts she had heard, and Turner too went about her business as if nothing unusual had happened the night before.

Four days later, Crane again heard the domestic storm begin to rage. On Monday, April 1, she'd had oral surgery at the dentist's office, where she was given sodium pentothal and Demerol painkiller pills. After the surgery Turner had driven Crane home and tucked her into bed to rest. But before long, as Crane lay there in a Demerol haze, she'd heard the shouting begin again. It was Stompanato once more, but with heightened menace in his voice. Perhaps emboldened by the drugs, this time Crane took the plunge. She called to her mother and asked what was going on. Turner burst into Crane's room and insisted that everything was fine, that Stompanato was just leaving. But Crane noticed that one of her mother's cheeks looked puffy red and that she had those trembling hands again.

When Crane heard Stompanato threatening to cut up Turner's famous face, she called out once more to her mother. And once again Turner called back that everything was all right. But minutes later, after the front door had slammed loudly, Turner was standing in Crane's doorway. Crane beckoned her in, and in a scene that the daughter would later describe as a "lingering close-up," Turner blurted out the nasty truth about Johnny Stompanato—and asked the Baby's help.

On a rainy Good Friday—April 4, 1958—Cheryl Crane sat in her bedroom in her mother's newly rented house on Bedford Drive and tried to do some homework. Although Crane was still on her Easter vacation, she had a physiology term paper due the following Monday—a paper on the human circulatory system—and she had not yet started to write it.

Downstairs her mother and two guests—Del Armstrong and a businessman from Hawaii named Bill Brooks—were sitting in the bar having drinks. It was a quiet, almost gloomy gathering. Stompanato, who'd been around almost constantly for the past few days, had left the party after

some hard words—the coziness of the tipsy little group had infuriated him, as had Turner's plans to dine alone with Brooks the next evening.

As Crane sat trying to study, her mother called to her from downstairs. The guests had left, and she wanted to talk. Crane went down to find her mother pacing the floor, furiously drawing on a cigarette—anger that millions of fans had seen again and again in Turner films. Hers was not the fury of a woman scorned, however, but of one deceived on a point of painful sensitivity: age. Brooks had recognized Stompanato—they'd been at Kemper Military School together. After Stompanato left to run some errands, Brooks

A tree casts an ominous shadow across the second-story window of Lana Turner's pink master bedroom in this newly rented mansion on Beverly Hills' North Bedford Drive.

had cautioned Turner about her man. He'd been in the class of '43 with Johnny; the guy had been a snake, a thief, a troublemaker; he was a dangerous man. Turner heard the warning, but not nearly so sharply as the arithmetic of that graduating class. If he'd been in the class of 1943, Johnny Stompanato wasn't 42, as he'd alleged, but almost 33. "Which makes me five years older than he is!" she reportedly exclaimed to Cheryl. "I'm such a fool!"

Back in her bedroom, dressed in fuzzy pink slippers and an old nightie after a long shower, Crane tried again to apply herself to her physiology paper. She flicked on the television—a distraction that helped her concentrate—and tuned to "Sergeant Bilko." Phil Silvers, the star of the comedy series, was a friend of her mother's.

The front door slammed suddenly; Stompanato was back. Soon the adults were shouting at each other again. Crane called out to let them know she could hear them, but her mother told her to return to her homework. "Johnny's just leaving," Turner yelled up the stairs.

But Stompanato lingered. Minutes later, after another exchange of explosive shouts and threats, Turner entered Crane's room with Stompanato trailing, splendid in a flashy gold cardigan. "Johnny's going to leave now," Turner announced again.

My God, Cheryl, what have you done?

JOHNNY STOMPANATO

"Not so fast, lady," he growled from behind her.

"I stared at him, and in one chilling moment I saw for the first time what he looked like when he was angry," Cheryl Crane wrote later. "He seethed. He clearly hated her. It was controlled anger, but his neck veins stood out and he breathed from one side of his mouth. He hunched his shoulders as though he were going to pull out a pair of six-shooters, while the hands at his sides clenched and writhed like a snake's tail in death. He never once looked at me, but burned his glare into Mother, who stood in profile between us."

As the confused Crane watched, Turner bluffed her way through the confrontation. She scolded Stompanato for arguing "in front of the Baby" and Cheryl for doing her homework in front of the TV. She announced that Stompanato was leaving, and that she was going downstairs to get another vodka and tonic and then return to her bedroom. Stompanato trailed her, shouting that she'd broken her promise to go to a movie with him, chiding her for drinking too much.

By the time the pair returned to Turner's bedroom, the battle had resumed in earnest. Crane scuttled back and forth along the passageway between her room and her mother's closed door—the barrier she'd once regarded as a moat designed to keep her out—listening to the crescendo of threats building inside, knocking on the door now and then to try to interrupt. Then the familiar drama took a frightening turn. According to Crane, Stompanato growled, "You'll never get away from me. I'll cut you good, Baby. You'll never work again. And don't think I won't also get your mother and your kid." The threats, interspersed with her mother's desperate screams, became too much for Crane. She ran downstairs in a panic, into the kitchen, and grabbed a tapered, nine-inch carving knife that lay on the sink—one of the brand-new kitchen knives chosen by Stompanato himself on a recent shopping spree with Turner.

What happened next has been clouded by the two women's slightly different reports. Crane said that she stood outside Turner's room, desperately urging the pair to stop fighting, and then the door flew open—Crane remembered that Turner opened it; Turner recalled that her daughter pushed it open. Both women agreed, however, that what Crane saw at this point was Stompanato approaching Turner from behind, his arm raised as if to strike.

"Because we had originally planned to go out," Turner explained, "John had brought over a shirt and a jacket earlier in the day. They were on his own hangers, heavy wooden ones." When Cheryl entered, Stompanato had his clothes slung over his shoulder; but she saw, as Turner put it, "that upraised, threatening hand, and what appeared to be some kind of weapon."

Crane said that she then took a step forward and raised the carving knife, inverted, with the cutting edge up. "He ran on the blade," she wrote. "It went in. In! For three ghastly heartbeats, our bodies fused. He looked straight at me, unblinking. 'My God, Cheryl, what have you done?'"

Within seconds of the stabbing Stompanato was supine on the floor, and Crane had fled to her bedroom. Minutes later, after a ghoulish rattle that Turner described as "weird gasping," Stompanato was dead. The knife had made a small, vertical puncture just below Stompanato's right nipple. It was a small wound, but it opened upon catastrophic damage within. Later, an autopsy would show that, aided by Crane's upside-down hold on the weapon, the knife had punctured Stompanato's abdomen and kidney before his spine deflected it upward in an arc to the heart, where it sliced the aorta. As lethal as a perfect bayonet thrust, the wound virtually guaranteed Stomapanato's death.

The sudden, violent demise of Johnny Stompanato filled the world's newspapers the next day. "Daughter of Lana Turner Kills Man" screamed a front-page headline in the *Los Angeles Times,* adding in a cascade of smaller heads: "Johnny Stompanato, Constant Companion of Actress, Stabbed," "Child Once Ran Away From Home," "Actress Spent Acapulco Visit With Victim." The police were quoted, saying Cheryl Crane would be "treated no different than any other girl. She will be booked like any other juvenile and will be kept in Beverly Hills jail overnight"—in the Juvenile Hall with which, according to her memoir, Lex Barker had once threatened her. Lana Turner was said to have retained attorney Jerry Geisler, "famous filmland defense lawyer," within an hour of the stabbing.

In fact, Turner's first telephone call had been to her mother. She couldn't remember her doctor's number, Turner later explained, so she'd called her mother to get it. Mildred Turner had then quickly called the family doctor, John B. McDonald, herself—although she was so flustered she gave him the wrong address. In the meantime Cheryl Crane, from the sanctuary of her own bedroom, called her father,

Stephan Crane. He had been the first of those summoned to arrive and see Stompanato, seemingly lifeless, sprawled on his back. When he turned to his daughter and asked her what had happened, Cheryl answered: "I did it, Daddy, but I didn't mean to. He was going to hurt Mommie."

Mildred Turner was the next to reach the scene. When she saw Stompanato's inert form she immediately dropped to her knees and tried to administer mouth-to-mouth resuscitation. "Mother, don't touch him!" Turner said she screamed at her mother. "I didn't want her mouth on his."

The doctor followed Mildred Turner by a few minutes. After finding no pulse in Stompanato, he administered two shots of adrenaline straight to the victim's heart. When nothing happened, he motioned Turner toward the telephone. "Call Jerry Geisler," he advised, referring to the Hollywood lawyer who'd successfully defended actors Errol Flynn and Charlie Chaplin against charges of statutory rape. Geisler showed up a short while before the police, an ambulance, and Beverly Hills Police Chief Clinton Anderson, a longtime friend of the family's. Reporter Jim Bacon told police he was the coroner and bluffed his way into the house just as Turner stood pleading with Anderson. "Can't I take the blame for this horrible thing?" he heard her say. Anderson told her she could not.

When it was clear nothing could be done for Stompanato, McDonald tended to Cheryl Crane, injecting her with a sedative. As the teenager changed out of her nightclothes and prepared for her ride to the police station, Mildred Turner intervened as wardrobe mistress. She'd dressed her daughter for success; now she would do the same for her granddaughter. She chose a schoolgirl blouse, a wool skirt, flat shoes, a white head scarf, and a camel's hair coat. No make-up, she insisted. "She knew what she was doing," Crane recounted. "When she finished dressing me, I looked the tall, gawky young girl that I was, ready to be displayed to the world press who were now clamoring on the lawn."

Crane was charged with murder and held in Juvenile Hall. Bail was refused for her, perhaps because the Beverly Hills Police Department still smarted from accusations that they'd given preferential treatment to a Hollywood producer who'd wounded his wife's lover. Chief Anderson's friendship with Stephan Crane and Lana Turner only reinforced their determination to handle Cheryl like anyone else.

Not everybody was comfortable with Crane's story, however. Mickey Cohen rushed to the morgue to identify the body, then talked to reporters: "I don't like the whole thing," he said. "Johnny's been around a long time, but if what they tell me is true, he made no effort to dodge the knife. It just doesn't jell with me."

Not long afterward Stompanato's apartment at the Del Capri Motel was broken into and a shaving kit was stolen that contained the cache of love letters Turner had sent to Stompanato from London. Although Cohen denied burglarizing the apartment, he proudly took credit for turning the steamy letters over to the press, saying he wanted to "show that Johnny wasn't exactly 'unwelcome company' like Lana said." Coached by Cohen, Stompanato's brother Carmine told the press he was "not satisfied with the current version of the story." The hour's delay before the police arrived particularly upset Carmine, he said, as did the image of a 14-year-old girl fatally stabbing his Marine Corps-trained brother. Rumors of all sorts inevitably began to circulate. Some said that Lana Turner had killed Stompanato herself after finding him in bed with her daughter. Some said that Crane, out of love or fear, had taken the fall for her mother.

The press happily squeezed every source they could find. From Cheryl's retired Scottish nanny, the beloved Nana, they extracted: "I cannot believe my little darling would be capable of such a terrible thing." From Lex Barker, then filming in Italy, they heard that he'd warned Turner about her daughter. "I said, 'Watch out for Cheryl. That girl will end up in great trouble.' Time has proved me right." Barker died of a heart attack on a New York sidewalk several years before he could see what Crane would write about him.

The stars of the deadly drama huddled in the calm eye of the media storm raging about them. Crane was secluded in Juvenile Hall. Turner was in virtual hiding in her home, besieged by the press and the curious public. Stompanato had gone back to Woodstock. Spiffily dressed, as always, he'd been buried in Woodstock's Oakland Cemetery. His funeral services had opened with a poem — "In the Desperate Hours" — and ended with an American Legion honor-guard salute and the playing of "Taps." Mickey Cohen paid for the service. A few tough-looking cronies attended.

The coroner's inquest was scheduled for 9 a.m. on Friday,

*I did it, Daddy, but I didn't mean to.
He was going to hurt Mommie.*

CHERYL CRANE

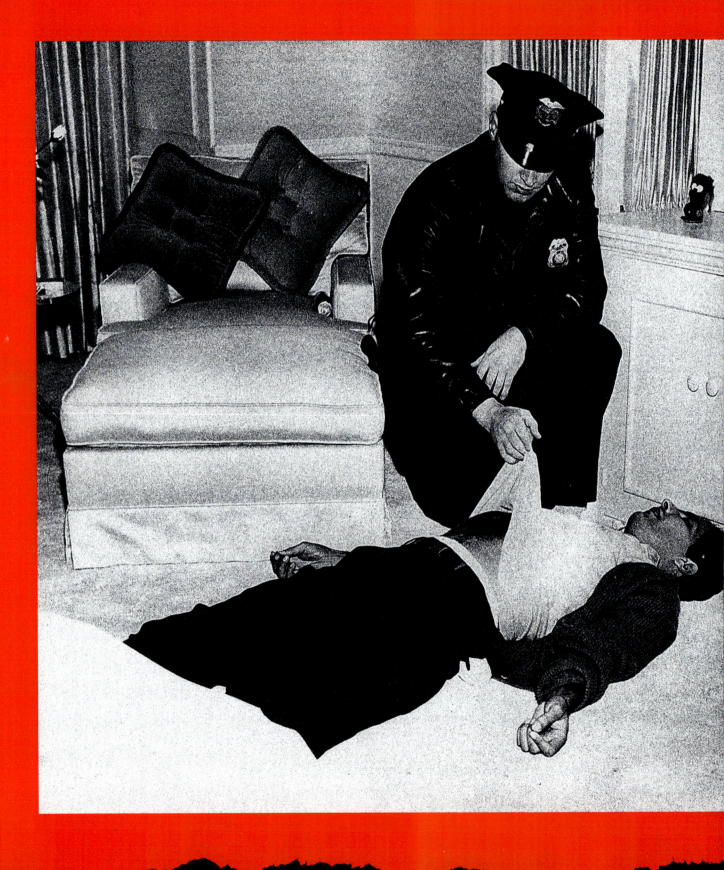

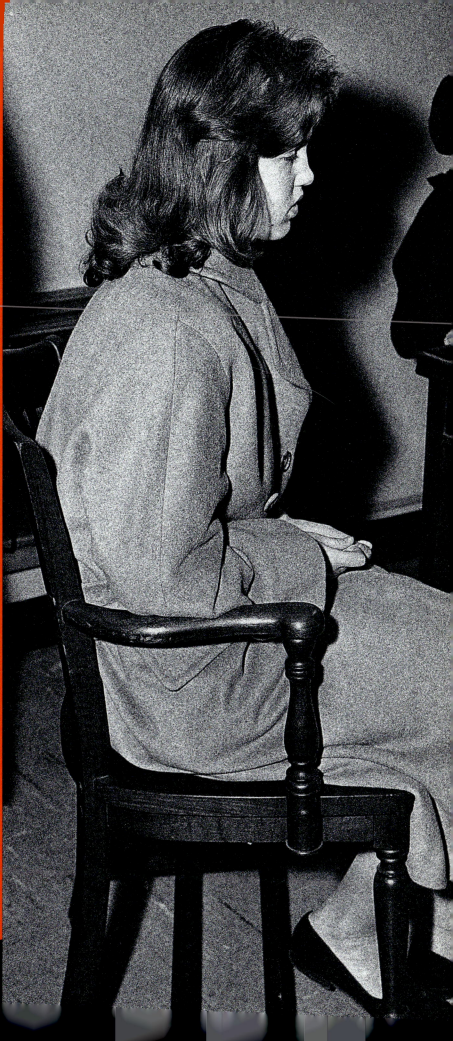

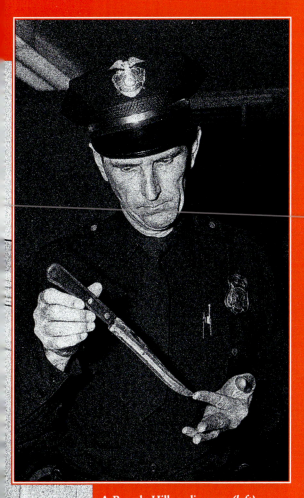

A Beverly Hills policeman *(left)* lifts Stompanato's gold sweater to examine the seemingly minor puncture wound that dropped the ex-Marine onto the mauve carpet of Lana Turner's boudoir. Inflicted by the thrust of an inverted nine-inch carving knife *(inset),* the injury ripped through Stompanato's vital organs, causing him to bleed to death internally. Traumatized teen Cheryl Crane *(right),* drained of grown-up glamour by the night's fatal events, waits to be booked in Los Angeles County Juvenile Hall.

In what some have cynically called the courtroom performance of her life, a carefully coifed Lana Turner dramatically demonstrates how Stompanato clutched his abdomen after the fatal stabbing *(right)* and describes his dying moments *(top inset)* during the nationally televised April 1958 inquest in Los Angeles. After her wrenching, hour-long testimony, she collapses in tears next to defense attorney Jerry Geisler *(bottom inset),* mouthpiece to the stars. The jury reached its verdict in only 30 minutes: justifiable homicide.

April 11. ABC and CBS had already agreed to pool their resources in order to film the event for television and to broadcast it live on radio. By 6 a.m. on April 11 a crowd had gathered outside the big eighth-floor courtroom in the Los Angeles Hall of Records where the inquest would be held. Most of those who waited would not get a seat inside — of the 160 spaces, 120 were reserved for the press — but they might catch a glimpse of the deliciously scandalous screen beauty when she arrived.

Mickey Cohen was called as the first witness and launched the event with a madcap twist when he refused to identify the body of Stompanato "on the grounds that I may be accused of this murder." Cohen, as he'd intended, was promptly dismissed. The autopsy report followed. Then Turner took the stand.

A hush fell over the crowd as the famous actress sat down, removed one white glove, and filled her lungs with a deep, steadying intake of air. For the next 62 minutes she sat with her impeccable posture, answering questions. Her performance was flawless, expert in its timing and expressiveness. Photographers, desperate for better shots, stood on their seats, on the arms of their seats, and even on window sills. Soon almost everyone in the crowd was standing on the seats. "In their precarious, picturesque position," one journalist reported, "the audience soon grew frozen and hushed and, except for the click and clatter of the desperately laboring photographers, the throaty, halting voice of Lana Turner seemed to be the only living thing in the room." She made good use of her training, pausing dramatically at key points and struggling to contain her tears. Midway through her description of how the dying Stompanato made "the most horrible noises in his throat and gasping" — she took a fortifying sip of water. When her ordeal was finally over, she returned to her seat next to Geisler and collapsed in tears.

The stream of witnesses who followed Turner's performance were all anticlimactic and included Stephan Crane, Mildred Turner, and a police captain who read the statement Cheryl Crane had given to Police Chief Anderson on the night of the killing. Crane herself was not present, but back at Juvenile Hall watching *Seven Brides for Seven Brothers* with her fellow inmates.

The jury of 12 was not long about its business. After 30 minutes they returned a verdict of justifiable homicide. As their decision was announced, shouts of joy and applause

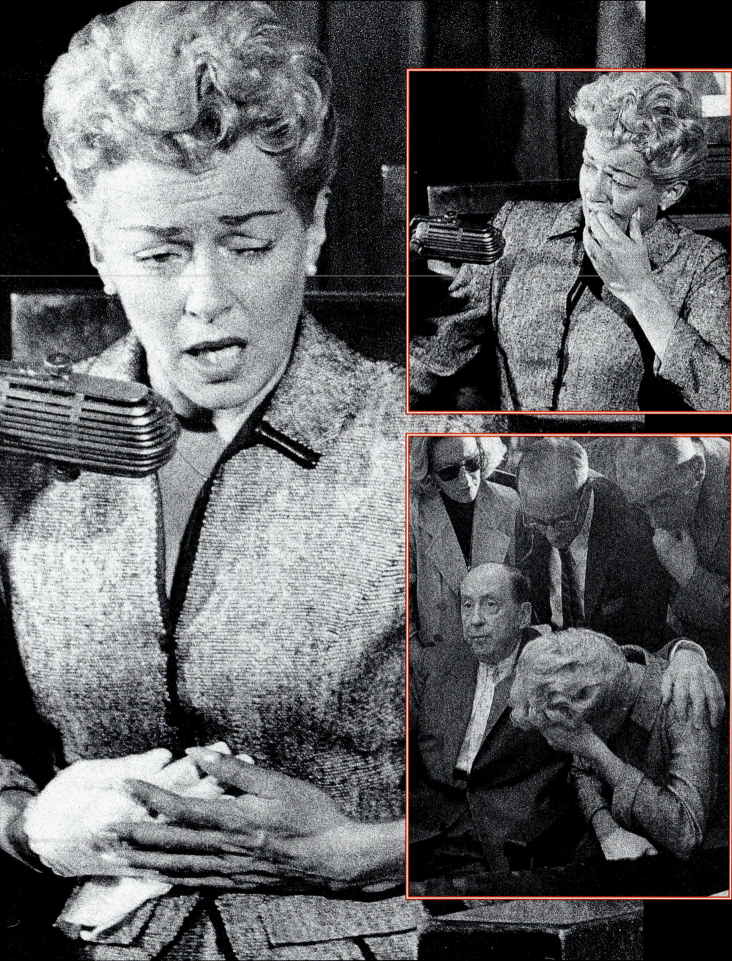

erupted in the courtroom. Stephan Crane burst into tears of relief. But Lana Turner, the star of the day, was not around to hear it. Exhausted, she was already slumped in the backseat of the green limousine that was carrying her home.

The next day Mickey Cohen remarked to reporters: "It's the first time in my life I've ever seen a dead man convicted of his own murder. So far as that jury was concerned, Johnny just walked too close to the knife." But his was almost the only dissenting voice. "In the turnover of husbands and wives, lovers and mistresses, the Cheryls are the misplaced baggage, lost and found and lost again," opined the *Los Angeles Times*. "In the Turner case Cheryl isn't the juvenile delinquent: Lana is." Declared columnist Hedda Hopper, long an antagonist of Turner's, "My heart bleeds for Cheryl!" Cynics condemned Turner's testimony at the inquest as the "performance of her life" and gleefully pointed to all the celluloid court scenes that had prepped her for such an event. Only columnist Walter Winchell stood by the former Sweater Girl. "She is made of blue-eyed sunshine, taffy tresses and swaying charms," he wrote. "Give your heart to the girl with the broken heart."

Beneath the buzz of outrage, the public tingled with the thrill of this look into the inferno of fame, transforming indiscretions into a very marketable public product. The scandal had boosted newspaper sales; receipts for *Peyton Place*, released four months earlier, jumped 32 percent. And there was always some new squib of news to ignite further interest in Lana Turner. Cheryl was made a ward of the court and entrusted to the custody of her grandmother, after a judge deemed she had no proper parental guidance at home. Stompanato's brother Carmine launched a $752,250 civil suit against Turner on behalf of Stompanato's 10-year-old son. Juiciest of all, the police found a cache of Stompanato's belongings stored in a warehouse. Mingled with a stack of unpaid IOUs and mementos from Turner were sexually explicit photographs of various women, and nudes of Lana herself. Because none of the women seemed to know they were being photographed, police took the photographs to be the secret stuff of blackmail. They also found Stompanato's little brown book with the names and numbers of many stars. But his preying days were over.

Producer Ross Hunter helped Turner cash in on some of this residual publicity in 1959 by casting her in *Imitation of Life,* the story of a Broadway star who spoils but neglects a daughter who then falls in love with her mother's boyfriend. It was the top-grossing film of her career and, according to Crane, saved financially troubled Universal-International Pictures. Turner would go on to make several more self-cannibalizing box-office hits, including *By Love Possessed, Portrait in Black,* and *Madame X.* The last was a film in which the actress portrayed a woman who winds up in prison after being convicted of killing a blackmailer.

If the actress could re-create her own misadventures for the screen, she remained unable to learn from them. During the years between 1960 and 1970, she married and divorced three more times: wealthy rancher Fred May in 1960, then producer Robert Eaton in 1965, and finally "nightclub hypnotist" Ronald Dante in 1969. "I expected to have one husband and seven babies," she wrote in her autobiography. "Instead I had seven husbands and one living baby, my darling Cheryl."

Unlike the seemingly indestructible Lana Turner, that one living baby had embarked on a trajectory of destructive behavior that would last for another five years. Although she'd been acquitted of a charge of murder and thereby escaped the gas chamber, Cheryl Crane still had to survive what she would call her detour through hell—a dark odyssey that was rooted in her childhood, grimly punctuated by a stepfather's assaults and the killing of John Stompanato. It would include reform school, arrests, mental institutions, and suicide attempts. "So much of the tragedy in my life was my own doing because I was carrying a terrible burden of guilt," Crane would tell a reporter in 1988. "Not just from Stompanato but from the child abuse. Children do that to themselves, they feel guilty and so they try to punish themselves."

At the time of that interview, Crane was 44 years old and had just published *Detour,* her autobiography. A businesswoman with successful ventures in real estate and the restaurant world, by this time Crane had also spent 18 years in an open lesbian relationship with a woman named Joyce LeRoy. Few other players have survived. In 1993 Lana Turner, aged 72, battled throat cancer in her modest Hollywood home. After 1970 she reconciled with her daughter and God, and she claimed to be abstemious of alcohol and men. Of the leading men in Turner's life, Greg and Artie, Stephan, Bob, and Tyrone, and Fernando, Lex, and Johnny are dead. ◆

Stompanato's personal effects *(inset)* included a wrist watch, pendant, and identification bracelet, which bears an inscription by Turner in Spanish. Translated, it reads: "Papa Johnny, my sweet love, when you read this remember it is a little piece of my heart that will be with you always. And also remember 'careful.' My life for all time for me. With all my soul. Lanita." The dead man's wallet contained this photograph of a veiled Lana Turner, inscribed: "For Johnny, my love and my life-Lanita."

Para Juanito mi amor y mi vida - Lanita

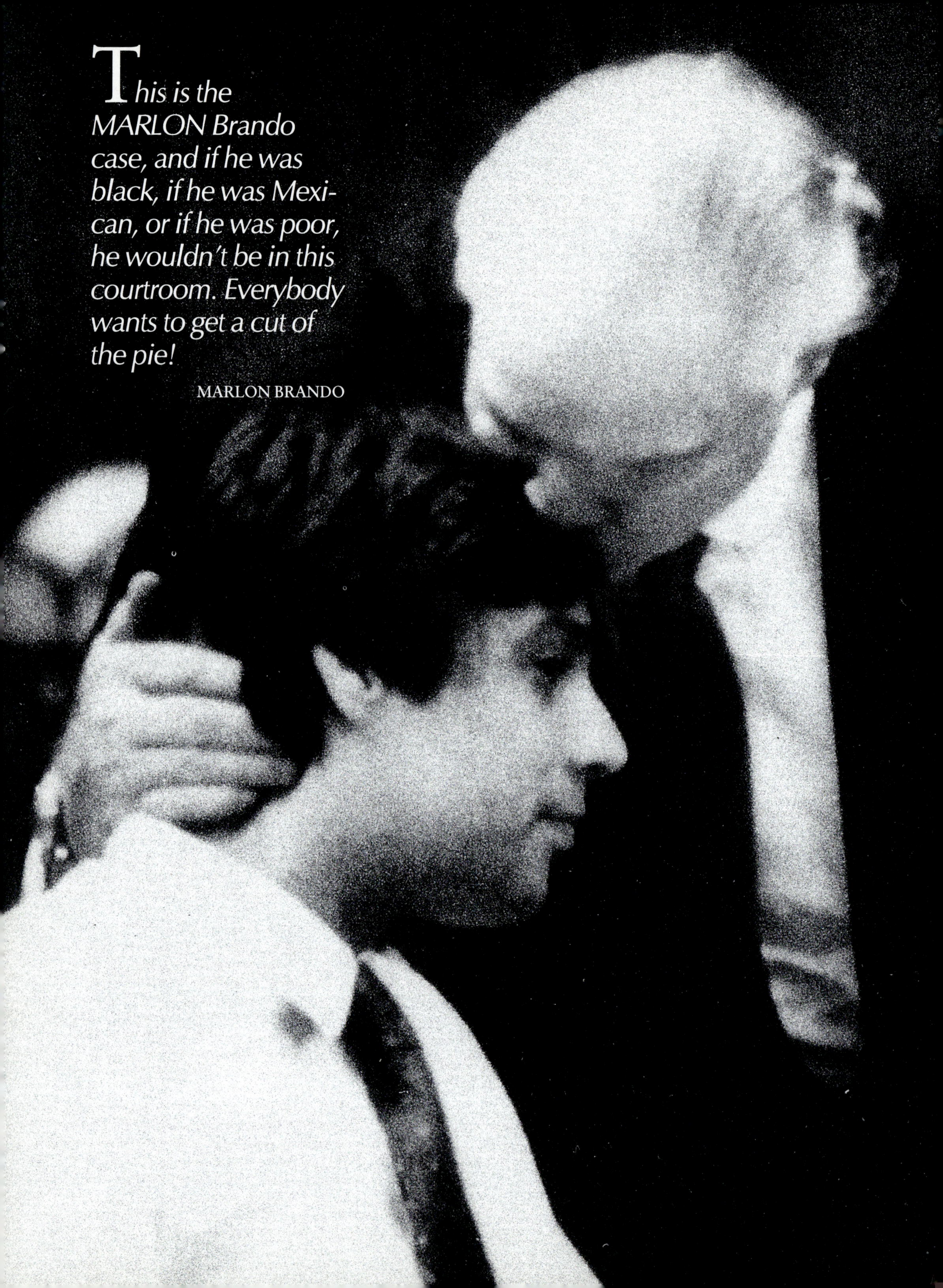

This is the MARLON Brando case, and if he was black, if he was Mexican, or if he was poor, he wouldn't be in this courtroom. Everybody wants to get a cut of the pie!

MARLON BRANDO

4

Lost Boy

The old man filled the witness box, both with his presence and his bulk. "I think that perhaps I failed as a father," he said. His breathing was slightly labored, perhaps because of emotional distress, perhaps because of his ponderous weight. "I'm certain that . . . that there were things that I could have done differently, had I known better at the time, but I didn't. I did the best I could."

In the wan glare of ceiling lights in this crowded, wood-paneled courtroom in Santa Monica, California, the witness, dressed all in black, looked worn and beaten. His sparse gray hair was slicked back into a little ponytail, and his broad face was pasty and lined. Still, it was an arresting face. Beneath the age and the bloat lingered hints of how startlingly handsome Marlon Brando once must have been: the straight brows and long, slitted eyes, the high cheekbones, hawknose, and chiseled mouth. He sat heavily in the padded swivel chair, the courtroom microphone pulled close to his face, and spoke softly—in the characteristic mumble that, while barely audible, would nevertheless have been recognized instantly in most of the civilized world. His answers to questions were long and rambling, and sometimes he winced as he groped for a word. He'd been in this same courtroom, he said, about 18 times before, in custody battles with his ex-wife over their son, Christian. But that was years ago, and now the son, his eldest child at 32, was in serious trouble. He had shot another man to death.

The testimony this father had heard about his son had taken its toll. Witness after witness—experts as well as people who'd called themselves friends—told of a boy gone astray, wandering through his life, destroying himself with drugs and alcohol. The big man barely stirred, looking ashen as an onslaught of testimony forced him to review his own life over the past three decades. Like many another distracted professional man leading a complex life, he had too often been away when his son needed him.

In its basics, the story was rather commonplace: Well-to-do parents part in a bitter divorce. Their child, tossed brutally between them and coming of age in the permissive 1970s, looks for answers in drugs and booze and winds up with more problems. Once on his own, he strays into deeper trouble, lands in the hands of the police, and the parents' ugly memories become testimony in court. Usually only the local newspapers took notice of such modern morality tales. But this case was different, its principals giving it an extra measure of riveting drama. The father on the witness stand, seeming to hold himself there by a sheer act of will, was world-famous, after all. As he answered questions from his son's lawyer, describing the boy's early life, his pain was almost palpable.

"Some people have reported," the lawyer probed gently, "that Christian is the spoiled son of a rich and famous man. What would be your comment to that?"

"Either they're a lying son of a bitch," the father spat, "or they don't know what they're talking about." Of all his children, he said, Christian "from the very beginning has been the most independent. I've offered money to Christian because I knew he didn't have any money. And he wouldn't take it. He's been very, very proud." The young man sometimes even declined to use his last name, the father said. "He wanted his own identity, and he worked hard to get it and he's still struggling with that, with all the reporters who . . . who . . ."; suddenly his anger burst forth. "This is the MARLON Brando case," he said bitterly, "and if he was black, if he was Mexican, or if he was poor, he wouldn't be in this courtroom. Everybody wants to get a cut of the pie!"

Indeed the Marlon Brando pie had been tempting to many people for more than 40 years. At 23, a powerful young actor bursting with vitality and virility, Brando had flared into stardom in 1947 with his electrifying performance in Tennessee Williams's *A Streetcar Named Desire*. Onstage, and then in a movie version, his steamy rendering of sweaty, sexy Stanley Kowalski created a sensation and soon had college boys all over the country bawling his trademark line, "Hey, Stella!" outside their girlfriends' windows. "Brutally convincing," one critic called his portrayal;

"almost pure ape," said another. Brando's acting was raw, the emotions elemental; it was a headlong departure from the drawing-room gentility of other actors of the day, and it catalyzed a revolution in theater and the movies.

As Brando's talent unfolded over the following decades, his performances won him awe-struck reviews and countless imitators, both onstage and off. "Marlon is just the best actor in the world," summed up Elia Kazan, who directed him in the stage and screen versions of *Streetcar* and in Brando's Oscar-winning performance in the 1954 film *On the Waterfront*. "The most exciting person I've met since Garbo. A genius," said Joshua Logan, directing him several years later in *Sayonara*.

Brando's personal life was as outsize as his talent—sprawling, untidy, and, some would say, chaotic. He was driven by huge appetites, for knowledge, for food, for sex. Since his expulsion from a Minnesota military school at 19, he'd read voraciously—everything but fiction. He'd been known to down a gallon of ice cream at one sitting; his weight ballooned in his later years to more than 250 pounds. He acknowledged fathering six children and adopted four more. He had made headlines with his crusades for social causes, his contempt for Hollywood, his despair at the uselessness of acting. Yet his acting, when he cared to exert himself, still defined the craft. In 1989 critic Roger Ebert mused that "Marlon Brando has learned, over the years, to dominate a scene more completely than any other living actor. He is not performing, he is there. He is a fact."

In the California courtroom, on February 28, 1991, Brando's mastery of his art was, perhaps, a hindrance as he pleaded for leniency for his son. Some of those present—the victim's parents, in particular—mistrusted him in his role of concerned parent. They felt he was giving his most studied performance. "Brando is an actor," the victim's father said acidly, "and even in his private life he is always acting. He can cry and lie like a horse can run."

The arena for the performance, if such it was, was a presentencing hearing, convened to consider the proper punishment for Christian Brando's crime. He had admitted shooting Dag Drollet, his half sister's boyfriend, in Marlon Brando's secluded Beverly Hills house, in what Christian described as a struggle over a gun. He said that his half sister, Cheyenne, told him that Drollet (pronounced *dro-lay*) had been beating her. In a plea bargain that reduced the charge against him from first-degree murder, Christian

Brando waived his right to a trial and pleaded guilty to voluntary manslaughter.

Much of what was heard in the proceeding wouldn't have been admissible as evidence at a trial. But the point of the hearing was to inform the judge, as thoroughly as possible, not so much about what Christian Brando had done, but about what kind of man he was—and what kind of boy he'd been. In pursuing this task, the hearing sent out ripples well beyond the courtroom: It shattered Marlon Brando's cherished privacy, and it exposed to the world the sins and foibles of several members of the Brando clan. It opened the Brandos, and the victim's family as well, to the relentless glare of publicity. And the way of life it laid bare had none of the glamour that immense talent, wealth, and fame are supposed to confer.

Assuming the stand again after a recess, Marlon Brando began with an apology for his emotional outburst. "Sorry if I offended anybody in the courtroom," he murmured into the microphone. "I give you my apologies. I was kind of hysterical."

Brando had already told the court that Christian's mother, former actress Anna Kashfi, was "as negative a person as I have met in this life, as cruel." It is the "tincture of what her character is," he said, that "she's not in this courtroom today." He added, "I have never said anything bad to Christian about his mother. I've always tried to tell him that his mother was ill, that she was disturbed, and that she might come around. And at this very time, if she were to call me, I would send her to get psychiatric help."

As the hearing continued, the actor testified that he owned several rifles, which he always kept under his bed, that he originally bought a handgun because he'd had "at least seven" intruders "come in while I was sleeping, standing right there, some of them nuts—well, all of them nuts." His life had been threatened, he said, and people had threatened to kidnap his children. So, though he claimed he didn't believe in guns, he bought them and kept them.

Christian's lawyer, Robert Shapiro, asked whether Brando knew his son had guns.

"Oh, yeah."

"Did you ask Christian to bring his guns to your house?"

"You bet," Brando affirmed, "I didn't want to have him drunk and fooling around with weapons. Alcohol and weapons don't mix."

After pleading guilty to a charge of voluntary manslaughter in the death of Dag Drollet, his half sister's Tahitian boyfriend, a dejected Christian Brando *(left)* listens to the February 1991 testimony of his famous father. Grimacing with powerful emotion, Marlon Brando *(above)* recalls his troubled son's painful childhood for the court.

"Did Christian bring up his weapons to your house?"

"Damn right he did." But Christian knew where they were kept, added Brando, and he "snuck some away. Then I checked and I looked and I said, 'There's some guns missing. Bring the God . . .' " the actor caught himself. " 'Bring the guns here.'

"As a matter of fact, I asked him that night before he went to dinner. I said, 'Did you bring me *all* of your guns?'

"He said, 'Yes, all except my automatic.' "

"And I said, 'I want that, too, Chris, you gotta bring that to me. Pick it up and bring it over.' "

Christian Brando's automatic — a SIG Sauer .45 — discharged the single bullet that killed 26-year-old Dag Drollet on May 16, 1990. Drollet, a Tahitian playboy, was a guest at Marlon Brando's estate. He'd accompanied Brando's 20-year-old daughter, Tarita Cheyenne Brando, and her mother, Tarita Teriipia, from their home in Tahiti. Cheyenne, six months pregnant with Drollet's son — Tuki would be Marlon Brando's first grandchild — had been depressed and suicidal since a car accident in 1989, in which her face was slashed and scarred.

At the presentencing hearing, Shapiro asked Brando

about Cheyenne, who was in the house when the killing occurred. "What was her mental, emotional state" at the time of the shooting?

The actor replied that a neighbor had found Cheyenne eating Comet cleanser. "She was sniffing it, and she was licking her hand. I saw her do it." He said he called the poison control center and learned that about two table-spoons could be lethal. "So I was very concerned. So we hid all the knives." Visiting Cheyenne in Tahiti some weeks before, he said, he'd seen her lash out at people around her, slapping her sister, throwing a Coke bottle at another girl— "completely nut-case behavior."

The lawyer reminded Brando that his daughter and son had gone out to dinner together before the shooting, then returned to the house.

"I was watching television in the TV room," Brando related. "Christian came into the room. I asked him what he had for dinner, if he had a good time. He said yes. I asked him if he brought the gun back. He said yes he did. I said, 'Where is it?' He said, 'It's in the kitchen someplace.' And I said, 'What did Cheyenne say?' And there was a pause, and he said, 'You don't want to know, Pop.'

"And I turned to him and I said, 'Listen, I want to know everything that Cheyenne says. Every single scintilla of information that you've got, I want to know what it is.'

"He said, 'Believe me, Pop, you don't want to know.' And he got up and left the room."

"When was the next time you saw Christian?" the attorney inquired.

"Five minutes later." Then, "He came into the room, and looked weird and said, 'I killed Dag.' I said, 'What are you talking about?' And he said, 'He's dead, Pop. I didn't mean to do it. He went for the gun and it went off.'"

Brando struggled to go on. "And then, I had the impression—first of all, I wanted to . . . I started to . . . I said, 'Do you have the gun?'" He said he told Christian to unload it, then "I smelled the gun. It had been fired.

"I looked at him and went right in the other room where Dag was." At this point Brando seemed to be fighting back tears in an emotional display that apparently failed to convince all present. He glanced at someone in the courtroom and growled, "I'm not lying. I swear to Christ on Tuki's life, on his soul, I saw Dag lying there. And I tried to get ahold of myself. And I felt his pulse on his neck." Again he seemed to weep. Drollet's parents, Jacques and Lisette, looked on

grimly. "He still had a pulse. And I breathed into his mouth. And I called 911. The police came, and the firemen came.

"I got some Valium because I knew that I had to be as reasonable as possible, as collected," Brando went on. "Tarita was hysterical. I gave them to Tarita and I took two—5 milligrams of Valium. I don't know where Christian was. It was—uh—pretty much of a blur."

The lawyer asked if Brando knew whether his son was drinking after the shooting.

Brando shook his head.

And as the body was being carried out?

For a moment, Brando seemed unable to reply. Then, "As much as it may not be believed, by Jacques and Lisette—I loved Dag," he said. "He was going to be the father of my grandchild." Struggling with tears, Brando continued. "When they brought him out, I asked some officers to unzip the bag, and I wanted to say good-bye to him properly. And I—uh, I kissed him and told him I loved him. And," he whispered, "that's all."

The killing of Dag Drollet ripped apart the Drollet and Brando families in a brutally public way. But then, Christian Brando's family had never been whole, nor had its troubles been private. Some people familiar with the case saw Christian as a victim himself, a young man who'd never had a chance at an ordinary life. Some said his whole life, lived in the shadow of one of the world's legends, was one long extenuating circumstance.

The seeds of Christian Brando's misery were sown before he was born, in the colossal, tempestuous mismatch of his two egotistical parents. When they met, in 1955, Marlon Brando, at 31, was a major star, acclaimed for his screen performances in *Streetcar, The Wild One,* as Mark Antony in *Julius Caesar,* and as Napoleon in *Desirée.* He'd won an Oscar for his role as a crude but gutsy longshoreman in *On the Waterfront.* As the most famed of the new actors turned out by Stella Adler's Actors' Studio in New York, he would soon command record salaries and demand expensive indulgences on the set.

Offstage, Brando irritated the Hollywood establishment with his aggressively unstarlike behavior, his preferences for black leather jackets and motorcycles over black-tie and Jaguars, and his basic bad manners. He used his Oscar as a doorstop. And he played his animal appeal to women for all it was worth—which was quite a lot. "I had a real Ford

A solemn wedding portrait taken in October of 1957 betrays the cooling passions between 33-year-old Marlon Brando—his hair bleached for a role in the 1958 film *The Young Lions*—and Calcutta-born actress Anna Kashfi. Kashfi, 23, was three months pregnant at the time.

assembly line going throughout much of my life," he would later tell a reporter. "If you're rich and famous, getting laid a lot isn't that difficult." He was partial to young brunettes, exotic Latin or Asian beauties.

Anna Kashfi filled the bill. Calcutta-born and convent-educated, the graceful, almond-eyed starlet had modeled in London and was, at 21, under contract at MGM, where she costarred with Spencer Tracy in *The Mountain*. Although Brando was keeping company with several actresses and engaged to another at the time, he made a play for Kashfi.

It was a stormy courtship, in which he might arrive at her place unannounced at two in the morning for a quick bedroom interlude and leave just as suddenly, without a word. Erratic as it was, their passion endured through her bout with tuberculosis and his long stays in Japan to film *Teahouse of the August Moon* and, later, *Sayonara*. But he still saw other women, and the relationship with Kashfi was cooling when she told him she was pregnant. They were married in a secret ceremony on October 11, 1957. He took the matter seriously enough to wear a suit and tie; she wore a green sari. "I didn't want Christian to be an internationally known illegitimate child," he explained years later, asserting that the pregnancy was the only reason he married Kashfi. "Today it doesn't make any difference." As on most things, Anna's version differed. She claimed, in her confessional biography, *Brando for Breakfast*, that neither she nor Marlon regarded illegitimacy as a stigma nor saw it as a spur to wedlock.

Predictably, the marriage was no more tranquil than the courtship. Almost immediately, reporters suggested that Anna Kashfi's Indian heritage was mostly fabricated. True, she was born in Calcutta. But her father, some alleged, was not, as she claimed, an Indian architect named Devi Kashfi—there was no record of such a man—but a British railway supervisor named William Patrick O'Callaghan. In fact, Kashfi's studio paychecks were made out to Joan O'Callaghan. Brando, furious at the lie and resulting loss of privacy, had his public relations man, Walter Seltzer, grill Anna, and she was reduced to hysterical tears, "probably sufficiently ill," Seltzer said later, "to raise questions about her competency. We never got the same story from her."

Kashfi's mother was apparently Anglo-Indian, an unenviable condition in Britain—so much so that O'Callaghan denied there was Indian blood anywhere in the family. According to some reports, Anna herself had displayed the

111

same disdain of her mixed heritage in her schoolgirl days; when the family left India and settled in Wales, she denied she was part Indian and shunned her Indian classmates. In a turnabout at age 19, she apparently embraced her Indian heritage as she traveled by train from Wales to London, where, she hoped, an exotic identity would help her break into the world of acting and modeling.

As Anna clung stubbornly to her story of Devi Kashfi, even telling reporters he had died the previous summer, a brooding Brando hired private detectives in England, France, and India to ferret out the truth. He never, Anna contended, told her what he learned.

The incident established several themes that would weave through the relationship of Christian Brando's parents. Relentless publicity would attend everything they did; Kashfi would be dramatically unstable and unreliable on even the basic things; and Brando would demand that everyone play by his rules—which didn't necessarily apply to him. In his early Broadway days Brando had made up his own biography, as outlandish as he could make it, for the program notes of every play he was in, once even listing Calcutta as *his* birthplace. He insisted that this practice was no mere self-dramatizing but was rather part of his rebellion against conventional notions: He was making a statement that such factual details as age and origins had no importance.

In fact, he was born in 1924 in Omaha, Nebraska, the youngest of three children born to a philandering, abusive limestone-products salesman and a long-suffering but notoriously drunken mother. Although he said it didn't matter, he apparently shared Anna's buried wish to replace a shadowed past with something brighter.

Brando and Kashfi stayed together, but they took to complaining about each other in the press. Marlon told a Hollywood columnist, "I can't really talk to Anna. She is so emotional, so immature." Anna in turn told reporters, "Living with Marlon is like an afternoon at the races—short periods of orgiastic activity followed by long periods of boredom and anticipation. He's almost never home." Her next remark revealed her accumulating bitterness and jealousy in the most unflattering terms: "He attracts women like feces attract flies."

After the pregnant Kashfi fell downstairs twice, winding up unconscious on at least one occasion, the couple managed to agree to move from their West Hollywood house to a Japanese-style bungalow—12 rooms all on one floor—at 12900 Mulholland Drive, atop a ridge that runs through the Hollywood Hills. It was to be the first house Christian lived in, and the one where Dag Drollet died.

According to Kashfi, Brando suggested before the baby came that she might "move to Hawaii and live there." She asked why she should do that, and he replied, "There is so much prejudice here in America, it might be wiser to avoid it. Also, you being Indian and I American, we have to think of the baby—we don't know what color the baby will be when it is born, do we?" When the baby came, on the evening of May 11, 1958, at Cedars of Lebanon Hospital in Los Angeles, Brando wasn't there to see it. Kashfi had to drive herself to the hospital, since her husband was out with a girlfriend. When he came to visit his wife and child the next afternoon, she greeted him with, "I hope he's the right color for you."

They immediately argued over what to name him. Anna insisted on Devi, "to perpetuate my father's name," and Brando wanted Christian, after a friend, French director and actor Christian Marquand. They settled on Christian Devi, but Anna never called him anything but Devi. Now that the baby had come, Brando vowed to be a more devoted husband. But only weeks later he came home with an actress on his arm. The assembly line was still rolling along.

It was all too much for Kashfi. Soon after Christian's birth, she later wrote, she turned to alcohol as "an automatic resource for dulling emotional pain," and used barbiturates such as Seconal and Nembutal to "lift the anxieties of insecurity and paint a fuzzy glow over the sharp edges of daily conflicts." She lived on the brink of "furious temper tantrums wherein I tore at Marlon's hair, threw dishes at him, and assaulted his ears with obscenities." Her husband, she wrote, "would thrust out his chest at me: 'Go ahead, do whatever the hell you want.' "

To the household staff—cook, chauffeur, two gardeners, and Kashfi's private maid, Sako—Brando now added a nurse, ostensibly to care for the baby. But Anna found out that the nurse was trained not in baby care, but in psychiatry. Enraged at the thought that Marlon had hired the woman "more to chaperone me than the baby," Kashfi fired the lot, except for Sako and one gardener, then fled with Christian to New York. When she returned three weeks later, "Marlon took no more notice of it than he had of my departure." That summer—Christian's first sum-

mer—passed, Kashfi later wrote, between "rages and chills of studied silence, between drinking and bouts of seeming madness. The intervals of tranquility" became "fewer and shorter." It took a death on a hot September afternoon to break the spell.

Sako went outside for a swim while Anna and Christian napped, and Kashfi awoke to find the maid facedown on the bottom of the pool. She summoned police and firemen, and the would-be rescuers mistook the lifeless victim for Mrs. Brando—and Anna for the household help. Amid radio reports of Anna's drowning, with reporters swarming on the lawn and in helicopters overhead, Brando burst into the house and was stunned to find Kashfi. " 'Good God,' he sputtered, 'you're still alive,' " and on his face, Anna said, she read "shock, apprehension, disappointment." On that day, weeks short of their first anniversary, she picked up Christian and left for good.

Kashfi announced the separation in October of 1958, and in March of 1959 she filed for divorce on grounds of extreme cruelty. When the divorce was granted on April 22, she got custody of their son, child support of $1,000 per month, and alimony of $500,000 over the next 10 years. Brando stayed in the house on Mulholland Drive and Kashfi took a house in Coldwater Canyon. Arrangements for Christian were spelled out in the property settlement agreement, and indeed the boy became a trophy—or a bone—over which his parents would fight savagely and publicly for the next 14 years.

Within two weeks, as Kashfi later recalled it, the couple exchanged blows in the nursery on one of Brando's court-allowed visits. In November, they were in court again. Brando charged that back in August she'd assaulted him in

Marlon Brando's sprawling Mulholland Drive mansion was Christian's first home and the scene of Dag Drollet's death. The shooting occurred in Christian's former bedroom.

his bed at 2 a.m., tried to run him down in her car, thrown a log through a window, and left his house only under police escort. For his part, she countered, Brando continued the pattern he'd established during their courtship, showing up unannounced at all hours, hammering the door like the animalistic Stanley in *Streetcar,* and demanding to get in—only now it was to see his son.

It was just the beginning. For years to come the pair would communicate through a more or less steady flow of suits and countersuits, private investigators, affidavits, and contempt charges, Brando labeling Kashfi as unstable, and Kashfi trying to prove Brando "morally unfit"—whether for teaching Christian bad words or for having too many girlfriends. An ever-changing parade of judges and lawyers tossed the boy back and forth like a rag doll. It was, Marlon Brando would say on the witness stand, "a classical situation where a divorced woman very often—or a divorced man—tries to hit the other parent over the head with the child." But, he said, "I had no choice in the matter; I couldn't just back off and say, 'All right, I won't see my son—to hell with him, let her have him.' I couldn't leave a child alone."

But though Brando and Kashfi fought to get him, each would leave Christian in the care of a succession of nannies, nurses, secretaries, and schools—or on his own. The headmistress of Christian Brando's Montessori preschool reported rushing to Kashfi's house after a phone call from a neighbor. There she found the little boy unattended by the swimming pool while his mother was in the house, "passed out, lying in her own vomit."

Kashfi's alcohol and drug dependencies grew, and her acting career—which she had resumed after the divorce and

On location in Tahiti in 1960 for *Mutiny on the Bounty,* Brando plays a scene with Tarita Teriipia, who would become his common-law wife and mother of Teihotu and Cheyenne Brando.

which amounted to a role in a TV movie in 1960—withered. While the former no doubt contributed to the latter, she blamed Brando. Producers afraid of displeasing him "consigned me," she later said, "to the leprosarium of untouchable actors."

Meanwhile, Brando's love life continued to be busy and newsworthy. In the summer of 1960, when Christian was two, Marlon married again, this time to Movita Castenada, a Mexican actress with whom he'd started a typically tempestuous affair before marrying Kashfi. Now Castenada was pregnant with his second child, a boy they named Miko. The couple would never live together, and the marriage, at first kept secret, would end eight years later, after the arrival of a daughter, Rebecca.

As the domestic drama was reaching fever pitch in the States, Brando was in Tahiti, embarking on what would be another long-term liaison with a young actress. In 1960 and 1961, Brando spent several months on the South Pacific island

filming *Mutiny on the Bounty.* There he met 18-year-old Tarita Teriipia, who became his costar, his mistress, and his common-law wife; in Tahiti's relaxed way of living, she never saw the need for a ceremony. She would present him with another son, Teihotu, and in 1970 with his second daughter, Tarita Cheyenne.

Whatever the other twists and turns of Marlon Brando's not-so-private life, his feud with Anna Kashfi over Christian continued to make headlines. On one occasion Kashfi, angered by a judge's decision, took a swing at Brando in the corridor outside the courtroom. She fought not only with him, but with his household staff, with court officials, and with police officers, once screaming that she would "subpoena the judge and the whole damn court" to continue the battle over Christian.

Despite the public spectacle that surrounded his oldest child, Brando tended to avoid the press himself, and he shielded the rest of his brood from publicity so successfully that for years no one was quite sure how many offspring he had. "Several," was his answer to one reporter; "My children are flowers in a great meadow of love," and he just wanted everyone to get along. He especially wanted all his children to play together, which Kashfi found very upsetting—and apparently so did Christian. For all her professed sophistication on questions of legitimacy, she disliked his "mixing wives, mistresses, ex-mistresses, legitimate and illegitimate children in various combinations," and she took her complaint to court as further proof that Brando was a "morally unfit father." Christian Brando would later call it his "weird, spaced-out" family. "We'd have new additions all the time. Like I'd sit down at the table with all these strange people and say, 'Who are you?'" Once, Kashfi wrote, after his father kept urging the boy to "kiss the baby," the three-and-a-half-year-old Christian socked his half brother Miko on the nose.

A period of peace began in 1962 when Christian was four and his mother was under treatment for what she called "ep-

Her Indian heritage questioned by the press, vacationing Anna Kashfi leaves a London hotel in December 1959 with 19-month-old Christian Devi Brando. It was one of many wrenching displacements.

ilepsy and incipient alcoholism." Brando invited Anna Kashfi and the boy for a month's vacation in Tahiti, where he was negotiating to buy Tetiaroa, an atoll some 30 miles from the main island. Kashfi later sneered at Tahitian life as "a wasteful, vacuous existence," but Christian loved it. The following year he spent another month there with Brando and came home saying it was "more fun than a month at Disneyland with Donald Duck." It was one of the happiest times in his life, and he was especially impressed to see his father punch out a shark. They were wading along a reef when Brando spotted a four-foot shark cruising nearby. He frightened it away with a single punch on the snout. Years later, Christian would still be saying that "Pop will duke it out with anybody."

Tahiti became Marlon Brando's haven. Living beach-comber style in his island paradise, in a thatched bamboo hut with the bare minimum of furniture, he found refuge from an intrusive world. He also found an uncharacteristically peaceful relationship with Tarita Teriipia, a woman nearly 18 years his junior. Once Tetiaroa was his, he began to develop the island as a simple tourist resort. He was also full of ideas and plans for food production. With solar energy, wind power, and aquaculture, he hoped to help bring self-sufficiency to Tahiti and make Tetiaroa a Third World model of ecological harmony.

But the peace ended late in 1964, with Kashfi's dangerous slide back into drug abuse. On December 7, 1964, Christian called the police when he couldn't wake his mommy. They took her to a hospital, where she was treated for an overdose of barbiturates. Brando took Christian to the house

Fond of animals as a child, a giggling four-year-old Christian Brando drapes a cooperative black cat around his neck. The boy's menagerie included dogs and even a stray raccoon.

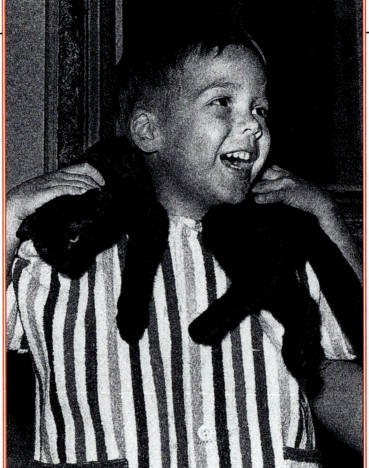

on Mulholland Drive, where the next day Kashfi burst in, having left the hospital against her doctor's orders. Brandishing a loaded gun, she assaulted Brando's secretary, Alice Marchak, threw a table through a plate-glass window, grabbed Christian, and fled with him out the smashed window, to take refuge in the Bel Air Sands Hotel. When Brando arrived with an emergency court order and an L.A. policeman to retrieve Christian, a fight broke out. Kashfi, clad in a sheer nightgown and light robe, ran screaming through the hotel lobby, then punched the officer and was arrested.

Brando dashed to court and got temporary custody of Christian, on the ground that Kashfi's conduct—and her gun—presented a danger to the child. Anna replied with a petition to regain custody, arguing that Marlon and his live-in Tahitian lover, Tarita, formed an unsuitable household for her son. In February 1965, the court, fittingly enough, looked to see what shape Christian was in. A psychologist told the court he was "a tense, fearful, terrorized youngster who is very hypersensitive and is unable to maintain attention or relate well to most adults."

Kashfi admitted that she'd tried to kill herself with pills. She was put on probation for six months, to be spent in psychiatric evaluation and drug rehabilitation. Judge Laurence Rittenband awarded custody to Brando, on condition that the boy go and live for six months with Marlon's sister Frances—then married to artist Richard Loving—and her family on their farm in Mundelein, Illinois. The Lovings had two daughters, one older than Christian, one younger.

Christian's Aunt Frances reported on his progress in regular letters to Judge Rittenband. Her letters provided startling, poignant contrasts between ordinary, quiet family life and the turmoil that was the norm in Christian's world. He arrived in March, and two months later she wrote, "He has been very alert to our relationships with other adults and has asked many questions about our feelings toward them. His reaction has been one of surprise that we like the people we know (our friends, the teachers, shopkeepers, household help, carpenters, etc.) and that we don't hate any of them, haven't fired any of them or gone to see lawyers.

"He asked us about grown-ups fighting and if we ever fought," the letter continued. "When he was told that the most fighting we ever did was to get annoyed with each other occasionally, which he had already seen, he said, 'That's good—I hate fighting.'"

Yet conflict had been the only constant in Christian's life, and thus he seemed to have a neurotic need to keep things stirred up. "From the beginning, Christian has used every kind of situation to try to establish a point of emotional conflict between himself and other people (adults and children)," Frances Loving reported.

At school Christian was put back from first grade to kindergarten. Even though he was seven years old, he was behind the other children his age in learning and in social skills. He had little self-control and had to master such basic classroom conduct as sitting in his chair when the other kids sat in theirs. His teacher at first placed him "at the extreme end of the scale" of restlessness, and Richard Loving called him "an absolutely wild child." But the boy calmed down considerably during that spring.

At home Christian enjoyed doing all sorts of ordinary things—walks in the woods, simple carpentry, pancake-making for Sunday breakfasts. The Lovings had hired a crew to add a room to their house, and the child was fascinated to see the carpenters, bricklayers, and other craftsmen doing their work. It was his first glimpse of the sort of active, physical labor that he'd find so satisfying later on.

For his seventh birthday there was a party and a visit from his father, but no word from his mother. She was busy with her drug rehabilitation program, and in July she was tried and convicted of assault and battery for the incident at the Bel Air Sands and fined $200. In the strangest event of his stay on the farm, Christian and the Lovings made and buried an effigy of Anna, as if to put an end to her influence.

Saying that Christian had endured "a great deal of arbitrariness and whim in his short life—probably an inevitable result of constantly changing hired help," Frances Loving told the judge she felt "very strongly that he will continue to need this shelter from the conflicts of his early life," and she hoped he would have enough time with her family "to find himself before he has to go back to an unsettled life." But it was not to be. Later that year another judge, convinced that no mother should be separated from her child, gave full custody back to Kashfi. Testifying 25 years later at

Anna Kashfi prepares to blindside an unsuspecting Marlon Brando as the warring parents leave the Santa Monica courthouse in 1961 after an acrimonious hearing over the custody of Christian Brando.

Brando and 13-year-old Christian enter the Santa
Monica courthouse in March 1972. The father
received sole custody of the troubled boy after
Anna Kashfi secretly consigned her son to a hippie commune in Baja California.

Christian's presentencing hearing, Marlon Brando called
this a "barbarous decision."

Kashfi's rehabilitation was a failure, and Christian's
nightmare was far from over. Virginia Hardy, a neighbor of
Anna and Christian's, told the court at the hearing what she
saw of their life together. "I don't know if it was alcohol or
drugs, or pills, but she was constantly ailing," Hardy said,
adding that Christian "served as a 24-hour nurse to her."

Hardy told of seeing Anna rush into Christian's bedroom
one night "and snatch him up from a deep sleep and slap
him, just continuously, right and left, and yell at him hys-
terically for him to apologize to her. And he didn't know
why. And he kept saying, 'Well, Mommy, I would, but I
don't know what I'm apologizing for.' And she said, 'You
just apologize to me.' And so then he would say, 'Okay,
Mommy, I apologize.' And then she would scream at him,
'What are you apologizing for? What did you do? Why are
you patronizing me?' "

Despite such harrowing incidents, for a few years things
were quiet on the custody front. Brando had visitation
rights, but he saw Christian only irregularly; he was busy
with social causes and films—after a decade of mostly un-
distinguished, unprofitable movies, he was about to revive
his faltering career with a towering performance as Don
Vito Corleone in 1972's *The Godfather*. Christian was enrolled in a military school in Los Angeles where, he remembered, he got into trouble a lot and carried a rifle high over
his head as punishment. After that he was enrolled in the
Ojai Valley school, a boarding school north of Ventura.
Then came the kidnapping.

Anna Kashfi picked up 13-year-old Christian from his
boarding school one Friday afternoon in February
1972. Within a few days, she had turned him over to a man
who was supposed to take the boy to Mexico. She later
claimed a double motive: to liberate Christian from the Ojai
school and to get him to a climate that would help ease an
attack of bronchitis. According to Anna's account, she and
the man were supposed to meet in Mexico several days
later. But he never showed up, and somehow Christian ended up with a group of American hippies in Baja California.

Kashfi reported her son missing, and Brando flew home
from Paris, where he was filming *Last Tango in Paris,* a
controversial X-rated film that would add a new dimension
to his superstardom. A private detective hired by Brando

located the boy in the hippie encampment and, with a con-
tingent of Mexican federal police, raided the camp and retrieved him. His hosts included six men and two women,
and they had enough provisions to last for several months.
They told police that Kashfi had promised them $10,000
each to hide Christian. The boy, frightened and confused,
thought the detective was kidnapping him and tried to run
away from him several times en route to Los Angeles.
Meanwhile Kashfi, traveling back to California from Mexico with a woman friend, made a scene on an interstate bus,
was arrested for drunk and disorderly conduct, and spent a
night in jail. Anna Kashfi was not charged with kidnapping.

After this bizarre episode Brando got sole custody of his
son and, despite further skirmishes with Kashfi, would remain Christian's sole guardian until the boy was 18 and on
his own. He took Christian with him when he went back to
Paris, and he recalled at Christian's hearing that after *Last
Tango* wrapped up, Christian asked, "Dad, could we live
here in Paris?"

They returned instead to Mulholland Drive, where, said
Brando on the witness stand, "I tried to keep some measure
of consistency in his life." But Christian was a very troubled
boy, "a basket case of emotional disorders," his father told
the court. Christian's feelings toward his father became a
mixture of love, awe, and fear. He idolized his father,
longed for his approval, and never quite got it. Adding to
the youngster's confusion were the mixed signals about his
importance in his father's life. Brando spent a great deal of
time away, working on movies and offering muddled support to various social causes. When he traveled he left Christian behind in the care of his longtime personal secretary,
Alice Marchak, or other employees, or sometimes the girlfriend of the moment.

When they were together, Brando clearly wanted to win
Christian, wanted the boy to like him and prefer him to his
erratic, abusive mother. But Brando was no model of propriety, responsibility, or paternal understanding. His own
upbringing had given him no model of normalcy or nice-
ness. He tried to win Christian by being both macho and
permissive—a co-conspirator, a fellow adolescent. With
crude shared pranks he attempted to be a pal—although at
48 a much bigger, more experienced one—to his teenage
son. But then he would suddenly play the strict patriarch,
banning the boy from the house in the name of discipline,
even hitting him. Christian Brando was willowy and slen-

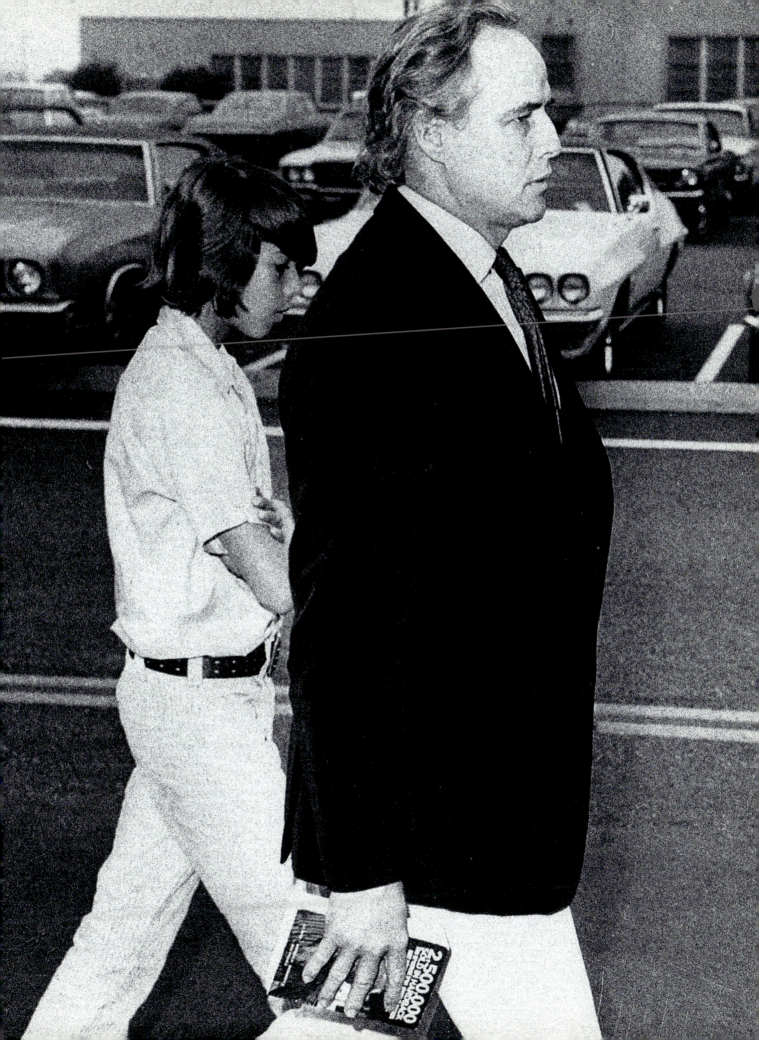

der, like his mother, not brawny like his dad, so there was never a fair contest between them.

According to Kashfi, the father and son dealt in pranks laced with a certain bullying cruelty. On one of their ski trips, for example, a freshly showered Christian was shoved out onto the balcony, wearing only a towel; Brando locked the sliding glass door after him. The shivering boy banged on the glass, shouting oaths and demanding to be let back in. Brando dropped his pants and pressed his bare rear against the glass, yelling, "Here, climb into this!"

But the father could also play the buddy. Once Christian swiped a yield sign from a local intersection. When police came to the house to inquire about it, Brando stood at the door, keeping the officer outside on the doormat, and played the shocked parent while Christian huddled gleefully nearby, holding the purloined sign.

Christian also showed himself capable of cruelty, according to his mother. To taunt her, he'd provoke her over the phone into a hysterical outburst, catch it on tape, and then play it back to amuse his friends.

But the boy's real demons were just beginning to assemble in his life. By the time he'd reached his early teens, Christian Brando had a drinking problem and was also using drugs. "I knew that he was drinking" his father testified later. "And he was smoking pot. So I said, 'If you're gonna smoke pot, if you're gonna drink, do it at home. I don't want you sneaking around.' "

Yet Brando's next effort to handle his son was the essence of sneaking. "I hired an ex-police officer to bug Christian's room because I wanted to know what was going on with him and his friends," he told the court. Christian finally asked him to turn the tape recorder off because the noises it made were keeping him awake. "I'd torn the wall out and everything, and I'd thought I was so clever, but I wasn't so clever," Brando said. In 1974 police picked Christian up for possession of marijuana, but he was never formally charged. Not until much later would Brando insist that the young man get treatment for his addictions.

Christian had continued his disjointed schooling at California Preparatory, an exclusive day school in Encino. In the spring of 1976, granting a rare interview in his Tahitian hideaway, Marlon Brando told *Time* magazine he was pleased with his relationship with Christian, who, he said, would enter college in Los Angeles. "I not only love him, I like him," Brando said. "We spend a lot of time together."

By the time the interview appeared, however, Christian had turned 18 and quit school, dropping out without finishing 10th grade. College became just another plan that never panned out. Venting his displeasure, Brando told his staff to bar Christian from the house on Mulholland. "I didn't have the heart to keep him out," an aide said later, "so every night I'd let him come up. But he never slept there; he went off and slept on friends' couches." In fact, throwing Christian out was one of Brando's misguided disciplinary tools. "He'd kick him out for 10 days because he wouldn't get up in the morning," another family associate noted. "Of course, neither did Marlon, but his line was 'Don't do what I do, do what I say.' "

In an effort to instill a work ethic in his children, Brando would employ them during the summers at his flourishing tourist hotel in Tahiti. Christian was a pearl diver: He washed dishes. Brando was spending about half the year on Tetiaroa in those days. "I'm convinced the world is doomed," he had told the *Time* reporter. "The end is near. I wanted a place where my family and I could be self-sufficient." His children Teihotu and Cheyenne lived on the main island, Tahiti, with their mother but would visit on weekends. "I don't think I will let them go to the States," he told the visiting reporter. "As Tahitians, they are too trusting. They would be destroyed in the pace of life in the States." The words would prove sadly prophetic.

The pace of life in the States—in Los Angeles, at least—was just as destructive of the actor's non-Tahitian son. Christian Brando returned to Los Angeles in the spring of 1977, after about a year of working for his father in the islands, and he might have settled into his former routine, except that the senior Brando intervened once more. He asked friend Louis Kemp, an associate of folk-rock singer Bob Dylan, if he could find something for Christian in his fishing operation in Alaska. The remoteness, Brando indicated, would be good for the boy. By summer 19-year-old Christian had a job with Kemp & Paulucci Seafoods, doing odd jobs in the company's packing plant in Bethel, a cluster of shacks and shops on the Kuskokwim River, in the southwestern corner of Alaska.

That first season in Alaska went well for Brando. Former coworkers remember him as a hard worker who, year by year, learned the fish-processing trade without entirely shedding his aura of restless peculiarity. "Most people," recalls

Tom Hyland, a former Kemp & Paulucci bookkeeper, "would think of him as flakey. He was hyper, definitely hyperactive, in my mind. But the more you got to know the guy, the phrase 'He'd do anything for you' could be attributed to him." While still a greenhorn, Brando got the distasteful job of grinding up a bargeload of spoiled fish and did it without complaining. Some thought he played his radio and sang too loud, but the people who knew him in Bethel seemed to have liked the odd young man from Hollywood. For one thing, he was careful not to use his father's fame as leverage; like most people along the Kuskokwim, he was considered down-to-earth by his neighbors.

In fact, Christian Brando seemed to have been ready to settle into a life spent in the remote corners of America. The short Alaska season, from April to September, left him free to roam in winter. The next summer, however, he was back in Bethel with Kemp & Paulucci, and in the process of moving north permanently, to a cabin near Washington State's Mount St. Helens, about 140 miles south of Seattle. Possibly aided by his mother, Brando bought the densely timbered, five-acre spread for $12,500 in 1978, with an eye to living there between Alaskan fishing seasons, supported by unemployment checks and odd jobs. For the first time in his life, Brando had a place—and a life—of his own.

The now-seasoned hand returned to Bethel for the 1979 season, this time to pilot one of the fish barges that the company sent up and down the Kuskokwim, visiting Eskimo villages to buy their fish. It was good, responsible work, requiring Brando to strike bargains, then weigh, pack, and ice the purchased fish before hauling it back to the Bethel seafood plant.

During this idyllic interlude, another person colored Christian Brando's life. Mary McKenna and Brando had been friends for a decade—they'd met in 1969 when McKenna and her family were Anna Kashfi's neighbors in West Hollywood. Friends since they were 11 years old, the two had been together, off and on, ever since, and by the end of the 1970s, their friendship had blossomed into love. In some respects, the pair were tailored for each other: Neither had finished high school, and both liked life on the edge. But after visiting the forest cabin in 1979, McKenna balked at the pastoral life. A pretty woman with long, dark hair and an exotic Greekness from her mother's side, Mary McKenna was a makeup artist, and with her sister she owned a Hollywood cosmetics store called Vanity. She felt her business prospects were far better than Christian's, and she talked him into moving back to California in 1980.

Abandoning his hard-won freedom, Brando took Mary McKenna to live with him in his father's house. In January 1981, acting on impulse, they married. Marlon Brando supported the move, giving his daughter-in-law several thousand dollars to pay store debts. Christian got along for a while running errands for his father and working sporadically. He trimmed trees for Brando's longtime neighbor Jack Nicholson, worked as a mechanic at a Ford dealership, and learned and taught heli-arc welding at an adult vocational school. Mary McKenna's mother would remember her daughter's months at the Mulholland Drive house as the good times—Christian and Mary seemed to have eluded their problems.

But now another presence entered Christian Brando's life. Through a mutual friend, local cable talk-show host Skip E. Lowe, Brando met Bill Cumpanas, a professional tree surgeon and sometime actor and model known to everyone as Bill Cable. Twelve years Christian's senior, macho and swaggering, Cable took Brando into his tree-trimming business and taught him, he says, to "really climb, how to get in there with the ropes and do the stuff." And the two became, said Cable, "brothers. We were really close." They'd get together for jobs several times a week, and after work they'd drink and—despite the fact that Brando was married and Cable in a serious relationship—meet women. Observed Cable, "It was easy to get laid, especially if your father was legend." To Brando, Cable was always "Cabe." And despite Christian's aversion to his burdensome surname, Cable dubbed him Brandoling.

In fact, the shadow of a famous father still loomed over Brandoling. Over the next few years, try as he would to establish a direction in his life, Christian would find himself drifting, moving through the landscape in a meandering, aimless way. Like many another celebrity's child, he suffered from comparisons, and he remained entrenched in an ambivalent struggle with his larger-than-life father.

At the presentencing hearing, Christian Brando's defense painted a portrait of a passive and insecure young man of low self-esteem, a fellow who let things happen to him and was often overtaken by events. This was the Christian Brando that many folks in Los Angeles got to know in the 1980s. He spent a lot of his time partying with pals, picking

up women; he earned some of his living as a freelance tree surgeon and welder, and he took halfhearted stabs at modeling and acting. By the time he was 30—an age at which his father was already an acclaimed star—Christian Brando had barely explored the difficulties of breaking into show business, even with a famous parent and his own dark good looks.

In his pursuit of good times, Brando used enough alcohol and recreational drugs to damage his brain. At his presentencing hearing, psychologist Saul Faerstein testified for the defense that Christian Brando's mental faculties were slowed permanently. His mental deficiencies could only have added to his feelings of inadequacy. Friends recognized him as a gentle guy who showed tenderness for animals and generosity toward other people. But they also told of a man with a sudden and violent temper.

During these years Christian showed a determination, on the surface at least, to be independent of his father. He would introduce himself as Christian Smith, so people would react to him as a person and not as the son of a celebrity. He refused money from his father and tried to make his own way. But he still depended on Marlon Brando's generosity, living rent-free in a house the actor owned.

The senior Brando's own ambivalence created a tremendous push-pull in Christian's efforts to find a direction. Marlon, in his disillusion with show business, hoped his children would not be contaminated by what he viewed as a neurotic, decadent industry. When his son began to have acting aspirations, Brando said he had to make it on his own. But when Christian had a project under consideration, his father would insist on examining and reshaping it, sometimes killing it altogether.

Christian had developed another compelling interest: guns. Bill Cable fed his friend's preoccupation with firearms, and helped him assemble the arsenal police later took from Brando's house: a shotgun, a .44-caliber carbine, two unregistered automatic weapons—an Uzi submachine gun and an M-14 rifle—in addition to the .45 Christian used to shoot Drollet. In December 1983 police picked up a rifle-wielding young Brando for trespassing at an abandoned antiaircraft missile site. He wasn't charged.

Friends since 1969, newlyweds Christian Brando and Mary McKenna *(far left)* pose happily after their 1981 marriage. In 1985, only a year away from divorce, Mary *(near left)* mugs with Christian and partner-sister Paule outside Vanity, their Hollywood cosmetics shop.

The friendship between Cable and Christian Brando was deepened in 1984 by an unexpected opportunity in Tahiti. A tropical cyclone had devastated Marlon Brando's hotel there, and he asked the two men to come and clear the downed trees and fell others on nearby islands to furnish lumber for rebuilding the resort complex. For several months the young men shared beer, hard work, and adventure—on one occasion, in the lagoon, Cable said, he'd pulled his friend out of the way of a threatening shark after Christian's timber-laden raft capsized.

While the two men labored in paradise, however, the frayed edges of Christian's marriage began to disintegrate; when he returned to Los Angeles in early 1985, it was over. During their marriage, Mary McKenna's business had prospered while Christian's tree work didn't pay his bills. The couple had moved into their own apartment, but Christian, following Bill Cable's example, would live with his wife only until they had an argument, then move out and stay with a friend—sometimes a girlfriend—until things calmed down. At times he would sleep in his car rather than go home to his wife or his father. According to McKenna's mother, the pair constantly fought "like brother and sister."

Brando's violent outbursts of temper did nothing to help his marriage. McKenna would charge in her divorce action that Christian had slapped her around, threatened to kill her, pointed a gun at her mother, and jumped on her car to keep her from driving away. When questioned at her ex-husband's presentencing hearing about these incidents, however, she downplayed their importance, saying that she might have been exaggerating. Their divorce was granted in February 1987.

Meanwhile, Christian had started seeing a tall, blond actress named Laurene Landon, and the couple had a relatively happy arrangement, perhaps because they had their own places. Brando lived on Wonderland Avenue, next to Laurel Canyon, in a hilltop house that his father had bought him in 1985. Landon lived on Hollywood Boulevard. She was earning enough as an actress and model to help Christian, buying him a new, expensive chain saw when he needed it for his business. Landon became pregnant in 1987, and they were disappointed when she miscarried.

In his Wonderland Avenue neighborhood, Brando was a magnet for a group of neighborhood toughs who became known as the Down Boys. Mostly unemployed, many homeless, they were down-on-their-luck guys who spent their time and what little money they had on drugs and beer. They hung around a Laurel Canyon convenience store that Brando visited nearly every day to buy cigarettes and beer. "They were always saying, 'It's Marlon Brando's son,' and Christian would give them money, he felt sorry for them," one friend said. According to Skip Lowe, Brando chose these companions "because he wanted to try to be rough. But he wasn't. He was a boy, a shy boy, a skinny little guy." Christian was, Lowe said, "trying to be Brando, like his father." Bill Cable was succinct on the subject of the Down Boys, calling them a bunch of losers and leeches.

Brando let the Down Boys crash at his house on Wonderland, which Lowe called a "terrifying pad, terrifying. It was never clean, you would not believe it. It was just a bunch of guys hanging around, sleeping there and carrying on." Lowe thought Laurene Landon sometimes cleaned the house—but added that "Laurene wanted to be Marlon Brando's daughter-in-law; she tried to help her career." And Lowe was not alone in thinking Landon had ulterior motives. Christian Brando could point to little that hadn't come to him because of his father.

By then the young Brando was making noises about getting into acting. Aided by Lowe, he attracted the attention of Italian producer Carmine DeBenedittis, who offered Christian the part of a hit man in a low-budget Italian gangster movie called *The Issue at Stake*. The producer found parts in it for Cable and his wife, Shirley, too. But the Americans had barely landed in Rome when Marlon Brando called them back to Los Angeles for conferences about the project. "When I went to meet Marlon Brando," said De-Benedittis, "I noticed that when Christian is near his father, he seems to shrink, he becomes a gnat. He seems to be crushed by the force of his father's personality. It's a very heavy load, to be called Christian Brando."

The movie was made, and although it was never released outside Italy, Christian was paid $30,000 for five months' work. The experience, recalls Cable, "got him past that point of being afraid to try," and got him excited about doing other movies. "He had a taste of working on a film and making some good bucks." He began exploring a joint project with Cable called *Buddies*, an adventure movie growing out of their experiences in Tahiti. "But nobody ever came across with the dough," Cable said. The father, meanwhile, had been working on a script for a movie called *Jericho* about the Central Intelligence Agency's involvement in the international drug trade, and there was a part in it for Christian. But that project was eventually scrubbed.

"That kind of hurt Christian," Cable says, "because he was really looking forward to that. And then it was just back to trimming trees again and back to a nowhere life of just doing physical labor." Friends said Brando was depressed and was drinking more heavily. His father got him into a detoxification program, but Christian couldn't stay with it. A nasty fall from a tree wrecked his knees, and he had to give up tree surgery, so he turned to freelance welding. He liked welding, he would say later, because "I get to be the boss. I'm in control of the situation." He wasn't in control of much else.

"When we came back from Italy," Cable later recalled, Christian "started getting threatening phone calls. Someone would say, 'I'm gonna kill your whole family, and I'm gonna start with you.'" The younger Brando already had a pair of assault rifles that he'd bought with Cable's advice, but even so he didn't feel safe. So when Cable decided to get a new SIG Sauer .45 automatic, Brando got one too, and they had "sister SIGs," as Cable called them.

Then came the money. On May 11, 1988, Christian Brando turned 30 and began receiving interest income from the half-million-dollar trust his father had long ago set up for him. This money made him even more of a mark for the Down Boys. With their encouragement, Christian was doing drugs, drinking malt liquor—as many as

two dozen Colt 45s a day—and just hanging around.

One childhood pal of Brando's remembered seeing him drunk and armed several times at the Wonderland house, the loaded .45 stuck in his waistband. Once, the gun went off accidentally, but no one was hurt. Christian kept the pistol on a shelf in his bedroom and would sometimes take turns with a friend shooting it in the house, aiming at logs on either side of the fireplace.

Beyond that, Brando was doing some welding. His agent was getting him occasional readings, and he was considering an acting workshop, but nothing was panning out. Buoyed by the steady income from his trust, he lived aimlessly in his Laurel Canyon setting. Then, in the autumn of 1989, his world shuddered: His friendship with Cabe, his big brother, suddenly came to an end.

Bill Cable had split from his wife, Shirley Cumpanas, and wandered up to Brando's Wonderland Avenue house, he recalls, "to go cry on his shoulder." He found Christian on the bed with Shirley, but clothed. Furiously rejecting their protestations of innocence, Cable stormed out. "And then I'd call Christian up and say, 'If I ever see you around, I'm going to kick your ass.' As much as I love Christian, I would never hurt him, but I wanted to scare him. And I had him running scared for eight months, thinking I was going to kick his ass."

Brando was scared, all right. He moved out of his house on Wonderland and into a small apartment, and he hired

Sometime actor, tree surgeon, and gun enthusiast Bill Cable *(left)* unwinds with buddy Christian Brando after a 1985 appearance on a Hollywood cable television program.

a bodyguard. He chose a guy called Frank, "one of the cleanest of the Down Boys," Shirley Cumpanas recalled, "but also one of the baddest. He was the one to handle Big Bill if he walked in with a gun, and he became Christian's best friend. He wouldn't have batted an eye about blowing Bill's head off." Reasoning that they had nothing to lose, Shirley and Christian began a short affair.

The brew was becoming more dangerous. To the volatile combination of money, guns, and alcohol, Cabe's departure added paranoia. As Christian felt his control over his life lessening, his temper seemed to become more violent. His rage flared one night when he had some of the Down Boys over, drinking, and he got into a shoving match with a fellow named Luke over a 12-string guitar. As Down Boy William Smith told it, Luke started to fall and grabbed at Brando to steady himself. Believing Luke was hitting him, Brando ran out of the house yelling, "That's it, that's it," and came back swinging a hammer. "And Luke is sitting here, completely drunk on the ground," Smith continued. "He didn't even see him coming with the hammer." When Brando took a swing, Smith caught his arm and told Luke to run. Brando chased Luke, throwing rocks at him, then used the hammer to smash his car's headlights, and told him to get out.

By February 1990, Christian Brando had returned to his hilltop house on Wonderland, and it was again Party Central. The Down Boys kept showing up with drugs or beer, usually both, and staying for days, sometimes stealing things—even Brando's welding equipment—and Brando was having more and more trouble handling them. Finally, one February night, he took a shot at one of them, a 56-year-old unemployed propman named Ricardo Alvarez. William Smith described the incident on the witness stand during Christian's hearing.

The story began in the afternoon, when several of the Down Boys and Brando spent time at Wonderland, drinking, before their host chased them off. That evening Smith, Corey Kronick, and Alvarez came back, bringing beer to share with Christian. Smith got out and approached the front door, just as Laurene Landon came running out yelling that Brando was "going off." Then Christian came out with his .45 in his hand, yelling at them to leave. He fired three shots over Smith's head and kicked him with his steel-toed construction boots.

Alvarez, Smith recalled, was in the backseat of their car,

"obliviated." When the man spoke to Brando, he found the .45 stuck in his face. The gun went off, the bullet carving a gash across Alvarez's left temple and burying itself in the seat. The friends fled as fast as they could, avoiding the police and the hospital because they were all drunk and stoned and Alvarez didn't want to antagonize the Brandos.

The story of this shooting broke only after Christian Brando's arrest for the murder of Dag Drollet, when some of his friends sold information to a tabloid newspaper. After reading the paper's account, the district attorney launched his own investigation. "About the best that can be said for Christian," the prosecution would later say after describing these violent incidents, "is that he usually warns his victims to leave before he tries to kill them."

A worried Marlon Brando kept trying to help his son. He got him into another alcohol rehabilitation program, but Christian again dropped out. Brando arranged for a tutor to come to Mulholland Drive so father and son could get their high-school equivalency diplomas together. But that didn't work out either. In January 1990, California's new gun-control law took effect, tightening restrictions on assault weapons. Worried by his son's blending of guns and alcohol, Brando ordered Christian to bring all his weapons to the house on Mulholland Drive for safekeeping. By May he'd succeeded in getting all but one of them: the .45.

Things seemed to be looking up for Christian Brando in May 1990. He had long since ended his fling with Shirley Cumpanas and was getting back on good terms with Laurene Landon, whom he'd invited to his 32d birthday party on May 11. Two days later, Bill Cable called. He'd made up with Shirley and had decided to patch things up with his old friend. Cabe and Brandoling shot some pool and had some beers, just like old times. And on May 16, Brando was going to see his pregnant little sister, who was in town from Tahiti.

Tarita Cheyenne Brando had led a sheltered and privileged upbringing in the closed, island society of Tahiti. She and her older brother, Teihotu, grew up mostly with their mother in Papeete, the Tahitian capital on the big island, flying to their father's atoll to spend weekends with him—when he was there.

To Brando, this beautiful daughter was a princess, but many described her as spoiled. She once flew into a rage at some fishermen who'd beached their boats on Tetiaroa, and

Photographed in Tahiti about 1988, Tarita Cheyenne Brando *(near right)* began living with playboy Dag Drollet *(far right)* soon after meeting him at a nightclub in 1987. Ignoring their occasional strife, one French writer called the pair Romeo and Juliet in Paradise.

she smashed their fragile canoes with a rock. When this happened, Brando simply bought the fishermen new boats.

Early in 1987 Cheyenne had run into Dag Drollet, a former schoolmate of her brother Teihotu's, at a nightclub. Days later they began living together on the first floor of Drollet's stepfather's house overlooking Papeete. She was 17, he was 23. Drollet was in the midst of building a house, and when it was finished the couple moved there.

Drollet was the son of a prominent Tahitian family, but his father, Jacques, an influential educator and politician, had divorced his mother, Lisette, when Dag was a child. Lisette Drollet then had married Albert Lecaill, a builder, and when Dag grew up he sometimes worked for his stepfather. When Drollet started dating Cheyenne Brando, he already had a baby daughter, Tiairani, from another liaison. The infant lived with the Lecaills. Drollet had attended a university in Paris but found he preferred Tahitian life and returned home. He was a big man—six-feet-five and powerfully built—and fond of rugged activity. He went to work for the Tahitian government, provisioning heavy equipment on the outer islands, but he lived the life of a playboy, spending lots of time surfing, diving, and enjoying Tahitian nightlife. He was also a champion motorcycle racer and often took Cheyenne around Tahiti on his bike.

Death first cast its shadow over their affair in March 1989. They were out driving in a car when Drollet ran down and killed a pedestrian. Criminal charges were dropped because the pedestrian was found to have been drunk, but civil charges against Drollet were still pending when the victim died. And this tragedy was not the first of the couple's troubles.

From the beginning, relations between Drollet and Brando were passionate, stormy, and by some accounts, occasionally violent. His father, Jacques Drollet, would sum it up at Christian Brando's court hearing: "Dag and Cheyenne lived like two scorpions in a glass. They were looking at each other, jealous of each other, saying silly and nasty things of each other." And the nastiness didn't always stop with mere words. Yet Dag told his father: "I love her, I have her under my skin."

As early as 1988, Cynthia Garbutt, Marlon Brando's longtime business manager on Tetiaroa, saw a bruise on Cheyenne's face when she returned early from an island-hopping trip with Dag. She told Cynthia they'd argued while tripping on ecstacy, a hallucinogen. Cheyenne Brando

seemed to be changing. Formerly "sweet and sensible," according to Garbutt, she became "nervous" and took to breaking things, smashing glasses. But another automobile accident, this one in August 1989, multiplied these disturbing changes in Cheyenne and magnified the strains between the lovers.

Driving her brother Teihotu's Jeep, Cheyenne Brando lost control and the vehicle swerved off the road and rolled. She was thrown from the car onto jagged coral rocks, badly slashing her face. Her head injuries included several broken skull bones. Her father flew her to Los Angeles for months of painful reconstructive surgery and psychiatric counseling. Although her beauty was largely restored, she didn't believe it; she felt her looks were gone. And the accident caused a deeper kind of damage as well. Family and friends said that Cheyenne was emotionally changed, simply not the same person, after the crash. She began to make up stories about her loved ones; friends said she was depressed.

Concerned about Cheyenne, Dag Drollet took what was to be a two-year leave from his government job in October of 1989 and went with her to live on Brando's atoll, with a view to becoming a permanent part of Marlon's hotel operation. Lecaill thought his stepson and Marlon Brando got on well together. In December, Cheyenne announced she was pregnant and the couple seemed happy.

But one night that same month, Cheyenne's mother, Tarita Teriipia, would later tell Tahitian authorities, "I heard Cheyenne crying. I went to her room and found Cheyenne on the floor and Dag hitting her. They didn't give me any explanations, but Cheyenne told me that this wasn't the first time that this had happened because Dag was very jealous." Around Easter in 1990, Drollet moved back in with the Lecaills and Cheyenne returned to her house next to her mother's. Drollet still visited, when she asked him to, but they never lived together again after that. Despite her pregnancy, Cheyenne Brando evidently continued using drugs.

Her father grew alarmed about Cheyenne's deteriorating mental state and visited Tahiti to see her. He hoped to take her back to Los Angeles where he could keep an eye on her and get her to a psychiatrist he trusted. Brando went home without Cheyenne, but then Drollet helped talk her into going for a visit and offered to go with her; "Cheyenne felt protected by Dag," said his stepfather. Cheyenne and Dag flew to California on tickets that Brando paid for. Tarita

Teriipia joined them later, after Cheyenne called from Los Angeles and asked her to come.

By that time, Drollet's father would later tell the press, Dag had decided his relationship with Cheyenne was going nowhere, and they should separate. The elder Drollet felt even more strongly about it. "I said, 'You're going to meet a tragedy with that girl, your life together smells of tragedy, it smells of death.'" As Jacques and Lisette saw their son off to the States, they thought this would be his one last act of support for Cheyenne Brando after an affair that had lasted more than three years.

At Brando's Mulholland Drive house, Cheyenne was distant from Dag, sleeping apart from him in a room off the kitchen. Drollet bedded down on a mattress on the floor in a den that had been Christian's room—the room in which Dag would die. She discouraged Drollet from going with her to her gynecologist, saying, according to Garbutt, "Don't worry yourself. It is not your baby." Dag had taken the jibe as an effort to punish him for having implied that she'd been unfaithful.

On May 13 Dag Drollet telephoned his mother to say that he and Cheyenne Brando were still having problems; he also told her that he planned to fly back to Tahiti on May 25 for a hearing on the 1989 pedestrian death. The next news the Lecaills had from California came just three days later: Dag was dead.

May 16, the evening that would end tragically for Marlon Brando's two troubled children, began on a promising note. Christian had made plans to go to Mulholland Drive and pick up Cheyenne for dinner. "I guess Pop told her she'd been driving him plain nuts," he later told police. "I brought her a couple of presents, a couple of T-shirts, cheer her up, take her out, you know, hanging out with her big brother. That's rare for her." And it was. Christian and Cheyenne had never been particularly close—the 12-year age difference and the geographic separation alone could account for that—but several of Brando's friends talked about how protective he was of Cheyenne. Perhaps he hoped to find a kindred soul in his half sister. She would later tell police how surprised and pleased she'd been that Christian arranged to see her; to her, they had always seemed from different worlds.

Christian had a job that day, welding brackets at a private residence. When he got home, around three in the afternoon, he indicated later, he drank "almost all" of a six-pack of Colt 45. "This is what I would generally do when I got off work in the afternoon. It was not unusual for me." Then he picked up Laurene Landon and the two went shopping at a surplus store, where he bought some work boots and two T-shirts to give to Cheyenne and Dag. He dropped Landon off at her place around 5 o'clock and went to his father's house.

He asked Drollet to come along to dinner, but he declined, and Christian drove Cheyenne in his pickup truck to Musso and Frank's Grill, a popular Hollywood restaurant. Over dinner, Cheyenne would later say, she told her brother that she and Drollet had a good relationship, even though they sometimes fought. But what Christian heard her say, he would declare later, was that Dag was "whacking her around." During dinner, Christian had at least three potent negronis—gin, vermouth, and campari—and the drinks fueled his growing anger. When, hours after the shooting, police gave Christian a Breathalyzer test, he would show .19 blood alcohol, more than twice the drunk-driving threshold in California.

After dinner brother and sister left the restaurant and drove to Laurene Landon's place; Christian said he wanted to introduce the two women. Cheyenne waited in the truck while Brando went inside, where he collected his .45 automatic and a knife. Cheyenne later told police he seemed upset and recalled Christian saying repeatedly, "I'm gonna bust on Dag." This seemed like vain bravado coming from Christian, who at six feet even and 160 pounds was five inches shorter than Drollet, and 65 pounds lighter. When Landon walked outside to meet Christian's baby sister, she found her curled up on the seat, asleep.

Leaving Landon, Christian stopped at a market and bought some beer. Cheyenne again stayed in the truck, and this time while she waited she handled the gun, thinking it was not loaded, or that it was a toy, because it was so light. Cheyenne reported one more stop, when Christian pulled off the road by some dunes and "drank several gulps of beer." And he continued to make threats against Drollet, according to Cheyenne. Then he drove on to Mulholland Drive, successfully negotiating the winding, treacherous road, and followed Cheyenne into the house. It was sometime after 10 o'clock.

How the next few minutes unfolded is perhaps eternally unclear. Cheyenne Brando told Los Angeles police that she and Christian were in the house less than a minute before she heard a shot in the den; then Christian came into her room, just off the kitchen, and said, "I killed him." She summed up her opinion for Detective Andrew Monsue, saying "It's a murder, in case you didn't know it." Sometime after that, she would tell Tahitian officials that she and her brother had been in the house for 10 to 15 minutes before the shooting occurred.

As Marlon Brando remembers it, and as he testified, Christian first came into the room where his father was watching television, and Marlon asked him about the dinner and about Cheyenne. Then Christian went to the den at the other side of the house and confronted Drollet, returning to his father's room in another five minutes to say that he'd killed Dag.

As police interrogated Christian that night in an exhausting series of interviews between midnight and dawn, they heard three versions of the events leading up to the shooting. While never denying that he'd been holding the gun when the single shot killed Dag Drollet, the gun, he said, had been "where I always kept it," hidden under a cushion of the sofa that the young Tahitian lay on, and that it was in getting the gun from its hiding place that he'd struggled with Drollet. Pressed on that point, he admitted that he'd brought the .45 into the house that night and concealed it in the couch. Finally, Christian admitted that he hadn't hidden the gun at all—it had been in his hand when he walked into the den, where Drollet was watching television.

Christian Brando told police he'd had three negronis but denied he was walking strange or talking strange. Later in the interview, however, he said, "I was drunk; I was blasted. Pretty soused."

The rest of Christian's story was pretty jumbled, too. He said he didn't know Dag Drollet well, didn't even know his last name, and hadn't wanted to hurt him. Months later, he would say he met Drollet for the first time that evening. But as detectives worked on him that first night, encouraging him to get all the truth out, he allowed that he'd been "pissed off" by the time he got to Mulholland that night, and that he "hated" Drollet. Brando said his preference would have been to see his sister's lover "in a wheelchair all busted up than to have him dead," and he added a bit of macho bluster: "I didn't, I mean, go up to him and go BOOM! in my dad's house. If I was going to do that, I'd take him down the road and knock him off." Brando also talked of how he might have taken Drollet "out to Death

Valley, no clothes on, and give him three gallons of water. 'Get a suntan.' "

Of Cheyenne, he said, "I love her to death," then, pleadingly, "How do I get out of this? I mean, I didn't want to kill the guy, I didn't mean to kill the guy." Chain-smoking Marlboros, nervous and scared, Christian Brando told police he'd had words with Drollet. He said that he and Dag struggled for the gun, and it went off. He said he was sorry.

When police had arrived at the Mulholland Drive house on May 16, they'd found Dag, dressed in shorts and a shirt, sprawled on the sofa, a comforter across his lower legs. His left hand held a bag of tobacco, a throwaway lighter, and a packet of cigarette papers; his right index finger rested on the remote control for the television set. The bullet had entered the young man's left cheek and exited the back of his neck. To police eyes, as Detective Monsue would testify, there was no sign of a struggle. The path of the bullet, as shown by the entry and exit wounds, seemed to show that Drollet had been shot while sitting, leaning back, and at very close range.

Early in the morning after the shooting, Christian Brando was charged with murder and, as a result of a search of his father's house, with illegal possession of a machine gun and illegal possession of a silencer. At his bail hearing police pointed out that his first impulse after the killing was to run, and that it was only Marlon Brando's parental authority that persuaded him to stay and wait for police. Christian was, they said, still a flight risk, with friends in other countries and means of getting to them. The judge denied bail, over the protests of Christian's first attorney, William Kunstler, famed for his civil-rights work in the 1960s and long a friend of the young man's father. Brando went back to the county jail, where he stayed for 90 days. He was soon isolated from the prisoners who had taunted him with cries of "Hey, rich boy, think your Godfather daddy's going to take care of you now?"

Marlon Brando was anything but the Godfather at that moment. Monsue, who'd interviewed the actor in his bedroom at length the night of the shooting, described him to writer Peter Manso as "sad, very humble, very meek; he was like a tired old man. There was a sense of being beaten about him, and he cried several times." He told Monsue that Christian had always had trouble controlling his temper and would erupt violently when he got angry.

Because of her mental fragility, police left Cheyenne Brando alone for nearly a month. On June 15, three days after giving a brief statement to officials, the young woman flew to Tahiti, beyond the reach of Los Angeles subpoenas. At the end of June, two months prematurely, she was delivered of a son and named him Tuki.

But Tahiti was no refuge for Cheyenne. Drollet's father could not reach Marlon or Christian Brando, but he could reach Cheyenne. He brought charges against her, under French law, of complicity in the killing of Dag, a French citizen. When the magistrate questioned her, her answers were full of extravagant accusations and contradictions. She accused her father of planning to have Drollet killed because "he was jealous of my life and my happiness." She told the judge to see *The Godfather,* and "you will understand everything." She misdated Tuki's birth by six weeks, insisting he was born on Dag's birthday in August.

Marlon Brando was, in fact, recovering his Godfather energy, trying to take charge of his son's defense. Breaking a lifelong taste for silence, he began a marathon of interviews with the press, giving news conferences in front of the courthouse and calling favored reporters with exclusive comments. He angrily took the media to task for portraying Christian as what he called a "mad-dog killer." When in August bail was finally set at $2 million, Brando put up his $4-million house on Mulholland to cover it; under California law, property used as bail must be worth twice the amount set. He also announced that he was setting up a million-dollar trust fund for Dag Drollet's four-year-old daughter. As if in answer, Jacques Drollet, Dag's father, slapped Christian Brando with a wrongful-death suit on behalf of the child.

I didn't, I mean, go up to him and go BOOM! in my dad's house. If I was going to do that, I'd take him down the road and knock him off.

CHRISTIAN BRANDO

Killed by a bullet through his left cheek, Dag Drollet *(left)* still clings to a throwaway lighter, tobacco pouch, cigarette papers, and a television remote *(inset)* in this Los Angeles police photograph taken May 16, 1990. Prosecutors would argue that the relaxed position of the body and the objects gripped firmly in one hand indicated that Drollet had been ambushed, and was not involved in a struggle that caused the pistol to discharge accidentally, as alleged by Christian Brando.

A police crime scene photograph shows the computer-room sofa in which Marlon Brando said he concealed his son's SIG Sauer .45 automatic and magazine *(inset)* after the shooting. The actor had asked Christian to bring the pistol to his Mulholland Drive home for safe-keeping, he told investigators.

Haggard from a hangover and a night of intense interrogation, Christian Brando was photographed and booked by Los Angeles police. When this mug shot was released to the media, Marlon Brando angrily charged that prosecutors were trying to portray his son as a "mad-dog killer."

BK1998049 05-17-90

LOS ANGELES POLICE = W/LA

In court with his interim counsel, noted civil-rights attorney
William Kunstler *(left)*, Christian Brando is charged with first-
degree murder at his May 18, 1990, arraignment.

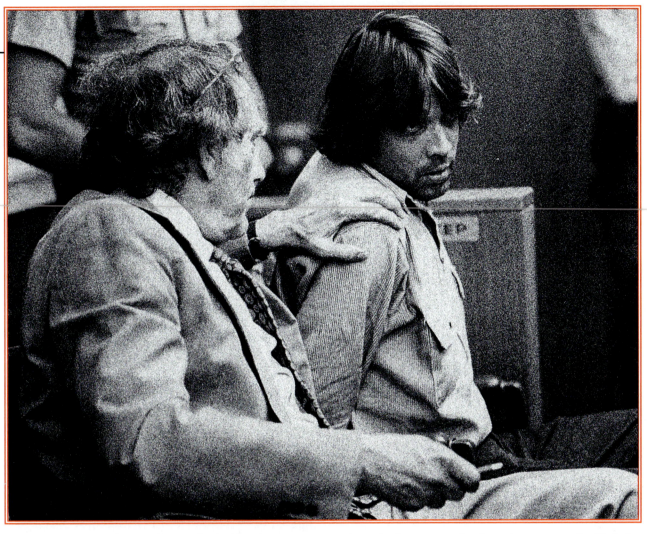

By now, however, the murder case looked hard to prove. Christian's entire taped statement to police had been ruled inadmissible as evidence. The officer reading him his rights at the beginning of the interrogation had assumed that Marlon Brando's son would have no trouble finding the money to hire legal counsel and neglected to finish the litany with: "If you cannot afford one, an attorney will be appointed for you without charge before questioning." Moreover, the major witness was unavailable. Cheyenne, still in Tahiti, had made two suicide attempts—once by taking pills, once by trying to hang herself with a dog chain. She'd wanted, she said later, "to rejoin Dag." In and out of a mental hospital, she seemed permanently unable to travel. "She's not crazy," Jacques Drollet protested; she "knows things and wants to tell the truth," but "her family and Marlon Brando are keeping her away."

In early January a plea bargain was struck. Christian Brando would plead guilty to voluntary manslaughter, forgoing a trial; in exchange, the gun-possession charge against him would be dropped. Thus the only courtroom proceeding would be the three-day presentencing hearing.

The event was a media circus. Marlon Brando, rebellious to the end, refused to be sworn in as a witness with the usual oath to tell the truth "so help me God." He did not believe in God, he said, in "a conventional sense." He offered to swear on his grandchildren, then ended up taking an alternative oath that required him only to promise to tell the truth on pain of perjury. In a packed courtroom, a parade of other witnesses revealed painful details of Christian Brando's appalling childhood. Forensic experts traded opinions on whether the gun could have fired accidentally

133

Members of the extended Brando clan look on while Christian is denied bail as a flight risk in a May 22, 1990, hearing. From left are Miko and Rebecca, Brando's children by Mexican actress Movita Castenada; Brando; Tarita Teriipia, his common-law Tahitian wife; and her son Teihotu, Cheyenne Brando's older brother.

during a struggle, on whether there could have been a struggle, on how close Dag Drollet's hands had been to the gun when it went off.

Christian Brando did not testify, but defense lawyer Shapiro told the court how he had answered when a probation officer asked why he took his gun to Drollet: "Because that's what my mother did to me," evidently referring to her threatening, bullying, violent behavior. "And no one would listen. No one would help me. And I couldn't let that happen to my sister. So I wanted to scare him. I wanted to let him know what fear is really like."

At the end, Marlon Brando faced Dag Drollet's parents across the courtroom. Speaking to them in French, he said, "I cannot continue with the hate in your eyes. I am sorry with my whole heart." After Drollet's parents and stepfather made bitter replies, Christian Brando's statement was brief. To Dag's parents, he said, "If I could trade places with Dag, I would, right now." To the judge he murmured, "I'm very prepared for the consequences. Whatever's fit."

The judge saw fit to choose the middle ground. The prosecution had not shown enough malicious intent, he said, to merit the maximum 16-year prison sentence prescribed by law; nor had the defense shown enough mitigation to justify a minimal three-year sentence or probation. On February 28, 1991, Judge Robert Thomas sentenced Christian Devi Brando to 10 years' imprisonment: six years for manslaughter, four for using a gun.

Christian Brando began serving his time in the California Men's Colony in San Luis Obispo and would be eligible for parole in 1996.

After the hearing, members of the Brando clan maintained virtual silence about the case. Christian and most of those close to him refused requests for interviews. But intriguing information continued to leak out. For instance, there was the matter of the fatal bullet. Although Marlon Brando testified at the hearing that he'd found the bullet underfoot eight days after the shooting, *Entertainment Weekly* magazine reported in late 1992 that the actor had actually found it the day after the shooting and had his staff help him rip up the carpet and rearrange the furniture in an apparent effort to reconstruct the bullet's path.

Cheyenne Brando continued to exemplify the family penchant for tragedy. She got permission to leave Tahiti in January 1991, but only to move to another mental hospital, this one in France. When eight months later she skipped out of the clinic, Interpol tried to trace her and send her back to Tahiti, but her father took her on the lam, and for weeks they shuttled through the French countryside. Police finally trailed the actor from a little café where he dined alone back

Flanked by father Marlon and half brother Miko, Christian Brando steps into the light after 90 days in the Los Angeles County Jail. Marlon Brando put up his $4-million Mulholland Drive estate as collateral for the $2-million bail.

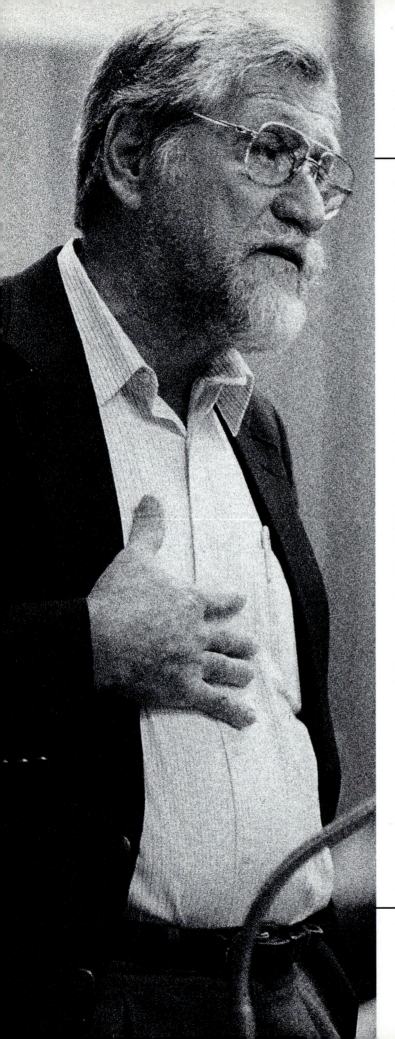

Unmoved by Marlon Brando's emotional apology to his family, an implacable Jacques Drollet urges skepticism and stern justice at Christian Brando's 1991 presentencing hearing.

to a well-appointed house outside Orléans where Cheyenne was hiding. Brando returned to Los Angeles, and a French military jet took Cheyenne to Tahiti. In August 1992 she got permission to move into a 12-room house that her father had bought her in Los Angeles. There she lived as a near recluse, with occasional visits to a nearby psychiatric hospital. A nurse there was suing Cheyenne for beating her up in a locker room at the hospital. Three years after the shooting, on May 26, 1993, the complicity case against her in Tahiti was dropped.

Tuki was in the care of Cheyenne's mother and others at Brando's Tahitian hideaway. Concerned about Cheyenne's claims that the infant was not really Dag's, Jacques Drollet sought a DNA test to verify the child's paternity. As late as mid-1993, his request had not been granted. "I had a very strong sense of revenge," Drollet says. "You cannot take someone's life for nothing. I may just as well quiet down and wait for destiny to take care of the culprit."

Mary McKenna, Christian Brando's ex-wife, talked to Christian the Sunday after he went to jail. According to her mother, he told her not to cry, that he would have some kind of life in jail. He would even have a garden. He hoped people would forgive him, and he said he prayed every day. McKenna herself had a nervous breakdown after the trial, her mother said, and later went to Spain, to try to forget.

By late spring of 1993 Bill Cable, Christian's self-styled big brother, had not yet been to see the friend he called Brandoling in jail. "I was going to see him a few times, but to tell you the truth," he said, "I just can't bear to see him in jail, you know. And I can't call him on the phone. And to go there you've got to send for some kind of an application thing. What am I going to say? 'Wish you were out'? 'I'm having a great time out here'?"

As for the great actor at the center of this grim play, the shooting of Dag Drollet brought terrible grief and irreparable damage to the two young people he may love most in all the world. Had a dramatist been writing the Brando saga, it would have read like a Greek tragedy, full of murder and madness, replaying the ancient theme that mortal genius and greatness carry destruction as their price. This meeting of life and art in his own family might have escaped Marlon Brando, the suffering father. But Marlon Brando the actor must have understood it perfectly. In his old age there had finally come a role worthy of his grand, brooding talent. It was a part that only Brando could have played. ◆

I cannot continue
with the hate in your
eyes. I am sorry with
my whole heart.

MARLON BRANDO

*S*id and Nancy,
we were partners in
crime, we helped
each other out.

NANCY SPUNGEN

THE BO[...]KS

HERE'S [...]

5

Knives and Pistols

England's outrageous Sex Pistols were the quintessential punk rock group, producing a brutal, obscene sound fashioned from the wreckage of rock-and-roll and reggae, punctuated with onstage mutilations and anything else that would shock. Their writhing audiences wore the uniforms of their movement—studded black leather and chains, hair spiked and vividly colored, pierced skin, and a vampirelike paleness beneath a war paint of mascara. Arising in a time of high unemployment and shrinking opportunity, their common cause had to do with futility, death, and nihilism; they lived only to tear down convention. Most outsiders shrank from the awful emptiness evoked by these young legions of the punked out. Others attacked, providing the tonic of danger and pain demanded by punks, male and female alike.

In December 1977, the Sex Pistols' imaginative—some would say exploitive—manager, underground clothier Malcolm McLaren, had a vexing problem. The Pistols, embarked on their short, ballistic exploration of fame, were just a month away from an American tour. But 20-year-old John Ritchie, abruptly famous as Sid Vicious, the band's bass guitarist, had become hooked on heroin and on the woman who introduced him to it—Nancy Spungen, a brilliantly manipulative but poorly balanced 19-year-old addict from Philadelphia.

Since March 1977, she and Vicious, reigning briefly as the king and queen of punk, had torn up hotel rooms and lurched in and out of hospitals, rock clubs, and courtrooms. The two were inseparable, as hungrily and violently attached to each other as they were to the smack and other drugs they consumed. McLaren correctly feared that the self-destructive Spungen was going to destroy the equally out-of-control Vicious unless something was done, and quickly. She had to be ejected from Sid's life.

To Malcolm McLaren, haberdasher for the angry young, every practical problem had an impractical solution. They would save Sid—and thus the band—he decided, by kidnapping Nancy Spungen and putting her on a plane—to America. "It was completely mad," recalled McLaren's office manager, Sophie Richmond, somewhat understating the absence of logic.

One afternoon in December, while Vicious was showing his neglected teeth to his dentist, McLaren had Richmond suggest a shopping trip to Spungen. Nancy agreed to go along, but her antennae, as always, listened for the sound of betrayal—she had the junkie's itchy sense of conspiracy unfolding everywhere.

By the time the pair had covered the mile from London's King's Road to Kensington High Street, Nancy's alarms were ringing. McLaren and John "Boogie" Tiberi, the Sex Pistols' principal road manager, suddenly appeared and, aided by Richmond, tried to shove Nancy into a waiting van. "She started screaming in the middle of Kensington High Street," McLaren later told the London *Daily Express*. Then Spungen took off on foot, as McLaren and Tiberi gave chase through startled crowds of holiday shoppers. The pursuit ended in a standoff, with all parties yelling at one another. There had never been the slightest possibility of putting Nancy on an airplane against her will.

The abortive kidnapping was just bad thinking. No one was going to weaken Nancy Spungen's hold on anything she wanted, much less on anyone she loved. The screams and tantrums and single-mindedness of this five-foot-one-inch fireball had been making the world turn for 19 years; all her troubled life, in a sense, had been preparation to be Sid's girl. Nothing that McLaren or anyone else did would arrest—or even slow—the deadly trajectory she and Sid were traveling. Nothing.

Nancy Spungen had always been at war. She'd entered life like a warrior parachuting into battle, fighting from the instant she touched down in Philadelphia on a sleety February morning in 1958. She was born five weeks premature, and blue—cyanotic—from the umbilical cord twisted around her tiny neck. Hours after her delivery, the infant had turned a jaundiced yellow—her blood type was incompatible with her mother's. Massive transfusions were required to save her. The first needles went into Nancy's veins on that first desperate day of her desperate life.

Doctors assured 23-year-old Frank Spungen and his wife, Deborah, 20, that their six-pound-five-ounce firstborn had safely weathered her traumatic beginning. The transfusions had done their work. There appeared to be no brain damage from either jaundice or the strangling umbilical cord. She was a perfectly normal, healthy infant, they said. The Spungens set out on the parental sea, like all new parents, with no experience and grand expectations. Both had attended the University of Pennsylvania. Frank was an accountant who went into paper sales. At the time of Nancy's birth, Deborah was completing her degree in foreign languages. She'd later run her own business and then work as an executive for Western Union. They were, according to Deborah Spungen's memoir of life with Nancy, middle-class, moderate liberals, just religious enough to celebrate major Jewish holy days.

Nanki-poo, as the new father liked to call his baby girl, began immediately making her presence felt. She slept little and cried almost incessantly when with her parents; a nanny might soothe her, but the mother could not. Nancy's first pediatrician guessed the mother wasn't producing enough milk and suggested giving the baby formula instead. When that didn't work, the doctor recommended a dietary switch to solids. Nancy ate voraciously and put on weight. But she continued to scream, holding her parents hostage to her penetrating cries.

After three months of sleeplessness, Deborah Spungen took her daughter to a new doctor, the beginning of a medical odyssey that would last for 18 years. This physician accused the mother of overfeeding—and spoiling—the child. If she'd ignore the squalling, he advised, it soon would stop. The Spungens spent a week steeling themselves against the angry din from the nursery. That did no good, either, against Nancy's herculean stamina.

Finally, the doctor came up with a certain means of silencing Nancy: phenobarbital. The mother administered the red fluid orally every four hours. Her daughter would continue shrieking for a half-hour, finally nod off for an hour or two, then wake up screaming until drugged again. With the clarity of hindsight, physicians would note later that this may have trained the girl's mind and body to seek chemical solutions for life's problems. But at the time no one

seemed to care. It was enough to have her briefly silenced.

A baby sister, Susan, arrived in September 1959; brother David would follow two years later. In 1960 the growing family moved to a larger house on Welsh Road in northeast Philadelphia. Nancy bracketed the move with tantrums that gave new, horrible meaning to the Terrible Twos. She writhed on the floor, hammering at her face with tiny fists, and whipped around madly when a parent tried to hold and calm her. When she wasn't drugged—the sedative therapy continued into her second year—she seemed to be consumed by endless, explosive rage.

Nancy began suffering recurrent nightmares. In one of them, a strange man tried to dynamite her bedroom. In another, a rabbit bit her. So real were these phantasms to the terrified little girl that she sometimes wore bandages over her rabbit "bite" all day. Her mother was allowed to remove the bandage only to replace it.

In 1962 Nancy underwent her first mental evaluation. The Spungens were heartened to hear that their four-year-old daughter didn't seem to have any serious emotional problems, at least none that she shouldn't easily outgrow. Moreover, although Nancy's motor-visual development was a bit slow, she was extremely bright; her IQ measured 134. "My feeling," a psychiatric social worker told the parents, "is that time and the structured environment of school will be the answer for Nancy." His final advice: "Take her home and love her."

School, as predicted, was tonic. Nancy enjoyed the classroom and looked forward to school each day. She also confirmed her high test scores with exceptional progress. In fact, the child was so far ahead of her age group that her second-grade teacher recommended that Nancy skip straight into the fourth grade, where she continued to perform well—academically.

Outside the classroom, however, she grew stranger and increasingly violent. An ungainly youngster, heavy for her age and ill proportioned, she was socially awkward, often hostile, and so difficult that her peers shied away from friendship. At home, Nancy verbally abused both her younger siblings, and on occasion she attacked them physically. Her little sister's first sentence, according to Deborah Spungen, was "Nancy, leave me alone."

Nancy also had moments of grand tenderness. When her mother developed kidney trouble after David's birth, the child was an angel of help and gently took care of her brother when he became ill. But most of Nancy's life, it seemed, was spent prowling for those things that would thwart—and madden—her.

Mystified by their daughter, Nancy's parents decided that a change of environment might help. In 1967 they moved the family from their semidetached town house on Welsh Road to a two-story, four-bedroom colonial on quiet Red Barn Lane in suburban Huntingdon Valley, about 15 miles north of Philadelphia. But the plague of destructive behavior raged on. Hoping to bring the girls closer together, the Spungens moved Nancy and little Suzy into the same bedroom. Nancy's response was a carefully controlled rampage that made a shambles of Suzy's half of the room. She employed caprice like a scythe, demanding that the family go where she wanted, *now,* then changing her mind, keeping everyone eternally off balance. It was as if she could read her parents utterly, for she could always outbid them—if they

escalated to a rare reprimand she was capable of countering with a frightening self-destructive act. At 10, Nancy held the entire family in her little fist.

Now, the formerly complacent psychiatric examiners began rewriting the parameters of Nancy's malady. The parents learned that their firstborn viewed interactions with others as either emotionally sterile or discordant—she perceived no middle ground between rage and nothing. The doctors spoke of emotional hunger, a sense of receiving less than others—indeed, of being a receptacle that was impossible to fill—and anger, anger, anger.

The doctors could offer Nancy nothing but drugs that dulled the senses. But soon the young girl learned of another antidote for her inner discord. One afternoon, Deborah Spungen played for her daughter the cast album from the new Broadway rock musical, *Hair.* The child, she wrote later, was drawn into the music, as if it spoke directly and

**Actors inscribed with "Love" and "Trip Out"
portray hippies at a Be-In on the incense-veiled
stage of the 1960s musical *Hair,* Nancy Spungen's first compelling contact with rock.**

I'm gonna die before I'm 21. I'm gonna go out in a blaze of glory. Like . . . like headlines.

NANCY SPUNGEN

distinctly to her. Nancy listened to *Hair* in its entirety at least a half-dozen times a day for months afterward. Then she heard the Beatles for the first time and asked for their *White* album for Hanukkah. Rock soon became an obsession. The Doors. Cream. Jimi Hendrix. Led Zeppelin. The harder, the hipper, the harsher the better. "It seemed to hypnotize her," Deborah Spungen wrote. "The rock musicians were coming from where she wanted to be."

Nancy had discovered another world, one of sounds that touched her deep interior, where people sang the lyrics of the young, alienated, and angry. She let her chestnut hair grow long and began to affect a hippie look. At the age of 10, she read the poetry of Sylvia Plath and Richard Brautigan, both suicides. She plumbed the drug-enhanced quests for truth described by Carlos Castaneda, followed the disconnected youth portrayed by J. D. Salinger, and saw, in Ken Kesey's work, how madness could be a kind of heightened sanity after all. She liked F. Scott Fitzgerald, possibly for his famously psychotic wife, Zelda. She followed news reports of America's war in Vietnam and sided with the growing legion of protesters. Everywhere that Nancy looked, it seemed, she found evidence that her behavior was not that extraordinary.

But Nancy was losing the few, frail restraints she possessed. On a family outing to New York City in 1967 the Spungens happened upon a free first-anniversary performance of *Hair* in Central Park. Nancy insisted upon staying for the show. When told that the family had to head home for Pennsylvania, she didn't protest. She simply disappeared into the crowd. Frantic to find her, the parents gave their daughter's description to the police. At the intermission, *Hair* producer Michael Butler personally took the stage and asked that the missing Nancy Spungen please come forward. "Come backstage," Butler said. "That's where your mom is. She's waiting for you."

Nancy didn't respond. An hour after the performance concluded, a patrolman found her sitting alone and silent on a park bench, her face a perfect blank—a hooded, unhappy expression already well known to her parents. As she often had before, Nancy professed not to remember the incident. Perhaps she didn't. Or perhaps she was merely confounding her family again.

Then as before, the mental health professionals to whom the Spungens more and more frequently turned for guidance declared that Nancy's problems were the parents'

fault. They'd handled the situation badly. They should have been more firm, said the shrinks, who persisted in viewing the youngster as simply fractious and poorly disciplined.

Two weeks after the concert, sitting on a lawn with some neighbor girls stringing glass-bead jewelry, Nancy dropped her work into the grass and couldn't find it. She immediately began howling, "It isn't fair! It isn't fair!" By the time her mother arrived at the scene, Nancy was crazed, facedown, pulling her hair out and shrieking out of control. Her little friends looked on, aghast. Unable to control the fit, Deborah Spungen rushed Nancy to a hospital emergency room. The moment she was left alone in an examining room, the 10-year-old jumped down from the table and shut and locked the glass door. When a security guard arrived to open it, Nancy sat on the examining table, laughing. "I'm smarter than you," the girl told the doctor. "I'm smarter than all of you."

It would take more than stern parenting to contain Nancy, as became clear to her therapist during one appointment in 1969. Nancy tore up the woman's office, pitched a clock through the window, and doused the psychologist with a bottle of blue ink. A doctor examining her following the episode believed that he detected the emotional and behavioral skewing of the severe mental disorder called schizophrenia—but perhaps out of compassion, he neglected to tell the Spungens.

Then Nancy assaulted her mother with a claw hammer. As before, chemistry—dispensed from the hands of yet another doctor—provided a temporary recourse; the powerful sedative Thorazine was prescribed for the young girl.

Early in 1970, unable to find a special school nearby that could accommodate their troubled daughter, the Spungens heard about Barton, a private boarding school for disturbed children in western Connecticut. At great cost, they enrolled 11-year-old Nancy there, and for the spring semester, the child seemed to find her equilibrium and did well. The siege of the Spungen household was lifted for a time; spirits revived. By the following autumn, however, Barton had become more crowded, and a new director had come aboard who was not as adept at handling Nancy's case. As volatile as nitroglycerine, Nancy exploded.

Home for Christmas, Nancy told a favorite male cousin that she'd become a heroin addict and had aborted a pregnancy; she may have been sharing her aspirations, for, as experts have noted, heroin addiction is the mark of true seriousness among the drug dependent, and few things disturb a family more than news of unwanted pregnancy. The Spungens moved their daughter to another school in 1971, this one closer to home and more academically challenging. But little changed. By the time 13-year-old Nancy came home for Thanksgiving, she'd begun smoking cigarettes, and she boasted of getting stoned on marijuana and dropping acid, activities she supported by stealing and selling her mother's jewelry, including her wedding band. Nancy had become sexually active with a number of the boys at school, and at one point, mistakenly convinced that her prepubescent organs held a fetus, she performed a coat-hanger abortion on herself, puncturing her uterus in the process. And she went through the preliminaries of suicide: Twice she slashed veins in her forearms, once coming within a few minutes of death.

The Spungens by this time had come to fear, love, and despise their eldest child for the chaos she created. They recognized that Nancy was bent on self-destruction, and they also realized that they were powerless to stop her. They were therefore both apprehensive when, at 16, Nancy completed her high-school coursework and was accepted into the freshman class at the University of Colorado at Boulder. There were many dangers on a big college campus for someone as dysfunctional, and vulnerable, as Nancy. On the other hand, she'd be nearly 2,000 miles away from the site of her worst behavior, in a kind of small-town Shangri-la perched among the eastern foothills of the Rockies, breathing clean air and surrounded by healthy people.

It was more of the same. "Why don't you just leave me alone?" the teenager snarled at her parents the day they brought her to Boulder. "Get out!" she shrieked as they strolled through the pretty little town. The Spungens fled back to Pennsylvania, their home life once more revived by a relief from Nancy's siege. It was a brief respite. Before the year was out, Nancy was arrested for stealing ski equipment and faced charges for drug possession. Frank Spungen, through a local attorney, agreed to withdraw his daughter from school in return for all charges being dropped and all records of the arrest erased.

When her mother urged her to try another college, Nancy gave a frightening illumination of the landscape she saw ahead of her. There was no point in going to college, she replied. "I'm gonna die before I'm 21. I'm gonna go out in a blaze of glory. Like . . . like headlines." The Spungens had begun to believe in their daughter's matter-of-fact prediction—their firstborn's only real interest seemed to lie in her own destruction.

Within a week of her return from Colorado, Nancy had totaled her mother's Volvo. Shortly after that, while unpacking her daughter's things, Deborah Spungen came across Nancy's heroin setup of syringes, rubber catheter, and spoon. The girl had stepped into the world of the junkie, a life reckoned in fixes, a life spent scratching for ruined veins huddled near the bone, a life spent serving what one addict has called the invisible mouth of heroin addiction—a mouth that must be fed three or four times a day.

The parents watched hopelessly as their eldest child slipped into ever-greater drug dependence. Nancy spent more and more time in Philadelphia and in New York, where she'd discovered a vibrant new world that seemed to have been designed with her in mind. She bragged to her little sister Suzy of having slept with members of rock bands as various as The Who and the Allman Brothers; she did whole bands, she said. Her claims may have been exaggerated, but certainly they contained a grain of truth: At the age of 17, Nancy already wielded a hardhearted promiscuity like a club.

By December 1, 1975, nearly three months shy of Nancy's 18th birthday, her family had reached the end of its tether. It was time to cut Nancy adrift. The parents made one last desperate offer: If Nancy wished, they'd set her up in a New York City apartment and help her with the rent. She enthusiastically accepted the deal. She still dreamed of headlines, and New York was the place to make them.

Nancy took a small apartment on West 23d Street, in lower Manhattan's Chelsea district, where art and music were thriving. At first she seemed to settle into her new haunts; the apartment shone, and she enrolled in a city program that offered methadone, a less-debilitating opium derivative, as a substitute for heroin. Inevitably, however, her demons returned.

This time it required little less than a month for the slurred phone calls to begin, the drug-slowed gibberish punctuated by silences and pleas for money. Heroin became more and more the central element in her existence. Soon she was calling three or four times a day, every day, and late into the night, begging for money, demanding it. When her parents refused to help support what had become a $100-

Newly arrived in England, punk groupie Nancy Spungen attends the March 21, 1977, debut of Sid Vicious, the outrageous new bass guitarist for the Sex Pistols, at London's Notre Dame Hall.

a-day habit, Nancy turned to topless dancing in Times Square dives to pay for her fixes.

"She and my friend were topless dancers," recalled rock photographer Bob Gruen. "Nancy was working in a kind of brothel in an upper East Side town house. She used to beat bankers." According to Gruen, the New York Nancy reflected the best qualities of the Huntingdon Valley Nancy. "She was a nice person, she had a way about her. When I had a cold once she came over to my house for a couple of days and took care of me, made me tea and toast." His only really bad memory of Nancy is that she whined. "She had a way of whining that used to drive everybody crazy," he remembered. The whine was the adult counterpart of the infant's steady scream.

The other half of Nancy's life was music, and musicians. But this was a new kind of music, a roaring rock pulse that defied categorization. Loud, basic, and darkly hostile, the form had arisen in the late 1960s as a reaction to what the disaffected perceived to be the homogenization of mainstream rock—the increasingly slick and predictable corporate products heard on the top 40. Underground bands had begun experimenting with a new sound, harsh and deliberately primitive, but also raunchy and weird. Created by self-styled, often adolescent, misfits for like-minded youth, it hammered away the nights in such downtown Manhattan clubs as Max's Kansas City at 17th Street and Park Avenue and CBGB—for Country, Blue Grass, and Blues—in the Bowery. For a time these became the main outposts of Nancy Spungen's existence.

Among the first of the new radicals were singer Lou Reed and the Velvet Underground, whose signature piece, "Heroin," exalted the smack high. In the early 1970s came the New York Dolls, perhaps the first band to refer to themselves as punk. The Dolls, five young men who dressed in spandex, high heels, and full women's makeup, epitomized glitter, or glam, rock. Their stage costumes, like their brash and amateurish music, were meant to offend.

Nancy Spungen was a vital part of this defiantly different scene. She befriended Deborah Harry, locally famous lead singer of the rock group Blondie, which was also popular at Max's and CBGB's. Nancy became friends with Jerry Nolan and Johnny Thunders of the Dolls. She dated Richard Hell, lead singer for another major band, Television. "She was a fairly typical suburban girl who worshipped rock stars," Hell wrote later. "She had an exceptionally

large drive to be where the action was. Nancy just wanted to be somebody (not necessarily herself). And you've got to hand it to her. She made it."

Others recall Nancy Spungen less amiably. "She was a total junkie prostitute," asserted Leee—with an extra e—Childers, then manager of a group called the Heartbreakers. She hung around clubs, Childers remembered, offering sex for drugs and drugs for sex.

Although Nancy had found a kind of niche in New York's punk rock underworld, she hadn't penetrated to the center of her new domain. In fact, the center was not in America, with its relatively friendly variant of punk. It was in England, where the collapsing welfare state had spawned a generation of youth whose ruined expectations expressed themselves in a more violent, feral form of rock and roll.

The major British punk groups of the time were the Clash and the Sex Pistols, the latter led by singer John Lydon, called Johnny Rotten. In November 1976 the Sex Pistols had released "Anarchy in the U.K.," a hard-rocking anthem that rocketed the group to instant stardom. The following month, 18-year-old Nancy announced to her family her own intention to visit England. "The whole *thing* is there," she told the Spungens over dinner in New York. "It's like everybody from here is there now. That's where it's all happening. *Everybody's* there!"

Nancy had again weaned herself from heroin and was looking comparatively healthy when she left New York for London in early March of 1977. The needle tracks on her arms had healed, which meant that she could dance nude again—nobody liked to watch a girl with tracks. She thought she might be able to find some sort of work in the music business and, after a week in London, planned to play bass fiddle for an all-girl band then forming to tour the Continent. To Nancy it didn't matter that she'd never played an instrument before; she'd learn.

As in New York, however, she kept to the fringes, roaming London's punk hangouts in search of Jerry Nolan, her friend from the New York Dolls. The band by then was defunct, and Nolan was in London drumming for the Heartbreakers. Leee Childers emphatically warned her to leave Nolan alone. "The last thing I needed was Nancy Spungen with her bag full of drugs," Childers told one chronicler of those times. "So I told her, 'Over my dead body you will see Jerry Nolan.' And she turned around and she walked away. She wasn't hurt. Almost immediately I

heard that she had found Sid and hooked up with him. A cold chill ran down my spine when I heard."

Sid was Sid Vicious, just shy of 20 years old, the newest member of the Sex Pistols, and one of the hottest rock celebrities in England, which really meant in the world. At a gaunt six-foot-two, he had a drooping eyelid and black spiky hair, sepulchral paleness, a vast tolerance for pain, and a sneering, androgynous aspect. Sid Vicious embodied everything in the world that Nancy Spungen esteemed.

The boy who would become Sid Vicious had not entered the world angry so much as disenfranchised. He was born John Simon Ritchie in London on May 10, 1957. Anne Randall, the boy's unconventional mother, had been abandoned as a child. By the time she met John Ritchie—father of the son she'd call Si, or sometimes Sime—Randall had been in and out of the Royal Air Force and a first, failed, marriage.

They resided in a ground-floor garden flat in Lee Green, a working-class neighborhood near Lewisham, in southeast London. But home was not a structured environment. As his mother described Si's life, "He was never in a stable situation. It was like a mirror of my early life."

In the summer of 1960, the Ritchies planned a vacation together on the island of Ibiza in the Mediterranean, a favored British holiday destination off the east coast of Spain. Si and his mother went first; John Ritchie was to arrive later. Meantime, he'd send money. As it happened, neither funds nor Ritchie arrived in Ibiza, and Anne Randall realized she was alone with a toddler to raise.

Characteristically, she didn't panic. Rather, mother and child remained for several months on the sunny, free-spirited island, moving from town to town by bicycle, enjoying Ibiza's laid-back ambiance. Randall found occasional employment as a typist and "earned money rolling joints for people," as she put it. During the stay, little Si discovered alcohol. On one occasion, the boy downed two or three glasses of curaçoa, an orange-flavored liqueur. On another, he finished off what his mother described as an "enormous" brandy. He also began cultivating the limited but lusty vocabulary that would serve him well as a Pistol.

When poverty finally ended their island idyll, Randall returned to London, where she went to work in a Soho jazz club and established a home of sorts for her and Si on Drury Lane—a two-room cold-water flat with an outdoor toilet.

In an era of beehive hairdos and hemlines two inches below the knee, Randall wore her hair severely bobbed and her dresses short. "I got every remark you could think of," she recalled, "and Simon heard all this. I tried to inculcate into his psyche: 'You are you, you can do anything you like providing you don't hurt anybody else while doing it.'"

Soon the boy began what his mother calls "this fidgeting and twitching stage. All the time you were talking to him he'd be at it." At his first school, St. Peter and St. Paul, located according to one biographer in "one of the most corrupt, prostitute-ridden square miles in Britain," the only subjects that interested Si were art, music, and history. Because of his tics and his frailty, Si was also prey for the bullies of St. Peter and St. Paul, as, in later life, he would be for London's Teddy Boys—the 1970s reincarnation of the 1950s' zoot-suited, working-class tough guys—and the roving thugs of New York City.

In 1964 the nomadic Anne Randall moved with Si to Oxford where she met and, after a brief courtship, married a man named Chris Beverley. Si, just seven at the time of the February 1965 nuptials, may have looked forward to a life of greater stability. Indeed, the new stepfather was in the process of adopting the boy when Beverley died suddenly in August of that same year, leaving mother and son once more on their own—or nearly so.

Beverley's family in Tunbridge Wells, about 30 miles southeast of London, made it possible for Si to attend a local private school there. He once caused a classroom stir when he announced that he doubted God's existence. Otherwise, according to his mother, he passed several unexceptional years with her in Tunbridge Wells. "He used to laugh a lot, and he was fascinated by music," she recalled. "But being an only child like that meant that he was very wrapped up in himself. He first started taking an interest in clothes when he was about 13, and as he got older he became more and more outrageous. He desperately wanted to be noticed." He had his mother's appetite for attention.

"I helped him dye his hair the first time," Anne Beverley said. "He wanted to have it bright green, so I bleached it first, then we dyed it. It got him in a certain amount of trouble, but because he could run very fast he used to clear off quickly. He felt that this was far more sensible than bravery. He wasn't at all aggressive in those days. That was brought on by drugs and alcohol."

From Tunbridge Wells, the intinerant pair moved south-

Young Sime

John Simon Ritchie began life as a much-loved, much-photographed child, romping with his parents—Anne Randall and her common-law husband, John Ritchie—in the garden of their ground-floor flat in Lee Green, a working-class neighborhood in southeast London. But the infant's idyll did not last long. By the time the boy was three years old, his father had abandoned the family, and Sime, as Anne Randall often called her son, had been swept away into his mother's nomadic, nonconformist life.

John Ritchie and Anne Randall present their new son, John Simon, in the summer of 1957.

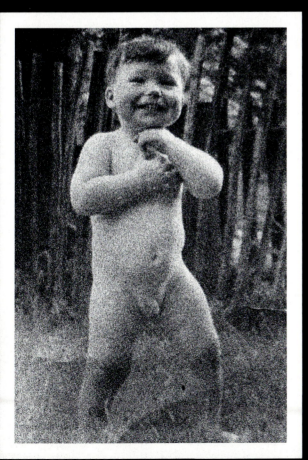

Anne Randall cuddles her 14-month-old son in her sister's South London garden.

In photographs that capture the mercurial moods of toddlerhood, a strapping 16-month-old Simon Ritchie frowns in a photo with his mother *(above),* and at two he smiles obediently for a portrait in his aunt's garden *(right).* Soon the disintegrating bond between John Ritchie and Anne Randall cast mother and son into poverty.

On Ibiza in 1960 Sime poses with his Alsatian mix, C. P. *(above),* and dines with his mother at a quayside cafe. Abandoned by Ritchie, the pair returned to England, drifting until Anne's 1965 marriage to Chris Beverley *(near right)* in Oxford, where the couple is seen with Beverley's brother and nephew and Simon *(center),* who wears his latch key.

given him by his friend and partner in poverty, John Lydon—later Johnny Rotten. Attracted by art and photography, a newly permed Ritchie stands outside London's Hackney College of Further Education *(inset)*, where the maturing punker staged dramatic self-portraits *(below)*.

ALL VISITORS PL ASE
ENQUIRE AT OFFICE
STAIRCASE 'A'

ALL STUDENTS PLEASE
USE STAIRCASE 'A'

west for a time to Clevedon, not far from Bristol on England's south coast, and then back to London and Stamford Hill, a seedy northeast London neighborhood. Si's last formal studies were at Albion Road Secondary Modern School where, at the age of 15, he completed his education in 1972.

Young Ritchie's first job was at a Daks Trousers plant on Kingsland Road in central London. He started out on menial chores, then was given a trial as a trainee cloth cutter. Starting out on pockets, which were machine-cut from clamped piles of folded material, he managed to ruin hundreds. "Simon fell about laughing when he told me," recalled his mother. "Some of the pockets were so small you couldn't even get a thumb in them." But Daks was not amused and fired him.

There might also have been a problem at Daks with Si's appearance. David Bowie by now was his idol, and posters of the rocker hung in Si's bedroom. To the extent he could, Si emulated the androgynous dress, makeup, and primary-colored hair favored by Bowie. "He was a Bowie fan," schoolmate John Lydon observed to one rock historian. "He'd do silly things to get his hair to stick up, because it never occurred to him to use hair spray. He'd lie upside down with his head in an oven."

Si met Lydon at the Hackney College of Further Education, where Si had been accepted as an art student after the Daks debacle. Lydon, a year older than Si, also was a working-class kid with a similarly hostile opinion of formal education, and of society in general. It was he who nicknamed his friend Sid, after Lydon's hamster. John Lydon later added the Vicious as an ironic afterthought: "Sid was the least vicious and least screwed up person that I'd ever met then or have met since. Hence Vicious."

The rechristened Ritchie, who has been variously reported as loathing and loving his new name, dropped out of art class and left home, intermittently, over the next two years to live in what his contemporaries called the squats, a catch-all term for any vacant, free shelter around central London. This went on for two years until, as Anne Beverley described it, she finally ordered him out of the house for good.

Sid and John squatted for a while in a West End brothel operated by a lesbian prostitute, Linda Ashby. The two friends also found refuge behind the tube—or subway—station in Hampstead in northern London. "Really desperate people lived up there," recalled Lydon. "It was awful. I liked it: it was better than home. I don't remember a great

deal from that period because I loved getting wildly drunk. It was good fun: it was freedom." To pay for his new freedom, Lydon worked in a shoe factory. Sid tried prostitution.

The point of their existence, of course, was its very pointlessness—an outlook that Sid and John shared with many working-class youths in a country whose dismal economy and class stratifications offered little to those who lacked salable skills or union affiliation. Working-class kids who peered into the future saw little or nothing waiting for them there. The best job Sid had been able to find was the brief spot with Daks. Lydon, although a hard worker, had not found much either. At home he'd worked with his father, pouring concrete, and made a relatively good wage at it. Before taking the shoe-factory job he'd worked as a sewage plant rat exterminator.

Undirected, disaffected, and broke as Sid and John and the rest of their generation's outcasts generally were, the two nevertheless found the hardscrabble life in a London squat infinitely preferable to the brutish, stultifying sameness of home. "It was freedom," as Lydon observed, for which privation wasn't too steep a price to pay. It was also a world of absolute and wonderful spontaneity—everything was improvised.

On a Saturday in August 1975, green-haired John Lydon, wearing his shredded jacket with crisscrossed safety pins all over it, wandered into Sex, a clothing store on King's Road in Chelsea. There he met the owner, Malcolm McLaren, as well as Steve Jones, Paul Cook, and Glen Matlock, three customers and part-time sales clerks who, under McLaren's guidance, were trying to form a rock-and-roll band they would call the Sex Pistols.

Startlingly pale with wild red hair, Malcolm McLaren was a former art student who esteemed the music and fashions of the 1950s. In 1971, at the age of 25, he and 30-year-old Vivienne Westwood, his companion and the mother of his child, opened the King's Road store, calling it Let It Rock. Later, it was renamed Too Fast To Live, Too Young To Die, then Sex, which seemed to say it all.

McLaren carried practically nothing that was generally in fashion. The store's varied collection featured Teddy Boy zoot suits and Edwardian styles, studded, armless T-shirts, ripped and torn attire of many sorts, S-M paraphernalia, rubber fetish gear, and even the odd swastika. It was John Lydon's sort of place.

Malcolm McLaren also was a self-styled rock impresario. In 1974 he'd moved to New York, where for a while he managed the New York Dolls, which were then fading into eclipse. Back in England in May 1975, McLaren hired Steve Jones, a frequent shopper (and shoplifter) at his store, and Paul Cook, Jones's close friend, who were trying to start a new band. Although Jones and Cook outfitted the group—partly, it was said, with instruments stolen from David Bowie—the band was having trouble coalescing. McLaren set about remaking it. He named it the Sex Pistols and jettisoned the bassist for Glen Matlock, another of his employees at Sex, who was talented both at bass guitar and at songwriting.

Then McLaren went looking for a lead singer. Johnny Thunders of the defunct Dolls was considered, as was Richard Hell from Television. The Sex Pistols insisted, however, that their singer be British, which led to the improbable auditioning of John Lydon. He'd become well known to all of them, but as Johnny Rotten, thanks to Glen Matlock. "He used the word rotten all the blasted time," Matlock once explained, "everything was rotten. Not just, How are you feeling? Rotten! but every damn thing. So I christened him Rotten, and it stuck." Credit for giving Lydon his new surname, however, was claimed by many.

According to British rock historian Jon Savage, one evening in a bar, McLaren, Jones, and the rest of the band handed Johnny Rotten a showerhead as a prop microphone, and told him to sing along with Alice Cooper's "Eighteen" on the jukebox. "I was terrified," Lydon said. "It never occurred to me that the music biz could be a place for me to vent whatever talent I had." Vent was just the word for it. "Lydon launched into a sequence of hunchbacked poses," wrote Savage, "screaming, mewling and puking, until his first audience dissolved into laughter. The group wasn't sure, but McLaren was. 'I had an eye,' he says, 'and my eye saw Rotten's ability to create image around himself. It was a gut feeling. I knew he had something.'"

That something had little to do with musicality; Johnny Rotten couldn't carry a tune. What he brought to the group was raw, almost cosmic, indifference and wonderful anger. He performed drunk, or stoned, or both. He'd forget words or forget to sing altogether. From their first gigs in tiny rooms without stages Rotten would delight in offending their equally tiny audiences, or baiting members of other bands. The Sex Pistols were as much an event as they were a rock-and-roll group; it was often difficult to tell where the band stopped and the audience began.

"Boiling with energy," was how Caroline Coon, a writer for the British rock magazine *Melody Maker,* remembered the Pistols. "Boiling with anger. They were a rock band and their anger was theatrical. Furious at what was happening to society. The Punks were taking the place of street rebellion."

The term *punk,* already used on the street, was codified that autumn by a pair of Americans, Legs McNeil and John Holmstrom of Cheshire, Connecticut, who decided *Punk* was a perfect title for a rock-and-roll magazine devoted to the new music pounding away on both sides of the Atlantic. McNeil explained that punk was what TV cops like Kojak always called their arrestees. "It was what your teacher would call you," McNeil said. "It meant that you were the lowest."

As Coon saw it, "The tenets of the Punk tribe were anarchic; it was annihilating, it had to do with destroying rather than creating." Punk musicians "were adolescents with really very acute emotional problems," she said. "They were going to performances, gigs, with razor cuts down their faces, with blood dripping."

Caroline Coon met Sid Vicious, then still a fan, at early Sex Pistol gigs and felt the punk scene "was absolutely what Sid was looking for in terms of identity." He was "very, very tall, that white, beautiful white skin, beautiful eyes, he was utterly unaware of how beautiful he was," she recalled. "He was wearing skin tight jeans, a really battered old Harley Davidson-type motorcycle jacket, and a kind of like rag of a tee shirt. I guess he was living in the squat. He was not very well fed or very well washed. His hair was all kind of like crunched up and dirty."

According to rock legend, it was Sid who invented the unofficial punk dance, the Pogo. During a Sex Pistols' December 12, 1975, appearance, Sid began hopping up and down, feet together, arms flailing, in an unwitting emulation of someone jumping on a pogo stick. That was Sid's irrepressible goofy side.

The vicious side of John Ritchie, submerged until now,

A King's Road haberdashery of faddish costumes and bizarre apparatus, Sex *(left)* was the brainchild of fiery-haired punk impresario Malcolm McLaren, manager of the Sex Pistols. Below, Sid Vicious hangs out at Sex in October 1976 with, from left, co-punkers Simon Barker, Marco Pirroni, and Sue Catwoman.

burst into view during the summer of 1976. In the midst of a Sex Pistols performance at the 100 Club, located at 100 Oxford Street, he tried to provoke a fight with rock journalist Nick Kent. When Kent didn't rise to his taunts, Sid uncoiled a bicycle chain from his waist and whacked the writer over the head with it, opening a bloody gash. Some-

time later that summer, in a gesture of disdain toward a band called The Damned, Sid reportedly pitched a beer mug at the band. The mug shattered over the front of the stage, hitting the lead singer's girlfriend in the eye. Sid was arrested as a result of the incident and, according to Caroline Coon, was badly beaten by the London police on his way to jail.

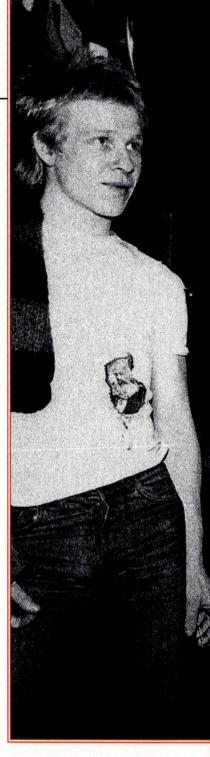

The Sex Pistols punk it up for a publicity shot in early 1977. From left to right are drummer Paul Cook, lead vocalist Johnny Rotten, new bass guitarist Sid Vicious, and Steve Jones on electric guitar.

Although he was jealous of his friend Johnny Rotten's success, 19-year-old Sid Vicious was almost content to be the Sex Pistols' First Fan. The only greater fulfillment would be to become a Sex Pistol himself. While he waited in the wings, Vicious drummed for a while in a group called Siouxsie and the Banshees. In the autumn of 1976 he joined the otherwise all-female Flowers of Romance as their singer, sax player, and songwriter. Sample Sid titles: "Brains on Vacation" and "Piece of Garbage."

In the meantime, the Sex Pistols had signed a recording contract with EMI, one of Britain's preeminent music companies, and in November 1976 released "Anarchy in the U.K.," their first single and one of the first serious punk hits. Sales were boosted by priceless publicity. On December 1, the Sex Pistols appeared on "Today," a live London evening television program, where, coaxed along by host Bill Grundy, they put their rough vernacular on the air. The British tabloid press predictably was outraged on behalf of its readers. "It was hilarious," Steve Jones said later. "From that day on it was different. Before then it was just music: the next day it was the media."

The incident helped establish the Sex Pistols as punk's brashest band, a reputation that manager Malcolm McLaren fostered. Central to McLaren's scheme was creating and sustaining the Sex Pistols' convulsive chemistry. That meant the relatively unflappable Glen Matlock had to go. Matlock's main liabilities as a Sex Pistol were his competence, his professional approach to music, and the fact that he regarded punk rock not as an apocalypse but as fun. He strongly disapproved of Rotten's onstage drunkenness—just the sort of unbuttoned behavior that Malcolm McLaren wished to encourage. Worse, Matlock admitted to admiring certain of his mainline rock forebears, including the Beatles. One day in February 1977 he actually admitted a taste for the Fab Four's work. It was treason.

McLaren sent a telegram to Derek Johnson, news editor at *New Musical Express*. "Derek," it read, "yes, Glen Matlock was thrown out of The Sex Pistols because he went on too long about Paul McCartney. EMI was too much. The Beatles were too much. Sid Vicious, their best friend and always a member of the group but as yet unheard has been enlisted. His best credential is that he gave Nick Kent what he deserved many months ago at the 100 Club. Love and peace. Malcolm McLaren."

Sid Vicious—whose band, Flowers of Romance, had never played a public performance and were history by February 1977—suddenly was famous and comparatively well off. In the brief interval that the Sex Pistols had existed, McLaren had built up a pot of money for himself and his boys, despite the fact that record companies quickly dumped the Pistols once they got to know them. Between advances, earnings, and goodbye handshakes from four different record companies, the Pistols accumulated over £200,000 in one year. Virgin Records' release of "God Save the Queen" sold in excess of 200,000 copies and rose to Number 2 on the British rock charts.

Cushioned by more money than he'd ever dreamed of having, Sid Vicious was in clover—and in love. Back in March, he'd met someone very special at a party in his friend Linda Ashby's West End flat, an American girl who shared his taste in everything: Nancy Spungen, the love of his short life.

Deborah Spungen saw her daughter's boyfriend for the first time on television that summer. "With his drooping eye and malevolent expression," she later wrote, "he had to be the creepiest-looking young man on the face of the earth." She added, however, that "Nancy was genuinely happy, possibly the only time she had been in her entire life."

Anne Beverley was no more favorably taken with Nancy, whom she knew as Nauseating Nancy. "I'll never forget when Simon first brought her round to the house," his mother recalled. "Here was a blond, plumpish, dirty-clothed American girl, who didn't shut her mouth, ever. She never talked of anything but herself. She simpered and cooed in a way that said: How could you do anything else but like me? But it was a very thin and insincere front—she was hard as granite."

Nevertheless, it was clear to all, mothers and friends alike, that Sid and Nancy were inextricably bound. "Simon," Beverley later explained, "was never a very loving sort of person. He didn't reveal himself to many people, and he could be very cold, but he loved Nancy very dearly. He loved her with all his heart, and that had to be very big to take what he did from her."

Mainly, what Sid took from her was a heroin habit. Like most early punks, he was only fleetingly familiar with hard drugs — the narcotics of the hated rock establishment. By the end of March 1977, however, he was hospitalized with hepatitis that doctors indicated was needle related. The two lived with Anne Beverley for a couple of months, then took a flat in Chelsea. Their life increasingly revolved around feeding their heroin addictions; they also fed their appetites for hard sex and dangerous living — they played with knives constantly and liked to cut each other. And they didn't flinch from violence on the street; drugs seemed to embolden Sid, who once ran away from the blows of schoolyard bullies. According to one acquaintance, the surprisingly powerful little Nancy would pin an assailant's arms while Sid worked over the victim with a broken bottle or a knife.

In early July, Nancy appeared in a London court for carrying a truncheon, a clublike weapon she needed, as she explained to the judge, for self-defense. The need for some kind of deterrent was real, for punks were walking, jeering invitations to a brawl. Beginning in mid-June, Sid, Johnny, and the rest of the band members, as well as their entourage, were repeatedly attacked on the street by toughs that included, ironically enough, a new generation of Teddy Boys, whose fashions Malcolm McLaren featured at Sex. Nancy had sustained black eyes and a broken nose in one of the attacks as she tried to protect her 126-pound lover. Sid then had given her the truncheon.

Despite their seeming devotion to each other, the pair had arguments that often turned violent. In early November they were asked to leave a hotel after Sid dangled Nancy out a window. "I was screaming at him to let me back in," she told her mother, "and I guess it pissed off the other people in the hotel." Later in the month, according to the British press, the lovers argued in another hotel room. This time, the manager discovered Sid, and the bed, soaked in his blood. Exactly what happened is unknown.

All this could not have come at a worse time from McLaren's point of view. In the autumn of 1977 the Sex Pistols were considering a U.S. tour, to be sponsored by their North American label, Warner Brothers Records, which had signed a contract reportedly worth $700,000 with the band. Clearly, Sid Vicious could not perform on an American tour with Nancy present — indeed, there was some uncertainty as to whether he could perform at all.

In December McLaren arranged the bungled attempt to send Nancy back to the States, one way, but only succeeded in deepening the bond between her and Sid. Having failed to separate them, McLaren and road manager Boogie Tiberi turned their attention to spiking the tour.

Accordingly, they appended part of each band member's criminal record to his U.S. visa application: Johnny Rotten fined for possessing speed; Steve Jones and Paul Cook each convicted on several counts of theft; Sid's two assaults on policemen. Nevertheless, the U.S. government issued temporary entry permits to all four of the Sex Pistols. Some said that the government had been helped to its decision by Warner Brothers Records' lawyers. In the end, the only moderating influence that McLaren was able to exert on his fractious creation was to ban all women — including Nancy Spungen — from the tour.

On Thursday, January 5, 1978, the seven-city gig opened at the Great Southeast Music Hall in Atlanta before 600 people and five television crews. After the show, Sid ran out into the city to forage for heroin, scored, and wound up in an Atlanta hospital. The band retrieved Sid and went on to Memphis, an uneventful gig. At Randy's Rodeo in San Antonio, their third stop, drunk patrons pelted the band with beer cans and bottles; one can caught Sid square in the mouth. Roderick Gilchrist, entertainment editor for the London Daily Mail, sat with Vicious on the lip of the stage after the San Antonio show. Surrounded by shattered beer bottles and blood, Sid kept slicing his bare arms with a razor blade as he spoke. "With every new cut," Gilchrist remembered, "rivulets of blood ran down to his fingers and he watched with a Neanderthal grin as his hand gradually turned a wet red. I asked him the only question: Why? 'Because it makes people take notice of me,' he said."

The fourth stop on the tour was Baton Rouge, Louisiana, where the band, exhausted by a long bus ride, played the Kingfisher Club. There, Vicious enlivened his performance by having onstage sex with an anonymous woman. Next, in Dallas, Texas, Sid performed shirtless with "GIMME A FIX" written in Magic Marker across his thin chest; a fan

Anything but vicious around children, Sid chats with
young London admirers between concerts in September
1977 as Nancy Spungen looks on.

Embarked on a seven-show American tour in January 1978, the Sex Pistols *(left)*, led by Vicious and Rotten, open in Atlanta. In Dallas, Sid *(inset)* bleeds after a head butt by a female fan. Despite the "GIMME A FIX" inked on his chest, Vicious is driven to drink *(above)* by a lack of heroin.

who'd driven from Los Angeles for the show gave Vicious a bloody nose and a date. On January 12 in Tulsa, gig number six, "Sid tried to kill himself," wrote *Punk* magazine cofounder John Holmstrom. "First, he smashed a gin bottle against a TV set. The bottle didn't break so he tried to jump out the window. That didn't work, so he asked if anyone had any drugs."

The Sid Vicious now swerving out of control across America bore scant outward resemblance to the awkward 19-year-old who just 13 months before had spontaneously invented the Pogo. Punk, for Sid, no longer had much to do with making noise and being outrageous. His friends and family and Malcolm McLaren blamed the change on Nancy. But Sid's budding addiction to violence had been acquired on his own; it was among the many things he shared with his girlfriend.

Tension among the band members was high. The next stop was San Francisco, and after that they were scheduled to head straight for another multicity tour in Scandinavia. But it seemed a tossup whether Sid would survive the journey, or if the rest of the band would survive Sid. After the Tulsa gig, Paul Cook and Steve Jones flew on to San Francisco with McLaren, while Sid Vicious and Johnny Rotten stayed on the tour bus.

Early on the morning of January 14, they pulled into a truck stop south of San Francisco. Sid went inside and ordered a steak-and-eggs breakfast. An African-American trucker caught his attention. "That nigger is as good as any white guy!" Vicious reportedly shouted to a pair of cowboys and their dates in the next booth.

"What do you know?" asked one of the men. "What do you do for a living, funny-looking?"

"I'm a guitar player," Sid answered with a grin.

"Well, where's your guitar, boy?"

"Up yer ass!"

The exchange continued. Then, with macho theatricality, the cowboy ground out a cigarette on the back of his own hand. "Come on, punk," he dared.

Like his lover, Sid was quick to escalate. Without flinching, he picked up his steak knife and seriously gashed the back of his left hand twice, allowing the blood to gush freely down into the rare steak and runny eggs in his plate. Without further comment the punker resumed eating. The cowboys became quiet.

The show that night in San Francisco was the wretched end to a blazing, brief chapter of rock history. "The Winterland gig," Steve Jones later told *Rolling Stone*, "was torture. My guitar kept going out of tune, breaking strings." Vicious was dead drunk, fell over at least five times, and once required a stagehand's help to put his guitar back around his neck. Johnny Rotten had the flu and was surly about Sid's greater share of the publicity. As the Sex Pistols staggered through the last song of what would be their last gig together, Rotten—he would soon change his name back to Lydon—looked out over the audience, smiled with his terrible teeth, and asked, wearily, "Ever get the feeling you've been cheated?" And that was it.

After the performance, San Francisco disc jockey Howie Klein attended a party in the Haight-Ashbury district, the city's old hippie enclave. "I was standing next to a closet," Klein remembers. "When I opened the door, Sid fell out. He'd been in there about 20 minutes."

Vicious had overdosed on heroin, but he recovered under a doctor's care. Several days later, McLaren's assistant, Sophie Richmond, took him to Los Angeles, where a second doctor gave the ailing punker enough methadone to get him back to England. Vicious promptly administered the full amount, however, and fell into another coma on the airplane to New York. There, he was hospitalized near Kennedy International Airport and partially detoxified before departing, in late January, for London.

McLaren had already issued the band's valedictory: "The group is bored with being a successful rock 'n roll band. Burning venues and destroying record companies is more creative than making it." The Sex Pistols were dead.

Reunited with his Nancy, Sid resumed the grim everyday routine of heroin addiction, a life passed in a sluggish fog of feeding a habit four or five times a day, not to get high, but merely to keep from feeling rotten. When the addict misses a fix, the pangs of withdrawal—chills, stomach cramps, diarrhea, vomiting—set in quickly. As one addict has written, if the withdrawal lasted only a few hours, or a day, it would be tolerable. But the sickness may go on for weeks. Few addicts can endure the long, agonizing haul between the onset of withdrawal and waking up clean.

Soon after Sid's return, filmmaker Lech Kowalski filmed Vicious and Spungen together in bed for his documentary *DOA*—dead on arrival. Both appear heavily drugged in the movie. Sid, weaving in and out of consciousness, plays with

Sid joins Nancy for a February 8, 1978, London court appearance on a charge of possessing a small amount of amphetamine. The charge was never fully resolved.

a large knife and repeatedly burns Nancy with a cigarette. Spungen, more alert, nags at Sid to stay awake. "Sid and Nancy," she says at one point, "we were partners in crime, we helped each other out."

Later that spring, Malcolm McLaren returned from Rio, where he'd begun setting up location shoots for a movie project he called *The Great Rock 'n Roll Swindle.* His idea was for the members of the Sex Pistols to appear on screen, individually, from different parts of the world for what would prove to be a sort of musical last hurrah: Cook and Jones from Brazil, Johnny Rotten from India. Sid's big scene would be filmed in Paris, to which McLaren sent Sid and Nancy that spring.

Sid by this time was as strongly disaffected from McLaren as his old friend Johnny Lydon had become; Lydon accused his onetime manager of skimming Sex Pistol profits. For Vicious, the irreconcilable offense had been McLaren's botched attempt to kidnap Nancy in December. According to one account, Sid only agreed to appear in *Swindle* after McLaren signed a document stating that he no longer managed Vicious.

"We eventually filmed it in a totally empty theater," said Julien Temple, whom McLaren hired to direct the picture. "We wanted him in a kind of destroyed version of dinner dress, and as long as he could wear his trousers and boots, he didn't mind anything."

In the scene, a spotlight discovers Vicious shirtless under a cream jacket, wearing his black pants and leather boots and walking down a staircase onto a stage. String music wells up, and Sid begins slowly croaking Frank Sinatra's "My Way." Then, halfway through the song, raunchy guitars kick in on the soundtrack and Sid flashes his trademark snarl. "My Way," finishes the punk way, at warp speed; Vicious even altered the lyrics, adding, "I killed the cat," for no discernible reason. At the song's end, he produces a handgun, pretends to blow away his "audience," and then insouciantly saunters back upstairs.

In Boogie Tiberi's view, the mock shooting was Sid's ultimate symbolic gesture. "Sid was getting demoralized," said Tiberi, "because the dream was broken. Not only the dream of being a pop star, but this thing, with which he was in love, as a fan, as a guy at the 100 Club with or without a beer glass. That's his PR. Rather than the group dying, the audience dies."

Julien Temple saw in the scene what he believes was Sid's

native affinity for the camera. "Sid," said Temple, "had a unique possibility to present things that no one else could present. I thought he was tremendous. His performance on 'My Way' was great." During the filming, Temple also witnessed the terrible dynamic of Sid's bond with Nancy: "I remember coming back one day and she'd cut her wrists. There was blood all over the bed and she'd faked up a suicide attempt to really make Sid feel he shouldn't leave her, even for a few hours, to do any filming." Such incidents, routine for Sid and Nancy, alternated with sentimental expressions of love. "It's so *beautiful* here," Spungen told her mother by telephone. Her Sid had bought her French lingerie, shoes, good meals in quaint restaurants; she was excited and happy. But their life together still proceeded very dangerously.

An April 1978 issue of *Record Mirror* magazine carried an interview with Sid in which he mused on the imminence of death. "I'll die before I'm very old," he told the magazine. "I don't know why. I just have this feeling. There have been plenty of times when we've nearly died." One of them came that June, when Nancy had to be hospitalized for badly infected fallopian tubes. In August Sid and Nancy stirred to consciousness one day to find a corpse in bed with them: 22-year-old John Shepcock, a friend, dead of a cocaine overdose. The survivors were too befuddled by dope to notice when Shepcock stopped breathing.

That incident scared the lovers back onto methadone for a while, and it may have helped restore Sid's balance enough to allow him to perform. After they returned to Britain from Paris in August 1978, he and Glen Matlock, the Sex Pistol bass guitar player Vicious had replaced in March of 1977, met in a London pub and decided to form a new group of punk superstars. They recruited a drummer and a guitarist from other well-known groups and called themselves the Vicious White Kids.

Nancy Spungen, who by now directed Sid's life in detail, had taken control of their money and the remnants of her man's career. The night of the Vicious White Kids' single performance before a paying audience, in the Camden Town section of central London, she even took the stage as a backup singer. Matlock, appalled at Spungen's voice, made certain her microphone wasn't plugged in.

The Camden Town gig notwithstanding, Sid was no longer a fresh face around London, or a particularly welcome one. When he and Nancy showed up late one night at John Lydon's house in Gunter Grove, Lydon refused to let them in. Sid started kicking the front door. One of Lydon's friends came after them with an ax. Nancy was soon on the telephone to her mother in Pennsylvania. "We're comin' back," she said. "I'm managing Sid's career now. He'll do better in the States, I figure." In New York, she promised, they would enter yet another methadone program, but this time they'd get clear of smack.

Wrote Deborah Spungen of her daughter's impending visit: "A knot formed in my stomach."

The Spungens met their daughter and her lover at the Trenton railway station on Friday, August 25, a day after the pair arrived in New York, where Nancy had secured a room at the Chelsea Hotel. She was very thin, dressed all in black, with bruised bluish-white skin and sores and scabs evident along her hairline. Sid matched her perfectly, his milky skin swathed entirely in black, set off by studded black-leather cuffs and collar. "They stood out as much as if they'd just arrived from another planet," recalled Deborah Spungen. "There was a total absence of life to them. It was as if the rest of the world was in color and they were in black and white."

On the drive home to Red Barn Lane, Sid sat limply in the backseat, holding hands with Nancy. He didn't stir until the Spungens pulled into their driveway and he first saw the family's unprepossessing suburban two-story. "It's a palace!" he exclaimed. Dinner—barbecued steak, corn, salad, and garlic toast—was served on the patio. Nancy cut Sid's meat for him. "Never have I had a meal like this, never," raved Sid. "Used to be I lived in a place with rats. Had to tie the food up in bags. High up, so they couldn't get at it. Never have I had a meal like this." Sid and Nancy finished about a third of their dinners before excusing themselves for the den.

The couple was staying at a local Holiday Inn that weekend. They surfaced the next afternoon and frolicked for a time in the Spungen swimming pool before Sid became exhausted and had to go inside and lie down. Sid and Nancy spent the balance of the day in front of the television, blurrily watching cartoons, and nodding off from time to time, dropping cigarettes on the couch. At one point Nancy did stir to ask if her "Mum," as she now called her, could find a doctor to remove stitches from her ear. She'd been beaten up by Teddys a few weeks earlier, and they'd ripped her ear off. A doctor had sewn it back on, she explained, but she'd neglected to have the stitches taken out. Her mother removed them herself.

Sid was a lightning rod for trouble, so rather than risk a public incident, the family ordered a takeout dinner for Saturday night. Waiting for the meal, Sid and Nancy drank vodka and tonic and groped each other on the couch. When Nancy caught her younger sister's look of wonder and repulsion at her behavior, she threatened her. Sid and Nancy watched TV as they nibbled at the spaghetti and meatballs they'd ordered, eating only a fraction of the meal. But Sid was full of praise: Again, it was the best food in his experience, the best ever.

On Sunday, Nancy decided it was time for them to go. "Thank you so much for having me," Sid told the Spungens on the way to the station. Deborah Spungen remembered a silence filling the car. Then, she wrote, "Nancy quietly said, 'I'm going to die very soon. Before my 21st birthday. I won't live to be 21. I'm never gonna be old. I don't ever wanna be ugly and old. I'm an old lady now anyhow. I'm 80. There's nothing left. I've already lived a whole lifetime. I'm going out. In a blaze of glory.'"

The pair had apparently arrived from London with as much as $10,000 in cash, and they moved into New York's venerable Chelsea Hotel on West 23d Street. The 12-story, red-brick Chelsea was an ironic, but apt, choice; it, too, had seen better times. Since its first day of business in 1884, the hotel had been a beacon for celebrated travelers; acclaimed writers, actors, and composers had stopped there. But age and abuse had caught up with the grand old place, famous for its wrought-iron balconies. By the time Mr. and Mrs. Ritchie, as the couple signed in, took a second-floor room, the Chelsea Hotel had become home to junkies, hookers, and hustlers.

Sid and Nancy enrolled in a local methadone program, as promised. Nancy, acting as Sid's agent, was able to promote several gigs for him, including one on September 7 at Max's Kansas City. Under the headline "Sid Vicious' Grand Farce," *Rolling Stone* reviewer Charles M. Young described Sid as "resplendent in black leather and chains" and noted that the punk rocker seemed free of mutilation marks, a newsworthy tidbit at any Vicious appearance. As for the 35-minute set, Young dutifully pointed out that Sid was terrible, then added, trenchantly: "Vicious has always insisted on his own talentlessness, presenting it as a chal-

lenge to anyone with a craving to be looked at on stage."

In New York City appearances later that month, Sid seemed wholly indifferent; one night he tried to leave the stage after only three numbers. In fact, both he and Nancy were being overtaken by their addiction to heroin and their huge intake of assorted other drugs. Around the city, Nancy's old acquaintances noticed how woebegone she looked. So vulnerable were the pair now that both suffered repeated physical attacks when they ran the gauntlet of street toughs on the way to the Spring Street methadone clinic in lower Manhattan. Sid and Nancy began to sink into a drugged variant of despair.

Late in September Nancy's father drove up from Pennsylvania with some of Sid's possessions, including a gold record that had been sent from England in care of the Spungens. He discovered Sid and his daughter together in bed in a dark room that was littered with half-eaten food and dirty laundry. They were watching cartoons. Neither took particular note of his presence. "Thank you, Daddy," was all Nancy said. It was a term of endearment he'd heard only rarely; he never heard it from Nancy again.

One night Sid fell asleep with a lighted cigarette and burned up their room; the Chelsea management moved them down the hall to Room 100. And there, in the rubble of their short, ruined lives, they overtook the fate that both had been chasing since childhood.

There are conflicting reports as to how Sid Vicious and Nancy Spungen spent their last few hours together. They were seen in the lobby of the Chelsea on Tuesday evening, October 11, 1978, with an unnamed girl who reportedly accompanied them to their room about midnight and then departed. In another version recounted to Glen Matlock by Stiv Bators, the since-deceased former lead singer with The Dead Boys, Sid and Nancy spent part of Tuesday night with Bators and Neon Leon, a musician and neighbor in the hotel. Bators told Matlock that they all bought knives that night. Nancy selected a folding model with a five-inch blade and made it a present to Sid.

Neon Leon, who lived down the hall from Sid and Nancy, would recount to police that Sid brought over certain of his possessions, including two gold records and his leather jacket, just after midnight and entrusted the items to Leon's safekeeping. At about 4:30 a.m., Nancy telephoned, looking for some marijuana. Neon Leon, who subsequently

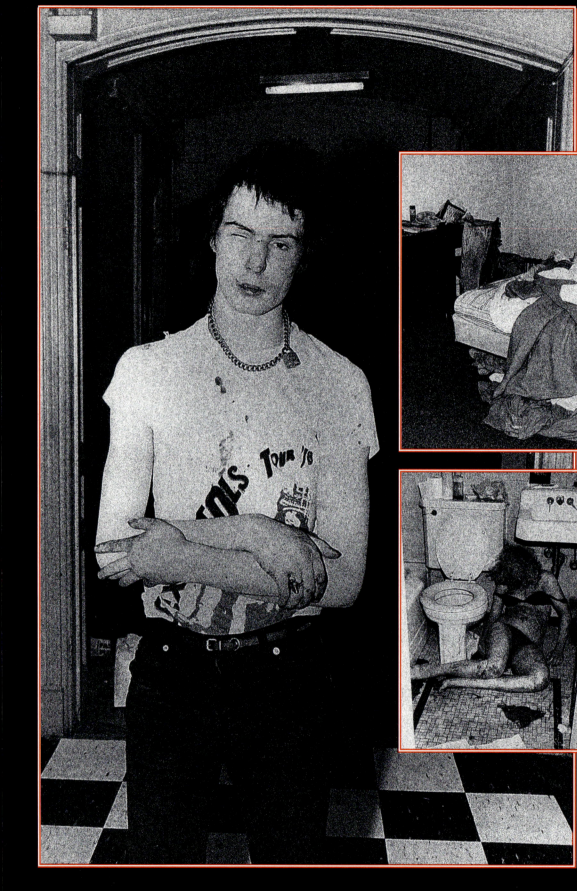

Rarely published New York police photographs portray Sid and Nancy's Chelsea Hotel room as a gallery of violent death. A trail of gore leads from the bloodstained bed *(above)* to the bathroom, where Spungen *(inset, left)* sits crumpled under the sink after bleeding to death from a knife wound in her lower abdomen. At left, Sid Vicious, bleary with drugs and still smeared with blood, is photographed by police before his arrest for Nancy Spungen's murder.

dropped out of sight, told the British paper *New Musical Express* later that morning that Sid, who recently had acquired a kitten named Socks, seemed content with his life of watching television and adoring Nancy. "He said she was the only real woman in the entire world," recalled the musician. "She was stronger than him and mouthed off to everyone. When they had fights, which were fights of extremist lovers, they were carried to the point of exhaustion or minor injuries. Then they made up."

A third witness, a drug dealer and addict known as Rockets Redglare, recounted in his statement that at approximately 1:30 that morning he delivered a small amount of synthetic morphine to Room 100, accepted several hundred dollars from Spungen to acquire more the next day, and then left Sid and Nancy, alive, in the room sometime between four and five o'clock. On the way out, said Redglare, he'd seen yet another dealer, Steve Cincotti, arrive. According to Cincotti, he sold Sid and Nancy the powerful barbiturate Tuinal on his visit.

About six hours later, Sid Vicious placed a panicked call to the Chelsea front desk, shouting in anguish for an ambulance. "I'm not kidding!" he cried. But it was too late.

When the police arrived, they found Nancy Spungen on Room 100's blood-spattered bathroom floor. She was clad in a black bra and black underpants and was seated upright with her back against the wall, underneath the sink. She'd suffered a single stab wound one inch below her navel. The five-inch knife she'd just bought for Sid lay on their bloody bed. It had been wiped clean of fingerprints. Her time of death was estimated at somewhere between five and nine o'clock that morning.

According to the police, Vicious admitted the murder that morning. Later, he'd claim to have no recollection of it. In press interviews he said that he had awakened sometime in the night to see Nancy playing with the knife she'd given him. Hours later he awoke again to find blood everywhere and Nancy in the bathroom, dying. That was when he called for the ambulance.

Hardly anyone who knew the pair believed that Sid Vicious could have murdered Nancy Spungen. Some held that a third party committed the murder—the knife had been wiped clean, a coherent act that was likely beyond Sid at any time after three o'clock that morning. Also, several people reported that Sid and Nancy had been flush with cash that night and, as was their custom, had left wads of bills out in plain sight. After the slaying, no money was found in their room. Perhaps, some say, a drug dealer, identity unknown, came into the room some time after Cincotti departed, grabbed the money, and killed Nancy, framing Sid for the homicide.

Anne Beverley has offered an alternative theory that echoes Shakespeare's Romeo and Juliet. Sid overdosed on the Tuinal he'd bought from Steve Cincotti and passed out; Nancy, also full of drugs, mistakenly believed Sid was dying and stabbed herself.

Others believed there was a suicide pact that fizzled—the two had talked about wishing to die together. Handing over Sid's belongings to Neon Leon the night before is consistent with such a plan. Perhaps Nancy persuaded Sid to stab her, but he could not sustain his nerve long enough to join her. Rock journalist Joe Stevens claimed that Sid later described a variation of this scenario. According to Stevens, a week following Nancy's death, after slicing his arms open in an attempted suicide, a distraught Vicious told him that the night of the killing he'd made a racket at the Chelsea, banging on junkies' doors, trying to score a fix. There were complaints. Sid was making a nuisance of himself. As a result, a bellboy punched him in the nose, a not-unusual event in recent weeks.

Later, in bed, he and Nancy had been playing with his new knife when suddenly Nancy slapped him, hard, on the nose, right where he'd just been punched. Sid angrily warned her that if she did it again he would take her head off. He told Stevens that Nancy then shoved her stomach at him "right in front of my knife." Vicious said that at the moment he hadn't noticed anything dire. But sometime later, he awoke and left the room in search of methadone. While he was gone, the mortally wounded Nancy crawled out of bed and into the bathroom, leaving a trail of blood behind her. That's where he'd found her, he said, seated under the sink.

The New York City police authorities took the simpler view that Sid had murdered Nancy, an assumption that was shared by private investigator Andrew J. Tuney, Jr., whom Sid's lawyers hired on his behalf. "There's no question in my mind that he did it," said Tuney, who tried to find evidence to the contrary. "Let's put it this way, there was no third party." Tuney spoke with Vicious as he escorted him to and from the methadone clinic. "He just seemed out of it to me. He was in a daze all the time. But he did seem very sorry.

He more or less said, 'I'm sorry it happened. I didn't mean for it to happen. Next thing I knew I found her there.' Words to that effect. He did not remember doing it."

Sid was charged with second degree murder on Wednesday, October 12, 1978, and was sent to New York's Riker's Island lockup. His heroin demons went with him and plagued him for nourishment; he spent the weekend with the nausea, goose flesh, and cramps of cold-turkey drug withdrawal.

Malcolm McLaren flew in from London the moment he heard of Nancy Spungen's death and worked through the weekend to persuade Virgin Records to front Sid's $50,000 bail, which the record company agreed to do on Monday. In spite of his rift with Vicious, McLaren was one of the few people still willing to help Sid. Of course, there was also a major, lurid news story to exploit. On King's Road in Chelsea, Vivienne Westwood instantly produced a T-shirt bearing Sid's likeness and the line: "She's dead, I'm alive, I'm yours."

Nancy Spungen was autopsied and her remains released to Frank and Deborah Spungen for burial in Philadelphia. They chose a cherrywood casket, decorated with autumn flowers. Her burial dress was the lime-green jersey with the bare midriff that she had worn, defiantly, to her senior prom. At her sister's behest, Nancy's hair was dyed back to something approximating its true chestnut color for her private funeral on Sunday, October 16. That same day, Anne Beverley flew in from England and visited her son in jail.

Five days after his release, on Monday, October 22, Sid Vicious made his first suicide attempt while staying at the seedy midtown Seville Hotel with his mother. Joe Stevens called the ambulance that delivered Vicious to Bellevue Hospital, where he was put into a psychiatric ward. He called Nancy's mother. "I can't live. I tried to kill myself." Sid also wrote Deborah Spungen several intimate, heartbreaking letters, surprising in their articulate expression of his grief. "I worshipped Nancy," read one, in part. "It was far more than just love. To me she was a goddess. She used to make me kiss her feet before we made love. No one ever loved the way we did, and to spend even a day away from her, let alone a whole lifetime, is too painful to even think about. Oh Debbie, I never knew what pain was until this happened. Nancy was my whole life. I lived for her. Now I must die for her."

Bellevue discharged Sid back into his mother's custody. A judge ordered a psychological evaluation and allowed Sid to remain free on bail as long as he reported daily to the methadone clinic, and to the police. At a November 21 hearing, Sid appeared in court, holding hands with a new companion, an unemployed 22-year-old actress named Michelle Robinson, with whom he soon was seen around town. They had grief in common; her British boyfriend had recently died in a motorcycle crash.

On December 9 Sid Vicious showed up at Hurrah's, a new disco at 62d and Broadway. Around 2:30 in the morning, he provoked Todd Smith, brother of poet and rocker Patti Smith, into a fight. Smith landed a few punches. Sid responded with a broken beer bottle and sent Smith to the hospital for stitches. Police sent Sid back to Riker's Island, his bail revoked. While he was there, Mick Jones and The Clash gave a benefit performance for him in London, to help with his legal expenses.

At 1 p.m. on February 1, 1979, he was released once more. Completely detoxified, wearing an "I Love New York" T-shirt and accompanied by his mother, Sid said only, "I want a slice of pizza." But he had changed. "When he came out of jail," recalled photographer Bob Gruen, "I saw him and he saw me and he burst into a big smile and it was the first time he was completely off the dope, he was clean, straight, lively, there was such a difference. He'd given up dope for two months. He'd dried out."

Sadly, he wasn't dry for long. A party to celebrate his release was planned that night for Michelle Robinson's Greenwich Village apartment. Anne Beverley cooked spaghetti and brought heroin. Sid shot up that afternoon, and again after dinner. "Simon had a rose pink aura around his whole body," reported his mother. "I said, 'Jesus, son, that must have been a good hit.' He was elated, quietly so. Elated on the inside, coming out, creating the aura." Five minutes later, Sid turned blue and crumpled onto Robinson's bed. His mother and the others positioned him on his side, hoping he'd revive. "I covered him with a blanket," Beverley told the *Daily Express*, "and every few minutes came out of the party and felt his pulse. He was having difficulty breathing, but he seemed okay." Sid regained consciousness about 40 minutes later. "We all had a good laugh," said Beverley.

Vicious slept with Robinson that night, but he arose before dawn to shoot up once more. Though an experienced heroin user, he made no allowances for the drug's potent purity, or for the fact that abstinence had reduced his tolerance for it—what had been an ordinary fix two months earlier could be fatal now. But Sid knew what he was doing.

The next morning, his mother went in to awaken him for his daily meeting with the police. Robinson lay asleep under the covers. Sid lay on his back, uncovered, and very still. She bent to kiss him awake, her lips brushing his forehead. It was cold. "I felt for his pulse and there was none," she told the newspaper. "After a couple minutes, Michelle woke up and I told her Sid was dead."

Sid Vicious, born John Simon Ritchie, was cremated before his mother found what she believes was a handwritten suicide note in his pocket. "We had a death pact," it read. "I have to keep my half of the bargain. Please bury me next to my baby. Bury me in my leather jacket, jeans and motor cycle boots. Good bye."

The Spungen family would not allow it, nor even disclose the site of Nancy's resting place. But Anne Beverley found the grave. One day she visited the Philadelphia cemetery, carrying the several pounds of cremation ash and bone pellets that remained of Sid. She scattered them over Nancy's headstone. ◆

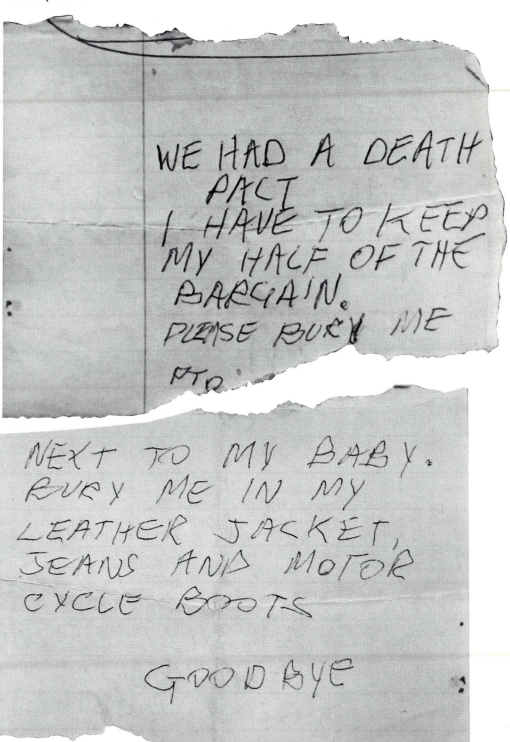

Acknowledgments

The editors wish to thank these individuals and institutions for their valuable assistance:

Wayne Alexander, Los Angeles, Calif.; Max Baer, Jr., Van Nuys, Calif.; George Barclay, Vancouver, B.C., Canada; George Barris, Hollywood, Calif.; Stephen M. Barshop, Santa Monica, Calif.; Molly Basler, Santa Monica, Calif.; Bill Brooks, Honolulu, Hawaii; Don Bullough, Vancouver, B.C., Canada; Glen Bystrum, Sacramento, Calif.; Bill Cable, Los Angeles, Calif.; Colleen Camp, Los Angeles, Calif.; Mario Casilli, Altadena, Calif.; Jefferson Wortham Clark, Jr., New Smyrna, Fla.; Caroline Coon, London; Alex Cox, Culver City, Calif.; Dr. Stephen Cushner, Scottsdale, Ariz.; Dirk Dirksen, San Francisco, Calif.; Jacques Denis Drollet, Punaauia, Tahiti; Andre DuVal, Los Angeles, Calif.; Mel Farr, Oak Park, Mich.; Harvey Fuqua, Las Vegas, Nev.; Robert Giannageli, Los Angeles, Calif.; Michael Goldberg, San Francisco, Calif.; Jeffrey Good, Venice, Calif.; Marilyn Grabowski, Los Angeles, Calif.; Bob Gruen, New York; Ingrid Hammond, Rome; Bill Harrison, Kemper Military School and College, Boonville, Mo.; Michael D. Hermes, Ojai, Calif.; James David Hinton, Los Angeles, Calif.; Ken Honey, Vancouver, B.C., Canada; Mary Thorton House, Los Angeles, Calif.; Robert Houston, Beverly Hills, Calif.; Tom Hyland, Duluth, Minn.; Lori Jacobsen, Los Angeles, Calif.; Larry Johnson, House of God, Lexington, Ky.; Ken Johnstone, Vancouver, B.C., Canada; Alan Jones, London; Rosanne Katon, Los Angeles, Calif.; Howie Klein, Burbank, Calif.; Jeffrey Kruger, Sussex, England; William LaChasse, Eagle Rock, Calif.; Susan LaChasse, Eagle Rock, Calif.; Elaine Lodge, Los Angeles, Calif.; Skip E. Lowe, Los Angeles, Calif.; Jim McEachran, Vancouver, B.C., Canada; Paola McKenna, Los Angeles, Calif.; Robert Martin, Los Angeles, Calif.; Bud May, Longview, Wash.; Estella Mayberry, Lexington, Ky.; W. L. Melville, Coquitlam, B.C., Canada; Al Messman, Woodstock, Ill.; Joy Metcalfe, Vancouver, B.C., Canada; Uwe Meyer, Vancouver, B.C., Canada; Steve Mirkovich, Bernaby, B.C., Canada; Jennifer Miro, San Francisco, Calif.; Elizabeth Earhart Norris, Chicago, Ill.; Hugh O'Brian, Los Angeles, Calif.; Paul Odermatt, Coquitlam, B.C., Canada; Fondazione Pasolini, Rome; Clarence Paul, Las Vegas, Nev.; Taylor Pero, Los Angeles, Calif.; Jerry Phillips, Washington, D.C.; Howard Rasch, Los Angeles, Calif.; Jim Reber, Sacramento, Calif.; David Redlick, Vancouver, B.C., Canada; Calvin Reynolds, Vancouver, B.C., Canada; John Riley, Beverly Hills, Calif.; Lloyd Sandstrom, Bethel, Alaska; Isabelle Sauvé-Astruc, Conservateur des Collections Historiques de la Préfecture de Police, Paris; John Savage, London; Michael Schiff, Los Angeles, Calif.; Larry Shaeffer, Tulsa, Okla.; Curtis Shaw, Los Angeles, Calif.; Dave Simmons, Los Angeles, Calif.; Chester Simpson, Alexandria, Va.; Horace Smith, Kemper Military School, Boonville, Mo.; David Snider, Vancouver, B.C., Canada; Evelyn Snider, Vancouver, B.C., Canada; Andrew J. Tuney, Jr., Boston, Mass.; Arnold Wattum, Richmond, B.C., Canada; Abbe Wool, Los Angeles, Calif.

Acknowledgment is given for permission to reprint the lyrics from "Let's Get It On" by Marvin Gaye and Ed Townsend. Copyright February © 1973 by Jobete Music Co., Inc./Stone Diamond Music Corporation.

Bibliography

Books:

Anderson, Clinton H., *Beverly Hills Is My Beat.* Englewood Cliffs, N.J.: Prentice-Hall, 1960.

Bateson, Keith, and Alan Parker, *Sid's Way.* London: Omnibus Press, 1991.

Bogdanovich, Peter, *The Killing of the Unicorn: Dorothy Stratten (1960-1980).* New York: William Morrow, 1984.

Brando, Anna Kashfi, and E. P. Stein, *Brando for Breakfast.* New York: Crown, 1979.

Burroughs, William S., *Junky.* New York: Penguin Books, 1977.

Capote, Truman, "The Duke in His Domain." In *A Capote Reader.* New York: Random House, 1987.

Carey, Gary, *Marlon Brando: The Only Contender.* New York: St. Martin's Press, 1985.

Cohen, Michael Mickey, as told to John Peer Nugent, *Mickey Cohen, In My Own Words: The Underworld Autobiography of Michael Mickey Cohen.* Englewood Cliffs, N.J.: Prentice-Hall, 1975.

Coon, Caroline, *1988: The New Wave Punk Rock Explosion.* London: Omnibus Press, 1982.

Crane, Cheryl, with Cliff Jahr, *Detour: A Hollywood Story.* Thorndike, Maine: Thorndike Press, 1988.

Davis, Sharon, *I Heard It through the Grapevine: Marvin Gaye, The Biography.* Edinburgh: Mainstream, 1991.

DeCurtis, Anthony, and James Henke, eds., with Holly George-Warren, *The Rolling Stone Illustrated History of Rock & Roll.* New York: Random House, 1992.

Fong-Torres, Ben, *The Motown Album.* New York: St. Martin's Press, 1990.

Fox, Ted, *Showtime at the Apollo.* New York: Holt, Rinehart and Winston, 1983.

Grobel, Lawrence, *Conversations with Brando.* New York: Hyperion, 1991.

Higham, Charles: *Brando: The Unauthorized Biography.* New York: New American Library, 1987.

Merchant of Dreams: Louis B. Mayer, M.G.M., and the Secret Hollywood. New York: Donald I. Fine, 1993.

The Holy Bible. Iowa Falls, Iowa: World Bible Publishers, 1971.

Kaplan, John, *The Hardest Drug: Heroin and Public Policy.* Chicago: University of Chicago Press, 1983.

Lait, Jack, and Lee Mortimer, *U.S.A. Confidential.* New York: Crown, 1952.

Leff, Leonard J., and Jerold L. Simmons, *The Dame in the Kimono: Hollywood, Censorship, and the Production Code from the 1920s to the 1960s.* New York: Grove Weidenfeld, 1990.

Markman, Ronald, and Dominick Bosco, *Alone with the Devil.* New York: Doubleday, 1989.

Monk, Noel E., and Jimmy Guterman, *12 Days on the Road: The Sex Pistols and America.* New York: William Morrow, 1990.

Morella, Joe, and Edward Z. Epstein:

Brando: The Unauthorized Biography. New York: Crown, 1973.

Lana: The Public and Private Lives of Miss Turner. New York: Citadel Press, 1971.

Nash, Jay Robert, *Murder among the Rich and Famous: Celebrity Slayings That Shocked America.* New York: Arlington House, 1983.

The New York Times Directory of the Film. New York: Random House, 1971.

Parish, James Robert, and Ronald L. Bowers, *The MGM Stock Company: The Golden Era.* London: Ian Allan, 1973.

Pero, Taylor, and Jeff Rovin, *Always, Lana.* New York: Bantam Books, 1982.

Ritz, David, *Divided Soul: The Life of Marvin Gaye.* New York: Da Capo Press, 1991.

Savage, Jon, *England's Dreaming: Anarchy, Sex Pistols, Punk Rock and Beyond.* New York: St. Martin's Press, 1992.

Schickel, Richard, *Brando: A Life in Our Times.* New York: Atheneum, 1991.

Spungen, Deborah, *And I Don't Want to Live This Life.* New York: Villard Books, 1983.

Turner, Lana, *Lana: The Lady, the Legend, the Truth.* New York: E. P. Dutton, 1982.

Vermorel, Fred, and Judy Vermorel, *Sex Pistols: The Inside Story.* London: Book Sales Limited, 1987.

Wood, Lee, *Sex Pistols Day by Day.* Ed. by Chris Charlesworth. London: Omnibus Press, 1988.

Periodicals:

Arrington, Carl, "Ailing but Never Out, a Troubled Marvin Gaye Finds Out What the Doctor Ordered: Sexual Healing." *People,* Jan. 24, 1983.

Bangs, Lester, "A Sid Vicious Story." *Village Voice,* Oct. 23, 1978.

Banks, Sandy, and Robert W. Stewart, "10,000 Fans Mourn Gaye; Father Appears in Court." *Los Angeles Times,* Apr. 5, 1984.

"Battle of Brando, Ex-Wife Takes New Twist." *Los Angeles Times,* Mar. 10, 1972.

Bernstein, Paul, with Bob Eisner, "Marvin Gaye: Paradox Makes Perfect." *Crawdaddy,* July 1973.

"Brando's Ex-Wife Seeks Son's Custody, Cites Role in 'Tango.'" *Los Angeles Times,* Apr. 12, 1973.

"Brando Wins Sole Custody of Son, 13." *Los Angeles Times,* May 7, 1972.

Carpenter, Teresa, "Death of a Playmate." *Village Voice,* Nov. 5-11, 1980.

Cass, Julia, "Punk Pal." *Philadelphia Inquirer,* Feb. 15, 1978.

Cass, Julia, and Marc Schogol, "Punk Guitarist Charged in Area Girl's Death." *Philadelphia Inquirer,* Oct. 13, 1978.

Christian, Frederick, "Legend of the Sweater Girl." *New York Journal-American,* July 7, 1963.

Cohen, Jamie Alison, "Marvin Gaye Shot, Killed." *Los Angeles Herald Examiner,* Apr. 2, 1984.

Collier, Aldore, "Marvin Gaye: What's Going On with His Family Five Years Later." *Jet,* May 15, 1989.

Dacre, Paul:
"I Held Sid's Heroin." *Daily Express,* Feb. 5, 1979.
"Sid's Drug." *Daily Express,* Oct. 16, 1978.

"Daughter of Lana Turner Kills Man." *Los Angeles Times,* Apr. 5, 1958.

Davis, Merlene, "Acquaintances of Singer's Father Shocked at Charge." *Lexington Herald-Leader,* Apr. 22, 1984.

"Dignity and Honor Marked the Last Rites for John Stompanato." *Woodstock Sentinel* (Woodstock, Ill.), Apr. 10, 1958.

Fazio, Jeff, and Rodger Claire, "The Battle of Sunset." *Los Angeles* magazine, Nov. 1988.

Feldman, Paul, "Brando's Daughter Has Gone to Tahiti." *Los Angeles Times,* June 26, 1990.

Fong-Torres, Ben, "With Marvin Gaye." *Rolling Stone,* Apr. 27, 1972.

"For the Record—Marvin Gaye." *Los Angeles Times,* Sept. 29, 1990.

Freed, David, and Dean Murphy, "Brando a Hard Act to Follow." *Los Angeles Times,* May 18, 1990.

"Gaye Skips Princess Margaret's Dinner without Explanation." *Variety,* July 16, 1980.

Gehman, Richard, "Mrs. Marlon Brando: Who She Really Is." *McCall's,* July 1959.

George, Nelson:

"Author Sues Gaye over 'Sexual Healing' Copyright." *Billboard,* July 9, 1983.
"The Power and the Glory." *Village Voice,* May 8, 1984.

Gilchrist, Roderick, "The Adolescent Who Really Believed Punk Joke." *Daily Mail,* Feb. 3, 1979.

Gillman, Peter, and Andrew Stephen, "Sid Vicious: The Making of a Monster." *Sunday Times,* Oct. 22, 1978.

Gilmore, Mikal, "Marvin Gaye Declares Bankruptcy." *Rolling Stone,* Nov. 30, 1978.

Hell, Richard, "Excess." *Spin,* Dec. 1986.

Heron, W. Kim, "Complexity Marked Gaye as Artist, Man." *Detroit Free Press,* Apr. 8, 1984.

Hobbs, Michael A., and Julia Cass, "Sid Vicious Jailed." *Philadelphia Inquirer,* Oct. 14, 1978.

Hobbs, Michael A., Julia Cass, and Art Carey, "Two Lives in the Fast Lane." *Philadelphia Inquirer,* Oct. 15, 1978.

"Hold Stompanato Rites Wednesday." *Woodstock Sentinel* (Woodstock, Ill.), Apr. 7, 1958.

Holmstrom, John, "The Harder They Fall." *Nerve,* 1983.

Janos, Leo, "Brando Between Takes: The Private World of Marlon Brando." *Time,* May 24, 1976.

"Johnny Became Moslem." *Los Angeles Herald Examiner,* Apr. 8, 1958.

Johnston, Laurie, "A Walk Through Chelsea's Literary Past." *New York Times,* May 25, 1979.

Jones, Jack:
"Brando Flies from Paris; Mystery over Son Grows." *Los Angeles Times,* Mar. 11, 1972.
"Court Allows Brando to Take Son to Paris." *Los Angeles Times,* Mar. 14, 1972.
"Jury Clears Lana Turner's Daughter; Slaying Justifiable." *Los Angeles Times,* Apr. 12, 1958.

Kent, Nick, "Life in the Vicious Circle." *New Musical Express,* Oct. 21, 1978.

Kifner, John, "Sid Vicious, Punk-Rock Musician, Dies, Apparently of Drug Overdose." *New York Times,* Feb. 3, 1979.

Kinnersley, Simon, "Sid Vicious and Nancy." *London Times Sunday Magazine,* Sept. 18, 1983.

" 'Kiss Me . . . Thousand Times,' Lana

Writes." *Los Angeles Herald Examiner,* Apr. 8, 1958.

Klein, Patricia, and Mitchell Fink, "Two Versions of Gaye's Death." *Los Angeles Herald,* Apr. 8, 1984.

Kunen, James S., Robin Micheli, Dan Knapp, and Logan Bentley, "Brando's Son Faces Murder One." *People,* June 4, 1990.

"Lana's Daughter Held for Slaying." *Los Angeles Times,* Apr. 6, 1958.

"Lana's Plea for Daughter Is Real-Life Drama Triumph." *Life,* Apr. 21, 1958.

"Lana Turner's 'Love' for Stompanato Told." *Los Angeles Times,* Apr. 7, 1958.

Landau, Jon, "A Whiter Shade of Black." *Crawdaddy,* Sept./Oct. 1968.

Lisners, John, and Gloria Stewart, "I'll Get Out of Jail Free Says Sid Vicious." *N.O.W.,* Jan. 21, 1978.

McMillan, Penelope, "Missing Letter Led to Gaye Shooting, Police Say." *Los Angeles Times,* Apr. 4, 1984.

Malnic, Eric, and Scott Harris, "Marlon Brando's Son Held in Fatal Shooting." *Los Angeles Times,* May 18, 1990.

Manso, Peter:
"The Brando Demons." *Vanity Fair,* Aug. 1990.
"The Trials of Marlon Brando." *Entertainment Weekly,* Jan. 25, 1991.

"Marvin Gaye Faces Jail for Contempt in Alimony Dispute." *Variety,* Aug. 18, 1976.

"Marvin Gaye Is Shot and Killed; Pop Singer's Father Faces Charge." *New York Times,* Apr. 2, 1984.

"Marvin Gaye's Father Freed on Bail." *Los Angeles Times,* June 21, 1984.

Mieses, Stanley, "Sid's Bail." *Melody Maker,* Oct. 21, 1978.

Morrison, Patt:
"Drollet Was Trying to Break from Brando Clan, Relatives Say." *Los Angeles Times,* July 18, 1990.
"Maximum Term Sought for Brando." *Los Angeles Times,* Feb. 22, 1991.

Murphy, Dean, and Louis Sahagun, "Brando's Son Faces One Charge of Murder." *Los Angeles Times,* May 19, 1990.

"Names & Faces." *Detroit Free Press,* June 20, 1984.

Park, Jeannie, and Robin Micheli, "As He Copes with His Son's Murder

Rap, Marlon Brando Is Dealt a Second Blow: Daughter Cheyenne's Suicide Try." *People,* Nov. 19, 1990.

Prince, Al:
"The Brando Saga Returns to Tahiti." *Tahiti Sun Press Magazine,* Jan. 1992.
"Brando's Son Arraigned in L.A. Shooting Death, Victim Was Boyfriend of Brando's Pregnant Daughter." *Tahiti Sun Press,* May 26, 1990.
"Cheyenne Brando Attempts Suicide 2nd Time in Tahiti, Father Tells L.A. Times." *Tahiti Sun Press,* Nov. 17, 1990.

Randerson, Middy, "Setting the Record Straight." *Houston Post,* Mar. 9, 1988.

Rhodes, Richard, "Dorothy Stratten: Her Story." *Playboy,* May 1981.

Sahagun, Louis, and John H. Lee, "Bail Request for Brando's Son Denied by Judge." *Los Angeles Times,* May 23, 1990.

Segell, Michael, "Sid Vicious Accused." *Rolling Stone,* Nov. 30, 1978.

Sippel, John, "Gaye Files Two Bankruptcy Pleas." *Billboard,* Oct. 7, 1978.

Smith, Bob, compiler, "Brief on Janis Gaye filing for divorce," *Detroit Free Press,* Sept. 23, 1979.

"Soul Singer Marvin Gaye's Former Home in Hidden Hills, Calif., Valued at $1 Million, Goes on Sale." *Wall Street Journal,* Nov. 17, 1982.

"Stabbed to Death in Home of Lana Turner." *Woodstock Sentinel* (Woodstock, Ill.), Apr. 5, 1958.

"Starbabies." *Murder Casebook* (London), No. 96.

"Star Sent 'Kiss Notes' from London." *Los Angeles Herald Examiner,* Apr. 8, 1958.

Stevens, Joe, "The Vicious Affair." *New Musical Express,* Oct. 21, 1978.

Stevens, Joe, and Dan Oppenheimer, "I Don't Want to Go to the Chelsea . . ." *New Musical Express,* Oct. 21, 1978.

Stewart, Gloria, "How Punk Went Rotten." *The Sun,* Oct. 23, 1978.

Stewart, Robert W.:
"Gay Found Mentally Able to Stand Trial in Singer's Death." *Los Angeles Times,* June 13, 1984.
"Plea Bargain Talks in Gaye Slaying Held." *Los Angeles Times,* Sept. 6, 1984.

Stolberg, Sheryl, "Brando's Son Pleads

Guilty to Voluntary Manslaughter." *Los Angeles Times,* Jan. 5, 1991.

"Stompanato Brother Here to Claim Body of 'Adonis.' " *Los Angeles Times,* Apr. 6, 1958.

Svetkey, Benjamin, "Marlon Brando." *Entertainment Weekly,* Oct. 2, 1992.

Talbert, Bob, "Five Times around Marvin Gaye, Trying to See All the Man." *Detroit Free Press,* Aug. 15, 1971.

"Tammi Terrell, 24, Rock Music Artist." *Philadelphia Inquirer,* Mar. 17, 1970.

"Tammi Terrell" (obituary). *Variety,* Mar. 18, 1970.

"Tammi Terrell Dies—Brain Tumor?" *Rolling Stone,* Apr. 16, 1970.

Tempest, Rone, and Penelope McMillan, "French Arrest Brando Sister in Drollet Case." *Los Angeles Times,* Nov. 16, 1991.

Thackrey, Ted, Jr., and Claire Spiegel, "Singer Slain; Father Arrested." *Los Angeles Times,* Apr. 2, 1984.

Timnik, Lois:
"Brando Ends Silence, Defends Son." *Los Angeles Times,* Aug. 10, 1990.
"Brando Says His Daughter Tried to Hang Herself." *Los Angeles Times,* Nov. 13, 1990.
"Brando Son Gets New Lawyer." *Los Angeles Times,* June 12, 1990.
"Brando Son Pleads Not Guilty to Murder." *Los Angeles Times,* Aug. 8, 1990.
"Brando's Son Ordered to Stand Trial for Murder." *Los Angeles Times,* July 25, 1990.
"Case against Brando Erodes." *Los Angeles Times,* Oct. 26, 1990.
"Christian Brando Tells of Remorse and Hopes." *Los Angeles Times,* Feb. 26, 1991.
"Hearing for Brando Begins." *Los Angeles Times,* Feb. 27, 1991.
"Judge Gives a Sentence of 10 Years to Brando." *Los Angeles Times,* Mar. 1, 1991.
"Probation Study Calls for 3-Year Term for Brando." *Los Angeles Times,* Feb. 25, 1991.
"Violence by Brando Disputed." *Los Angeles Times,* Feb. 28, 1991.

Timnik, Lois, and Patt Morrison, "Drug Overdose Leaves Cheyenne Brando, 20, Comatose, Source Says." *Los Angeles Times,* Nov. 2, 1990.

Townsend, Dorothy, "Brando's Missing Son Back in U.S., Border Police Say."

Los Angeles Times, Mar. 12, 1972.

"Tragedies Reflected in Lana Turner's Tears." *Los Angeles Times,* Apr. 6, 1958.

Wilkinson, Tracy, "Brando Is Released from Jail." *Los Angeles Times,* Aug. 16, 1990.

Young, Charles M., "Sid Vicious' Grand Farce." *Rolling Stone,* Sept. 1978.

Other Sources:

Anna Kashfi Brando v. Marlon Brando, Superior Court of California for the County of Los Angeles. Case No. SMD18492. Filed Apr. 22, 1959.

Arrington, Carl, "Marvin Gaye." *People* dispatch, Apr. 3, 1984.

Brando, Christian, Videotapes of *The People of the State of California v. Christian Brando,* Case No. SA 003367 (Court TV). Courtroom Television Network, New York, 1991.

Christian Devi Brando v. Mary McKenna Brando, Further Judgment on Reserved Issues After Bifurcation, Superior Court of the State of California for the County of Los Angeles. Case No. WED 47145. Filed May 4, 1987.

Complaint #6735, Nancy Laura Spungen Homicide Reports, New York Police Dept., Oct. 12-13, 1978.

Cox, Alex, Notes taken for the film *Sid and Nancy,* courtesy of Alex Cox and the University of California, Los Angeles Theatre Arts Library.

Gay, Marvin, Sr., Transcript of Probation Hearing. Los Angeles County Court, Nov. 2, 1984.

Gay, Marvin Pentz, Certificate of Birth. Oct. 1, 1914, Jessamine County, Kentucky.

Gaye, Marvin, Jr., Autopsy Report. Department of Chief Medical Examiner-Coroner, Apr. 2, 1984, Los Angeles, California.

Gaye, Marvin Pentz, Jr., Los Angeles Police Department Preliminary Investigation of Murder, OR 84 0714137. Apr. 1, 1984.

Hoogstraten, Dorothy Ruth, a.k.a. Dorothy Stratten, *Autobiography.* © 1979 Peternella Eldridge, Administratrix of the Estate of Dorothy Ruth Hoogstraten, also known as Dorothy Stratten, also known as Kristin Shields, deceased.

Internal Revenue Service Court Papers filed Jan. 23, 1985, Los Angeles, California.

Interview with Christian Brando by Bill Cable, *Skip E. Lowe Looks at Hollywood* (Public Access Cable Television Program). Los Angeles, California, 1985.

Kemper Military School and College Class Records. Boonville, Missouri.

Kruger, Jeffrey S., © Unpublished manuscript. London, England.

Lester, Peter, "Marvin Gaye." *People* dispatch take two, Feb. 22, 1979.

Lilly, Melinda, "Marvin Gaye." *People* dispatch, Apr. 5, 1984.

Lilly, Melinda, "Marvin Gaye." *Time* dispatch, Apr. 5, 1984.

Lorie Kligerman v. Cheyenne Brando, et al., Assault and Battery with Intentional Infliction of Emotional Distress. Case No. SC21857, Superior Court of the State of California for the County of Los Angeles, filed Feb. 16, 1993.

Marc Goldstein v. Playboy Enterprises, Inc., et al. Deposition of Susan Patricia LaChasse. Superior Court of the State of California for the County of Los Angeles. No. WEC 069 349: Volume I, Mar. 30, 1982; Volume II, Apr. 8, 1982.

Marc L. Goldstein v. Playboy Enterprises, Inc., et al. Deposition of Albert William LaChasse, Jr. Superior Court of the State of California for the County of Los Angeles. No. WEC 069 349. Volume I, Apr. 9, 1982; Volume III, Apr. 28, 1982.

Marlon Brando v. Anna Kashfi Brando. Superior Court of the State of California for the County of Los Angeles. Case No. SMD18492. Apr. 22, 1959.

"Marvin Gaye." *People* dispatch, take five. Apr. 2, 1984.

"Marvin Gaye's Death." *People* dispatch take four, Apr. 2, 1984.

The People of the State of California v. Christian Brando. Sentencing Memorandum, Superior Court of the State of California for the County of Los Angeles. Case No. SA003367, filed Feb. 20, 1991.

The People of the State of California v. Marvin Pentz Gaye, Sr., Superior Court of the State of California for the County of Los Angeles. Probation. No. A751295. Filed Nov. 5, 1984.

Proof of Claim for Internal Revenue Taxes, Superior Court of the State of California for the County of Los Angeles in the Matter of the Estate of: Marvin P. Gaye (deceased), Jan. 24, 1985. Probate No. P-688 909.

Riley, John, and Laura Bernstein, "The Girl Next Door Is Dead." Unpublished article.

Ritz, David, "Portrait of an Artist." Liner notes to Motown Marvin Gaye box set.

Stompanato-Utush Marriage Certificate. Foreign Service of the United States, National Archives, Suitland, Maryland.

Stratten, Dorothy, private letters sent to Elizabeth Norris.

Index

Picture Credits